Who Will Provide?

Who Will Provide?

The Changing Role of Religion in American Social Welfare

edited by
Mary Jo Bane, Brent Coffin,
Ronald Thiemann

Center for the Study of Values in Public Life
Harvard Divinity School

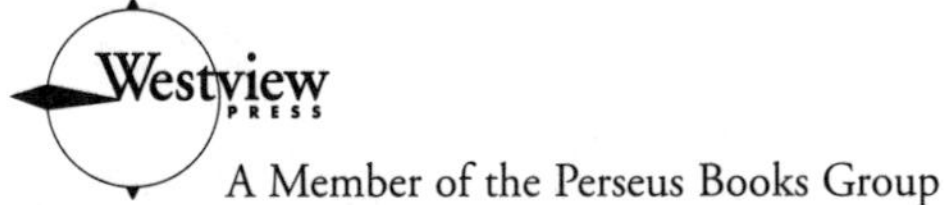

A Member of the Perseus Books Group

Published in 2000 in the United States of America by Westview Press, 5500 Central Avenue, Boulder, Colorado 80301–2877, and in the United Kingdom by Westview Press, 12 Hid's Copse Road, Cumnor Hill, Oxford OX2 9JJ

Find us on the World Wide Web at www.westviewpress.com

Library of Congress Cataloging-in-Publication Data
Who will provide? : the changing role of religion in American social welfare / edited by Mary Jo Bane and Brent Coffin.
p. cm.
Includes bibliographical references and index.
ISBN 0-8133-3876-X (alk. paper)
1. Social service—United Sates. 2. Church Charities—United States. 3. Public welfare—United States. 4. Nonprofit organizations—United States. I. Bane, Mary Jo. II. Coffin, Brent.

HV91 .W497 2000
361.7'5'0973—dc21 00-063303

The paper used in this publication meets the requirements of the American National Standard for Permanence of Paper for Printed Library Materials Z39.48–1984.

10 9 8 7 6 5 4 3 2 1

Contents

Foreword

David Little

Who Will Provide? is a collection of provocative and timely essays about the import of social welfare for the future of American democracy, a subject that has thrust itself into the center of American political discussion. These essays are aimed at striking the right balance between the government and religious and other nonprofit organizations in delivering public care and assistance to the poor and disadvantaged in American society. The book is the fruit of a series of discussions, sponsored by the Center for the Study of Values in Public Life, at the Harvard Divinity School, that took place over several years and involved members of the Harvard faculty from a wide variety of disciplines and fields of study.

The discussions were prompted by the passage of the Personal Responsibility and Work Opportunity Act of 1996, which, among other things, replaced a system of federal matching funds and entitlements to assistance with flexible block grants to states that require most welfare recipients to work and also limit federally funded welfare benefits to five years. To broaden the range of "charitable choice," the legislation also relaxed restrictions on funding faith-based organizations for purposes of providing social services and of helping administer the transition from "welfare to workfare."

In variously analyzing and evaluating the role of religious communities and other nonprofit groups in face of this new state of affairs, the interdisciplinary "multilogue" generated by the essays that make up *Who Will Provide?* illustrates richly the fundamental purpose for which the Center for the Study of Values in Public Life was established nearly a decade ago. The center was designed as a vital forum where faculty from across the university, as well as scholars and professional persons from near and far, could gather together in order to clarify and elevate topics of urgent public concern involving contested moral and religious values.

The authors included herein fulfill that mandate admirably. Among them are social scientists, moral theologians, scholars of the law and of public policy, several of whom have supplemented their academic work with practical experience in government or in religious or other nongovernmental organizations. In response to down-to-earth debates over social welfare policy, the authors shed light on broader issues surrounding the meaning of values in public life. The essays demonstrate, for example, an urgent need to reexamine and reformulate conventional distinctions between familiar notions like "public" and "private," "church" and "state," or "justice" and "charity." They also make clear that the problems posed by the new legislation are not completely novel, but are part of a long, if controversial, pattern of cooperation in regard to welfare policy between government and private sector organizations, including religious communities.

All the same, the essays also imply that simply recasting our definitions, refining our principles, and deepening our historical awareness will not automatically dissolve the perplexities—moral, religious, constitutional, and social—regarding responsibility for cultivating equal citizenship. These perplexities are hard to dispel, partly because they are so complicated, and partly because they touch the nerves of deep unresolved issues over the role of government and religion in American society. Following the example of the essays in this volume, perplexities like these can best be confronted and coped with by combining mastery of practical and policy detail with sensitivity to wider theoretical and conceptual issues, and by marking out major options in both areas. Such is the calling of the Center.

Preface

Mark H. Moore

POOR HUMANS! Blessed and cursed with self-consciousness, reason, and empathy, we find it difficult to know what we live for, and with whom we must live.

We feel an obligation to take care of those "near and dear" to us. But we are uncertain about how widely we should draw this circle of care. Are our obligations only to our extended family, and those we choose to have as neighbors and friends? Or do they extend to the fellow citizens with whom we share a common government, or to human beings throughout the world?

We long to achieve virtue, but many of us have come to believe that it is best to consider that quest a private affair and to leave the important questions of how to organize our collective life to reason and science divorced from moral argument or religious belief. Yet, partly as a consequence of this, we find that we are unpracticed in public discussions about the important purposes that we ought to be seeking. And without those purposes, reason and science alone provide little assistance to our restless minds and hearts.

While these issues have long troubled humans, recent history has given us a strong shove in a particular direction. The growth of markets and the rise of liberal political ideologies have all pushed in a consistent direction: toward individualism and away from interdependence; toward materialism and away from the pursuit of moral virtue; toward reason, science, and secular life and away from faith, spirituality, and religion.

One might easily think that this is all for the best — a triumph of human progress towards individual liberation and economic progress. And so it might be.

But there is also a price to be paid for these advances. One of these costs is a loss of "community" — that strong sense of both mutual vulnerability and mutual responsibility. With that loss comes both a loss to individuals who need communities to live well and flourish, and to the polity that needs communities and communal spirit to be able to do its work of helping to define and achieve collective aspirations. The result is less engagement in the public institutions and common life on which the health of our democracy depends.

Now comes a posse of Harvard colleagues to sound the alarm and to point to an unexpected source of help in resolving these modern dilemmas. The event that draws their attention is the recent debate about welfare reform — the public means we have relied upon to define and meet our collective responsibility to the poor. My colleagues are interested in the character of the debate and in the choices that were made. But they also use this case more broadly as an occasion to investigate the character of our current political culture and ideology. They explore in particular the ways in which religious ideas and religious institutions might have influenced that debate and society's capacity to feel and respond to a commitment to the poor.

The trick, of course, is to recognize that when religious values come into public life, they must negotiate the plurality of our common life. Religious participants in public debate must recognize that they lack absolute moral authority over the views of others. Their voices must be advisory rather than authoritative, patiently persuasive rather than dogmatically insistent. They must give up the claim of the "one true way" and look for common ground with others, even while retaining their own convictions. In short, religious views, organizations and spirit must become a part of civil society and democratic politics.

Those of us who are interested in the quality of our civic life—including the ways in which we talk to one another about what collective purposes we might choose to achieve, as well as how we might best achieve them—must open our minds once again to the important role that religious views, religious congregations, and other faith-based organizations play in shaping public debate about social provision. A strong liberal community has never been a wholly secular community. It has been one in which individuals could seek meaning for their own lives through different kinds of religious experience. It has also been one in which individuals could participate in the arduous task of self-governance as whole human beings—not being required to leave their religious commitments at the doorway to civil society. And it is one in which the role and tradition of religious "prophecy" could be relied upon as one source to remind us of our deep obligations to one another.

We owe a great deal to these authors for having the courage to put these issues before the polity as powerfully as they have done, and to begin the process of recovering the important role of religion in shaping the moral discourse and action potential that is contained in our civic life. It is significant, I think, that the process that produced these essays is itself a model of the kind of collective process that they believe holds much promise for the future. That process held a group of highly diverse scholars—those professionally committed to theology and the importance of faith as well as those committed to "secular humanism" and social science methods, those committed to a stern ethic of individual freedom and personal responsibility as well as those committed to a political ideology that insisted on the recognition of our mutual dependence and obligations to one another — tightly together in a joint effort to explore the values and the institutional arrangements that could guide our efforts to create a more just society. That they have succeeded as well as they have in bringing this effort to a coherent whole is a tribute to their leadership. It is also evidence of the ability of humans to reason together not only about what is true but also what is just and good and important to try to achieve together. Let's hope that this effort will be followed by many more of similar quality, and that the potential of religious faith to improve rather than divide our public life is fully explored.

Acknowledgments

THE CENTER FOR THE STUDY OF VALUES IN PUBLIC LIFE invited a diverse group of scholars to begin a dialogue in the aftermath of the 1996 legislation restructuring public assistance. Our aim was not to rehash welfare reform. It was to explore a broader perspective for assessing the current state and future direction of American social provision. An extraordinary conversation unfolded over the next three years, drawing on current work in a number of disciplines, and focusing on a question of deep concern to us all: Who will provide?

We are grateful to each of our co-authors in this volume for their willingness to present papers that often ventured across boundaries to explore a wider terrain. Those presentations would not have sparked such interesting and enjoyable exchanges were it not for the deeply collegial and thoughtful contributions of the colleagues who participated in the Harvard Faculty Seminar on Public Life and the Renewal of Democracy: Lawrie Balfour, Evelyn Brooks Higginbotham, Allen Callahan, James Carroll, David Ellwood, Marshall Ganz, Jon Gunnemann, David Hall, Stuart Hauser, Douglas Holt, Janet Jakobsen, Barry Karl, Elaine Kamarck, Christine Letts, Jane Mansbridge, Mark Moore, Katherine Newman, Linda Nicholson, Gary Orfield, Robert Putnam, Paula Rayman, Kathleen Sands, Juliet Schor, Elisabeth Schüssler Fiorenza, Jeffrey Seglin, Bernard Steinberg, Jim Wallis, Cornel West, Preston Williams, and Julie Boatright Wilson.

Like a good dinner with friends, a sustained conversation doesn't happen automatically. In this case, it was made possible by the dedicated work of Center staff. Donna Verschueren and Nancy Nienhuis provided steady support for this project amid many other duties. Sam Herring and Betsy Perabo assisted the seminar with a review of current literature and research on faith-based organizations and social services. Elizabeth Parsons provided skillful coordination and thoughtful reflection to turn draft papers into revised essays for publication. Sarah Moses furthered that process and prepared the integrated bibliography.

We are grateful as well to Rafael Sagalyn, our agent, who observed the seminar in action and helped to make the publication of its work a reality. Our special thanks are due to Richard Higgins who, amid the demands of family and journalism, carved out time and summoned patience to apply a clear mind to the task of final editing.

More than capturing different voices in a sustained dialogue, this collection of essays represents the guiding aim of the Center for the Study of Values in Public Life: to advance our understanding of how religion shapes critical debates and institutions in American public life. If that mission has been served at Harvard University through this project, it has been made possible by the generous support of the Lilly Endowment and the encouragement of its Vice President for Religion, Craig Dykstra. We hope these essays will honor their trust by contributing to a timely discussion, in many quarters, on the changing role of religion in how we provide for one another.

—*Mary Jo Bane, Brent Coffin, Ronald Thiemann*

Introduction

Mary Jo Bane and Brent Coffin

Who Will Provide?—for the hungry and the homeless, the widow and the orphan, the prisoner and the stranger? When the Hebrew prophets observed injustice, exclusion, and oppression in Israel, they raged in the name of God against an uncaring people. They took the whole community to task—the rich who oppressed their workers, the kings who did not provide for their people, the religious leaders who cared only about their own well being, and every person who passed by someone in need. They demanded that the people as a whole face up to their responsibilities and that every member and every institution contribute to the care of all.

America today is wary of prophecy. How could anyone today presume to speak of justice and compassion in the powerful language of faith to a wildly diverse and highly individualistic society? Who in a society enamored of the market and distrustful of government would pay more than passing attention to concepts like community, covenant, shared responsibility and the common good? How could a people that has by and large secularized and professionalized the work of feeding the hungry, sheltering the homeless, caring for the sick, and protecting the vulnerable hear a call for everyone to participate in caring through individual, community and government action? Does America want or need such prophets?

The essays in this volume answer: Yes, we need prophets. Yes, we need their religious voice and fervor behind a cry of concern to a society that too often seems not to care. Yes, we need a new network of social provision that encompasses individuals, nonprofit organizations, and government and that does not shy away from including religious communities. Yes, we need a politics that includes every person, hears every voice and cares about justice.

The essays, of course, do not speak as one. They do not agree on one religious perspective, one set of policy recommendations or one model for organizing social care. Indeed they document the complexity of all these dimensions. But they do agree on the need for, and in some sense try to provide, a clear prophetic voice calling all of us to reexamine the obligations we have for one another.

The essays emerged from a seminar on public life and the renewal of democracy that came together at Harvard in 1996 under the auspices of the Center for the Study of Values in Public Life of Harvard Divinity School. The catalyst prompting the seminar was a common concern about the 1996 welfare reform legislation. The participants generally shared a perception that the legislation represented an abdication of federal responsibility for the poor and a failure of politics. They also shared a concern that the "charitable choice" provision in that legislation, which encouraged states to contract out welfare services to religious organizations, embodied a dangerous assumption that local communities and especially religious groups could alone fill the breach left by government.

From this starting point, the seminar went beyond just another case study in welfare reform. More than 25 scholars from seven Harvard schools and departments met regularly over three years. They did so because welfare legislation signaled for them the end of an era. Beyond changes in welfare laws and institutional strategies to deliver services, they encountered questions concerning the enduring moral obligations of all institutions and members of society. To grasp these questions, seminar participants sought a broader context encompassing issues of poverty and inequality that society has not figured out how to solve or whether to care about: growing economic inequality, the increased salience of both the "working poor" and the multiply disadvantaged dependent poor, the paradox of great hardship in the midst of great prosperity. Accompanying these issues were perplexing expressions of moral and spiritual impoverishment: the erosion of communities linking Americans across boundaries of geography, affluence and race; the inability to discuss and solve public problems in a constructive way through democratic politics; and the withdrawal of historic religious bodies as prophets and healers to the nation. As members of the seminar probed these deeper complexities, they continually encountered a pervasive absence of clear and vibrant voices in our public life calling us to the responsibilities we have toward one another as human beings and citizens of a democracy. To explore how such voices might be recovered in a period of profound change, seminar participants increasingly focused their discussions on America's religious communities and sought to understand them in a new perspective.

A New Perspective

The Religious Right insists that faith provides answers to the deepest problems of society. They tell us that our public institutions, policies, and even personal characters must be built upon the bedrock of divine moral absolutes. Only by returning to religious faith will our society solve the vexing challenges of failed schools, crime, drugs, poverty, and national drift. Yet with equal conviction the Secular Left insists that the re-emergence of public religion poses grave dangers for society. They warn that constitutional democracy is built on the freedom to hold diverse beliefs about what is ultimately good for individuals, communities and the nation. When one religion seeks to impose its truths on others, it endangers these most fundamental freedoms of democracy and erodes the tolerance that allows diverse men and women to work together. Those who regard religion as "the problem" find their fears justified by those who proclaim religion to be "the answer," and such fears distort the contributions of America's vast tapestry of religious communities.

Seminar participants, therefore, agreed on the need for a new perspective on public religion. They proposed to consider the contributions of religious communities toward revitalizing America's social caring in terms of four potential roles: relating men and women to the transcendent through spiritual traditions, shaping moral vision, creating community, and participating with other institutions in social provision. Each of these roles offers a useful way to move beyond the paralyzing standoff between the Religious Right and the Secular Left, and more fruitfully to explore the promises and perils of religious communities in the emerging era.

The vast majority of Americans understand themselves to be religious. At the same time they relate to the transcendent through varied and particular spiritual traditions. The Religious Right is correct to insist that deeply held beliefs and values find expression in both public and private realms of society; for a democratic society to thrive its citizens must dare to draw on their deepest values without embarrassment. Yet, contrary to the Religious Right, we believe there is a need for an ever deeper respect for the varied spiritual traditions in which men and women live in relation to the transcendent. Here, the Secular Left is correct to insisting on protecting the rights of all citizens, most especially those who are poor and in need, from even well intended efforts by religious citizens to impose their beliefs through the coercive power of the state. But the new perspective we propose need not be rooted in the Secular Left's fear and suspicion of religion as inherently dominating and intolerant of those who are different. Deeply held convictions and practices of faith can awaken consciences to those who are in need, inspire service to the poor in a spirit of respect, and build common moral ground for new partnerships among those who are rooted in profoundly different traditions.

A new approach also moves beyond the Religious Right and Secular Left in rethinking how public religion contributes to moral vision. The Religious Right properly calls us to understand that social care and provision involve more than economic and political dimensions; they also involve spiritual and moral dimensions. Yet a new perspective calls for critical scrutiny of how spiritual beliefs influence our understanding of the poor. Many on the Religious Right insist that better approaches to social provision require greater personal responsibility, and properly so. Responsibility for oneself and others is a sacred and essential feature of personal dignity and social welfare. At the same time, we must critically challenge religious groups that place the burden for overcoming destructive and unacceptable social conditions upon the poor themselves. The moral visions of the prophets began with divine judgment on those in power, who enjoy opportunity, who benefit from society's present conditions—but all the while turn their backs on those living at the margins of society. Like the Secular Left, a new perspective seeks to provide insights into structural injustices of inequality, race, and gender that exclude men and women and diminish community. Yet once again, it rejects the underlying assumption of the Secular Left that religion necessarily silences or merely mimics these critical insights. In diverse communities of faith, there are complex repertoires of memory and moral vision that connect charity to justice, privilege to obligation, personal responsibility to social transformation, personal service to public policy, impossible odds to enduring hope. If these moral resources are misused, religious communities can further injustice; if they are reclaimed today, those communities can provide moral vision to help all of us better recognize what we owe to one another.

A new perspective will also look beyond easy generalities about "faith-based organizations" to help us better understand how public religion creates community. Many social scientists tend to ignore religious communities. A few scholars have drawn attention to the functional values of faith-based organizations: supplying information, physical space, leadership skills, social networks; mobilizing human and financial resources for services such as soup kitchens, tutoring and mentoring programs, job training and placement, drug counseling; and in a number of cases, sponsoring community and economic development projects such a new housing, schools and businesses. In addition, a new perspective will be aided by those on the Religious Right who see religious communities as places for intrinsic values: worship, celebration, friendship, support, hope, and much more. But while seeking to understand the fullness and complexity of religious communities we must also heed an important warning from the Secular Left. Those who extol religious communities uncritically can promote a localism and voluntarism that will burden religious communities with more than they can bear, exempt the government from responsibilities it alone can bear, and harm those in need by the failures of both. Pressing beyond both the Religious Right and Secular Left, a new perspective on public religion must recognize that faith communities are being summoned to play an extremely important role in this moment of history, but one they can fulfill only through creative partnerships with other nonprofit organizations and the government.

Finally, from this perspective a paramount challenge is to identify the kinds of partnerships that build on the strengths of religious communities, secular organizations, and the government; that respect and preserve the integrity of each partner; and that advance social care and provision for all citizens. This approach believes that faith-based organizations must take care to preserve their distinct values and identities; indeed they must renew them in the process of developing partnerships that make a real difference for those in need. It encourages efforts now underway among local religious and government leaders to build new relationships and initiatives in a spirit of mutual accountability. At the same time, it rejects partnerships that allow religious groups to use the state to impose their beliefs upon others, or the state to co-opt religious communities into becoming their arms for service delivery. In short, a new perspective recognizes that partnerships will involve inescapable perils; but those perils should not be allowed to overshadow the promises religious organizations hold for renewing our obligations to one another. It is in this perspective that the following essays explore both the promises and perils of new partnerships in the current historical moment.

Welfare Reform in the 1990s

To set the context for these essays, it is important to recall the dramatic change in social welfare policy that took place in the 1990s. While welfare reform is a perennial topic on the policy agenda, in the early 1990s public anger about welfare seemed to reach new heights. Candidate Bill Clinton discovered that a pledge to "End Welfare as We Know It" brought very high approval ratings from polls and focus groups. Polls taken around the time of the 1992 election showed that the public supported nearly any alternative to the then current welfare system.[1] Clinton's powerful rhetoric and innovative ideas about welfare almost certainly contributed to his election.

Candidate Clinton tapped into both public attitudes and academic analysis. To some extent the public's anger almost certainly reflected prejudice and stereotype. It also, however, reflected a perception of unfairness: that many families struggled to support themselves and their children with two working parents and almost no government support, while the welfare system seemed to allow single mothers to stay home with their children and be supported by the public. Academic analysis, by both conservative and more liberal thinkers, argued that the incentives, rules and organization of the welfare system discouraged work and parental responsibility.[2] The early 1990s saw a number of proposals for welfare reform that were aimed at encouraging or requiring work, shortening stays on welfare and encouraging parental responsibility.

The early Clinton administration's welfare policy, reflecting these themes, had two prongs. One consisted in the granting of federal waivers to states to enable them to experiment with new approaches to welfare. By 1996 nearly all the states had passed some form of welfare reform. Most of the state plans included work requirements and also included increased financial incentives for recipients who worked. Many of the plans included some form of time limit on welfare receipt. Some included provisions aimed at increasing family responsibility, such as "family caps" (not increasing welfare benefits upon the birth of a child to a welfare recipient), requirements that teen mothers live at home and stay in school, and increased enforcement of child support.[3]

The second prong was an administration-proposed welfare reform bill that would have continued these themes and established a time limit for welfare receipt, to be followed by work, subsidized if necessary. The administration's proposal continued the basic framework or entitlement to cash benefits, federally enforced legal protections for recipients, and federal-state matching funding.

The proposal, however, became irrelevant after the midterm elections of 1994, when the Republican Congress took over the welfare agenda.[4]

The 1996 legislation. The Personal Responsibility and Work Opportunity Reconciliation Act, based on the Republican's Contract with America, passed the House of Representatives and the Senate in the summer of 1996 by large bipartisan margins after the president indicated that he would sign the bill that had been worked out in conference committee. The legislation was long and complicated, containing, among other things, detailed (and bipartisan) proposals for improving federal child support enforcement. The major features of the law affecting welfare per se included: abolishing of the federal entitlement to assistance and the federal matching-fund structure; establishing of a flexible block grant to states to be used for "Transitional Assistance to Needy Families;" requiring states to require most welfare recipients to work; and placing a five-year time limit on the receipt of federally funded welfare benefits.

Senator Daniel Patrick Moynihan, the Senate's long-time premier expert on welfare, denounced the bill as "welfare repeal" and predicted that its passage would lead to ". . . a third of a million children in the streets. . . children on grates, because there is no money in the states and cities to care for them."[5] Three officials in the Department of Health and Human Services with primary responsibility for welfare, including co-author Mary Jo Bane, resigned in protest after the president signed the bill. By and large, however, both Democratic and Republican members of Congress, even moderately liberal Democrats, not only voted for the bill but also denounced the old welfare systems and bragged in their reelection campaigns about their vote to reform welfare.

Under the new federal welfare rules, most states continued the reform policies they had begun to put in place under waivers, emphasizing work, time limits and parental obligations. Because of the construction of the block-grant formula, states received relatively generous funds, which some of them invested in supportive services. This, plus the fact that the 1990s saw robust economic growth and extremely low unemployment rates, shaped a benign environment for the implementation of reform.

Changed welfare. The combination of a very good economy and a new welfare policy resulted in changes in the welfare system that were far greater than most people had predicted. The actual operation of the welfare system changed in most states from a system that had been rightly criticized for focusing almost entirely on establishing and documenting eligibility for cash and in-kind benefits and on delivering them. The new systems, as documented by a team of implementation researchers from the Rockefeller Institute of SUNY Albany, saw caseworkers spending much more time emphasizing the transitional nature of welfare and both requiring recipients to work and supporting them in it.[6] In some states benignly and in other states quite punitively, recipients were discouraged from going on welfare, required to explore other means of support, and encouraged or pushed off welfare as quickly as possible.

These efforts were accompanied by, and partially caused, dramatic caseload declines. By 1999, welfare caseloads had dropped more than 40 percent from their high point in 1994, an unprecedented decline. In some states, caseload declines were as much as 80 percent of more.[7] At the same time, labor force participation and employment by divorced, separated and never-married mothers rose by about ten percentage points, after a long period of no change in these rates.[8] Numerically, by 1999, the increase in employment was only about half as large as the decrease in welfare caseloads. Clearly welfare was much less often seen and used as a primary means for family support. Further evidence of the declining importance of the welfare system came from the fact that Food Stamps and Medicaid rolls also declined much more than would have been predicted on the basis of the economy and the modest policy changes that occurred in those programs.[9] Apparently neither the system nor potential recipients distinguished the welfare system that had been reformed from the programs that were expected to continue to provide a safety net. Welfare as we knew it had indeed ended, and in many states welfare itself seemed on the road to ending entirely.

Persistent poverty. Although the welfare system had changed dramatically by 1999, the plight of poor families with children, especially female-headed families, had not. Poverty rates for children in single-parent families, though lower than in 1993, remained at a shocking 46 percent in 1998. Careful examination of trends in poverty rates by the Children's Defense Fund and the Center for Budget and Policy Priorities showed that, although some among the poor were better off because they were working rather than on welfare, others, neither working nor on welfare, were worse off.[10]

Despite the fact that systematic evaluation data are only beginning to come in, and despite the fact it is much too early to tell how welfare reform will play itself out over the long term, it is clear that important changes have occurred. The combination of declining caseloads, increased work, and stable poverty signals a movement of many of the welfare poor into the ranks of the working poor. Those who had or would have been welfare recipients are now in the low wage labor markets, mostly in insecure jobs without benefits or opportunities for advancement, many with irregular work hours and all vulnerable to an increasingly competitive and insecure labor market.

The dramatic changes in the welfare system pose new challenges and present new opportunities. Because the change in welfare has been so dramatic, and because it is perceived by so many people as basically positive, it is hard to imagine that the basic thrust of the welfare reform legislation will be reversed anytime soon. Though there may be modifications at both the state and federal level, it seems highly unlikely that entitlements to cash benefits will be restored, that work requirements or time limits will be removed, or that the federal government will exert strong new authority vis-a-vis the states.[11] But since the welfare system is becoming an ever-smaller part of the safety net, there may be an opportunity to refocus the social policy debate on poverty rather than welfare.

The new issues for poverty policy are the plight of the working poor, the lack of a safety net for the unemployed, and the problems of those (some of whom remain on the welfare caseload) with serious barriers to employment. The dramatic change in welfare means that policy need no longer focus on those who are able to work but are not in the labor force, but instead on those who are working but still poor, those who are out of work because of recessions, layoffs or lack of jobs, and those who cannot work or can barely work even in a good economy. Questions of cash or in-kind support for poor working families (e.g., the Earned Income Tax Credit, health insurance and subsidized child care) and also training and educational opportunities to help those in the low wage labor market advance will receive public and policy attention, as will developing better protection for the unemployed and safety nets for those who do not meet the current definitions of disability but nonetheless cannot work. This new context may provide an opportunity for a less angry, more compassionate and more inclusive politics. Public opinion is consistently sympathetic both to those who cannot work (as long as the barriers are not perceived as the "fault" of the person, as alcoholism, drug abuse and even emotional and mental disabilities often are) and to those who are working but still poor. Because a large proportion of the population has been left behind by a 1990s prosperity that has mainly benefited the top fifth of the income distribution, there may be more discussions of policies to share prosperity more broadly and fairly, discussions that could engage more voters around both ideals and self-interest than poverty or welfare policy ever did. This will not necessarily happen, of course, but the new context that has emerged after the 1996 welfare legislation would seem to provide a chance that it might.

The Historical Moment

To explore this possibility, it was necessary to refocus the social-policy debate more broadly around welfare reform. Accordingly, seminar participants explored new partnerships involving religious communities in light of six wider features of the historical moment: increasing and seemingly intractable economic inequality; gender and race inequalities that especially affect the most vulnerable families; a loss of confidence in the welfare state to provide adequate solutions; the reliance on choice frameworks for solutions to social needs; a widely voiced need to strengthen civil society; and a religious revival that increases the promise and peril of religion in the public square.

The 1980s and 1990s have been, according to many criteria, a time of unprecedented economic prosperity. But the prosperity has not been widely shared. Between 1970 and 1996, the mean income of the top fifth of American families increased from $131,450 to $217,355, while the mean income of the bottom fifth of American families decreased from $11,640 to $11,388.[12] During the same period, the portion of America's children under the age 6 living in poverty grew from 16.6 to 22.7 percent; and from 1976 to 1996 the portion of

Americans without health care coverage grew from 10.9 to 15.6 percent.[13] Despite these precipitous trends, most Americans do not seem to see economic disparity as a problem. They appear not to begrudge the wealthy their riches, perhaps because popular culture suggests that the rich have earned their rewards, perhaps because aspiring to riches seems such a part of human nature. But it is hard to see how American society, especially our sense of obligation to one another, can thrive in the face of the huge and growing inequalities that now exist. Between the period of 1978–80 and that of 1996–98, the average income of the top fifth of the population in terms of income grew by 33.3 percent, while that of the bottom fifth dropped by 6.5 percent.[14] In a "winner take all society," we fear that Americans will cease to regard the question of how we provide for one another as something that needs to be asked at all. In such a situation, how will we renew what has been an historically American commitment to building institutions such as public schools and hospitals, offering attainable health coverage and supportive work programs that provide all citizens genuine opportunity and shared prosperity?

Gender and racial inequities exacerbate the growing income gap in the United States. While the earnings gap between women and men has narrowed in the last two decades, the average female earner in 1996 still received just 73.8% the pay of her male counterpart in a comparable job.[15] As women continue to invest more time in paid work to support their households, they still bear a disproportionate responsibility for nurturing young children, elderly parents, and ailing family members. The most devastating expression of racial and gender inequities is evident in the lives of low-income women who have turned to welfare for sustenance. Since its inception in the 1930s, American social welfare has been a two-tiered system. The first tier, Social Security, has honored working Americans, who in the past, at least, have been disproportionately white and male by rescuing many from poverty in their elderly years with income support in excess of their contributions, and doing so without shame or intrusion. By contrast, the second-tier welfare programs have provided much lower support to families that lack a worker and have done so with terrible humiliation and control. The 1996 welfare reform legislation means that the large majority of single-parent families, headed by women, must now exit welfare roles for work, and most are eager to do so. Yet for the first time, African-American and Latino families comprise the majority of remaining welfare recipients, because they face additional obstacles arising from racial inequities. Taken together, class, gender, and race inequalities are producing a welfare reform story wildly unrelated to the American Dream. Welfare poor are becoming working poor, often no more able—quite possibly less able—to support and nurture their families than before. Ignoring gender and racial inequities will undermine our ability to find a better answer to the question, Who provides? Facing them will help working families across America to seek better ways of supporting one another.

Deep tensions over race, gender and income have fueled an often ugly politics of welfare reform. But the public ire animating such viciousness is symptomatic of the alienation Americans have come to feel from their government on the whole. Where a generation ago three quarters of the American public trusted the federal government to do the right thing most of the time, today only a quarter of Americans do so.[16] Few today are looking to the federal government to play a leading role in providing for those who lack affordable housing, safe communities, decent schools and hope for their future in America's democracy. This public loss of confidence in the national welfare state, accompanies a shift in the locus of responsibility for providing social services from the federal to the state and local levels and to private and nonprofit organizations. While devolution offers new opportunities for innovation and experimentation, it also poses new challenges to maintain national standards, to rebuild a sense of shared moral responsibility among citizens, and to reevaluate America's bold social experiment.

A fourth feature of the present historical moment is the almost unquestioned dominance of market-based choice models for meeting the needs of our citizens. Who should provide? In the first instance, individuals should provide for themselves. If they cannot, this argument holds, the void should not be filled by welfare state provision. Instead, the state should support the market by supplementing individual purchasing power. Choice and competition jargon now characterize strategies for providing care to infants, schooling to children, and Social Security to the elderly. Private retirement accounts, child care tax credits, and school vouchers are heralded as the most effective means of expanding the control individuals have over their lives, diminishing government interference, and improving the performance of institutions. Significantly, as the essays in this volume reveal, the choice motif actually opens the door more widely for religious institutions to provide services from schooling to drug counseling. At the same time, choice and competition rhetoric provide all too easy answers to the question on which these essays focus. If we are simply a society of separate individuals or small groups, each fulfilling our lives through private choices, then all we owe to one another is a well functioning and occasionally subsidized market. Once we can claim that choices exist, we can ignore the systemic inequities created by varying life opportunities and outcomes. But doing so runs counter to the great strides we have made in becoming a democratic nation that provides for all its citizens. An over reliance on choice and competition also inhibits the social caring and mutual obligations that have brought this country so far and upon which the future of our democracy will depend.

Perhaps because some lingering doubts exist in many minds regarding the market's ability to solve societal problems, the current moment exhibits a widely felt need to revitalize civil society—the institutions, voluntary associations, and practices of community involvement beyond the state. Evidence abounds that Americans are painfully experiencing a loss of community. Families are under strain as they struggle to nurture their young and care for their elderly. The sense of place and connection to others that has so long characterized neighborhoods seems non-existent in many locales. Large numbers of the younger generations are growing up with little affiliation to religious communities and opportunities for pondering transcendent meaning seem in scarce supply.[17] Despite these trends towards dissolution of traditional common bonds, those most loudly calling for renewal of civil society insist that vibrant local communities are the alternative to governmental responsibility for social provision. The authors in this volume reject this dichotomy as fundamentally flawed both historically and prescriptively. Instead, they maintain that vibrant voluntary associations linking citizens across local boundaries have generated moral and political support for advances in social welfare policy. In turn those advances have undergirded the capacity of Americans to sustain vibrant associations that express their values. Renewing private voluntary associations *and* generating public support for better social policy must be pursued as compatible and interdependent goals.

Related to all these features, the broad question of "Who will provide?" is now being reconsidered amidst indications of religious revival. There is mounting interest in what role religious communities will play in determining how a diverse democratic citizenry provides for one another, most especially those who are least advantaged and in greatest need. As in previous periods of religious revival, Americans of diverse backgrounds are today engaging in a search for transcendent meaning and purpose. Religious institutions continue to play a significant role, as they have from the nation's beginning, in building social networks of compassion, providing services, and expressing moral values in the public square. Moreover, the new policy environment after welfare reform is encouraging—perhaps even requiring—faith-based organizations to renew their social ministries. Soup kitchens and food pantries are in greater demand; parenting, job readiness, and drug rehabilitation programs are being offered by religious organizations with government contracts or through voluntary partnerships; and religious voices are seeking to articulate the "we" that unites a diverse people into bonds of mutual care and responsibility. This sixth feature – public religion shaping the future of our democracy –emerged as the central focus of these essays as they consider seriously both the promise and the perils of new partnerships for social provision in the emerging era.

The Promise and Peril of Religious Communities

The promise of religious communities to play a crucial role in revitalizing the social fabric and re-knitting the social safety net comes from three potential roles: creating community; shaping moral dialogue; and participating with other institutions in social provision. Underlying all three is the uniquely religious transcendent perspective that orients people of faith to a reality beyond themselves. This orientation shapes the motivation and the commitments of religious people as well as the grounding of their sense of community.

Faith-based organizations are in a unique position in American society to create community, both through their religious commitment to the brotherhood and sisterhood of all humanity and through their very practical activities of bringing people together. The vast majority of Americans belong to churches, synagogues and mosques. Significant numbers participate in religious activities in addition to worship—e.g., scripture study, fellowship groups, and a variety of service activities. We believe it is important to recognize that these activities are not "private." While religious congregations are private in the sense that they are constitutionally protected from control by government, they are vital public contributors to a wider civil society. Religious communities constitute genuinely "public meeting spaces" where people come to know one another and to act upon their common values. Religious communities are extraordinarily diverse and broadly based; they provide public meeting spaces in virtually every locale in the nation. We do not want to minimize the fact that religious congregations, where persons voluntarily choose to associate with others, are typically homogeneous in race and economic status. Yet historically religious denominations have been among the most vital associations connecting men and women across geographic, economic and social boundaries, and providing diverse people with experiences of belonging to and serving a larger civic community.

Religious communities also are in a unique position to help shape the moral dialogue about social caring and just provision for all persons. Religious traditions are irreducibly different; those differences at times have fueled tragic human conflict. Yet the great religious traditions share much in common; and they do so not merely at their boundaries but at their vital centers. According to Confucius, "What you yourself do not want, do not do to another person." According to Rabbi Hillel, "Do not do to others what you would not want them to do to you." Jesus of Nazareth said, "Whatever you want people to do to you, do also to them." Islam teaches, "None of you is a believer as long as he does not wish his brother what he wishes himself." Hinduism teaches, "One should not behave toward others in a way which is unpleasant for oneself; this is the essence of morality." Indeed, these great religious traditions differ in their beliefs about ultimate reality, their approaches to community, and the types of institutions they foster. Yet, for all their enduring differences, these traditions share central commitments: to the equal worth and sacredness of all men and women; to recognizing our shared vulnerability as finite creatures; and to our common needs for nurture and support to achieve our potential as creative participants in family, community and society.[18] The Torah, Bible and Koran especially stress that the covenant community requires of its members a special obligation to the poor and vulnerable; by their treatment the character of the entire community is measured. Religious communities thus bring to the question "Who provides?" their profound convictions that our common life is founded on a spiritual and moral dimension that cannot be left for safekeeping to government, markets, or special purpose organizations. It may be that the traditions of religious communities provide society's best hope for reviving and enlarging the circle of social caring upon which all parts of our society depend and for which all are responsible.

Finally, we believe that religious communities also have an important role in participating with others to actually do the work of feeding the hungry, sheltering the homeless and welcoming the stranger—and providing support and services to both welfare and working families. Service to one's brothers and sisters is part of the historic mission of faith communities. Religious motivation and committed has often generated models of service that are both more personal and more respectful than professional models. As we search for new ways to be with and support vulnerable families, many religious organizations have developed very powerful intervention and support strategies. They are helping people overcome addictions, develop effective work habits, become better parents, and regain hope for a better future. We believe religious communities should bring these talents to the larger table, as a way of both fulfilling their own mission and contributing to our democratic society. But they cannot and should not go it alone. We worry about the tendency to invite faith communities to expand their social ministries as an *alternative* to other private institutions and to the government renewing their commitments to social provision. "Dumping" social needs at the doorsteps of churches, synagogues and mosques will not enable religious communities to do what they do best, nor will it strengthen the social provision of inclusive democracy. Instead, religious communities must build upon their historic legacy of social caring by developing new partnerships with other groups and with the government.

Embracing a new perspective on public religion that moves beyond the Religious Right and the Secular Left, these essays stress the promise religious communities hold for helping us to find better answers to the question "Who will provide?" However, the promise of public religion cannot be separated from its perils. Religious communities may seek to renew themselves by serving their own members and ignoring—or worse, denigrating—those who are in greatest need. They may provide services to the hungry and homeless, or support networks for families struggling to exit welfare, but ignore underlying inequalities of income, gender, and race dividing our society. Religious congregations may provide services to the poor, or even protest on their behalf, but do so *for* them and not *with* them, thus reinforcing exclusion. They may form new partnerships with other organizations and government to deliver social services, but in the process lose their religious identities or their prophetic moral voices. Or they may reach out through spiritual ministries of healing and support, but in the process violate the constitutional freedoms of vulnerable persons. We believe these and other perils cannot be ignored. There are no easy answers to the question "Who will provide?" A better answer can be found only by facing the dilemmas that partnerships of social provision invariably pose.

Overview of the Book

The essays in this volume fall into three broad sections. Part One—"Social Provision in Historical Context"—addresses the need to recover a broader perspective on how we provide for one another as citizens in an evolving democracy. Historian and sociologist Theda Skocpol makes clear that religious associations and federations have historically played a central role in expanding the circle of America's social caring and provision. They have done so, however, not simply by each community taking care of its own. They formed trans-local associations that provided diverse people with a vivid sense of belonging to a larger moral and civic community; and they sought to secure social provision for all members of that community through both government and voluntary action. Theologian Ronald Thiemann, Sam Herring and Betsy Perabo further set the stage for a broader perspective by recalling that churches have engaged in diverse ministries of care and advocacy since the nation's founding, and they have done so precisely because of their religious identities. Such identities, Thiemann cautions, must be preserved in pursuing new partnerships of social provision.

Part Two—"Public Religion and Social Provision"—takes up the need for a new perspective on public religion. In actuality, a perspective that breaks with both the Religious Right and Secular Left is rooted in ancient traditions dating back to the Hebrew prophets and to the early Christian church. The contest over how we reclaim these traditions is joined here not by presenting a single theory of public religion, but by offering three examples of critical retrieval. In the first essay of this section, Catholic theologian Francis Schüssler Fiorenza notes how the contemporary focus on charity ignores the centrality of justice in the Christian tradition. The essay by Catholic moral theologian J. Bryan Hehir further shows the importance of interpreting religious traditions carefully. Challenging those who use the principle of subsidiarity in Catholic social teachings to justify recent trends in social welfare, Hehir argues that subsidiarity assigns moral responsibility to the state for meeting social needs that cannot be met by more immediate communities. In a third essay, Protestant ethicist Brent Coffin considers the public role of religious congregations, arguing that their practices shape who participants are and what kind of values they hold. While religious values are public, they need to be articulated in corresponding views of justice that are accessible to others in a pluralist democracy. Coffin illustrates the need to be "bilingual" religious citizens by showing how a religiously informed view of justice as participation would help to reframe a public debate over social provision after welfare reform.

Part Three—"Partnerships, Strategies and Inescapable Dilemmas"—takes up the promise and peril that public religion holds for helping us to answer the question of "Who will provide?" Religious communities are able to fulfill their potential only by working in partnerships with other civic organizations and with agencies of government. The essays in this section map the broad terrain of partnerships, examine specific cases, and analyze the dilemmas that leaders must navigate.

Constitutional scholar Martha Minow introduces the terrain by considering three invitingly simple answers to the question of who is responsible for the poor or for children: each community; the national government; no one outside the immediate family. Showing each to be unworkable, Minow turns to the constitutional constraints on partnerships between government and religious organizations, then explores the questions these more complex strategies raise in providing social services to the poor and schooling for children. Political scientist Anna Greenberg next surveys the types of government funding available to religious congregations in the post-welfare environment, and the ways states and local communities have responded to the recent welfare reform changes, showing that both federal resources and state/local initiatives are currently more limited than many assume. In the broad terrain mapped by Minow and Greenberg, nonprofit scholar Peter Frumkin looks directly at the dilemmas inherent in managing public-nonprofit partnerships. Beneath the rhetoric of partnership, there is no small danger that nonprofit organizations, whether religious or secular, will relinquish their independent character as they draw upon public resources and are held accountable for them. Such a danger is of great concern to religious leaders who, like Thiemann, believe their communities must retain their religious identities. Frumkin invites public managers to develop an approach that does not withdraw from partnerships but exercises public oversight with deliberate attention to the independent values of the nonprofit partners.

The importance of independent civic organizations embodying values and bringing them into partnerships of social provision is explored in three related essays. Sociologist Christopher Winship and co-authors examine a partnership between law enforcement and community leaders that reduced homicide rates 77 percent between 1990 and 1998. An important feature of the "Boston Miracle," they argue, is that the key community leaders in this partnership are ministers with inner-city congregations. As independent moral leaders, these clergy are able to use their authority to call trouble prone youth to personal responsibility and to challenge systemic injustices, to provide legitimacy for necessary law enforcement tactics and to expose abuses of police authority.

The story of religious leaders working with police to dramatically reduce youth violence makes clear that partnerships never occur in a vacuum; they take place in communities made up of families, social groups and civic organizations. The aim of partnerships, therefore, cannot be defined narrowly in terms of service delivery to those in need; it must include the development of communities. What models of community should partnerships seek to advance for disadvantaged youth and families? Poverty scholar Richard Weissbourd argues that a traditional model of the stable, sheltering community is no longer adequate for children, especially those who experience wrenching mobility but also the need to learn to manage multiple roles. He proposes a model of community that provides vulnerable children with lasting ties and access to more diverse communities beyond their own neighborhoods. Schools and religious organizations are positioned to address both facets, but they must give more attention to strategies that foster the second.

The importance of religious and civic organizations retaining their independent visions is further shown in an essay by legal scholar Lucie White. White seeks to understand the debate over social provision from the standpoint of low-income women of color, and therefore listens carefully to the voices of mothers who have participated in the Head Start Program. Not unlike the success stories illustrating the moral that leaving welfare leads to a better life, White hears in the voices of low-income women scripted narratives of isolation and empowerment. Running through these narratives are deep echoes of African-American spirituality that have shaped the culture of Head Start programs. Recognizing such influences, White asks how public programs can empower participants by drawing on their spiritual narratives while not excluding others for whom such traditions are foreign.

The final essay by poverty scholar Mary Jo Bane draws the book to a close by returning the focus directly to religious communities and looking to the future. Recalling the lack of grassroots participation by religious congregations in the last round of welfare reform, Bane asks what impact the new policy environment will have on faith-based engagement in social provision. Looking specifically at Catholic parishes, Bane envisions greater involvement taking three forms: new services to the poor and greater personal involvement with poor families; strengthening disadvantaged neighborhoods through congregation-based community organizing; and developing knowledge and skills in local parishes to shape the moral debate over social provision. While acknowledging the perils and dilemmas explored in these essays, Bane argues that greater participation in all three forms can strengthen *both* religious communities *and* the larger civic community. The perils do not overshadow the promise.

Whether or not new partnerships emerge will depend in great measure on those who exercise leadership in religious communities, civic organizations, and public agencies. It is the hope of the seminar members that their discussions, presented in these essays, will be helpful to leaders also working to find better answers to the question, "Who will provide?"

Notes

1. See R. Kent Weaver, *Ending Welfare as we Know It* (Washington DC: Brookings Institution, 2000) for an insightful discussion of the politics around welfare reform in the early 1990s.

2. For example, Charles Murray, *Losing Ground: American Social Policy* (New York: Basic Books, 1984); David T. Ellwood, *Poor Support: Poverty in the American Family* (New York: Basic Books, 1988).

3. Information on waivers is available at the web page of the Administration for Children and Families (ACF), Department of Health and Human Services: www.acf.dhhs.gov.

4. Mary Jo Bane's HHS and Kennedy School colleague David Ellwood wrote an illuminating perspective on the politics of the administration's welfare reform effort in "Welfare Reform as I Knew It," *The American Prospect* (May/June1996): 22–29.

5. Senator Moynihan in remarks on the Senate floor, August 2, 1996.

6. Richard P. Nathan, and Thomas L. Gais, *Implementing the Personal Responsibility Act of 1996: A First Look* (Albany: Nelson Rockefeller Institute of Government, 1999).

7. Statistics on welfare caseloads are available on the ACF website. See note 3.

8. Labor force and poverty data from the March Current Population Surveys, available on line at www.census.gov.

9. Excellent analyses of these issues are done by the Center for Budget and Policy Priorities, Washington DC, www.cbpp.org. See, for example, Kathryn Porter and Wendell Primus, *Recent Changes in the Impact of the Safety Net on Child Poverty,* CBPP, December 1999; and Wendell Primus, Lynnette Rawlings, Kathy Larin and Kathryn Porter, *Initial Impacts of Welfare Reform on the Economic Well-being of Single Mother Families,* CBPP, August 1999.

10. Poverty Statistics from the Current Population Survey. Analyses from Wendell Primus et. al., *Initial Impacts.* See also Arloc Sherman, "Extreme Child Poverty Rises Sharply in 1997," Washington, D.C.: Children's Defense Fund, August 1999.

11. This is prediction, not prescription. And it is possible that were there to be a serious economic downturn, the prediction might be proved wrong.

12. Marc Miringoff, and Marque-Luisa Miringoff, *The Social Health of the Nation: How America is Really Doing* (New York: Oxford University Press, 1999), p. 106.

13. Ibid., pp. 82, 93.

14. Jared Bernstein, Elizabeth C. McNichol, Lawrence Mishel, and Robert Zahradnik, Pulling Apart: A State-by-State Analysis of Income Trends (Washington, D.C.: Center on Budget and Policy Priorities, January 2000), p.8.

15. Miringoff, *The Social Health of the Nation,* p. 100.

16. Joseph Nye, Jr., Philip Zelikow, and David King, eds., *Why People Don't Trust Government* (Cambridge: Harvard University Press, 1997), p. 1.

17. See Wade Clark Roof, *A Generation of Seekers* (San Francisco: Harper, 1994).

18. See The Parliament of the World's Religions, "Declaration toward a Global Ethic" in Hans Kung, ed., *Yes to a Global Ethic* (New York: Continuum, 1996).

PART ONE

Social Provision in Historical Context

CHAPTER 1

Religion, Civil Society, and Social Provision in the U.S.

Theda Skocpol

The genius of U.S. voluntary membership federations was to make local and national commitments complement rather than oppose one another. When today's conservatives advocate local voluntarism apart from, or in opposition to, government, they advocate a break with the past, not a return to it.

GROUPS RALLY AND PARTICIPANTS PLEDGE to remake their lives. Older associations and religious denominations are besieged, while new groups multiply and flourish. Organizers issue clarion calls for volunteers to help individuals, embody fellowship, and pursue national salvation.

Is this the United States of the 1990s?—the America of the Million Man March, movements of church and community people to "Stand for Children," of stadium rallies for Promise Keepers; the America of proliferating evangelical and Pentecostal churches, the "thousand points of light," and the national Volunteerism Summit? Or is it instead the nineteenth-century United States, with its evangelical camps, crusades for temperance and against slavery, its Chautauqua meetings and wildfire foundings of Methodist and Baptist congregations, its waves of poor relief organized by benevolent and charitable societies?

Just posing this question reminds us that America has experienced repeated crusades combining quests for community and for individual and societal salvation. Again and again, established religious denominations have been overtaken by religious renewals; and Americans recurrently call for voluntary efforts to reform persons and society. Religious people, religious ideals, and religious ties figure prominently in American social movements and in the making and implementation of the nation's social-welfare policies.

But how, exactly? The challenge is to comprehend the full set of ways religion and religious folks have mattered in American democracy and social provision. This is not easy at a time when very tendentious and misleading claims are being made, both by those who would condemn and those who would celebrate the contributions of religion to our nation's social and political life.

Secularism versus Charity

These days, many on the liberal end of the U.S. political spectrum presume that religious instincts in public life are inherently small-minded and antidemocratic. Liberals often imagine that everything progressive in U.S. society and politics has been rooted in secular, economically grounded struggles. Celebrating the achievements of the New Deal and its immediate aftermath, secular liberalism downplays much that happened in the history of American democracy and social provision prior to the mid-twentieth century.

Almost in mirror image, today's self-proclaimed conservatives call for a moralistic revival, advocating a return to what they consider pre-New Deal fundamentals in the realms of civil society and social compassion. Some conservatives talk of revival in religious terms, while others speak more secular tongues. Yet regardless of idiom, the conservative revivalist hope is much the same. It is grounded in a vision of an allegedly simple authentic America of the self-sufficient family, immediate neighborhood, and local church. In this romanticized America, domestic government above the local level is thought to be unnecessary. Except for purposes of national defense, reliance on government and extralocal politics can be avoided as the source of corrupting social evil.

Battling liberals who celebrate a national, secular welfare state, conservative revivalists paint the twentieth-century "welfare state" as a bureaucratic demon. Modern welfare states spread "spiritual malaise," writes Irving Kristol, because they encourage dependence and decadence, undermining the "reverent" communal religiosity on which true personal fulfillment depends.[1] Religiosity also appears in the version of the revivalist argument advanced by Marvin Olasky. In *The Tragedy of American Compassion,* a book much touted by conservatives, Olasky outlines a twentieth-century-long process of social decline, as U.S. welfare-state builders turned away from an early American "understanding of compassion that was hard-headed but warm-hearted" and was based on a Calvinist understanding of a "God of both justice and mercy."[2] Olasky hopes there can be a "renewal of American compassion" through "faith-based charity"—person-to-person ministration by churches, community leaders, and ordinary citizens.[3]

Similarly, in their article issuing a clarion call for "A New Civic Life," Michael Joyce and William Schambra advocate repudiating America's entire misguided century-long, progressive-led "experiment" with national community and the "professional" and "bureaucratic" welfare state, returning instead to "the America celebrated and immortalized in Alexis de Tocqueville's *Democracy in America,*" the authentic America of local "island communities." In that America, Joyce and Schambra argue,

> A citizen's churches and voluntary groups reflected and reinforced his moral and spiritual values and imparted them to his children, surrounding him with a familiar, self-contained, breathable moral atmosphere. Voluntary social welfare associations ministered to the community's vulnerable according to the tenets of compassion and charity. A citizen's schools, whether publicly or privately funded, enshrined those values, and were run in accordance with them, with extensive citizen involvement and supervision. Critical public decisions were made in township meetings, ward conclaves, or other small, face-to-face gatherings in which the individual's voice was as important as his vote. The most important decisions about citizens' lives were made not by faceless others in some distant state or national capital; they were made among the citizens themselves, in gatherings of neighbors and acquaintances.[4]

Joyce and Schambra believe that their version of authentic America persisted throughout the nineteenth century, only to be compromised and damaged by twentieth-century progressives and liberals who tried to establish a false national community and disrupted genuine local bonds. "Whereas before, public affairs were well within the grasp of the average citizen, easily comprehended and managed by ordinary folk wisdom and common sense, now public affairs had allegedly been so complicated by modernity that, according to the progressive elites, the average citizen could no longer hope to understand and manage them."[5] In the name of a false "national community," progressive experts and bureaucrats "replace[d] civic and voluntary social programs" and turned citizens into "passive 'clients'."[6]

All of this reached its zenith in the Great Society anti-poverty reforms, say Joyce and Schambra. But then a return to American basics set in. Since the 1970s onward, they argue, Americans of all persuasions have been pulling back from the "apparently smoothly humming federal edifice." With "the moral foundations of the liberal project . . . eroding," the "federal government comes to be seen . . . as a distant, alienating, bureaucratic monstrosity." Americans yearn to "return to the idea of community that finds expression in small participatory groups such as the family, neighborhood, and ethnic and voluntary associations—an idea far more natural and easier to sustain."[7]

Many liberals tell much the same story of trends and shifts over time. They simply offer an opposite moral assessment, viewing the growth of a national welfare state during and after the New Deal as the high point of American democracy, and decrying tendencies before the 1930s and after the 1980s to "abandon" the poor to the vagaries of private charity.

A Distorted Picture

Before we accede to the terms of debate structured by these arguments we should notice that dubious understandings about the place of religion in the shaping of American civil society and public social policies underpin both of these points of view.

There may be bits of truth in both perspectives, yet each misses crucial religious contributions to American democracy and social provision.

Today's conservative revivalists imply that "original," healthy forms of civil society in the United States were local and apolitical, that churches and other voluntary associations developed apart from extralocal government, and that American social policy has been mainly about (better or worse) ways of helping the very poor. This focus on charity for the very poor makes sense to conservatives, because they simply presume that all nonpoor Americans have done just fine through a combination of market enterprise and salvationist religious faith rooted in voluntary local congregations.

To be fair, conservatives *have* underlined some important and somewhat forgotten truths. In recent years the academic literature on "social welfare policy" has been so dominated by leftist secularists that it has written out of the record positive contributions from religiously inspired service to the poor. If noted at all, such ministry has transmuted into machiavellian acts of class or racial domination. This is unfortunate, because much of redeeming value has been accomplished by religiously committed individuals and congregations delivering spiritual along with material aid to fellow members of congregations or needy persons beyond the existing congregation.

There can be little doubt that many religious congregations have flourished—both in the past and today—because they are communities for all of their members in both practical and spiritual realms of life. Today's evangelical "megachurches" feature huge arrays of support groups for adults and programs for children.[8] They also promise caring warmth. As a huge evangelical church complex on the outskirts of Presque Isle, Maine, blazons on its billboard: "Family Christian Center: An Oasis of Love."

As for care of the poor, Marvin Olasky's book details hundreds of examples throughout American history of volunteer efforts to minister to the needy or the wayward. From colonial days on, religiously motivated women, above all, have organized and undertaken these efforts. Whoever may have formally headed the countless "benevolent societies" of America's towns, women provided the footwork and the direct human contacts. Olasky bemoans that today, even religiously administered aid to the poor has too often become bureaucratized, dominated by professional social workers rather than volunteers. Although his fulminations against social workers are often misplaced, Olasky is right to suggest that there is still a need for personal and spiritual engagement along with the even-handed delivery of social services.

This point is poignantly made in *Not All of Us Are Saints* by David Hilfiker, a leftist physician and Christian who lives, worships, and delivers care amidst the poor of Washington DC.[9] As Hilfiker shows, a loving and demanding faith can often be the only effective means of redemption in a setting where access or material benefits alone cannot help disorganized and disorderly persons. Hilfiker also recognizes, however, that broader public institutions with adequate resources and procedures are also necessary, to support and surround faith-inspired personal engagement with the poor.

Despite important insights about religiously inspired personal ministry, conservative revivalism fails just as much as leftist secularism as a full account of the history of American civil society and social provision. American voluntary efforts, religious or secular, have never been just locally organized. Starting long before the New Deal, democratic civil society and public social policy alike have flourished at the intersection of government and voluntary associations. Successful social programs have as often been about mutual social support among average Americans, as about the delivery of aid to the desperate. Important programs have stressed mutuality and democratic inclusion, not just betterment of the down-and-out. And to the degree that professionally administered social services have developed in the United States, church-affiliated agencies have been at the heart of the process, as anxious as any other agencies to have funding and support from state and national governments.

Religious organizations and values have helped to shape broad features of U.S. voluntarism and shared social provision that today's secular liberals and conservative revivalists tend to overlook. Hardly restricted to a search for righteousness or salvation, religious beliefs have been the source of inclusive and nation-spanning values and organizations fostering shared and participatory citizenship. Periodically, too, religiously inspired Americans have led tumultuous movements for social justice and radical reform, even as they have continued to call for helping individuals one at a time.

Before returning to the ideological clashes and perplexing social and political trends of the current era, let me spell out this alternative story, at odds with both liberal and conservative orthodoxy. I first describe the core features of large-scale social provision in America, and then document that voluntary groups have often been extensive membership federations, not just local charities aimed at the poor. American civil associations managed to leverage religious values, ties, and resources, without ceding direct control to clergy or to any religious establishment. In this way, biblical religion in America nourished a lively democracy, which in turn demanded and benefited from public social programs aimed at broad categories of fellow citizens.

The Heart of U.S. Social Provision

Both conservatives and liberals today discuss "social welfare" in America as a set of federal government initiatives fashioned during the New Deal and the Great Society. Much of the argument between these camps focuses on programs for the very poor, which liberals view as essential aids to the least advantaged, while conservatives see anti-poverty programs as largesse distributed without regard for personal behavior or morals. In addition, today's liberals and conservatives argue about "entitlements," understood as unencumbered payments out of public funds to individuals. But both sides of these disputes are arguing about a very skewed picture of American social provision. Public social programs emerged and flourished long before the New Deal. And at all stages of the development of American social provision, the most extensive and expensive efforts have never dealt with the poor alone; nor have American social programs ever been justified in individualistic terms.

While some might quibble here or there, most would agree that America's finest social policy achievements have included the following milestones, spanning much of the nation's history:

Public schools: The United States was the world's leader in the spread of widely accessible public education.[10] During the nineteenth century primary schools, followed by secondary schools, spread throughout most localities and states.

Civil War benefits were disability and old-age pensions, job opportunities, and social services for millions of Union veterans and survivors. By 1910, more than a quarter of all American elderly men, and more than a third of men over 62 in the North, were receiving regular payments from the federal government on terms that were extraordinarily generous by the international standards of that era. Many family members and survivors were generously aided as well.[11]

Programs to help mothers and children proliferated during the 1910s and early 1920s. Forty-four states passed laws to protect women workers, and also "mothers' pensions" to enable poor widows to care for their children at home.[12] Congress established the Children's Bureau in 1912 and in 1921 passed the Sheppard-Towner Act to fund health education programs open to all American mothers and babies.[13]

Programs to help farmers and farm families, including subsidies for land-grant colleges, services provided through U.S. Department of Agriculture and its extension services, state-level agricultural programs, and the farm-price support programs of the New Deal and afterwards.

The *Social Security Act* was passed in 1935, including unemployment insurance and public assistance to the poor along with Old Age Insurance (OAI), which subsequently became its most popular part. OAI eventually took the name "Social Security" and expanded to cover virtually all retired employees, while providing survivors' and disability protections as well.[14] Most employees and their dependents were included in Social Security by the 1960s. Modeled in part retirement insurance, *Medicare* was added to the system in 1965.[15]

The *GI Bill of 1944* offered a comprehensive set of disability services, employment benefits, educational loans, family allowances, and subsidized loans for homes, businesses, and farms to 16 million veterans returning from World War II.[16] Subsequent "little GI bills" extended some aid to veterans of subsequent wars.

Although these giant systems of social support developed in different periods of American history and varied in many ways, they have several important features in common, each of which is worth a bit of elaboration. Taken together, these features add up to a formula for cultural and political viability for broad-gauged social provision in American democracy.

Major U.S. social programs have aimed to give social benefits to large categories of citizens in return for service to the community, or else as a way to help people prepare to serve the community. The most enduring and popularly accepted social benefits in the United States have never been understood either as poor relief or as mere "individual entitlements." From public schools through Social Security, they have been morally justified as recognitions of—or prospective supports for—service to the community. The rationale of social support in return for service has been a characteristic way for Americans to combine deep respect for individual freedom and responsibility with support for families and due regard for the obligations that all members of the national community owe to one another.

A clear-cut rationale of return for service was invoked to justify the veterans' benefits expanded in the wake of the Civil War and World War II.[17] Less-well understood, though, is the use of civic arguments by the educational reformers and local community activists who originally established America's public schools. They argued for common schools not primarily as means to further economic efficiency or individual mobility, but as ways to shape moral character and prepare all children for democratic citizenship.[18] American programs to aid farmers and farm families have always been justified as supports for those who perform essential national services, growing the country's food supply. Similarly, early twentieth-century programs for mothers were justified as supports for the services of women who risked life to bear children and devoted themselves to raising good citizens for the future.[19]

Today's Social Security and Medicare systems likewise have a profound moral underpinning in the eyes of most Americans.[20] Retirees and people anticipating retirement believe they have "earned" benefits by virtue of having made a lifetime of payroll contributions. But contrary to what pundits and economists often assert, the exchange is not understood as narrowly instrumental or individualistic. Most Americans see Social Security and Medicare as a social compact enforced by, and for, contributors to the national community. The benefits are experienced as just rewards for lifetimes of work—on the job and at home—not simply as returns-with-interest on personal savings accounts.

Major U.S. social policies have built bridges between more and less privileged Americans, bringing people together—as worthy beneficiaries and as contributing citizens—across lines of class, race, and region. Even if policy milestones started out small compared to what they eventually became, the key fact has been the structure of contributions and benefits. Successful social policies have built bridges, linking more and less privileged Americans. They have therefore not been considered or labeled "welfare" programs.

Public schools, for example, were founded for most children not just the offspring of privileged families as was originally the case with schools in other nations.[21] U.S. farm programs were open to richer and poorer owner-farmers alike, and sometimes to tenants as well. Civil War benefits and the GI Bill were available to all eligible veterans and survivors of each war. Although mothers' pensions eventually deteriorated into "welfare" payments to some of the very poorest mothers, they were not originally so stigmatized.[22] During the early 1900s a great many American mothers who lost a breadwinner-husband could suddenly find themselves in dire economic need. What is more, early federal programs for mothers and children were universal. The Children's Bureau was explicitly charged with serving all American children, and its first chief, Julia Lathrop, reasoned that if "the services of the [Sheppard-Towner] bill were not open to all, the services would degenerate into poor relief."[23]

Social Security and Medicare are today's best examples of inclusive social programs with huge cross-class constituencies. Although Social Security is the most effective anti-poverty undertaking ever run through the government in the United States, its saving grace over the past several decades—during an era of tight federal budgets and fierce political attacks on social provision—has been its broad constituency of present and future beneficiaries, none of whom understand it as "welfare."[24]

Broad U.S. social policies have been nurtured by partnerships of government and popularly rooted voluntary associations. There has been no zero-sum relationship between state and society; no trade-off between government and individuals; and no simple opposition between national and community efforts. The policy milestones I have identified were developed (if not always originated) through cooperation between government agencies and elected politicians, on the one hand, and voluntary associations on the other hand. I am not referring merely to non-profit, professionally run social-service agencies. I mean voluntary citizens' groups. The associations that have nurtured major U.S. social programs have usually linked national and state offices with groups of participating members living in local communities all across the country.

Public schools were founded and sustained by traveling reformers, often members of regional or national associations, who linked up with leading local citizens, churches, and voluntary groups.[25] The Patrons of Husbandry (the Grange) and the American Farm Bureau Federation were the largest of many farmers' associations that have been intimately connected to the creation, expansion, and administration of state and federal farm programs.[26] The movers and shakers behind early 1900s state and national legislation for mothers and children were the Women's Christian Temperance Union, the General Federation of Women's Clubs, and the National Congress of Mothers (which eventually turned into the PTA).[27] Civil War benefits ended up both reinforcing and being nurtured by the Grand Army of the Republic (GAR).[28] Open to veterans of all economic, ethnic, and racial backgrounds, the GAR was a classic three-tiered voluntary civic association, with tens of thousands of local "posts" whose members met regularly, plus state and national affiliates that held big annual conventions.

Social Security has had a complex relationship to voluntary associations. Back during the Great Depression, a militant social movement and voluntary federation of older Americans, the Townsend Movement, pressed Congress to enact universal benefits for elders.[29] But Social Security definitely did not embody specific Townsend preferences, and the movement itself withered away during the 1940s. Today over 35 million Americans fifty and above are enrolled in the American Association of Retired Persons (AARP), whose newsletters and magazines alert older voters to maneuvers in Washington DC that affect Social Security and Medicare.[30] The AARP does not have very many local membership clubs (though it is currently working to establish more of them). Still, many elderly Americans participate in locally rooted seniors' groups, including the union-related National Council of Senior Citizens, which has played a key role in advocating for Medicare. Moreover, along with unions and religious congregations, federal, state, and local governments have done a lot over the past thirty years to create services and community centers for elderly citizens. An important side effect has been to foster considerable social communication, civic volunteerism, and political engagement among older Americans.

The final example of government-association partnership in the expansion of inclusive U.S. social provision is perhaps the most telling. Conservatives and moderates often praise the GI Bill of 1944 for giving benefits in return for service, in ways that maximized the choices of individual veterans to enroll in any training program or college or university. All very true, and worthy of emulation. Yet the GI Bill took this shape only because a nationwide voluntary association, the American Legion, pressured conservatives in Congress as well as the somewhat elitist "planners" of the wartime Roosevelt administration.[31]

Organized after the First World War to associate veterans "for God and Country," the Legion was a locally rooted, cross-class and nationwide voluntary association that developed in close symbiosis with two very strong "federal bureaucracies"—the U.S. military and the Veterans Administration.[32] In the story of the growth and impact of the American Legion, there were no oppositions of state versus civil society—or of government versus individual autonomy and community engagement. The Legion grew up with the aid of government support after both the first and second world wars; in turn it aroused and coordinated mass voluntary efforts to influence the civic life of communities, aid veterans and their families, and shape national social legislation. Not all that the Legion did was praiseworthy; it adopted a truly repressive stance toward leftists and many unions. Nevertheless, the GI Bill of 1944 would have been a much more restrictive and elitist educational entitlement had not the popularly rooted American Legion pressured Congress to pass a bill open to millions of ordinary veterans and their families. It mattered that the Legion had a large, cross-class membership base. Legion leaders had to be sensitive to the aspirations of ordinary Americans—and millions of Legion members, in turn, were available to pressure Congress.

Partnerships of Government and Society

Today's liberals and conservatives not only argue about a restricted part of American social provision. Both camps also cling to misleading conceptions of the role that voluntary associations have played in American politics and social policymaking. When looking at the past, for example, leftist scholars stress the activities of trade unions, and overlook episodes such as the American Legion's decisive impact on the formulation and enactment of the GI Bill. Although unions and farmers' associations have certainly been important parts of popular associational life in the United States, there have also been many other kinds of popularly rooted associations. Women's associations, fraternal groups, veterans' groups, and many sorts of political and moral reform movements have mobilized large numbers of Americans across class lines, enabling them to shape civic and legislative affairs. American civil society simply cannot be analyzed solely or primarily in terms of class or occupationally based associations. Cross-class membership groups must be understood as well.

Contemporary conservatives, meanwhile, romanticize local and apolitical forms of charitable activity. But as the impact of associations such as the Woman's Christian Temperance Union, the Grange and the American Legion underline, many American voluntary groups have been active nationally and in the states as well as locally. Citizens' associations have often worked in close, complementary partnership with governments at all levels.

Conservatives often cite Alexis de Tocqueville in support of the notion that U.S. voluntary groups originally prospered as small-scale efforts apart from politics or government above the local level. This argument fails to do justice to the full subtlety of Tocqueville's argument in *Democracy in America*, where the great Frenchman repeatedly highlighted the ways in which early nineteenth-century U.S. electoral democracy promoted all sorts of voluntary associations.[33] What is more, recent empirical research underlines the importance of the U.S. federal government and democracy in promoting a vibrant civil society—a society in which extensive, translocal voluntary groups figured from the start along with local undertakings.

Between the establishment of the Constitution and the 1830s, when Alexis de Tocqueville visited our country, the fledgling United States enfranchised most adult men and established competitive elections for state and national offices. The American Revolution and subsequent electoral contests for state and national offices stimulated the formation of new voluntary groups in small villages and towns that otherwise might not have developed such groups.[34] The great religious movement of the Second Great Awakening had the same effect, because itinerant preachers and lecturers traveled far and wide across the fledgling nation to spread their moral messages and found groups of believers who would persist, and remain linked to one another, across many locales.[35]

The U.S. federal government had a lot to do with these developments, administratively as well as electorally. Recently, the historian Richard John has documented that the early America had an extraordinarily extensive and administratively efficient national postal system, encompassing even the remotest frontier hamlets.[36] Much bigger than the postal systems of the bureaucratic European monarchies of that time, the U.S. postal system created a network of communication and stagecoach transportation that facilitated commerce, subsidized the dissemination of countless newspapers, stimulated popular political participation, and encouraged the activities of thousands of local and extralocal voluntary associations. One early moral reform association, the General Union for Promoting the Observance of the Christian Sabbath, actually used the mail to organize a nation-wide movement to demand the closing of post offices on Sunday! And this was not an idiosyncratic undertaking, because temperance crusades and the anti-slavery movement operated in exactly the same way. A strong and effective national state and a democratic civil society grew up together in early America.

Scholars have documented major waves of voluntary group formation during two periods in the nineteenth century: before the Civil War, from the 1820s to the 1850s; and after the Civil War, especially from the 1870s to the 1890s, yet continuing to some degree until 1910.[37] Both waves of voluntary group formation started during periods of intense political party mobilization and highly competitive local, state, and national elections; and both waves coincided with periods of religious renewal and the spread of new denominations and congregations into "the west." The overall waves of voluntary group foundings coincided with periods of nationwide cultural and political debate—focused on issues of social morality and slavery before the Civil War; and on responses to industrialization and the rise of corporations during the decades between the Civil War and the Progressive Era.

In each great phase of American voluntary group formation, associated Americans—often religiously motivated sets of men and women working together across lines of class and region—called upon local, state, and national governments to work with them to pursue social betterment and moral reform. Although they often disagreed over goals and means, Americans active in all sorts of voluntary membership groups saw no contradiction between personal and local-group responsibility, on the one hand, and public, governmentally expressed responsibility on the other.

Part of Something Bigger

There have, of course, been many kinds of voluntary groups in America, ranging from particular associations that appear and fade in individual communities and workplaces, to endeavors organized strictly at the national level. Still, at the very core of American civic life, especially from the mid-nineteenth to the mid-twentieth century, were associations that *combined* local and extra-local activities. Historically, most locally present voluntary groups were directly or indirectly linked to parallel efforts across many communities, states, regions, and (often) the entire nation. People in local groups took heart or example from what others linked to them were doing at the same time elsewhere. People shared overarching values and ideas to which many individuals and local groups committed themselves.

Around the turn of the twentieth century, for instance, a movement called "Christian Endeavor" spread rapidly. The Society of Christian Endeavor was based in thousands of local groups linked to Protestant church congregations, yet it also included district, state, national, and international meetings. As the Christian Endeavor President Reverend Francis E. Clark explained, extralocal union brought "suggestion, inspiration and fellowship" to the local groups. He spelled out each facet in ways that suggests why many U.S. voluntary movements saw advantages in locality-spanning federation:[38]

> SUGGESTION: "If the members of the local society never look or go beyond themselves, they are in danger of growing short-sighted, narrow in their conception of duty and privilege, formal and routine in their 'endeavor,' and are liable to languish if not die of discouragement."
>
> INSPIRATION: "Bring together three or five hundred young Christians in a Local Union [district] meeting, and from one to three thousand at a State convention; let them look into each other's faces; let them warmly grasp each other's hands; let their voices unite in song; let them hear each other pray; let them report the Lord's doing with them in their several societies and churches; let them listen to personal testimony; above all, let them bow in humble confession and consecration; the *inspiration is untold.* Those who are present usually go back to their local societies and churches quickened and equipped for aggressive Christian work."
>
> FELLOWSHIP: "Young Christians, especially, need this. Living in comparative isolation, as many of them do, working in their own local field, which is often, as they feel, limited and little hopeful, the danger is that they will become lonely and disheartened. Bring them into contact with fellow Christians of their own age and 'endeavor;' they will see that a common bond of sympathy unites them. . . ."

This rational offered by Reverend Clark closely resembles the rationales for translocal associationalism developed by many other voluntary group builders in nineteenth and twentieth-century America.

Studying just one place at a time, contemporary social historians have at times mistakenly described locally present voluntary groups as purely idiosyncratic efforts. Fortunately, we scholars are now beginning to have the kinds of systematic data we really need to sort things out. Over the past two years Gerald Gamm and Robert Putnam have collected a rich data set counting all of the voluntary groups, including religious congregations, listed in city directories across 26 cities and towns for each decade between 1840 and 1940.[39] This gives us a much more complete picture of the changing array of locally present associations over a crucial century of American history.

Meanwhile, I am coordinating a Civic Engagement Project at Harvard that is assembling data on the emergence and growth of large voluntary associations throughout U.S. history. The members of this project have so far identified 58 U.S. voluntary membership associations, each of which enrolled one percent or more of American adults at some point (and in most cases over many decades) between 1790 and the present. Displayed in Table 1.1, these groups are listed in chronological order of their founding, so you can see that waves of foundings occurred in roughly the same periods for which other scholars have documented more general waves of voluntary group formation. The Civic Engagement group is developing a detailed "life history" of each of the large voluntary associations on the master list. Many of the points I make here are based on data from the early stages of this research

One might imagine that large, nation-spanning associations in America had little relevance for local voluntary group life. But this is not true. I have compared lists of national, regional, and state-level federated associations to lists of locally present voluntary groups for some of Gamm and Putnam's towns and cities, invariably finding that at least three-quarters of the locally present groups listed in the local directories they used were parts of translocal federations. Except for some recreational and elite-only clubs, most locally rooted American associations in the nineteenth and early twentieth centuries were parts of "something bigger." They were linked into regional or national networks of voluntary associations. As social historian Alexander von Hoffman has aptly summed up, "[s]ustained by both internal and local links, local institutions and organizations may best be understood as branch offices and local chapters. . . . the building blocs of a 'nation of joiners'.. . . Americans enlisted in local church groups, fraternal lodges, clubs, and other organizations that belonged to nationwide networks."[40] The link to state, regional, and nationwide associations was democratically empowering for local groups and individuals, much as Reverend Clark of Christian Endeavor explained.

During the entire "modern" era of U.S. voluntarism—stretching from the Civil War to around 1960—*the quintessential form of translocal U.S. voluntarism was the federation,* linking membership groups in cities and towns into networks with an organizational presence in each of 48–50 states, and at the same time tying the localities and the states into a national organization that ran conventions and disseminated publications. Until very recently, most large U.S. voluntary associations have had this kind of three-tiered federal structure, paralleling the three tiers of U.S. government: local, state, and nation. Details of the structure and how it worked through recurrent meetings at all levels are spelled out in little "constitution" books printed up by the millions during the nineteenth and early twentieth centuries, ready to be carried in the pockets of men and women who were members (or auxiliary affiliates) of temperance societies such as the Sons of Temperance and the Independent Order of Good Templars, and also the men and women who participated in the Patrons of Husbandry and the Knights of Labor, the Masons and the Eastern Star, the Odd Fel-

TABLE 1.1 Large Membership Associations in US History, Civic Engagement Project

Common Name	*Founding Date*	*Ending Date*
Ancient and Accepted Free Masons	1733	
Independent Order of Odd Fellows	1819	
American Temperance Society	1826	1865
General Union for Promoting Observance of the Christian Sabbath	1828	1832
American Anti-Slavery Society	1833	1870
Improved Order of Red Men	1834	
Washington Temperance Societies	1840	c1848
The Order of the Sons of Temperance	1842	c1970
Independent Order of Good Templars	1851	
Young Men's Christian Association	1851	
Junior Order of United American Mechanics	1853	
National Teachers Association/ National Education Association	1857	
Knights of Pythias	1864	
Grand Army of the Republic	1866	1956
Benevolent and Protective Order of Elks	1867	
Patrons of Husbandry (National Grange)	1867	
Ancient Order of United Workmen	1868	
Order of the Eastern Star	1868	
Knights of Labor	1869	1917
National Rifle Association	1871	
Ancient Arabic Order of the Nobles of the Mystic Shrine	1872	
Woman's Christian Temperance Union	1874	
Royal Arcanum	1877	
Farmers' Alliance	1877	1900
Maccabees	1878	
Christian Endeavor	1881	
American Red Cross	1881	
Knights of Columbus	1882	
Modern Woodmen of America	1883	
Colored Farmers' National Alliance and Cooperative Union	1886	1892
American Federation of Labor/ AFL-CIO from 1955	1886	
American Protective Association	1887	c1911
Woman's Missionary Union	1888	
Loyal Order of Moose	1888	
National American Woman Suffrage Association	1890	1920

(continues)

TABLE 1.1 *(continued)*

Common Name	*Founding Date*	*Ending Date*
Woodmen of the World	1890	
General Federation of Women's Clubs	1890	
American Bowling Congress	1895	
National Congress of Mothers/National Congress of Parents and Teachers	1897	
Fraternal Order of Eagles	1898	
German American National Alliance	1901	1918
Aid Association For Lutherans	1902	
American Automobile Association	1902	
Boy Scouts of America	1910	
Veterans of Foreign Wars of the United States	1913	
Ku Klux Klan (second)	1915	1944
Women's International Bowling Congress	1916	
American Legion	1919	
American Farm Bureau Federation	1919	
Old Age Revolving Pensions, Ltd. (Townsend movement)	1934	1953
Congress of Industrial Organizations	1938	1955
National Foundation for Infantile Paralysis/March of Dimes	1938	
Woman's Division of Christian Service/ United Methodist Women	1939	
American Association of Retired Persons	1958	
Greenpeace USA	1971	
National Right to Life Committee	1973	
Mothers Against Drunk Driving	1980	
Christian Coalition	1989	

lows and the Rebekahs, the Knights of Pythias and the Pythian Sisters, and other nationwide federated associations.

For classical U.S. voluntary associations, the three-tiered federal form was extraordinarily resilient and flexible. It allowed local participation and democracy to be combined with group decision-making at state and national levels. It allowed voluntary groups, if they chose, to relate as citizens, not just as clients, to all levels of U.S. party politics, public administration, and legislative decision-making. This three-tiered federal form also allowed for pluralism within a shared program—or "Unity Within Diversity" as the motto of the General Federation of Women's Clubs puts it—because local and state groups in particular parts of the country could pursue their own purposes, while at the same time cooperating for other purposes and sharing an overall identity with state and local groups in other places.

The great civic women's associations of the late-nineteenth and early twentieth century all developed federal structures: the Woman's Christian Temperance Union, founded in 1874; the General Federation of Women's Clubs, founded in 1890; and the National Congress of Mothers (which later became the National Congress of Parents and Teachers), founded in 1897. In all three of these cases, married women found that they could inspire state-wide and nation-wide movements to aid mothers, children, homes, communities, by combining voluntary efforts tailored to particular local conditions with campaigns coordinated at higher levels, campaigns designed to have a powerful impact on American society as a whole. The women who created and led these associations would find the current writings of Michael Joyce and William Schambra utterly mystifying, for these women believed strongly in combining Christian morality and local voluntarism with public commitments undertaken in cooperation with state and national governments. As Mrs. G. Harris Robertson of Tennessee explained to the National Congress of Mothers during a 1911 speech in support of mothers' pension laws, the forerunners of Aid to Families With Dependent Children: "Do not rise up in indignation to call this Socialism—it is the sanest of statesmanship. If our public mind is maternal, loving and generous, wanting to save and develop all, our Government will express this sentiment. . . . [E]very step we make toward establishing government along these lines [i.e., passing mothers' pensions] means an advance toward the Kingdom of Peace."[41]

Throughout much of the twentieth century, major American voluntary associations such as the American Legion, the American Farm Bureau Federation, the Knights of Columbus, the Elks, and the PTA deployed the federal associational form and partnership with government to perfection. Local groups supervised youth activities, helped to administer social or economic programs, celebrated religious or civic occasions, and otherwise contributed to and took vitality from communities across America. At the same time, the state and national parts of these federations deliberated about—and then spoke out on—state and national issues. Some of the things that particular membership federations have advocated or done may not be appealing. But that's not the point. The point is that, in their heyday, the American Legion, the PTA, the Knights of Columbus, countless fraternal groups, and many other U.S. voluntary federations—demonstrated that local community involvement and an intense commitment to encompassing identities and purposes could go hand in hand in American democracy. The genius of U.S. voluntary membership federations was to make local and state and national commitments complement—rather than oppose—one another. When today's conservatives advocate local voluntarism apart from, or in opposition to government, they are advocating a break with the past, not a return to it.

Religious Inspiration without Clerical Control

Religion mattered along with U.S. federal democracy in shaping the associational tradition I have just described. As the examples of early women's federations and the American Legion underline, experience with a democratic polity and the federal form of U.S. governance were an important source of inspiration for builders of voluntary associations. At the same time, Biblical religious values—along with institutional religious conditions specific to the United States—promoted active membership recruitment and "unity in diversity" as a strategy of association-building. Transdenominational Protestantism was, for good and ill, the primary cultural influence. Yet in the U.S. context, Catholic and Jewish people and groups often turned to some of the same ideals and associational methods as their Protestant counterparts.

The formula for success in American civic association-building was a combination of patriotic themes and federal-representative and popular-elective arrangements borrowed from the polity with ethical objectives and quasi-religious rituals borrowed (at least in large part) from the Bible. (There were also classical cultural referents, as in the story of the friendship of Damon and Pythias at the heart of the ritual of the Knights of Pythias.) The synthesis of representative government and Biblical religion gave citizens' voluntary associations the capacity to speak for broad moral goals and identities. At the same time, it allowed them to separate themselves from direct clerical control. The most successful associations were not the captives of any single hierarchy of priests or ministers. Indeed, most federated membership associations routinely included *elected* "chaplains" or "prelates" among their sets of elected officers. These were usually men and women with important ritual responsibilities, including responsibilities for readings from the Bible or the enactment of Bible-inspired rituals. Yet among Protestants, at least, chaplains and prelates were usually lay persons elected by fellow members, not religiously appointed clerics. Ordinary Americans thus took ownership of religious themes and rituals for themselves, drawing inspiration and energy from Biblical religion, but not submitting to overt religious institutional control.

Voluntary citizens' membership associations flourished historically in the United States at the interstices of a divided and competitive system of religious institutions. No religious orthodoxy in the United States has ever been legally established, so top-down bureaucratic strategies have not worked to attract members or stabilize or expand denominations. The U.S. Bill of Rights guarantees religious freedom, but forbids any religious monopoly, forcing denominations to struggle among themselves for adherents. A compelling, inclusive moral message, coupled with vigorous grass-roots organization have been the approaches used by all successful American religious movements, creating a model for religious-related citizens' associations as well.[42]

The primordial example—arguably the one that spurred other denominations into emulative strategies of expansion—was American Methodism. From the late eighteenth century through much of the nineteenth century, Methodists were on the move in a rapidly growing, westward-expanding America. Evangelical Methodists went beyond a settled, elite, highly educated clergy, throwing thousands of travelling itinerant preachers into the fray. Preachers traveled, gathered audiences, gave emotionally moving sermons—and then identified local lay leaders who could keep local congregations going and growing.[43] Methodism offered a universal, energizing, shared vision of personal and social salvation. At the same time, it used organizational methods that encouraged and supported grass-roots leaders and congregations. with their itinerant preacher-organizers.

Other religious denominations in America soon had to emulate Methodist methods or face permanent decline. Religious movements in America have almost never been purely local or idiosyncratic. They have sunk strong roots in local gatherings or congregations, yet also sought to link these up into broader networks of ongoing faith and communication and mutual aid. Starting with temperance and other moral reform movements, and spreading to many other kinds of endeavors after the Civil War, citizens' associations adopted organizational strategies similar to expanding religious denominations, stressing both grass-roots participation and the involvement of local groups with district, state, and national federations.

Contemporary conservative revivalists like Marvin Olasky look back at American history and see the religious contribution to building U.S. civil society as mainly one of local congregations or righteous individuals doling out charity and personal advice to the poor. But this overlooks the much broader contribution of religious values and institutions—especially of evangelical Protestantism, but the other Biblical religions as well. Groups such as temperance crusades, Christian Endeavor, the (Roman Catholic) Knights of Columbus, and the various "sons" and "daughters of" associations among "Hebrews" all were in the business of building horizontal, inclusive ties that strengthened the strand of democratic community in America, linking middling Americans to one another, and also linking many elite Americans with ordinary white and blue-collar working people. The vision of brotherhood and sisterhood in God was an important to the building of such civil solidarities. Both religious denominations and religiously linked associations had to compete and reach out, if they were to flourish in a huge, expanding nation with no official religious monopoly. Citizen-led voluntary associations loosely linked to each denomination were able to carry the "reaching out" process furthest of all, often crossing the boundaries of particular Protestant denominations or the boundaries of particular Catholic ethnic churches.

Religious congregations, religiously inspired voluntary associations, and—finally—other voluntary movements that picked up on religious methods—all sought to inspire full individual participation in interactive groups. In a formulation characteristic of many American voluntary associations, the pledge young men and women made when they joined the Christian Endeavor clubs enjoined democratic participation along with individual righteousness: "As an

Active member I promise to be true to all my duties, to be present at and to take some part, aside from singing, in every meeting unless hindered by some reason I can conscientiously give to my Lord and Master, Jesus Christ."

Recruitment was another area where voluntary associations as well as religious movements stressed the role of individual members in addition to leaders. Characteristically, for its fiftieth birthday, the Woman's Christian Temperance Union issued the "Jubilee Membership Campaign Songs," reproduced here, one of which was to be sung to the tune of "Coming Through the Rye":

> If a body meet a body
> Coming through the year;
> Shall a body ask a body
> Join us now and here?
> Yes! our membership we'll double
> Jubilee is near,
> We'll never count it trouble
> Coming through the year!

Whatever the aesthetic (de)merits of the Jubilee songs, it is clear that they celebrated individual commitment to one-on-one recruitment.

Today, associations may recruit via computer-derived mailings to isolated individuals. But in the classic era of association-building, American voluntary federations used missionary-style person-to-person methods. With the aid of this approach, they were able to activate and strengthen people's pre-existing connections to one another, in churches, neighborhoods, occupations, and previous translocal federations (new ones almost always built off of earlier ones), and at the same time link those ties into broader networks. Millions of people in tens of thousands of localities and states could be mobilized and linked together in shared organizations through this approach to creating and expanding both religious denominations and religious and secular voluntary associations in the United States.

Brotherhood and Sisterhood Under God

Today's conservatives correctly remind us that social aid may work optimally when it is delivered in a context of mutual moral commitment. But contemporary conservative intellectuals too often regard religiously inspired community as a personalistic drama played out only in face-to-face groups, even as they disproportionately stress aid for the very poor instead of mutuality among fellow citizens, or among all persons as children of God. Conservative revivalism along the lines of Olasky attributes to American religion an overly restrictive vision of community; and it largely overlooks the critical, prophetic role of religion.

There has been an odd convergence between right and left. Even as conservatives attempt to use religion to justify localist personalism, leftist secularists

PHOTO 1.1 Good Templar postcards. "Males and Females, Old and Young"
(top) Leaders of the International Order of Good Templars, a Christian temperance association that was interdenominational and was also one of the first voluntary associations in the country to accept women as full members.
(bottom) Boys and girls who belonged to the Good Templars, which was founded in 1851. Some of the group's adult leaders are in the back row.

sometimes imagine that religious groups in America have always been racially or creedally exclusive. Exclusion did often happen, of course. Black and white American Christians have usually worshipped and organized separately because, historically, majority whites insisted upon that course. Moreover, gender segregation was the norm in U.S. associational life before the 1970s. And Protestants excluded Catholics and Jews from many voluntary activities, religious or secular.

Nevertheless, we should not overlook the surprisingly early urges toward inclusion and equality that did occur in America. Moves toward inclusion were often inspired by biblical religion. For example, an early transdenominational Christian temperance association, the Independent (later "International") Order of Good Templars (IOGT), was one of the very first large voluntary associations in the world, let alone the United States, to accept men and women together as full members of gender-integrated local groups. I have an old handwritten logbook from an IOGT lodge in East Machias, Maine in the 1870s. It shows "brothers" and "sisters" alike functioning as officers, and both genders speaking during the weekly meetings (held on Saturday nights, when other East Machiasers, no doubt, were at the saloons). The IOGT's practice of gender inclusion proved infectious, at least in the world of temperance associations. Before long, the Sons of Temperance changed its policies and admitted women members, too. The IOGT itself was even more daring. For considerable periods of its history, the IOGT tried to reach across the racial divide in America, including African-American lodges along with white lodges in the same supra-local federation.[44]

Another kind of civic inclusiveness grew up historically in the leading Catholic voluntary association, the Knights of Columbus. The Knights started out among Irish parishioners in New Haven. Yet when the Knights of Columbus sought to expand nationally—as a competitive counterweight to Protestant-dominated fraternals—it managed to bridge ethnic divisions among Catholics, first reaching out to Italians, and eventually to other groups, such as French Canadians in Maine.[45] To spread a Catholic civic fraternity across all of the U.S. states and thousands of communities, the Knights of Columbus *had* to appeal to many ethnic varieties of Catholics. Interestingly, the Knights of Columbus changed its organizational structure, to adopt exactly the same kind of three-tiered local-state-national federated form as the Protestant voluntary associations it competed against. This happened even though American Catholics probably would have found urban-centered, diocesan structures a much more "natural" form of institution-building. The capacity to reach out coincided with the adoption of a federated structure and was accompanied by a loosening of influence of Bishops and priests in the fraternity.

Religiously inspired American women tended to be pioneers in creating associational partnerships across denominational, ethnic, and racial lines. Such partnerships have been recorded from the side of black Baptist women by historian Evelyn Brooks Higginbotham.[46] Similar outreach (however incomplete by the lights of the 1990s) also came from religiously inspired white women. The Woman's Christian Temperance Union had separate black and white local and state unions, but they could choose to meet together, and at times did.

TABLE 1.2 Virtues Featured by Major American Fraternal Orders

Fraternal Group	*Virtues*
Independent Order of Odd Fellows	Friendship, Love, Truth
Improved Order of Red Men	Freedom, Friendship, Charity
Ancient Order of Hibernians in America	Friendship, Unity, True Christian Charity
Order of Sons of Temperance	Love, Purity, Fidelity
Junior Order of United American Mechanics	Virtue, Liberty, Patriotism
Knights of Pythias	Friendship, Charity, Benevolence
Benevolent and Protective Order of Elks	Charity, Justice, Brotherly Love, Fidelity
Ancient Order of United Workmen	Charity, Hope, and Protection
Royal Arcanum	Virtue, Mercy, Charity
Knights of Columbus	Unity, Charity, Fraternity
Loyal Order of Moose	Purity, Aid, Progress
Fraternal Order of Eagles	Liberty, Truth, Justice, Equality

Christian values and ideals offered them the rhetoric they needed to promote sisterhood in the name of love for every person. Ironically, some national meeting programs for women's groups such as the General Federation of Women's Clubs or the National Congress of Mothers also suggest that Protestant American women could find in Christian values justification for reaching out to Catholic and Jewish "sisters" or "fellow mothers," too.

Meanwhile, we know that many early Jewish women's groups advocated social supports for a wide range of families in their communities, non-Jewish as well as Jewish. Both Catholic and Jewish church-related associations have, as well, been leaders in political struggles for general, governmentally mediated social provision in America. Jewish associations often led the way in agitating for benefits such as mothers' pensions or old-age pensions. And the Catholic Church articulated a strong rationale in support of wage and hour protections for working men and women.

Even apparently exclusive voluntary associations—such as the great fraternal groups with memberships restricted to white men—celebrated Biblically inspired ethical values. Sometimes the male fraternals referred to Christian values and made Christian adherence (or, more narrowly, Protestantism or Catholicism) an explicit requisite for membership. At other times, as in the case of the Knights of Pythias, Jews (and Unitarians) were incorporated by making "belief in a Supreme Being" the key to belonging. Either way, American voluntary membership associations featured sets of values (usually a trilogy of them, with obvious resonance to Christian trinitarianism).

For major male fraternal orders from the Odd Fellows (founded in America in 1819) through the Fraternal Order of Eagles (founded in 1898), I have listed a few of these sets of featured values in Table 1.2. Note the recurrent combina-

PHOTO 1.2 Badge

tions of religious and patriotic themes: "For God and Country," as the more secularized American Legion would put it in the twentieth century. Fraternal featured values were proclaimed on public occasions, and they were spelled out in didactic ceremonies and rituals within each association. We can take them with a certain grain of salt, no doubt. Yet stories and performances illustrating these values were constantly invoked in all aspects of fraternal activities.

Associational values were emblazoned on banners and regalia proudly carried or worn by group leaders. And individual members wore group badges carrying the same messages. "Friendship, Love, and Truth" were, for example, the virtues celebrated by members of the Independent Order of Odd Fellows, as proclaimed by this beautiful example of badges worn by members of the Odd Fellows lodge in Stoyesville, Pennsylvania. This ribbon-badge is unusually explicit, spelling out the names of the Odd Fellow virtues and not just giving their initials or symbols, a more prevalent design. Yet in one or another format, millions of badges such as this were worn by American men, proudly proclaiming their association's featured virtues on countless public as well as intramural occasions. American men participating in these groups were told—and proclaimed to others—that manliness included religio-ethical inspiration as well as martial courage, charity as well as patriotism. They were rewarded for practicing mutuality and service both within and beyond their lodges. The message was constantly drummed home that men were "brothers under God" and "fellow citizens," not just bosses and workers, and not just people from varied ethnic backgrounds.

Prophecy for Social Justice

Finally, of course, the contributions of biblical religion to American democracy go beyond the justification of broad community, even beyond the expression of brotherhood and sisterhood as an ethical underpinning for fellow citizenship and mutual assistance. Throughout American history, Biblical religion has also been the wellspring of radical moral and political efforts to bring about social change and equal justice.

American religion has been as much about prophetic, critical voice as personalized charity or mutuality. Religiously inspired and organized people have challenged as well as succored. They have reached outward as well as inward, and they have shaken as well as reinforced the political status quo.

At times, to be sure, people speaking in the name of religion have called upon government and their fellow citizens to exclude or punish those deemed different. An instance like the Ku Klux Klan reminds us of this. But it is even easier to cite examples of religiously inspired movements in America that have called for relatively inclusive moral reforms and the extension of community support or citizenship rights to the excluded.

Anti-slavery movements in nineteenth-century America were religiously inspired and often led by ministers or devout laypersons. Crusades for temperance and prohibition, for woman suffrage, and finally for Civil Rights for African Americans, all were spearheaded by religious people and justified in Biblical terms. In each of these cases, people called for justice and inclusion for socially excluded groups, or called for new forms of government action that might prove unpopular, or both. They did so in the name of God, as they understood divine purpose. They also used networks of church people to recruit members and leaders, and to bolster people's resolve to challenge dominant powers-that-be. As sociologist Aldon Morris has written about the role of African American churches in the southern Civil Rights movement:

"Successful social movements usually comprise people who are willing to make great sacrifices in a single-minded pursuit of their goals. The black church supplied the civil rights movement with a collective enthusiasm generated through a rich culture consisting of songs, testimonies, oratory, and prayers that spoke directly to the needs of an oppressed group. Many black churches preached that oppression is sinful and that God sanctions protest aimed at eradicating social evils."[47]

In the Civil Rights case and many others throughout American history, both religious ideas and religious institutions afforded indispensable leverage against entrenched economic and political elites determined to maintain the status quo.[48] Recurrent Biblically inspired movements for social justice appealed to the national polity to become more democratic and inclusive, and urged the national government to act on behalf of the excluded and the disadvantaged.

Religion and Social Politics Today

Against the backdrop of this revised understanding of the role of religion in American democracy, we can revisit what is happening in contemporary U.S. civil society and social welfare politics. In recent decades, there have been some sharp changes—changes that help explain why secularists and conservatives are so much at odds today and that also threaten some of the best past achievements of American social provision and civil associationalism.

History certainly bears out the contemporary conservative claim that religious Americans, past and present, have made vital contributions to caring for the poor and building loving communities, that government action, in isolation, cannot substitute for such voluntary, religiously inspired efforts. Indeed, empirical research confirms that churchgoing Americans remain now, as probably in the past, more likely than others to join and contribute to voluntary activities in general.[49] The United States remains the nation in the democratic-industrial world where the most people go to church and volunteer regularly.[50]

Nevertheless, as I have tried to show, today's conservative revivalists put forward the false notion that American religious activism was traditionally apolitical, localistic, and separate from government. Historically, there was a positive-sum, not a zero-sum relationship between voluntary efforts and the undertakings of democratic government. And the most important religiously inspired voluntary efforts in American history were citizens' movements, not just charitable efforts to reach and reform the poor.

Partial and misleading as they are as guides to history, contemporary conservative visions have some grounding in real-world denominational and demographic changes. As the sociologist of religion Robert Wuthnow has ably documented, evangelical Christians are on the rise today, because their congregations are growing, in part because their birthrates are higher, while "mainline" Protestants and Catholics are, relatively speaking, falling behind. In a fascinating study of the involvements of various groupings of Americans in churches, church-related voluntary groups and other civic associations, Wuthnow finds that today's evangelical Christians tend to combine active participation in national elections and politics with intense involvements in groups within their local congregations. They concentrate on Bible study groups and on volunteering and charity channeled through their local congregations. Mainline Protestants and Catholic women, by contrast, are more likely to engage in extra-congregational civic activities and volunteering, reaching out to—and obviously helping to build or sustain—larger communities. This is the same thing that old-line Protestants tended to do historically, back when they were the rising forces in American religion, during the nineteenth century.

Clearly, conservative revivalist intellectuals—writers like Olasky—are speaking to a certain reality experienced by people in their current social and doctrinal base. They speak especially for and in resonance with the daily experiences of Southern and Western rural and suburban evangelical Protestants—

people who do, indeed, mainly find community among like-minded fellow congregants in growing megachurches.

Less appealingly, conservatives calling for a "return" to simple localism speak for people who feel oppositional to much of what the federal government has tried to do in the wake of the Civil Rights and gender transformations of the 1960s and 1970s. Today's conservatives are actually part of a nationwide political effort to disable a national government that they feel went astray when it started actively supporting rights and social supports for blacks. They are promoting anti-governmentalism in ways that yesterday's conservatives—let alone religious movements—hardly ever did in America. Furthermore, today's conservatives are promoting a turning inward by many evangelical Protestants, contrary to the calls for inclusion and universalism that similar Protestants advocated in earlier phases of American history.

But conservatives are not the only ones to break with important parts of religious tradition. These days, liberals and leftists want to maintain political and governmental activism on behalf of social justice, but *without* explicit religious underpinnings for calls to moral activism and renewal. It is not clear, however, that this can be done. The last successful movement for social justice in America was the Civil Rights struggle, which did centrally appeal to people's sense of religious brotherhood and sisterhood, engaging individuals' moral values, not just their economic interests. That movement also built upon religious social ties and institutional resources.

Since the end of the Civil Rights upheavals of the 1960s, class and economic inequality has become much greater in America. Many Americans have moral concerns about such growing inequality. But leaders on the liberal or leftist end of the spectrum have barely even tried to use explicit religious or moral appeals to mobilize a democratic movement to redress growing inequalities. Fearing religion as "divisive," or as inherently tied to conservative activism, liberals fall back on secular arguments about individual or group economic self-interest. Such arguments, however, may be too anemic to serve as a basis for a bold new movement for social justice in America, a point Brent Coffin makes in Chapter Five when he considers the intersection of religious and public values.

Somewhat beleaguered Mainline Protestants and Catholics still engage in some of the kinds of outward-looking and linking associational activities that flourished in the classic era of U.S. civil society from the Civil War through the mid-twentieth century. But this classic tradition of unity in diversity, of outward-looking as well as locally grounded civic involvements, is endangered today. Many Mainline Protestants are now privileged upper middle class people who have become wary of frank religious advocacy in the larger world, even as associational life, both secular and religious, has become more fragmented and money-driven.

As the research of Sidney Verba and Kay Lehman Schlozman (and their associates) shows, popular religious participation, important as it may be for ordinary citizens, no longer counts for as much in the national political equation as giving money.[51] National electoral and civic life are increasingly tilted toward the wealthy, and toward those who give money rather than time. Although some of the privileged may remain active via their churches and synagogues, most of the civic activism of the privileged, at all points in the political spectrum, is channeled through check-writing to support professionally run advocacy or social-service groups.

To be sure, Americans still volunteer a lot by international standards; this is especially true among older, retired or semi-retired Americans. But much of today's voluntarism is managed by professionally run agencies and involves short-term or one-shot commitments from rank-and-file contributors. More important, volunteering here and there in social service efforts or professionally coordinated drives is not quite the same thing as the sustained participation in associations and civic as well as charitable activities that earlier generations of Americans engaged in through giant, nation-spanning, cross-class federations. Missing in the versions of voluntary associationalism that may be spreading in the United States today are the face-to-face membership groups and the outward-reaching, locality and class-spanning linkages that were so prominent in America's civic past.

In short, whether Americans today are concentrating on involvements within their evangelical congregations, or volunteering for church-run or professionally coordinated secular activities to help the poor, it is not clear that the best egalitarian traditions of American civic voluntarism are continuing to flourish. Evangelical Christians may be building new communities of love—but mainly congregation by congregation, without strong ties that include, bridge, and reach out. Old-line religious groups may still have some capacity to encourage broad civic voluntarism among their adherents. But these groups are dwindling in numbers, energy, and resources; and they may not be promoting the kind of full brotherhood and sisterhood under God that once nourished a democratic civil society, and through inclusive social provision.

Progressive-minded Americans, meanwhile, are shying away from religious or moral calls for social change, viewing them either as irrelevant, or inherently particularistic, or as socially and politically divisive. But this leaves Americans who want social justice lacking for arguments and institutional ties needed to energize broad majorities of fellow citizens on behalf of visions of fellowship and social justice—this, at a time when growing inequalities call out for a moral response.

In a democratic society, fragmentary efforts to "do for" the poor by the privileged can never be a full substitute for all of the children of God associating—"doing together"—as they struggle to move toward the promised land of a just and loving community, and a more complete democracy. Misguided as some contemporary appeals to cramped versions of religious ideals may be, no one has yet found any substitute for the democratic energy unleashed historically by the best in America's tradition of Biblically inspired associationalism. Nor has anyone found a way to justify broad and inclusive social provision without appealing to moral ideals of community as well as the economic calculations of individuals. All Americans, therefore, have a strong stake in reconnecting with—and reinventing in new forms—the best traditions of religious and moral inspiration for democracy and generous social provision in our nation's history. Unless such reconnections happen, it is hard to see what can stop the march of inequality and pure market individualism from undercutting American democracy and shared social provision for the future.

Notes

1. Irving Kristol, "The Welfare State's Spiritual Crisis," *The Wall Street Journal*, Monday, February 3, 1997.
2. Marvin Olasky, *The Tragedy of American Compassion* (Wheaton, IL: Crossway Books, 1992), p.8.
3. Marvin Olasky, *Renewing American Compassion: How Compassion for the Needy Can Turn Ordinary Citizens into Heroes* (New York: The Free Press, 1996).
4. Michael S. Joyce and William A. Schambra, "A New Civic Life," in Peter L. Berger and Richard John Neuhaus, eds., *To Empower People: From State To Civil Society* (Washington DC: AEI Press, 1996), p. 12.
5. Ibid., p. 15.
6. Ibid., p. 17.
7. Ibid., pp. 25-26.
8. Charles Trueheart, "Welcome to the Next Church," *Atlantic Monthly* 278(2) (August 1996): 37-58.
9. David Hilfiker, *Not All of Us Are Saints: A Doctor's Journey with the Poor* (New York: Hill and Wang, 1994).
10. Arnold J. Heidenheimer, "Education and Social Security Entitlements in Europe and the United States," in *The Development of Welfare States in Europe and America*, Peter Flora and Arnold J. Heidenheimer, eds.,(New Brunswick, NJ: Transaction Books, 1981), pp. 269-304.
11. For the full analysis, see Theda Skocpol, *Protecting Soldiers and Mothers: The Political Origins of Social Policy in the United States* (Cambridge, MA: The Belknap Press of Harvard University Press, 1992), pp. 129-35.
12. Mark Leff, "Consensus for Reform: The Mothers' Pension Movement in the Progressive Era," *Social Service Review* 47(3) (September 1973): 397-417.
13. Molly Ladd-Taylor, *Raising a Baby the Government Way: Mothers' Letters to the Children's Bureau, 1915-1932* (New Brunswick, NJ: Rutgers University Press, 1986).
14. Martha Derthick, *Policymaking for Social Security* (Washington DC: The Brookings Institution, 1979).
15. Theodore R. Marmor, *The Politics of Medicare* (Chicago, IL: Aldine, 1973).
16. Theodore R. Mosch, *The G.I. Bill: A Breakthrough in Educational and Social Policy in the United States* (Hicksville, NY: Exposition Press, 1975); and Keith W. Olson, *The G.I. Bill, the Veterans, and the Colleges* (Lexington, KY: University of Kentucky Press, 1974).
17. Skocpol, *Protecting Soldiers and Mothers*, pp. 148-51; and Davis R. B. Ross, *Preparing for Ulysses: Politics and Veterans during World War II* (New York: Columbia University Press, 1969).
18. Mustafa Emirbayer, "The Shaping of a Virtuous Citizenry: Educational Reform in Massachusetts, 1830-1860," *Studies in American Political Development* 6 (Fall 1992): 391-419; and David Tyack and Elisabeth Hansot, *Managers of Virtue: Public School Leadership in America, 1820-1980* (New York: Basic Books, 1982).

19. Skocpol, *Protecting Soldiers and Mothers,* part III.

20. Eric R. Kingson, Barbara A. Hirshorn, and John M. Cornman, *Ties That Bind: The Interdependence of Generations* (Washington DC: Seven Locks Press, 1986); and Stanley B. Greenberg, "The Economy Project" (Washington DC: Greenberg Research, 1996).

21. Ira Katznelson and Margaret Weir, *Schooling for All* (New York: Basic Books, 1985), chapter 2.

22. Skocpol, *Protecting Soldiers and Mothers,* chapter 8.

23. From a letter quoted in Louis J. Covotsos, "Child Welfare and Social Progress: A History of the United States Children's Bureau, 1912-1935" (Unpublished Ph.D. dissertation, University of Chicago, 1976), p. 123.

24. Hugh Heclo, "The Political Foundations of Antipoverty Policy," in Sheldon H. Danziger and Daniel H. Weinberg, eds., *Fighting Poverty: What Works and What Doesn't* (Cambridge, MA: Harvard University Press, 1986), pp. 312-40.

25. Tyack and Hansot, *Managers of Virtue,* part I.

26. D. Sven Nordin, *Rich Harvest: A History of the Grange, 1867-1900* (Jackson, MS: University of Mississippi Press, 1974); and John Mark Hansen, *Gaining Access: Congress and the Farm Lobby, 1919-1981* (Chicago, IL: University of Chicago Press, 1991).

27. Skocpol, *Protecting Soldiers and Mothers,* part III.

28. Ibid., chapter 2.

29. Abraham Holtzman, *The Townsend Movement: A Political Study* (New York: Bookman, 1963).

30. Charles R. Morris, *The AARP* (New York: Times Books, 1996).

31. Ross, *Preparing for Ulysses*; and Theda Skocpol, "The G.I. Bill and U.S. Social Policy, Past and Future," *Social Philosophy & Policy* 14(2) (Summer 1997): 95-115.

32. William Pencak, *For God and Country: The American Legion, 1919-1941* (Boston, MA: Northeastern University Press, 1989).

33. Alexis de Tocqueville, *Democracy in America,* edited by J. P. Mayer and translated by George Lawrence (Garden City, NY: Doubleday, Anchor Books, 1969; originally 1835-40).

34. Richard D. Brown, "The Emergence of Urban Society in Rural Massachusetts, 1760-1820," *Journal of American History* 61(1) (June 1974): 29-51.

35. Donald G. Mathews, "The Second Great Awakening as an Organizing Process, 1780-1830: An Hypothesis," *American Quarterly* 21(1) (Spring 1969): 23-43.

36. Richard John, *Spreading the News: The American Postal System from Franklin to Morse* (Cambridge, MA: Harvard University Press, 1995).

37. See the discussions in Mary P. Ryan, *Cradle of the Middle Class: The Family in Oneida County, New York, 1790-1865* (Cambridge and New York: Cambridge University Press, 1981), chapter 3; and Gerald Gamm and Robert Putnam, "Association-Building in America, 1840-1940" (prepared for the conference on "Civic Engagement in American Democracy," Portland, Maine, September 26-28, 1987).

38. Rev. F. E. Clark, "The United Society of Christian Endeavor: State and Local Unions" (Boston, MA: United Society of Christian Endeavor, 1892), p.4.

39. Gamm and Putnam, "Association-Building."

40. Alexander von Hoffman, *Local Attachments: The Making of an Urban Neighborhood, 1890-1925* (Baltimore, MD: Johns Hopkins University Press), p. 121.

41. Mrs. G.H. Robertson, "The State's Duty to Fatherless Children," *Child-Welfare Magazine* 6(5) (January 1912), p.160.

42. Roger Finke and Rodney Stark, *The Churching of America, 1776-1990* (New Brunswick, NJ: Rutgers University Press, 1992).

43. Mathews, "Second Great Awakening as an Organizing Process."

44. David M. Fahey, Temperance and Racism (Lexington, KY: University Press of Kentucky, 1996).

45. Christopher J. Kauffman, *Faith and Fraternalism: The History of the Knight of Columbus*, revised edition (New York: Simon and Schuster, 1992).

46. Evelyn Brooks Higginbotham, *Righteous Discontent: The Women's Movement in the Black Baptist Church, 1880-1920* (Cambridge, MA: Harvard University Press, 1993).

47. Aldon D. Morris, *The Origins of the Civil Rights Movement: Black Communities Organizing for Change* (New York: Free Press, 1984), p.4.

48. This argument is compellingly made for women by Constance H. Buchanan, *Choosing to Lead: Women and the Crisis of American Values* (Boston, MA: Beacon Press, 1996).

49. This is carefully documented in Robert Wuthnow, "Mobilizing Civic Engagement: The Changing Impact of Religious Involvement" (Paper prepared for the Conference on Civic Engagement in American Democracy, Hotel Portland Regency, Portland, Maine, September 26-28, 1997).

50. A point stressed in Andrew Greeley, "The Other Civic America," *The American Prospect* 32 (May-June 1997): 68-73.

51. Sidney Verba, Kay Lehman Schlozman, and Henry E. Brady, "The Big Tilt: Participatory Inequality in America," *The American Prospect* 32 (May-June 1997): 74-80.

CHAPTER 2

Responsibilities and Risks for Faith-Based Organizations

Ronald Thiemann, Samuel Herring, and Betsy Perabo

Communities of faith function, in part, to provide a view of reality at odds with that of the larger culture, society, or government. They must retain the ability to be communities of dissent, should the historical moment demand opposition to governmental policies or cultural mores.

WITH THE PASSAGE OF WELFARE REFORM LEGISLATION in 1996, the nature of government-sponsored social welfare provision has fundamentally changed. While the federal government will continue to be involved in funding social and human services, it will now do so primarily in partnership with other agencies. Section 104 of the act includes the so-called "charitable choice" provision which allows the granting of government funds to faith-based organizations; thus partnerships between government agencies and religious institutions may grow significantly as we move further into this new era of social provision.

The notion that faith-based social service providers can offer effective and cost efficient solutions to America's social ills has gained widespread support among politicians in both parties. The idea that social service agencies must address the human and spiritual dimensions of poverty has become remarkably nonpartisan. Republican Governor John Engler of Michigan, an early supporter of government support for faith-based agencies, has argued that welfare reform is not "just about reforming broken systems, but about reforming what is broken in the human character."[1] Senator Dan Coats, Republican of Indiana, has extolled organizations like the Gospel Mission, a faith-based drug-treatment center for homeless men. "The Gospel Mission succeeds because it provides more than a meal, more than a drug treatment. It is in the business of spreading the grace of God."[2] Vice President Al Gore and Governor George W. Bush of Texas have both voiced strong support for faith-based social service agencies. In endorsing the recent expansion of the charitable choice provision, the vice-president insisted that faith is often "essential to spark a personal transformation and to keep that person from falling back into addiction, delinquency, or dependency." He added that if he is elected, "the voices of faith-based organizations will be integral to the policies set forth in my administration."[3]

Proponents of this new development of social provision in the United States have touted it as a fundamental change in the relationship between government and the religious non-profit sector. While the expanded charitable choice option has introduced a new mode of governmental funding for faith-based initiatives, it is important that we not lose sight of the long tradition of faith-based social service provision throughout American history. The effort to address the human and spiritual dimensions of poverty, homelessness, juvenile crime, and drug and alcohol dependency is extremely important, and religious institutions are uniquely positioned to offer this kind of assistance. Still, serious empirical, legal, and theological issues involved in the relationship between faith-based organizations and governmental agencies remain to be addressed. This chapter seeks to provide an overview of these important issues.

A Brief History of Faith-Based Social Service Provision in the United States[4]

As Theda Skocpol notes in the preceding chapter, scholars of American social history and religion agree that current proposals for introducing religion to social policy demonstrate an ignorance of the rich history of religion as a force in American social service provision. Robert Wineburg writes, "If scholars and planners looked closely at the evolution of human services in communities across the United States, they would find a changing but continuous thread of religious activity in helping people in need."[5] Similarly, Robert Wuthnow asserts that the recent proliferation of "special purpose" religious groups, many of which function as social service providers, does "not signal a new invention, nor can they be considered unique to the United States."[6]

In the early years of European settlement of the colonies, informal networks of family, neighbors, and community were the primary means of support for the poor and destitute.[7] In her book, *It Takes A Nation,* Rebecca Blank documents the continuation of this trend to the present day; (in fact, she estimates that direct transfers to low-income families from relatives are a greater source of income for the poor than private charity).[8] In addition to providing family support, a number of colonial religious institutions also served the poor. In Anglican Virginia, church officials (who were also officers of the municipal government) provided care for children, the elderly, and the sick. In Pennsylvania, the Friends Almshouse, the Pennsylvania House and the Philadelphia Bettering House—religious institutions that received both government and private funds—tended to the colony's sick and housed the poor. Furthermore, "friendly societies, organized along religious lines, relieved public officials of the necessity for caring for their community's poor by supplying mutual aid to members and dispensing charity to certain categories of beneficiaries."[9] Wineburg notes that this sort of church-municipality arrangement has endured to the present: Habitat for Humanity receives land from the government to build houses at below market prices; government agencies give food to local faith communities to distribute to the poor; and faith-based organizations such as the Salvation Army administer federal emergency heating assistance money to the needy and use federal housing money to make improvements to their homeless shelters.

Although examples of religious institutions organized to serve the poor during the colonial era are not uncommon, these institutions did not emerge in significant number until the beginning of the nineteenth century.[10] In their book examining the contract relationships between nonprofit organizations and the government, Steven Smith and Michael Lipsky write that "the antebellum period witnessed a veritable explosion" of agencies serving the poor, many of which were founded by evangelical Protestants or the fledgling Catholic Church."[11] The range of faith-based organizations that operated at this time was vast. Representative institutions from the era include the Female Domestic Missionary Society for the Poor, founded in 1816, which distributed Bibles and provided schooling for the poor in New York; the Catholic Maria Marthian Society which was founded in 1827 to deliver general assistance to the poor; and the Hebrew Relief Society, founded in 1831 to serve the sick and destitute in the Jewish community of New York.[12]

The number of national religious charities increased dramatically following the Civil War. The growth of these groups reflected a period of tremendous expansion of congregations in America. Between the Civil War and the advent of World War I, the number of churches grew from 70,000 to over 225,000. Religious membership more than doubled from less than twenty percent to over forty percent of the American population between 1860 and 1900. Factors contributing to this unprecedented growth include the influx of European immigrants totaling twenty million between 1870 and 1910, and the foundation and expansion of denominational bureaucracies which oversaw church construction, evangelism and charitable activities. The increasingly urban character of the nation (46 percent of the population lived in cities by 1910) spawned interdenominational ministries such as the YMCA and Salvation Army that provided religiously-motivated solutions to the social problems that came with industrialization and the expansion of America's cities. As testament to their success in meeting the needs of the urban poor, the Salvation Army quadrupled in size between 1890 and 1915, and the YMCA expanded from 10,000 to 263,000 volunteers between 1865 and 1895, reaching 720,000 by World War I.[13]

Following World War II, although a popular set of entitlement programs had been firmly established, there was little partnering between government and nonprofit organizations as contract service providers. In fact, despite the advances of the New Deal, there was little federal money spent on social services. For example, in 1953–54, the federal government spent just $124.1 million on social services, while states and local municipalities spent $605 million. Criticism of government social service programs arose throughout the 1950s, but increased public funding was slow to appear. Even by the mid–1960s, public funding had not become widely available to nonprofit social service providers. A 1965 study by the Family Service Association of America reported that public funds made up only 8 percent of nonprofit organization's income. Another study at the time of 800 service organizations found that 80 percent received no public funding.[14] In this context, the Catholic Church shifted its mission to emphasize political advocacy for the poor while still providing services as a privately-funded institution.[15]

However, the passage of the 1967 Amendments to the Social Security Act (known as Title IV-A) dramatically changed the relationship between the federal government and nonprofit social service organizations, because the law "specifically encouraged states to enter into purchase-of-service agreements with private agencies."[16] The result of this law was a proliferation of contracts with nonprofit organizations to provide government services. This new approach to delivering government services, what Lester Salamon calls "third party government," was financed by a threefold increase in federal social welfare spending from 1965 to 1970 ($812 million to $2.2 billion). Government contracting with nonprofits grew throughout the 1970s, increasing from 25 percent of total public social service expenditures in 1971 to 49 percent in 1978. The dramatic increase of government spending on social services led not only to the creation of a great number of secular and religious nonprofit organizations to deliver contract services; it also led to an explosion of special interest groups founded to combat or promote certain government policies.[17]

While the federal government was expanding social programs and creating new ways of delivering services, religious institutions such as the Catholic Church were undergoing major changes as well. As former immigrant Catholics joined the growing American middle class and thus no longer required charitable assistance from the Church, and the progressive social vision of Vatican II influenced whom the Church sought to serve, Catholic charities began to serve "a 'new' and largely non-Catholic poor." Furthermore, with the expansion of government social welfare programs in the 1960s through the War on Poverty and Great Society legislation, the Catholic Church, through its social service arm, Catholic Charities, expanded its provision of social services by winning government contracts to provide services for the poor.[18]

By the time Ronald Reagan took office in 1981, public funding had become a major source of nonprofit social service support, eclipsing private charitable sources and fee income. Lester Salamon writes that the Reagan administration had a prime opportunity to streamline the government relationships with nonprofit organizations that had developed haphazardly for over a decade. Instead, Reagan's administration chose to slash federal budgets in the name of supporting local "private sector initiatives." Salamon argues that these deep budget cuts (including a 20 percent reduction in the Social Service Block Grant, abolition of the Comprehensive Employment and Training Act, and major reduction in funding for community action agencies and neighborhood health clinics)[19] demonstrate a conceptual failure in Reagan's policy. By cutting federal spending,

Reagan jeopardized his prized "private sector initiatives" that were largely dependent on government grants. Cuts in federal social service spending were particularly damaging to the poorest Americans. To begin with, less than 30 percent of all human service agencies serve a primarily poor clientele. In his research, Salamon found that the greater the level of government funding a private agency receives, the more likely it is to serve the poor. Thus, those agencies that served the poorest clients were also those most affected by reduced government support. Furthermore, Salamon argues that Reagan administration's simultaneous tax cut did not achieve its stated goal of encouraging individuals to give more of their income to charity. The result of these policies has been the "marketization" of nonprofit service through fees, and increased competition between for-profit companies and nonprofit organizations, a situation which raises troubling questions about the affordability and accessibility of social services to the poor.[20]

What were the results of the Reagan administration's social service cuts for the poor and how did faith communities respond? Wineburg writes that Reagan's social policy and the economic recession of the early 1980s resulted in an increase in homelessness, hunger and poverty in America. For example, in 1988, there were eight million more people in poverty than there were in 1978. Wineburg argues that mainline churches rose to the social challenge of the mid–1980s "in a quiet and unceremonious way." The forms of service that religious congregations provided throughout the 1980s and continue to provide are direct service, assistance to community-based service providers, and increased financial support to religious national social service providers such as Lutheran Family Services and Catholic Charities. Citing his research of the Greensboro, North Carolina area, as well as the research of others, he finds that during the 1980s, "mainline religious congregations across the United States. . . fed the hungry, sheltered the homeless, and provided various kinds of assistance ranging from legal help to child and adult day care." For example, Wineburg's study of the Greensboro faith community's social service provision in the 1980s indicates that 40 percent of congregations made contributions to the local food bank, 34 percent provided volunteers to community feeding programs, and 22 percent started on-site programs in food, shelter, or cash assistance.[21]

The decade of the '90's has witnessed the continued expansion of faith-based services. The faith-based social service community encompasses not only small, local, congregation-based programs, but also, again as Skocpol notes, national service networks and other special-purpose organizations. According to a leading survey, faith-based service providers now spend more than 11 billion dollars a year to feed, house, and clothe the needy and provide a host of other services.[22] Some scholars have estimated that the actual dollar amount may be as high as 20 billion dollars per year.[23]

The 350,000 congregations in the United States are the largest source of both financial and human resources for faith-based social service programs. The American Association of Fund Raising Counsel estimates that Americans give $63 billion to churches and related organizations, and several studies indicate that congregations dedicate approximately 20 percent of this income to social service provision, for an annual total of $12.6 billion. In addition, volunteers in religious organizations, not including clergy, devote a total of 144 million hours per year to human services. More than 90 percent of congregations operate or support at least one social service program; the average number of programs per congregation is between 4 and 6.4.[24] These social services programs cover a wide range of needs. One-half to three-quarters of the congregations in the United States operate some kind of meal program.[25] Many also provide programs related to alcohol/drug treatment (47 percent); shelter (39 percent); support or counseling for abused women (30 percent) or children (26 percent); health screening (23 percent); support for health institutions (28 percent); teen pregnancy prevention (28 percent); support for migrants/refugees (23 percent); family planning (22 percent); day-care for children (24 percent) or seniors (21 percent); affordable housing (20 percent); housing for seniors (19 percent); after-school programs(18 percent); tutoring (20 percent); and foster care (16 percent).[26] In general, these programs serve all community members, not just members of the congregation that operates them or the denomination with which they are affiliated.

Finally, other religious organizations of many types also provide a vast array of services. These include local interfaith alliances involved in advocacy for the homeless; rehabilitation programs that focus on religion as an integral part of recovery; denominationally-affiliated homes for the elderly; and battered women's shelters that begin as offshoots of a church but become independent entities. The amount of money given to these organizations is difficult to estimate; probably upwards of a billion dollars, and possibly several billion.[27]

With such an impressive track record, faith-based organizations are now being urged to take on responsibility for an increasing amount of the social service burden. Many scholars argue, however, that it is unlikely that religious institutions can substantially increase their capacity to care for the needy. As previously noted, congregations already spend 20 percent of their income on social services. Also, they lack the resources to set up an infrastructure and to train staff and volunteers, and they do not have adequate experience to replace the safety net currently provided by the federal government.[28] Some scholars note that, despite their importance, religious-based efforts to provide social services are miniscule compared with governmental efforts. Rebecca Blank states that only about $12 billion of private charitable donations – which includes those to faith-based organizations – is spent to assist low-income families. In contrast, the government spends $200 billion per year on anti-poverty support.[29]

Furthermore, the amount of resources available and the quality of service provided vary between wealthier suburban areas and poorer urban and rural areas, as well as from region to region across the country. Julian Wolpert notes that despite the increase in the nonprofit sector, "the sector's real growth as a service provider is quite small" because there is growth in the suburbs but decline in city and rural areas; the independent sector is not structured to address these disparities. Thus, even when FBOs are able to gain access to additional financial and human resources, these resources may not reach the most needy.[30]

Proposals for increased involvement of faith-based organizations in the delivery of social services must address the issues of capacity and purpose of such institutions. Is it possible for religious not-for-profit institutions to expand sufficiently to meet the significant human service needs of the American population? Do such institutions possess the infrastructure, financial resources, and professional personnel to accomplish this task? Finally, *ought* faith-based institutions accept a larger share of the responsibility to provide for those in need? What ethical principles should guide our thinking about the shared responsibility among faith-based institutions, secular non-for-profits, and government agencies in provision for the poor and needy. There is, of course, a large role for faith-based social service providers to play in social service provision in America. However, public policy, civil society, and the religious institutions themselves will suffer if policymakers seek to abdicate their responsibility to the poor by simply claiming that it is no longer the responsibility of the government. The question "*who ought to provide?*" remains unanswered by the current proposals for increased involvement of faith-based institutions in social service provision.

The Distinctive Contributions of Faith-Based Organizations

While support for faith-based institutions has been most prominent among conservative politicians, others of a more liberal or even left-wing orientation have also recognized the potential of these organizations to make distinctive contributions to the body politic. The neo-Marxist and pragmatist philosopher Richard Bernstein has argued that there are "still the vestiges of community and community bonds in religious life" that might enable it to "play a role in the vitalization of public life."[31] Pointing to his own personal experience in the Civil Rights movement Bernstein notes, "The fact that there was *already* a pre-existing sense of communal religious bonds provided many individuals with the courage, hope, and conviction to join together in public action. It illustrates what I think is becoming increasingly evident in our time – that if there is to be a renewal of public life, a communal basis for individuals coming together, it is to be found outside those great impersonal abstractions of society and state."[32] In a remarkably similar mode Adam Michnik, the Polish intellectual and Solidarity activist, has highlighted the essential role of religion in providing counter-public spaces for those who opposed the tyranny of the Eastern European communist states. "In East Germany, Czechoslovakia, Hungary, as well as in Poland, the recovery of freedom, the revival of civil society, and the public presence of the churches were closely connected. . . . An active, public role for religion, therefore, would seem to be one of the preconditions of a vibrant democratic life."[33] Finally in his book *Democracy's Discontent* Harvard political scientist Michael Sandel notes that the work of the Industrial Areas Foundation (IAF), a network of community-based organizations devoted to teaching the poor the skills of political involvement, increasingly relies upon communities of faith as their organizational focal points. "In recent decades . . . most traditional bases of civic activity in inner cities have eroded, leaving religious congregations the only vital institutions in many communities. As a result . . . the IAF [has] organized primarily around congregations, especially Catholic and Protestant churches. . . . [These] parishes [provide] not only a stable source of funds, participants, and leaders but also a shared more language as a starting point for political discourse."[34]

These observations, like those of others from various points on the political spectrum, are suggestive, but they are more intuitive than analytical and critical. Appeals to common community bonds or shared moral language are important but require greater specification before they yield insights that can guide our thinking about the future of faith-based institutions. Each commentator has a different kind of religious institution in mind when extolling the contributions of FBOs. Bernstein has in mind an inter-faith special purpose political alliance, the Civil Rights movement. Michnik is referring to the role played by Eastern European congregations in providing space, moral courage, and political encouragement for the anticommunist protest movements. Sandel identifies alliances among congregations created by a special purpose group, the IAF. When commentators like Amy Sherman extol the role that "churches" can play in the post-welfare reform movement, they point to face-to-face programs sponsored by individual congregations or small faith-based special purpose groups. Indeed, this tri-partite division among *congregations, national denominational organizations, and special purpose groups*[35] is useful in identifying the distinctive contributions different sorts of FBOs might play in this new political context.

The previous historical review demonstrates that national denominational faith-based social service institutions have made and will continue to make essential contributions to the delivery of human and social services. Organizations like Catholic Charities, Lutheran Social Services, The Salvation Army, and the Jewish Federations may be able to expand modestly to respond to new state initiatives for faith-based services, but they cannot possibly absorb the enormous client base now served by governmental agencies.[36] Given the declining membership in most "mainline" Protestant denominations, voluntary contributions are also diminishing in these bodies. While these national organizations give no indication of reducing their commitment to social services, it is unlikely that they will direct additional revenues to these activities in the near future. In addition, the leaders of some national FBOs have argued against a larger role for their groups in the post-welfare context. Many are reluctant to increase the size of the bureaucracies needed to serve a larger client base and resist as well an increase in the dependence of their budgets upon government funds.[37] Most importantly, however, these groups often rest within theological traditions that assert the primacy of governmental responsibility for citizens in need.[38] While they are willing to continue their historic partnership with governments, they refuse to become the *primary* agents for social and human services to the most needy.[39]

Special purpose groups are the most difficult to analyze. They have grown dramatically during the last decade and no definitive study of the scope of their work is available. They range from national organizations like the Industrial Areas Foundation and the Gamaliel Foundation to tiny local initiatives run out of church basements with budgets under $10,000. Some are freestanding agencies, such as Charles Colson's national Prison Fellowship or Detroit's local Joy of Jesus recovery center. Others, like Michigan's Good Samaritan Ministries, are ecumenical social-service initiatives of local congregations. They serve widely diverse needs; persons with AIDS, addictions, and alcoholism, victims of violence and abuse, the hungry, the homeless, and those in prison all benefit from the work of special purpose groups. While some of these agencies—homeless shelters, food banks, and soup kitchens particularly – will accept government assistance, many others refuse it on grounds of principle. Their identities are defined precisely by their independence from government, and they believe that they provide a kind of unconditional, compassionate, face-to-face service that would be undermined by entanglements with the state. Just as importantly, many of these organizations are involved in advocacy work, and often they direct their protests *against* government agencies in the name of justice.

It is likely that we will continue to see growth in these groups in the coming decade. Already there is evidence that the decline in giving within "mainline" denominations has resulted in part from members' re-directing their contributions from the highly bureaucratized national agencies to smaller special purpose groups.[40] Evangelical Christians are especially likely to form freestanding social service agencies, since Evangelical Christianity is itself a trans-denominational movement. Many evangelical churches are independent of all denominational ties, and thus have no national denominational agency to support their social service ministries. These churches often have an ecclesiology, or doctrine of the church, that is strongly congregational in character and thus tend on theological grounds to resist large bureaucratized organizations. It is difficult to predict the degree to which special purpose faith-based groups would seek or accept the new funding that might be available through the "charitable choice" clause of the welfare reform law. Much more research must be done before reliable predictions can be made about the future relations between faith-based special-purpose groups and government funding.

Given the fact that the well-established national denominational agencies are not likely to grow significantly despite the availability of new governmental funds, the organizations most likely to show substantial growth over the next decade are the following: social services agencies sponsored by large congregations, ecumenical consortia of congregations, and freestanding, mostly evangelical, special purpose groups. Proponents of faith-based services point to a remarkably wide range of distinctive contributions FBOs can make to social service provision. Robert Wineberg identifies seven assets unique to faith communities in their work as social service providers: a mission to serve, a pool of volunteers, space for program use, fund-raising potential, political strength, moral authority, and willingness to experiment.[41] Nancy Ammerman lists fellowship, the development of civic skills, charity practices, and worship as key ingredients in the success of FBOs.[42] Stephen Warner notes that worship, religious education, mission, stewardship, and fellowship are the distinctive marks of faith communities involved in social service.[43] Despite the enthusiasm for the potential of FBOs, however, John DiIulio rightly observes that "we remain a long way from a definitive body of research evidence on the actual extent and the efficacy of church-anchored and faith-based social programs."[44]

One commonplace advantage cited for FBOs is their unique ability to address the fundamental social problem of "spiritual or moral poverty."

> [I]sn't it time we realized that there is only so much that public policy can do? . . . [I]sn't it time to realize that only a richness of spirit can battle a poverty of soul? Too many . . . charities dispense aid indiscriminately—ignoring the moral and spiritual needs of the poor and, in so doing, treating them more as animals than as people. The government of a pluralistic society is inherently incapable of tending to these spiritual needs, so the more effective provision of social services will ultimately depend on their return to private and especially to religious institutions.[45]

> What I have termed juvenile "superpredators" are born of abject "moral poverty," which I define as the poverty of being without loving, capable, responsible adults who teach you right from wrong. . . . Researchers have long known that urban poverty and joblessness are directly influenced by community norms and networks. Religious institutions consistently emerge as a key node of such networks.[46]

In the remainder of this essay, I will offer my understanding of the distinctive contributions faith-based communities can make within the national network of social service providers.[47] FBOs must be seen as expressions of the spiritual mission of the faith communities that sponsor them. Therefore I will treat these communities *theologically* as worshipping communities of faith and *sociologically* as religious voluntary associations. I will also review the opportunities and dangers that the new post-welfare context poses to such communities, and will conclude with some observations regarding the principle of the "separation of church and state."

Religious communities aspire to provide a basic framework of meaning through which participants understand themselves and the world. Meaning within such communities is mediated through stories, myths, and rituals which direct believers to "that which is more important than anything else in the universe."[48] Participants in communities of faith are engaged in a life-long process of learning and internalizing the knowledge, skills, and forms of behavior inherent in their religious traditions. The religious repertoire is complex, including the stories, wisdom, and moral instruction of sacred scriptures; the prayers, songs, and lore of tradition; the rituals of birth, initiation, commitment, and burial. Individuals and communities appropriate these rich and varied resources in sundry fashion in different times and places. Stories or moral precepts that might be central for one community at one point in history may become peripheral or nearly forgotten by communities at other times. Diversity is also a hallmark of contemporaneous religious communities. Though community leaders may seek to enforce orthodoxy or orthopraxis, diversity of religious belief and practice remains a given. In addition, although every community projects an ideal version of its belief and practice, actual communities instantiate that ideal imperfectly. It is also important to note that the cultural and social context of religious communities influences, often decisively, which stories and moral precepts are taken as authoritative. This is true whether the community understands itself as standing in fundamental agreement or in fundamental opposition to its host society. Consequently every analysis of the relationship between religion and society must attend to the organic principles that shape the beliefs and practices of a community as well as the critical principles that guide the selection, evaluation, and critique of those beliefs and practices.

Religious communities share at least the following four characteristics: a common story, a shared community life, an ethic of commitment, and a transcendent purpose. Within the Jewish and Christian traditions, the ethic of commitment, particularly in behalf of the poor and vulnerable, has been a defining feature. The prophets' injunctions to care for the "orphan, widow, and stranger"[49] and Jesus' teaching that we will be judged by our actions toward "the least of these our brothers and sisters"[50] have deeply influenced these communities and their host societies. This ethic of care is directed both toward members of the religious community and toward those "strangers" not of one's faith, clan, or nation. The well-known "parable of the Good Samaritan" teaches the importance of directing neighbor-love even toward those strangers who are also one's natural enemies. The New Testament describes Jesus' ministry as directed toward the poor and the outcasts on the margins of his society. The symbol of Jesus' radical ministry is his "table fellowship with tax-collectors and sinners," a visible and tangible sign of his special concern for those considered ritually unclean. Indeed, the "meal" has a special resonance within both Jewish and Christian communities. Messianic expectation within Israel is often symbolized by the "messianic banquet," the great feast at the end of time at which all sorrow, suffering, and hunger will cease. "On this mountain the Lord of hosts will make for all peoples a feast of rich food, a feast of well-aged wines strained clear. . . . Then the Lord God will wipe away the tears from all faces" (Isaiah 25:6,8). This theme is picked up within Christianity in stories like the "Feeding of the 5000"[51] and the "Last Supper"[52] and is then developed by St. Paul and others in the "agape meal" of early Christianity and in the succeeding eucharist or holy communion practiced by most contemporary Christian congregations.

Feeding of the poor, and other forms of ministry to those in need, are not simple "acts of charity" within the Jewish and Christian communities; rather, those acts resonate with symbols that define their basic communal identities. Moreover, such acts of compassion and justice are religious obligations, acts of devotion and commitment to God.[53] The Book of Deuteronomy enjoins Israelites to "justice for the orphan and the widow" in imitation of the God of justice, "the God of gods and Lord of lords, the great God, mighty and awesome, who is not partial and takes no bribe, who executes justice for the orphan and widow, and who loves the strangers, providing them food and clothing." Jesus says to those who stand before him on the last day, "I was hungry and you gave me food, I was thirsty and you gave me something to drink, I was a stranger and you welcomed me, I was naked and you gave me clothing, I was sick and you took care of me, I was in prison and you visited me. . . . Truly I tell you, just as you did it to one of the least of these who are members of my family, you did it to me."[54] The obligation to the poor in these communities is reinforced in readings, prayers, hymns, liturgical meals, and religious art. Thus the services which these communities provide are not simple "add-ons;" they are constitutive of the communities' identities.

In light of this brief theological overview of the Jewish and Christian ethic of care the long history of faith-based involvement in social and human service is hardly surprising. These communities are committed to service of the poor, independent of the availability of government funding. If such funding allows faith communities to carry out their mission without interference or conflict with basic religious principles, then the provisions of the new welfare reform legislation are consistent with the long history of government support for FBOs. Still potential dangers do exist in the new post-welfare atmosphere and with a review of those dangers I will bring this essay to an end.

Robert Wuthnow has recently surveyed the current state of American Christianity and has concluded that churches are in the midst of a crisis of finances and volunteer service.

> Behind the stained glass . . . a different picture emerges. Mission programs are being canceled. Homeless people are being turned away from soup kitchens because donations of time and money are too small. Pastors' salary increases are being postponed, sometimes for the fifth or sixth year in a row. Second and third calls are made to parishioners begging them to turn in their pledge cards. And at denominational headquarters and in seminaries, church leaders are projecting cutbacks and austerity-level programs well into the next century.[55]

While contributions to religious organizations continue at an extraordinarily high level, the percentage of those contributions as a proportion of family income has declined from an average of 3.1 percent in the late 1960s to 2.5 percent in the 1990s—this despite the fact that the middle classes have more money at their disposal that any time in America's history. Wuthnow argues that the middle classes, those from whom churches receive the vast majority of their funds, are giving less money and less time to their own congregations.

> Clearly, the churches are having to face new realities. Contributions are declining relative to parishioners' incomes. Family budgets are already stretched, and most

> families cannot count on their incomes rising as rapidly as they did a decade or two ago. With hard work and clever marketing, some churches can raise millions for new building and large ministries. But all churches are having to deal with higher fixed costs. Churches will be lucky if they can maintain staff and programs at their present size. The day is gone when churches can also build hospitals, nursing homes, retirement communities, and colleges. More and more people are dependent on churches for emergency meals, shelter, and counseling. But many churches are devoting meager sums to these efforts, and many needs are going unmet. Churches still enlist the help of large numbers of unpaid volunteers to teach classes, mow the lawn, visit the sick, and paint the belfry. But many parishioners are already working harder than ever before and have little energy left over for other commitments.[56]

Some might see this description as providing a further rationale for increased government funding of congregational initiatives. If volunteer time and treasure is waning, why not fill the gap with government dollars? To some extent this argument is perfectly reasonable. Yet the crisis of volunteer time means that congregations will have to rely increasingly on paid professional staff to deliver their services. Not only will this mean increased fixed costs for the churches, but it will also undermine one of the advantages most touted by proponents of government funding for FBOs: the involvement and compassionate care of church members for those most in need.

The potential dilemma raised by the new post-welfare situation is that government funding (with its attendant restrictions) could force churches to alter the manner in which they serve the poor and thereby diminish the very qualities – such as direct, face-to-face compassionate care – most desired in the current situation. On the other hand, if churches are allowed, as the new law stipulates, to "use principles originating in a religious tradition" to encourage "changes in behavior or attitudes,"[57] then government funding might be used to advance churches' conversion strategies, thereby running afoul of first amendment protections.[58] Notions like "spiritual and moral poverty" are particularly dangerous if they are used to characterize the poor as a degenerate class of persons in need of conversion. Undoubtedly, some recipients of social and human services do need a life transformation akin to conversion. They need to be introduced to a network of social support that will allow them to break the cycles of addiction, violence, or abuse that have characterized their lives. But all the poor should not be stigmatized as victims of "spiritual and moral poverty." As St. Paul reminds us, "All have sinned and fallen short of the glory of God" (Romans 3:23). Many of the poor have been victimized by a social and economic system that undermines their best efforts to hold jobs sufficient to support their families, but they are often remarkably virtuous people with deep and abiding spiritual and moral *wealth*.[59] Those whose ethical commitments have been shaped by the Jewish and Christian traditions should be particularly cautious about adopting the language of "spiritual and moral poverty" for the poor, since both traditions not only refuse to stigmatize them but often hold them up as models for the moral life. "Blessed are you who are poor, for yours is the kingdom of God. Blessed are you who are hungry now, for you will be filled. Blessed are you who weep now, for you will laugh."[60] For the Gospel writers it is *wealth* not poverty that indicates a deficient moral condition. "It is easier for a camel to go through the eye of a needle than for a rich man to enter the kingdom of God" (Matthew 19: 24, Mark 10:25).

The vital role that faith communities play within democratic societies requires their independence from governmental interference or control. *Theologically* faith communities are defined by their ultimate commitment to God; all other commitments, including that to the state, are by definition secondary or penultimate. *Sociologically* faith communities are voluntary associations within civil society; thus they must have the freedom to define their own purposes and goals. *Legally* the freedom of faith communities is protected by the religion clauses of the First Amendment; government is prohibited by the Constitution from interfering in the internal affairs of these communities. The vibrancy of faith-based institutions can be traced in large part to this legacy of independence. National denominational FBOs have demonstrated a remarkable ability to keep their religious values intact while still accepting substantial funds from governmental sources.[61] The new welfare reform act seeks to provide even more protection for the religious beliefs and practices of FBOs:

> Religious providers who accept government funds to help the poor retain their autonomy as independent organizations, in control of the practice and development of their religious mission, their organization structure, and their choice of officers and directors. They have the right to maintain a religious environment by displaying religious art, scripture, religious apparel, and other symbols. They retain their right to use criteria in hiring, firing, and disciplining employees, while remaining subject to other anti-discrimination laws.[62]

While these protections ought to be welcomed by FBOs, it remains uncertain how these principles will be applied. Smith and Lipsky, in their 1993 study, concluded that when the goals of government and contracted nonprofit agencies come into conflict, governmental priorities will inevitably hold sway. The nonprofit sector "now depends upon government to sustain it; [it] conforms to governmental expectation of service modes, standards, and client selection, and bends its internal structures toward ably performing as contracting partners. Critics who would see the private nonprofit sector as presenting an important alternative to state action must recognize that the sector is significantly compromised in its ability to offer clear alternatives."[63]

It is too early to tell whether the good intentions of the welfare reform act will result in a change of basic governmental practices toward FBOs, but since the freedom of faith communities is essential to their internal mission and external effectiveness, this issue will bear close examination in the coming months and years.

It should be apparent, in light of the evidence adduced in this essay, that the common phrase "the separation of church and state" hardly does justice to the complex relationship between government and communities of faith. In another work I have discussed the constitutional issues involved in this misleading notion,[64] but for now I simply want to point out the inadequacy of the phrase for guiding our thinking about the future of FBOs. Governments and communities of faith have been deeply intertwined with one another throughout the history of the republic. Government funding of FBOs has existed for more than one hundred and fifty years, and has expanded significantly during the past five decades. The new welfare reform law will not substantially change that historical relationship. Given the substantial entanglement between "church and state" in the social service area, it is important to remind ourselves of the meaning of the First Amendment Constitutional guarantees as they apply to this realm.

"Congress shall make no law respecting an establishment of religion or restricting the free exercise thereof." The religion clauses of the First Amendment are designed to protect the freedom of religion in its both corporate and individual expressions. These freedoms need to be guaranteed not because religion and government are separate in American democracy, but precisely because they are so deeply intertwined. At best the idea of separation identifies a single aspect of the relationship between these two entities; namely, that neither institution should exercise final authority over the values, beliefs, and practices of the other. But "separation" is surely an odd word to use to make that important point. Independence of authority is necessary because the institutions of religion and government are so interdependent in other ways. The government's extensive net of regulations encompasses religious institutions in countless ways; and communities of faith not only influence the values expressed in democratic government but also, as we have seen, carry out a significant portion of government's initiatives to assist the poor and needy. In order to understand the proper relationship between government and FBOs, we need to focus not on the notion of separation but on the issue of independence of authority.

Conclusions

We have entered a new period of experimentation in welfare provision in the United States. The devolution of responsibility from the Federal Government to the States and from the States to nonprofit organizations, including faith-based institutions, has just begun, and so we must be cautious about the projections we make for the future. But the following conclusions seem sound, based on the evidence and arguments of this essay.

1) Faith-based human and social service organizations emerge directly from the religious mission of their parent communities. Their effectiveness depends in large part on the protection of their fundamental religious identities.

2) FBOs have for more than one hundred years received support from state agencies. As long as the welfare goals of government and the mission goals of faith communities converge, a continuing fiscal relationship between the two ought to be encouraged. Political rhetoric notwithstanding, the welfare reform act need not be seen as a radical new departure in the relationship between government and faith communities.
3) FBOs (national denominational organizations, special purpose groups, and congregations) have clear limits on the degree to which they can expand to meet needs of the poor and needy. Those limits are theological, organizational, and financial. While we can expect modest growth in all three categories (probably the greatest growth should be expected in the special purpose groups), FBOs cannot expand, without danger to their religious identities, to encompass much of the welfare client base currently served by government.
4) The tendency to use quasi-religious or theological language to describe the plight of the poor ("conversion from spiritual and moral poverty") threatens to stigmatize the poor as specially in need of spiritual assistance. This tendency stands in direct contrast to the traditional Jewish and Christian emphasis upon wealth not poverty as the great threat to spiritual health.
5) The metaphor "separation of church and state" is inadequate to guide our thinking about the proper relation between FBOs and governments. The historic and continuing interdependence between the two, however, should make us particularly vigilant about the independence of authority the constitution has granted to both "church and state." Any effort by government to determine the identity or mission of a religious organization should be resisted, and any effort by religious organizations to use government funding or authority to assist in their evangelism or conversion efforts must be rejected.

Experiments and new partnerships between government and faith-based institutions will undoubtedly increase during the early years of the "post-welfare" era. In my judgment they should be encouraged, as long as the principles stated above are observed. But one thing is certain: the religious communities of America will continue to hold government to its responsibility for providing care for all citizens of the nation. Our constitutional democracy can allow significant entanglement between the state and faith communities, but neither "church" nor "state" will profit from a situation in which the *primary* responsibility for welfare falls to religious institutions. In order to make their distinctive contributions to our democratic polity, religious institutions must remain primarily communities of faith, witness, worship, and mission. When social service provision to diverse populations is consistent with a community's religious identity it should be supported with both volunteer citizen contributions and government grants. But such service or mission will always remain but a part of the larger fabric of a worshipping community. America's religious bodies will continue to play the role of good citizens, insofar as the commitment of citizenship does not conflict with the ultimate commitment "to that which is most important in the universe."

Communities of faith function, in part, to provide their members with a view of reality that stands at odds with that of the larger culture, society, or government. Communities of faith, therefore, must always retain the responsibility to be communities of dissent, should the historical moment demand opposition to governmental policies or cultural mores. If religious bodies become little more than extensions of government welfare policies, then their own moral and spiritual authority will be eroded and undermined. For the health of the nation as well as for the well being of faith communities, faith-based organizations must take their primary instruction from the stories, rituals, and moral teaching of their traditions. Those traditions themselves must be critically interpreted and applied; the history of America has been the story of the increasing (salutary) democratization of her immigrant religious populations. Democratic values and traditional religious values must stand in some tension with one another, so that the excesses of both can be curbed within their mutual relationship. In order for that creative tension to be maintained, each partner's independence of authority must be guarded. In the end all citizens of the nation must take responsibility for those who are in need. Thus government agencies and communities of faith, each in their own way, in partnership and in criticism, ought to provide for "the least of these" our brothers and sisters.

Notes

1. Amy L. Sherman, "Cross Purposes: Will Conservative Welfare Reform Corrupt Religious Charities?" *Policy Review* 74 (Fall, 1995): 58.

2. Randy Frame, "Religious Nonprofits Fight for Government Funds," *Christian Today* 39 (Dec. 11, 1995): 65.

3. May 24, 2000, campaign speech in Atlanta, Georgia.

4. Betsy Perabo and Sam Herring, research assistants at the Center for the Study of Values in Public Life, researched and drafted this section of the essay.

5. Robert J. Wineburg, "Social Policy, Community Service Development, and Religious Organizations," *Nonprofit Management & Leadership* 3:3 (Spring 1993): 286.

6. Robert Wuthnow, *The Restructuring of American Religion: Society and Faith Since World War II* (Princeton: Princeton University Press, 1988), p. 101.

7. Marvin Olasky, *The Tragedy of American Compassion* (Washington, D.C.: Regnery Gateway, 1992), pp. 6–13.

8. Rebecca Blank, *It Takes a Nation: A New Agenda For Fighting Poverty* (New York: Russell Sage Foundation and Princeton: Princeton University Press, 1997), pp. 201–203.

9. Wineburg, "Social Policy," 286–7.

10. Wuthnow, *The Restructuring of American Religion*, p. 103.

11. Steven Rathgeb Smith and Michael Lipsky, *Nonprofits for Hire: The Welfare State in the Age of Contracting* (Cambridge: Harvard University Press, 1993), p. 48.

12. Olasky, *The Tragedy of American Compassion*, pp. 15–17.

13. Wuthnow, *The Restructuring of American Religion*, pp. 21–23, 105–106.

14. Smith and Lipsky, *Nonprofits for Hire*, pp. 51, 53–54.

15. Dorothy M. Brown and Elizabeth McKeown, *The Poor Belong to Us: Catholic Charities and American Welfare* (Cambridge, MA: Harvard University Press, 1997), p. 9.

16. Smith and Lipsky, *Nonprofits for Hire*, p. 55.

17. Lester Salamon, *Partners in Public Service: Government Relations in the Modern Welfare State* (Baltimore: Johns Hopkins University, 1995), 3; Smith and Lipsky, 54, 55; Wuthnow, 114.

18. Brown and McKeown, *The Poor Belong to Us*, pp. 9, 195.

19. Smith and Lipsky, *Nonprofits for Hire*, p. 62.

20. Salamon, *Partners in Public Service*, pp. 7–10; considering Salamon's work, it should be noted that Peter Frumkin believes he does not adequately represent nonprofit organizations as anything more than contractors of government services. Frumkin urges thinking of nonprofits as "independent innovators," not simply "vessels" of the government. Peter Frumkin, "Rethinking Public-Nonprofit Relations: Toward a Neo-Institutional Theory of Public Management," Program on Non-Profit Organizations at the Institution for Social and Policy Studies, Yale University, April 1998, 35–36.

21. Wineburg, "Social Policy," 283–4, 290–1; Wineburg, "When Politics and Religion Meet on Main Street: Social Service and the Religious Safety Net," unpublished paper (February, 1998), p. 4; Wineburg, "Volunteers in Service to their Community: Congregational Commitment to Helping the Needy," *The Journal of Volunteer Administration* (Fall 1990): 35.

22. Hodgkinson, Virginia, Murray Weitzman, Arthur Kirsch, Stephen Norga, and Heather Gorski. *From Belief To Commitment: The Community Service Activities and Finances of Religious Congregations in the United States* (Washington, D.C.: Independent Sector, 1993), pp. 1, 78–79. In this study, less than one tenth of a percent of church funding is attributed to "government fees and contracts"(72). Peter Frumkin has criticized the methodology of IS studies, noting that in at least one case IS had included both public funds and the value of public services as part of an FBO budget. Eighty-six percent came from individual contributions, and 14 percent from program revenue such as fees for services and tuition. Frumkin also noted that IS, as a trade organization for nonprofits, should not be considered an independent research entity.

23. John McCarthy and Jim Castelli, *Religion-Sponsored Social Service Providers: The Not-So-Independent Sector*, Aspen Institute (1997), pp. 4, 17. The Aspen Institute estimates that congregations and other religious organizations spend between 15 and 20 billion of privately contributed funds per year on social services. The American Fund Raising Counsel states that 63.3 billion total was given to "religious congregations and related institutions" in 1995 (17). McCarthy and Castelli believe this does not include the 1.7 billion given to six major national networks.

24. IS says that the average is 6.4 programs; Robert Wineberg found an average of 5 in Greensboro, North Carolina, and Ram Cnaan found an average of 4 in Chicago (McCarthy and Castelli, *Religion-Sponsored Social Service Providers*, p. 12). Mark Chaves's 1998 National Congregations Study corrects some difficulties with the IS data; however, this study was released after the preparation of this essay. For some preliminary information on the NCS, see Chaves's "Religious Congregations and Welfare Reform: Who Will Take Advantage of 'Charitable Choice'?" in American Sociological Review 64 (6) (December 1999): 836–46.

25. McCarthy and Castelli, *Religioin-Sponsored Social Service Providers*, pp. 25, 23. Bread for the World estimate is 75 percent, IS estimate is 50 percent.

26. These data are taken from the McCarthy and Castelli reanalysis of Independent Sector report *From Belief to Commitment* (*Religion-Sponsored Social Service Providers*, pp.

12, 24). Mark Chaves has been critical of these data, in part since IS used the yellow pages to locate its sample, and in part because it asked close-ended questions with respect to the type of services provided (See "Religious Congregations and Welfare Reform," 836–46).

27. The Aspen Institute says congregations provide 12.6 billion, the six largest national networks provide 1.7 billion, and the total amount spent by FBOs is between 15 and 20 billion.

28. McCarthy and Castelli, *Religion-Sponsored Social Service Providers*, p. 6. Many other scholars have made similar observations.

29. Blank, *It Takes a Nation*, p. 308.

30. McCarthy and Castelli, *Religion-Sponsored Social Service Providers*, p. 53.

31. *Religion and American Public Life* (New York: Paulist Press, 1986), p. 46.

32. Ibid.

33. "Towards a Civil Society: Hopes for Polish Democracy," interview of Adam Michnik, *Times Literary Supplement* (February 19–25, 1988): 887.

34. Michael Sandel, *Democracy's Discontent: America in Search of a Public Policy* (Cambridge, MA: Belknap Press, 1996), pp. 336–7. Mary Jo Bane has reflected on this phenomenon in much greater detail in her contribution to this volume "Religious Communities and the Post-Welfare Reform Safety Net."

35. The Nonprofit Sector Research Fund of The Aspen Institute has developed a similar three-part scheme in its working paper entitled "Religion-Sponsored Social Service Providers: The Not-So-Independent Sector." The authors, John McCarthy and Jim Castelli use the categories congregations, national networks, and freestanding religious organizations. I prefer to use Wuthnow's category "special purpose groups" because these organizations are often not "freestanding." Bread for the World, for example, is an offshoot of Lutheran Social Services and still receives substantial funding from the Evangelical Lutheran Church in America.

36. John J. DiIulio, Jr., Statement Before the United States Senate Subcommittee on Youth Violence, February 28, 1996.

37. An exception to this trend can be seen in the decision of the Salvation Army to accept a $9.5 million grant from the State of Michigan to assist the homeless. For an analysis of the mixed results of this program see, Amy Sherman, "Cross Purposes," *Policy Review* (No. 74, fall, 1995): 58–63.

38. See, for example, Bryan Hehir's essay in this volume "Religious Ideas and Institutions in Social Policy: The Role of the Subsidiary Principle."

39. Catholic Charities of Baltimore, for example, refused the invitation of the State of Maryland to take over the management of the state's welfare program.

40. Robert Wuthnow, *The Crisis in the Churches: Spiritual Malaise, Fiscal Woe* (New York: Oxford University Press, 1997), pp. 14–17.

41. Robert Wineberg, "Welfare Reform: What the Religious Community Brings to the Partnership," *The Journal of Volunteer Administration* (Winter 1998): 21–24. Those of us who are veteran participants in congregations may remain skeptical of some of Wineberg's optimistic claims, particularly regarding the availability of volunteer time and churches' willingness to experiment.

42. Nancy Ammerman, "Organized Religion in a Voluntaristic Society," *Sociology of Religion*, 58:3 (1997): 203–215.

43. R. Stephen Warner, "The Place of the Congregation in the Contemporary Religious Configuration," in James P. Wind, and James W. Lewis, eds., *American Congregations, Volume 2: New Perspectives in the Study of Congregations* (Chicago: University of Chicago Press, 1994), pp. 54–99.

44. John J. DiIulio, Jr., "The Lord's Work: The Church and the 'Civil Society Sector,'" *The Brookings Review* 15:4 (Fall 1997): 29.

45. Marvin Olasky, "Beyond the Stingy Welfare State," *Policy Review* 54 (Fall 1990): 14.

46. John J. DiIulio, Jr., Statement Before the United States Senate Subcommittee on Youth Violence, February 28, 1996.

47. Ronald Thiemann is the author of the remaining section of this essay.

48. This phrase is used by the philosopher of religion William Christian to encompass the religious intentions of both theistic and non-theistic religious communities. See, William A. Christian, *Meaning and Truth in Religion* (Princeton: Princeton University Press, 1964).

49. Deuteronomy 10: 17–19.

50. Matthew 25: 31–46.

51. Matthew 14:13–21, Mark 6:30–44, Luke 9:10–17, John 6:1–13.

52. Matthew 26:17–29, Mark 14:12–16, Luke 22:7–13.

53. Thus it is astounding when the authors of the Aspen Institute study "Religion-Sponsored Social Service Providers" affirm that it is "the corporate culture created within Catholic schools, and not religious devotion, which make them effective," (p. 54), as if for Catholics the two could be divided!

54. Matthew 25: 35–37, 40. *The New Revised Standard Version.*

55. Wuthnow, *The Crisis in the Churches*, p. 4.

56. Ibid., p. 226.

57. *A Guide to Charitable Choice: The Rules of Section 104 of the 1996 Federal Welfare Law Governing State Cooperation with Faith-based Social-Service Providers* (Washington, D.C.: The Center for Public Justice, 1997), p. 6.

58. See Martha Minow's contribution to this volume "Welfare and Schooling After the Fall of the Welfare State: Who is Home in the Public Square?" See, also, Derek H. Davis, "The Church-State Implications of the New Welfare Reform Law, *Journal of Church and State* 38:3 (Summer, 1996): 719–731.

59. The *bas-relief* sculptures at the new FDR Memorial in Washington, D.C. depict Depression-era men standing with downcast eyes in a food line. Despite their difficult, even humiliating situation, they are depicted as the grandfathers, fathers, uncles, and brothers, of the viewers, i.e., they are "one of us." No attempt is made to stigmatize the poor or to make them the victims of spiritual or moral poverty. They are people who have "come on bad times" and who therefore elicit our sympathy. Contrast those images with those of the "welfare queen" so prominent in the 1980's or those in the need of spiritual or moral conversion, the image of the late '90s. Race, of course, is an important factor in this shift of imagery, but the FDR Memorial sculptures remind us that there is another, more compassionate way, to depict the poor.

60. Luke 6: 20–21. The Gospel of Matthew uses the phrase "poor in spirit," but even this more spiritualized phrase in no way makes the poor morally culpable for their own plight.

61. Roman Catholic hospitals, however, are finding increasing challenges to their ability to provide health care that is consistent with Catholic moral teaching.

62. *A Guide to Charitable Choice*, p. 4.

63. Smith and Lipsky, *Non-Profits for Hire*, pp. 206–7.

64. *Religion and Public Life: A Dilemma for Democracy* (Georgetown: A Twentieth Century Fund Book, Georgetown University Press, 1996).

PART TWO

Public Religion and Social Provision

CHAPTER 3

Justice and Charity in Social Welfare

Francis Schüssler Fiorenza

Throughout the history of Christianity, there are examples where the Christian churches express their concern about the poor and needy not simply by an appeal to voluntary charity but also by critique of imperial, municipal, and national state policy.

WHO CARES AND WHO PROVIDES are central questions concerning the nature and scope of social welfare. In seeking an answer, political and religious discourse in America today often sharply contrasts personal charity and societal justice, attributing a priority to the former over the latter. Advocates of charity praise its voluntary, personal, and religious nature in contrast to the involuntary, impersonal, and secular nature of justice. Moreover, they often presuppose a zero-sum game in which charity and welfare compete with one another, as if what is given in welfare detracts from what is given in charity or vice versa.

It is the merit of Theda Skocpol's essay in this volume to have demonstrated that several dichotomies, which are often assumed, are historically untrue. She illustrates that the usual contrasts between voluntary activity and governmental welfare, as well as between large and the small local groups, overlooks the varied and complex interconnections among them in the history of social provision in the United States. In addition, her essay highlights the varying understandings of social security, observing that while its critics see it as welfare, its recipients and defendents understand it not as welfare but as a just reward.

The distinction between charity and justice and the role it plays in discussions about social welfare is the subject of my chapter. I want to examine the contrast between justice and charity and the priority given to charity over justice by many critics of social welfare. To this end, I first examine the views of these critics, especially insofar as they entail a cultural and social critique of welfare. Since these criticisms elevate philanthropy over welfare and charity over justice, it is necessary to examine their cultural, philosophical, and religious presuppositions.

After a survey of these criticisms, I will seek to confont these criticisms through an interpretive reading of the Christian tradition and an analysis of the diverse conceptions of justice. I will then explore the distinctive and interrelated role that both charity and justice have for social welfare in a modern society. It is my hope that such an analysis will provide some religious and ethical guidelines and will thereby respond to the questions: Who cares and who provides? Such a response calls us to make a religious as well as ethical interpretation of the nature and scope of social welfare that highlights the significant role that the churches and religious traditions should have in in this arena.

The Advocacy of Charity and Philanthropy

Although the advocacy of charity and philanthropy is laudable, and, indeed necessary, it causes concern when the distinction between charity and justice leads to a devaluation of justice or is combined with a criticism of social welfare.[1] For example, in her survey of poverty in the nineteenth century, Gertrude Himmelfarb contrasts public welfare and private charity in order to suggest that philanthropy and charity rather than welfare will resolve social problems.[2] She argues that the Victorian principle of philanthropy, with its distinction between welfare and charity, has enduring value for us today. "An eminently non-Victorian society like ours," she writes, "can profit from the Victorian experience—all the more so at a time when the welfare society has proved to be bankrupt and when the institutions of civil society are being challenged to do what the state has so patently failed to do."[3]

Philanthropy in Contrast to Welfare

The advantages of voluntary charity over welfare, Himmelfarb contends, are that it is discriminating, morally uplifting, personally ennobling, and associated with religion. First, charity discriminates among recipients. Whereas welfare cannot distinguish between the "deserving" and the "undeserving" poor, philanthropy can make that distinction. It can thereby help those who would benefit from the assistance in order to better themselves. Second, charity leads to moral improvement. In contrast to public welfare, private charities in the nineteenth century could stipulate moral conditions for the reception of welfare: recipients had to avoid excessive drinking, keep a clean household, and even, in the case of religious charities, participate in religious services. In short, private charities could lay down conditions that would improve the morality of the recipients in a way that bureaucratic governmental regulations could not. The recipients had to become personally and morally self-sufficient individuals. Third, voluntarism shapes the character of the giver: it makes the giver a virtuous person. Welfare is limited to satisfying the needs of the poor, but the voluntariness of charity leads to a growth in virtue among those giving to the poor.

For this reason, voluntarism and charity can be treasured not so much as an economic means that cuts the costs of welfare, but as an activity that strengthens the moral character of the giver. (Jane Addams, the founder of Hull House, explained that her primary reason for establishing this charitable institution was to give meaning to her own life and only secondarily to help the poor.[4]) Fourth, voluntarism and religion are associated. Acts of voluntary charity were often carried out by religious organizations and were performed out of religious motives. In contrast, public social welfare is grounded in secular legislation. For all these reasons, Himmelfarb urges her contemporaries today to consider philanthropy as superior to public welfare, and charity higher than social welfare.

The Cultural and Social Critique of the Welfare Society

I would suggest that we view such a combination of the praise of philanthropy with the criticism of social welfare in relation to the cultural and economic critique of the welfare society that arose in the aftermath of the economic recession of the mid 1970s. This critique coincided with the renaissance of neo-*laissez-faire* and monetarist economic doctrines in the United States under Ronald Reagan and in England under Margaret Thatcher. This critique argued that the welfare state causes the very illness that it seeks to cure. Instead of curing the ills of the market society, it exacerbates them, because it prevents the forces of the market place from functioning positively, progressively, and with success.[5] This malaise results from disincentives integral to the welfare state: the disincentive to investment and the disincentive to work.

A welfare society needs financial resources to support its social welfare and social legislation to effect social change. To obtain such resources, a welfare society increases the burden of taxation, which then results in a popular disincentive to invest. Likewise, the burden of higher taxes upon businesses has the alleged effect of hindering the operation of small businesses and dampening the entrepreneurial spirit for the starting of new businesses. In addition, there is a disincentive to work that comes from receiving the welfare benefits of unemployment insurance and aid to families with dependent children. These welfare benefits in themselves, and especially when they are higher than wages, discourage persons from entering the workforce. Moreover, it is alleged that social legislation such as minimum wage laws have the unintended effect of diminishing productivity, as workers do not work as hard as they otherwise would, thus undermining the virtues of thrift and disciplined work.

In creating these two disincentives, the critics argue, welfare leads to a result that is the opposite of what is intended.[6] These disincentives are counterproductive and lead to a decline in the growth of the economy. They lead to increased expectations from the economic system at the same time that they lead to a decrease in the growth of the economic system. The economic system faces inflation, overload, and a lack of growth. It is even argued that the social legislation of the Great Society has led to increased poverty. Distinguishing between people in poverty (those below a certain standard) and latent poverty (those who would be below poverty except for welfare), Charles Murray has argued that the social welfare programs of the Great Society have led to an increase of the latter.[7] In short, the economic critique alleges that welfare stunts economic growth and in the long-run hurts welfare itself—a claim that is contested.[8]

In addition to the economic critique, there is a cultural critique of welfare, stemming from the right and left with their from different perspectives. The conservative critique of welfare society, rooted in a tradition of classic economics, argues that the civil liberties of democratic society and the economic individualism of the market economy go hand in hand. Individual autonomy and the market economy foster each other. From this perspective, it criticizes welfare for creating a culture of dependency that undermines individual autonomy and self-sufficiency. In contrast, the view from the left sees the cultural critique of welfare as resulting from the exhaustion of utopian energies and the shift of the middle class in their electoral preferences. In a specific way, the critique of welfare has been advanced by feminists who have argued that a welfare society often replicates the patriarchal division of the private and public sphere by the way it determines which needs are private and which are the objects of public welfare. Each of these criticisms needs further elaboration.

Culture of Dependency. The social welfare model of the state is criticized because it takes away from individual autonomy, and individual choice, and, thereby creates a culture of dependency. Rather than empowering the poor and needy, this argument goes, such a model disenfranchises them.[9] Welfare is not simply the result of a paucity of resources but is also a cultural and social problem. Critics of the social welfare model of the state argue that it creates the problem it seeks to solve or, if it is does not create the problem, it at least aggravates it. This critique raises an important challenge. By arguing that there are cultural and social as well as economic causes of poverty, it challenges one to ask: how welfare can be shaped so that it deals with all these conditions and causes of poverty and need. In the recent debates around welfare reform, a tension existed between the rhetoric of the critique and the reality of the legislation. The cuts in welfare were much greater than the resources made available for work programs and for child raising and household assistance so that women with dependent children would be able to work. If the rhetoric of empowerment were de facto at the basis of the reform, then one might expect welfare legislation to be shaped positively and constructively to make possible that empowerment.

Exhaustion of Utopian Energies. In his analysis of the welfare society, Jürgen Habermas points to the interconnection between the crisis of the welfare society and the exhaustion of utopian energies.[10] At the core of the welfare state is a utopian vision of an emancipated life that involves the transformation, or humanization, of alienated labor into self-directed activity along with guarantees that mitigate and compensate for the risks in wage labor (such as accidents, illness, loss of employment, and old age). The goal of full employment and the compensations for the risks of labor are parallel functions. Governmental intervention has to stimulate economic growth to mitigate economic crises, to support the compensations for the risks, and to safeguard jobs at home as well as economic competitiveness abroad.

The welfare society has had to deal with the perception that the costs of welfare impede the ability to invest and hence lead to increasing unemployment and economic stagnation. It also has had to address the problem that the national state cannot guarantee Keynesian economic policies in the face of the imperatives of a world market. In addition, the welfare society loses its social basis as upwardly mobile workers become a part of the middle class. They then tend to align themselves against the underprivileged and poor groups. For example, the electoral base of the Democratic party in the United States, the Labor party in England, and the German Social-Democratic party has become increasingly aligned more with the middle class than with the underprivileged in society. Furthermore, the administration of welfare through legal regulation and bureaucratic red tape seems to manifest a tension between the goals and methods of the welfare society. Although its goal is a vision of an egalitarian way of life enabling self-realization, the media of money and power appear unable to effect this goal.

Feminist Critique of Welfare. Feminists have criticized the practices of social welfare not in order to abandon it but to reshape it. One strain of feminist theory has taken up Jürgen Habermas's analysis of modernity, modifying his thesis about the colonization of the life-world through money and power. Feminists have used a nuanced version of this thesis of colonization to bring a feminist analysis to the interpretation of needs within the modern welfare society.[11] For example, Nancy Frazer underscores the dependencies created by welfare through her analysis of AFDC (Aid to Families with Dependent Children). She contrasts the differences in the interpretation of needs between the recipient of welfare and the administration of welfare. Because the AFDC shares assumptions about women's work with those of the wider society, it counterproductively boxes clients into their dependent positions. Alternative means of needs interpretation and communication must emerge from the experience, narratives, and life stories of the disenfranchised in order to challenge the assumption of a universal set of needs embedded in the bureaucratic administration of welfare.

The Religious Advocacy of Charity

There is also a religious advocacy of charity that serves to down play issues of social justice and welfare. Many reasons are proffered for this valuation of charity as distinctively Christian or religious and as superior to justice. One argues that justice deals with an abstract concept, whereas love deals with concrete individual persons.[12] Or, one contends that charity exhibits a personal, altruistic, and self-sacrificial love, exemplified in the Gospels by Jesus' death on the cross, whereas justice entails an abstract calculation of rights, a specification of obligations, and an impersonal law. The supererogation of charity stands over the calculation of justice. Those Christian theological traditions that separate or even contrast charity and justice view charity as the realm of grace and justice as the realm of law. Such affirmations of charity as a distinctive Christian virtue in contrast to law and justice are often unfortunately expressed in language that is also anti-Jewish, especially when law and justice is attributed to Judaism, whereas charity and grace are ascribed to Christianity. Moreover, the Christian practice of love is contrasted to the distortions of human nature and human law that are manifest in justice. Even charity itself becomes differentiated into a Hellenistic eros and a biblical agape, as in Anders Nygren's classic, *Eros and Agape*.[13] The Christian form of love is viewed as a specific form of generous love that contrasts both with an interested erotic love and with an interested justice. Underlying many of such modern theological contrasts is the distinction between a natural metaphysic or ethics and a Christian ethics or theology.[14] An ethic based upon metaphysics, natural law, or rational conceptions of justice is often contrasted with a specifically Christian ethic of love and sacrifice. The latter is viewed as a capacity for love "irrespective of circumstance."[15] For example, John Winthrop's sermon, "A Model of Christian Charity" is often quoted to praise a philanthropy based on love rather than a social welfare based on justice. [16] Such Christian love is described as helping people in a direct, personal, and concrete manner. Christian communities took care of the needy, caring for them primarily in their own homes and, only if that was not possible, in the household of others. This made charity personal and caring, familiar and communal. In contrast, our current age of social welfare is described as exercising charity through agencies, by paid professionals, who specialize in casework, and have hard and fast rules about the applicability of welfare standards to specific cases.

Christian Tradition in Relation to Charity and Justice

These social, cultural, and religious criticisms are intertwined insofar as the religious praise of charity is combined with cultural and economic criticisms of welfare to challenge the rationale of welfare. They raise issues and questions that require serious consideration in attempting to understand the role of charity and justice in social welfare and in answering the questions: who cares and who provides? To the extent that these cultural and religious criticisms charge that social welfare is self-defeating because it neglects religious and cultural dimensions of social welfare, they need to be examined.

The Ambiguities and Deceptions of Charity

The above contrast has historical and conceptual weaknesses. More importantly, such a praise of charity as the distinctive religious solution to social issues in contrast to social welfare and justice can lead to a self-deception in regard to charity, as Reinhold Niebuhr has so poignantly warned us: "American Christianity tends to be irrelevant to the problems of justice because it persists in presenting the law of love as a simple solution for every communal problem."[17] Niebuhr notes that Christianity has prided itself for advocating an ethic that goes beyond the mere requirements of law. Nevertheless, he points out that there is a sense in which love as philanthropy can indeed be not higher but rather lower than justice:

> Christian businessmen are more frequently characterized by a spirit of philanthropy than by a spirit of justice in assessing the claims and counterclaims of economic groups. Love in the form of philanthropy is in fact on a lower level than a high form of justice. For philanthropy is given to those who make no claim against us, who do not challenge our goodness or disinterestedness. An act of philanthropy may thus be an expression of both power and moral complacency. An act of justice on the other hand requires the humble recognition that the claim that another makes against us may be legitimate.[18]

Niebuhr notes that "the effort to make voluntary charity solve the problems of a major social crisis. . . results only in monumental hypocrisies and tempts selfish people to regard themselves as unselfish."[19] Niebuhr's political and moral realism shared with liberalism the idea that justice applies to all and goes beyond the limits of nations, communities, and interest groups.[20] Nevertheless, his interpretation of human nature saw that the distortions of self-interest and the corruptions of power made it much more difficult for the "children of the light" to accomplish their goals. Moreover, it made them sentimental and idealistic in their tendency to believe that a generous charity could easily overcome these distortions and corruptions rooted in the self-interest of humans.[21] With his critique of the sentimentality and idealism inherent in the emphasis on charity to the neglect of justice, Niebuhr made a significant contribution to American religious and political thought. His realism, however, engendering skepticism and pessimism, may have undercut social reform and led to conservatism in the face of social change, as subsequent critics have argued.[22]

The Practice of Charity and Justice in the Christian Tradition

Although voluntary individual charity is often advanced as the hallmark of the Christian tradition, the history of Christianity tells a much more complex story. A communal as well as a social justice orientation pervades the history of Christianity as a religious institution concerned with social issues.[23] It is not simply the case that only as a result of the emergence of capitalism or only after modern industrialization has Christianity been concerned with the civic and political dimensions of social welfare. Instead such a concern has persisted throughout Christian history, as salient examples show. One finds a double tendency even in early Christian communities of the New Testament period. On the one hand, Christians made social justice an integral part of the community's life and worship, as shown by the collection of goods for the poor during the offertory of the Eucharistic celebration. That these goods were collected during worship as offerings and distributed to the poor shows that concern for the poor was an act of the community as a community and actualized in its worship of God. Furthermore, the Acts of the Apostles presents an idealized picture of the social sharing of goods and property in Jerusalem. Here Luke presents his vision of an ideal Christianity in the first century. Such institutional caring for the poor finds its continuation in the medieval and modern periods. The use of monasteries as hospitals and hospices in the Middle Ages and the development of modern institutions of charity and health care indicate the institutional development of charity in concern for the poor and ill.

On the other hand, alongside this institutional and communal caring for the poor, an equally central practice in Christianity runs through its history of social and political criticism in the name of justice. There is a long history of criticizing civic and governmental institutions for unjust policies and for failing to care for the poor. Examples from four different historical episodes may help to illustrate the diversity and different contexts of this practice.

The first is the church's criticism of the tax legislation of the Roman Empire. The economic crisis of the third century and changed tax policies of the fourth century led to the impoverishment of farmers in the East. Synods and bishops witnessed the suffering that these tax policies brought to farmers, and they saw it as part of their task to criticize imperial policies, as St. Basil did in a paradigmatic way. Here the cause of the problem was neither local nor national but imperial. Imperial policies led to unjust social consequences and to social needs that church collections alone could not resolve. Hence, in addition to fostering innovative social institutions, the church engaged in a social justice critique of the Roman Emperor's tax legislation.[24]

Second, in the medieval church, various councils and synods were confronted with the growth of cities and their increasingly need to deal with the poor. Cities were facing social welfare problems and that the situation was quite different from the countryside with its landed monasteries. These Councils and Synods were very much concerned about how adequately the cities met the emerging social needs. Various Council decrees made it a prime duty of the bishop to watch over and to criticize cities if they failed in their civic obligation to the poor.[25]

Third, during the Renaissance era, the issue of outlawing begging became a primary concern. Was it against Christian charity to outlaw begging since it would deprive people of the opportunity to exercise the virtue of charity by giving money to people? The practice of outlawing begging began in Holland but was soon picked up by Charles V and became an imperial problem. The ostensible purpose of the laws was to pass social legislation so that beggars could be educated or receive training and not be dependent upon voluntaristic charity. (It is interesting to read the literature on this issue in the nineteenth century. The debate in this literature raged as to who was responsible for this social legislation. Lutherans claimed this legislation was a great contribution of the Reformation, whereas Catholics, pointing to legislation in Roman Catholic countries, claimed it was Catholic innovation. Both were probably influenced by the humanism of the Renaissance.) Yet this legal shift results from a changed attitude toward begging that is intertwined with a profound shift in the understanding of poverty and the attitude toward the poor.[26]

Fourth, there is the tradition of modern Catholic social doctrine and papal teaching dealing with the problems of industrialization and criticizing capitalism as well as socialism. This criticism of the market economy established a strain of social thought that affirms the significance of certain social rights, for example, the right to work, the right to a family wage, the right to organize in unions, and the right to a certain social security.[27]

These four historical examples speak against the contemporary tendency to equate or to reduce the role of religion to individual virtue and the role of virtue to charitable individual actions. Such a view represents a narrowing of Christian religious traditions and their past practices. The Eucharistic celebrations with the attendant sharing of goods for the poor were actually acts of a community and not so much acts of individual virtues. Social and political criticism, which was applied to Roman imperial tax laws, medieval urban social legislation, national legislation regarding begging, and the emerging conditions of industrialism (both in capitalism and in socialism), indicates that justice was viewed not simply as a habit of the mind of the individual (as George F. Will puts it), but as a concern with structures of society in relation to imperial, urban, national, and industrial economic systems.[28]

With this view of religious social practice within the history of Christianity, it would be a mistake to think that the church's relation to justice has been primarily one of voluntary acts of individual Christians or particular Christian communities. Likewise, it would be erroneous to think that somehow only in the modern period or in the post New Deal period was the charitable voluntarism of the churches replaced by governmental social policies that disparaged such voluntarism. Instead, the tradition of Christianity is a tradition that has combined communitarian elements of charitable voluntarism with the political demands of social justice made to the Roman empire, medieval cities, modern nation states, and economic systems.

An Interpretive Reading of the Christian Tradition

My interpretive reading of the Christian tradition sought to show that throughout the history of Christianity, there are examples where the Christian churches express their concern about the poor and needy not simply by an appeal to voluntary charity but also by critique of imperial, municipal, and national state policy. In offering this reading, there are two arguments that I have not made. I have not made a biblical argument from the preaching of Jesus or the direct discipleship and practical fellowship of Jesus in his option for the poor, as if these could provide certain and secure foundations for my position. Such a choice is deliberate. There are different strains among the earliest traditions of the New Testament in regard to eschatology. Which traditions go back to the earthly Jesus is highly debated within New Testament studies.

In the past, Jesus' ethic has been viewed as an "interim ethic" resulting from an imminent expectation of the end of the world. Today, it is more common to point to the interconnection between Jesus' proclamation of the *basileia* and creation—a proclamation that does not contain a specific social ethic but from which a social ethic could be developed. In addition, one finds in New Testament writings diverse approaches to ethics. The attitudes of Luke and Paul to the Roman empire appear quite different from that of the author of the Book of Revelation. The treatment of family life is very different in the early Jesus movement than in the Pastoral Epistles. These reasons suggest that one cannot simply quote or single verse or book or make an appeal to the "historical Jesus." Instead I have pointed to examples from the Christian tradition as interpretations of Christian faith in different social, political, and historical situations. I offer these examples as an interpretative reading of the Christian tradition.

Second, the "preferential option for the poor" is indeed an important theme that Latin American liberation theology has consistently developed.[29] Moreover, this formula has been adapted in papal encyclicals into the formula of "the preferential option or love for the poor." [30] These two formulas take up and reformulate in a new fashion a long standing tradition that goes back to the Hebrew Prophets in their concern for the widow, orphan, and stranger. However, what constitutes the prudent decision, practical consequence, and concrete policy that should flow from the option for the poor? What consequences result for a just social welfare policy from the option for the widow, orphan, and stranger? Part and parcel of the critique of social welfare is not only the advocacy of charity over welfare, but also the argument that welfare harms more than it helps. The critique, therefore, consists in a practical as well as an ethical argument. In my opinion, it is not sufficient for a religious tradition simply to link or to apply its beliefs to political policy in a direct fashion. In the welfare debate, it is necessary to take into account that the relation between experience and the tradition is not simply transparently obvious, but demands prudence and interpretation.[31] Instead, it necessary to take into account background theories as well as retroductive warrants from experience in arguing for the positions it takes. As I have argued elsewhere, theological method has to take into account several elements: reconstructive interpretations of the tradition, background theories, retroductive warrants, and communities of discourses.[32]

Interpretation of Society and the Welfare State

The issues revolving around welfare within a welfare society presuppose specific interpretations of the structure of modern society and entail a specific view about the nature of justice. The relation between a religious tradition and a society needs to be linked through a consideration of these two factors.

Functional Understanding of Society and Social Welfare

Traditional conceptions often view welfare in terms of the relation between state and society. A functional interpretation of welfare within modern society that views welfare in terms of its societal function provides a helpful background theory for understanding the issues.[33] The traditional view of welfare envisions the government as the provider. The government performs social welfare by providing extensive social benefits to particular classes. When the state needs to obtain the financial resources for the social benefits, but cannot do so, then a crisis in social welfare emerges. Such a diagnosis of the welfare state points to symptoms rather than to the underlying structural issues.[34] A contrasting view would interpret welfare as a function of society itself rather than as a function of the state toward society. Such a interpretation notes that modern society has become functionally differentiated in order to deal better with the risks, crises, and problems that modern society confronts.[35] Such a functional analysis suggests that "the realization of the principle of inclusion in the functional domain of politics ultimately leads to the welfare state."[36] It suggests that the welfare state is not just concerned with minimal standards of well-being for everyone. Instead, it seeks to deal with the specific problems and risks that modern society creates for itself in its decisions.[37]

A functional view examines how society and the bureaucracy of modern society uses law and money as the functional media to achieve its goals. The ability of welfare society to achieve its goals is depends in part on the ability of these functional media (money and law). Its success is conditioned by the advantages and disadvantages of money and law. The success or lack of success in carrying out welfare programs rests in the adequacies or inadequacies of the media of money and law to accomplish the desired goals. In relating the crises of social welfare to adequacy of these societal media of money and law, I am deliberately reshifting the problem away from that of the federal versus state governments. It is not simply that New York and California are larger than many nations. The emphasis on the states does not deal with the economic problems. Individual states faces the same competitive problems in terms of labor and welfare costs within the United States as nations face in terms of a competitive global labor market. The communitarian argument for the reinvigoration of local voluntary groups and local political institutions often fails to confront the problem of increasing growth of the international market. The effects of this market economy can makes individual communities and states noncompetitive if they increase social welfare just as it does for nations. The reverse argument could be made: just as the national power during the Progressive Era was used against corporate power structures, so what is needed today are new institutions of international governance to mitigate the negative effects of international capital upon national social welfare.

My focusing on the adequacy of these media rather than on the tension between centralized governmental programs and local programs of assistance takes issue with those who see the size of the federal government as cause of the crises of governmental social welfare programs.[38] The focus on the adequacy of law and money as the means of to deal with social welfare problems re-interprets the problem of social welfare. The decisive questions now become: In what way do these functional media have distinct advantages for dealing with social and welfare problems? In what way do they have disadvantages? These questions and this analysis provide the context for a proper understanding of the relation between charity and justice in social welfare. In order to answer these questions, we have first to consider the radical diversity in contemporary conceptions of justice.

Justice and Social Welfare: Entitlement or Equality of Opportunity

Whereas the advocates of social welfare equate social welfare and social justice, the critics of social welfare criticize this equation as presupposing a faulty conception of justice. They argue that the advocates of social welfare interpret justice primarily as redistributive justice. They fail to interpret justice as an individual's right to economic resources based upon his or her achievements and ownership. Instead, they explain justice in relation to "needs" and "deserts" that transcend or even override claims based upon private ownership.[39] Thus two very contrasting viewpoints of justice are present within the debates about social welfare.

These two conceptions of justice can be distinguished by the terms "equality of opportunity" versus "entitlement." The advocacy of social welfare operates with a conception of justice that seeks to compensate for differences so as to encourage equality of opportunity. Justice should not simply take into account the liberty, freedom, and achievement of individuals, but should also consider natural and social differences. It is for this reason that the social ethicist, John Rawls, for example, argues that justice has two basic principles. Justice entails not only a principle of greatest equal liberty as if libertarianism constituted justice. Instead, it includes a second principle that points to fair equality of opportunity.[40] This second principle of justice is defined by Rawls as such: "social and economic inequalities are to be arranged so that they are both (a) to the greatest benefit of the least advantaged, consistent with the savings principle, and (b) attached to offices and positions open to all under conditions of fair equality of opportunity."[41]

The critics of social welfare operate from a different understanding of justice: an "entitlement" conception of justice.[42] Such an "entitlement" conception of justice underscores the degree to which one justly deserves or is entitled to those rewards, goods, and earnings that one has achieved through the good fortune of one's industry, achievement, and property ownership. For example, Robert Nozick, as an advocate of an entitlement conception of justice, contends that notions of justice such as Rawls's fails to take sufficiently into account historical entitlements. Indeed, they are in principle incapable of doing so.[43] In addition, such a criticism objects to the centrality of redistributive elements in such an understanding of justice.[44] An entitlement conception often emphasizes individual rights in a way that the minimizing the role of government. It interprets rights as "side constraints" rather than as goals that one should seek to maximize.[45] It focuses on the distinction between freedom and coercion rather than on the contrast between the market and the state. Therefore, it argues that voluntary activities should contribute to the solution of welfare problems and that welfare goals are better achieved outside of the government. Moreover, it attacks the redistributive effects of a conception of justice that seeks to take differences of the disadvantaged into account. Therefore, Nozick critically asks whether a family would spend all of its resources on the most disadvantaged child of the family to the detriment of the brightest. The principle based upon difference and seeking equal opportunity can in this view produce counterproductive results for society, as this micro example illustrates.[46]

Justice, Solidarity and Democracy

This contrast between two theoretical conceptions of justice shows that any comparison between charity and justice needs to consider that justice is not a univocal or unambiguous concept that can be simply compared to charity. Conceptions of justice differ in the degree of valence that they attribute to a principle of entitlement or to a principle of equality of opportunity.[47] In citing these two contrasting conceptions of justice, I do not want to claim that one can argue abstractly for the superiority of one view over the other view. Instead, I want to emphasize that the assessment of these different conceptions involves more than an abstract evaluation. The assessment of these differences takes place within a context of differing historical traditions, both cultural and religious. How charity and justice relate to one another in issues of social welfare depends not only on one's understanding of the structure of society, but upon one's understanding of the nature of justice and its relation to one view of the good? Although one could argue philosophically for the superiority of one view over the other, one would make such arguments in the horizon of one's views about the good and about human life and in the framework of one's religious beliefs about the meaning of humanity and society.

In this regard, Martha Minnow's observation is, in my opinion, extremely relevant and to the point, when she argues that Rawls's view

> depends not on human nature abstracted from context but instead on an idea about human beings that was forged and is maintained by particular historical and cultural attitudes—an idea emphasizing the unique worth of each person, an idea often associated with humanism or with Immanuel Kant or with the Judaeo-Christian traditions. This idea contrasts sharply with the assumptions of utilitarianism, to name just one other view. Rawls's individual is specifically *not* a utilitarian—who would care about the worse-off person only to the extent that this person's well-being contributes to the well-being of all others.[48]

In concurring with this argument, I want to make an additional point. In view of these different conceptions of justice, what is needed is a communicative and discourse conception of justice in which one's principles of justice, as well as one's conceptions of what constitutes the good, well-being, and one's interests, enter into the conversation. In my opinion, Jürgen Habermas's approach takes us a step further than either Rawls or Nozick through a communicative understanding of justice. Habermas argues that in a communicative theory a close connection exists between justice and the concern for the welfare of other persons. The identity of a group is reproduced through the mutual recognition of other persons. Consequently, he argues: "Thus, the perspective complementing that of equal treatment of individuals is not benevolence but solidarity. This principle is rooted in the realization that each person must take responsibility for the other because as consociates all must have an interest in the integrity of their shared life context in the same way."[49]

In this view, justice and solidarity (not to be identified with benevolence) are two sides of the same coin, two aspects that supplement each other. Such a conception of justice seeks to serve a dual purpose. It protects the inviolability of socialized individuals by demanding equal treatment and respect for the dignity of each individual and it supports intersubjective mutual recognition by requiring solidarity within the community.[50] "*Justice* concerns the equal treatment of unique and self-determining individuals, while 'solidarity' concerns the welfare of consociates who are intimately linked in an intersubjectively shared form of life—and thus also to the maintenance of the integrity of this life."[51] One seeks to protect a person's equal freedom, rights, and dignity at the same time that one seeks to protect the welfare of other persons. In order for solidarity to function, its normative content must be universalized, lest normative obligations be limited to the family, tribe, ethnic group, nation, etc. There is not only an interrelation, but also a tension between justice and solidarity.

Such a conception emphasizes and develops further the interrelation between justice and solidarity insofar as it points out that social welfare and social welfare rights are significant for democracy. The effective use of political and civil rights depends upon social welfare rights. Civil and political rights do not exist in a vacuum. Instead, they depend upon social and material conditions, among which one condition is that citizens have their social and material needs met in order to be able to function as citizens and members within a political community.[52]

Social Welfare Between Charity and Justice

The context, therefore, for discussing charity and justice in relation to social welfare is constituted by the ambiguities of both societal structure and conceptions of justice. From a functional understanding of modern society, the organization of social welfare takes place through the media of money and legislation and it works not merely by compensating for the disadvantaged but also by furthering the functioning of the whole social system. Welfare has a function to stabilize society as a system. Its ambiguity, however, lies in the use of money and law to exercise this function. As binary models, money and law have the advantage of allowing the extensive scope of welfare. At the same time, however, they are limited to whatever areas and dimensions of life they can reach. Moreover, they can be overloaded (increased need for money; overregulation of law). The ambiguities of justice do lie just in the tension between entitlement and equality. They also lie in the relationship of justice to social solidarity and the disadvantages as well as advantages of money and law to deal with social problems and issues.

Charity Provides a Focal and Interpretive Vision for Justice

The relation between charity and justice is such that charity can be described as providing a focal intensity an interpretative vision of justice. The social ethicist, Nicholas Monzel, has proposed that charity enables the possibility of the vision of justice.[53] He bases this proposal on a phenomenological description of the relation between knowledge and love and between knowledge and affectivity. To realize what is just or unjust does not involve only an intellectual vision. It also entails volitional and affective elements. Pointing to the Hebrew word in the scriptures expressing the unity of knowledge and love, Monzel points out that love produces insight. Love can enable the economically powerful to see the conditions of the disadvantaged, to give up their advantage, and to indict an unjust economic order. Love enables one to break out of the limited vision of one's own dominant class and economic status and to identify with the other in poverty and need.[54] As has been noted: "Changes to a greater justice take place not only through a more exact intellectual 'knowledge' of conditions of injustice, but also through a changed 'consciousness' in which insight, affective valuations, and the good form an inseparable unity."[55]

This phenomenological insight needs to be interpreted and applied with care. It is not simply, as Reinhold Niebuhr suggests, that love can provide a more generous and inclusive vision than the limited calculated vision of a justice. It is not only that power tends to distort one's rational vision or one's morality to "weigh the standards of justice on the side of the one who defines the standard."[56] It is also that power distorts how and what we love. In my view, love as a life relation and love as a vision needs to be distinguished. One must attend also to the corruption of love. Power distorts both our relations of love and our relations of justice. Justice can, in practice, be weighed in favor of the person in power, just as love in practice, can involve nepotism, favoritism, and discrimination in situations of power. A vision of love and a vision of justice toward others can and should be equally inclusive if others are to be acknowledged and recognized in their dignity, both in mutual relations and in society. Visions of justice can correct our visions of love as much as as one suggests that love can correct justice.

Hermeneutical insights bear on our discussion. Human understanding does not take place in a vacuum, but takes place in the condition of a pre-understanding influenced by our life-relations and by the narratives, classics, and traditions of a culture. The importance of the narrative and religious traditions of a culture does not negate the attempts to develop discursively and democratically the basic principles of justice, as shown by John Rawness's theory of justice or Jürgen Habermas's discourse ethic. Nevertheless, thinking and acting take place in concrete traditions and within the horizon of the paradigmatic examples and ideals of those traditions.

Therefore, religious traditions, with their intertwinement between beliefs and practices, provide paradigms and ideals incorporating and exemplifying justice and charity. Insofar as religious communities discuss and teach their historical beliefs, morals, and ethical concerns, they engage in "thickening" of conceptions of the good within their particular communities and, thereby, indirectly for society at large.[57] In this way religious communities contribute to public political discourse insofar as a pluralist society necessarily rests not only upon a more general, common, "thin" conception of the good, but also upon individual communities and societies with their "fuller" or "thicker" versions of the good. An interaction takes place between religious communities as communities of discourse explicating the significance of their religious and ethical traditions and the more universalizable principles and conceptions of justice.[58]

Basic Human Dignity and the Religious Imagination

In addition to these religious traditions, anthropological, structural, and political considerations are at the basis of social welfare. Extreme physical and psychic needs affect human dignity so centrally that they cannot be left to the arbitrariness of private philanthropy.[59] If people cannot help themselves, they have a claim to the compassion and mercy of others. The social and economic order should correspond to basic principles of justice that seek to guarantee a dignified human life.[60] A structural analysis of society points out that the social welfare society works through the means of law and money. Law and money have the advantage that they can specify the conditions of availability, but are less effective when social problems presuppose and involve the self-cooperation of people in their own change, involving rehabilitation and socialization, what some call "people processing" issues.[61]

Religious beliefs and religious traditions play and should play an important role as a resource for cultural values. What is basic human dignity? The answer cannot be reduced to simple factual data. It does not simply result from empirical investigation or scientific analysis. Instead the answer to this fundamental question is in part provided in and supported through the cultural imagination, in which traditions play significant roles. Humans are not simply a complex set of neurological fibers that interact with their environment in a more evolved manner than other organisms. The Jewish and Christian traditions talk about the human person as created by God in God's own image. Religious traditions view human persons as children of God, such that, as John Calvin argued, an injury against another human person is an injury against God because a human person is an image of God. [62] It is no wonder that language about human rights arose out of the merger of Stoic, Christian, and Jewish traditions in the modern West.

How does one assess what human dignity is? One draws on examples and narratives from one's cultural traditions. Many of these narratives are drawn from religious literature in the West (and parallels can be drawn to narratives in other religious traditions elsewhere). The prophetic writings of the Hebrew Scriptures speak eloquently about the obligation to the widow, orphan, and stranger. Gospel parables spell out the conditions for salvation. They make actions on behalf of the least of the brethren and sisters actions on behalf of Christ (Matthew 25). One of the functions of the religious imagination is to cultivate cultural consciousness in ways that influence and shape it toward a greater sensitivity for the justice owed to others. Even abstract principles, underscoring human dignity, are both illustrated, understood, and applied through the paradigmatic narratives of religious traditions.

Contemporary philosophers as diverse as Martha C. Nussbaum and Richard Rorty have shown what a significant role the literary imagination has for civil and public life.[63] Nussbaum's phrase "poetic justice" highlights the function of this imagination. The literary imagination can highlight the cruelties and injustice of modern life in ways that formal rational consciousness often does not, for this imagination provides examples and stories. Moreover, it affects human emotions and motivates human action. So too does the religious imagination!

The religious imagination is a cultural resource for reflection and affectivity. Churches need to mobilize this resource for several reasons. It is not simply to advocate charity over justice, but rather to provide a horizon and tradition that illuminates the debates about the diverse meanings of justice. Moreover, the crises generated by the culture of dependency, the exhaustion of utopian energies, and the colonization of the life world are cultural crises and as such need the cultural and religious imagination as resources.[64] The religious imagination provides resources in the formation of character and personhood that counters a culture of dependency. The religious imagination combines to keep utopian vision alive. The religious imagination focus on the unconditionality of persons and thickens the moral discourse of societies.

The religious imagination has a significant role to play in shaping the welfare debate because there is a political imagination at work (perhaps "at war" might be a better term) in the debates about social welfare. A large part of the critique of welfare involves cultural criticisms and a large part of the public apathy or distrust of welfare stems from cultural stereotypes. The much cited image of the welfare queen who collects her welfare check in a Cadillac or the false belief that people on welfare stay on welfare permanently in a state of dependency, despite empirical evidence to the contrary, means the issue of welfare is not simply an issue of empirical data but of cultural imagination. This cultural imagination contains racist prejudices toward minorities as lazy or toward foreigners as not hardworking, which in turn plays an important role in the opposition of the popular cultural imagination to social welfare. These stereotypes are often latently re-inforced with the sound bites and images of political campaigns, with their "scientific" opinion polls. In addition, these stereotypes are often re-inforced by literature, claiming to have "scientific evidence," so that one is forced to ask: Is it a coincidence that a leading critic of social welfare, Charles Murray, is also the leading advocate of the racial inferiority of African-Americans?[65]

The issue of social welfare within our civic society is as much a cultural issue as it is a political or economic issue. When polls show such widespread opposition to social welfare within our culture, what does this say to churches? Does it say tailor your message and adapt your practice to the culture? Or does it pose a challenge to the churches themselves in the witness and testimony of their preaching and ministry? Churches are institutions of cultural formation. Therefore, the churches have a role to play within the culture through their weekly preaching, educational institutions, newspapers, bulletins, Sunday school classes, study groups, etc. One of their primary tasks as religious institutions is to articulate their religious and ethical traditions as they bear on human need and to bring this articulation into the cultural arena of civic society. This work involves not only a critique of the cultural racism and sexism that stereotypes the poor and needy, but also a formation into awareness of the importance of justice for all in civic society.

Churches and Voluntary Groups between Charity and Justice in a Welfare State

A functional analysis of the welfare society points to the advantages of law and money in terms of their ability to provide resources and to specify conditions for the availability of these resources. At the same time it points to the disadvantages of these media to provide motivation and self-help. The limitation of the media of law and money within welfare society indicates the role of certain institutions, communities, and groups that deal with motivation, formation, and communal life. The advantages and disadvantages of the media as well as the relation between justice and charity, therefore, help provide answers to the questions: who cares, who provides?

Law and money are important in providing basic social rights, however, where welfare involves the ability of persons to change themselves and to assist in their own formation, specific voluntary groups and churches in particular have important roles to play. In the previous sections, I have pointed to the cultural resources of churches with particular reference to Christian churches in terms of issues of justice and dignity. These cultural resources, however, are also involved in personal formation, transformation, and development.

There are crises in life that are not only material, but also personal and spiritual. If a person becomes seriously ill and if it becomes necessary for that person to be examined or healed with the most recent (and highly expensive) medical technology, then it is a question of justice as to what extent basic health needs are met, consonant with human dignity and a society's available resources. The functional media of money and law can provide such resources and their distribution can be considered just or unjust. However, a person who is critically, if not deathly, ill has fears and anxieties, experiences isolation and loneliness; these are also needs that must be met. Here is where churches and voluntary groups have important functions, for these needs are not simply met through legislation and money.

How are these obligations of justice or love related to one another in the practice and debates of social welfare? The question of what constitutes justice and what constitutes love is not an easy one to resolve. But we should also consider that we are all members of interlocking communities. Is helping a friend, a relative, or a member of our community in their time of need and illness solely an act of charity, as some might claim? I do not think that the usual definitions of charity and the distinction between justice and charity apply. One suggestion is that charity deals with supererogation and justice with obligation.[66] If we allow members of our family, our friends, or our community of associates in their hour of need to die, to be ill, or get old, alone and isolated, without companionship and friendship, have we then failed in acts of supererogation or have we failed in our obligations to treat other persons with the dignity and respect due them? Surely, we have obligations to others that in such circumstances that a failure is not simply a failure of supererogation.

Some try to define "Christian agape" in such a way as to underscore its characteristics as equal regard for the neighbor, self-sacrifice, and mutuality.[67] Such definitions are not totally coherent in themselves and in relation to justice. Can one not include equal regard and mutuality as obligations of what is justly owed to fellow humans if they are to receive the respect that they deserve from us and that we owe them? Paul Tillich is more to the point, when he writes: "The relation of justice to love in personal encounters can be adequately described through three functions of creative justice, namely, listening, giving, forgiving. In none of them does love do more than justice demands. In order to know what is just in a person-to-person encounter, love listens. It is its first task to listen. No human relation, especially no intimate one, is possible without mutual listening."[68] In underscoring this listening to the other in personal encounters, Tillich underscores the unity of justice and love. I have argued that this unity also exists in the unity of justice and love in the social solidarity of larger communities, where concern for social welfare rights is what makes possible the civil and political rights of others.

Conclusion

In analyzing the relation between charity and justice I have argued that one should not simply place the role of religion on the side of charity and the church on the side voluntary organizations of service. I have contended that an interpretive reading of the history of past religious practices and traditions has shown that Christian churches have not only engaged in voluntary services but have also been concerned that civic and political structures are just; they demanded justice from the time of the Roman empire's tax legislation, to medieval urban social legislation, to modern industrialization. Consequently, in asking what should be the role of churches in modern welfare society, I have argued for a complementary rather than contrasting, dualistic relation between charity and justice. Because modern societies use the functional media of money and law to deal with the risks, contingencies and crises that people encounter, it is necessary to ensure that this law be carried out and this money be distributed justly, and that churches should push for a conception of justice consonant with their tradition of concern for the other and the poor. The churches do proclaim charity as well as justice. Charity provides an interpretive focus on what is justice, and it reaches into areas of personal formation and motivation as well as depths of human need not covered by law and money.

The necessity of these diverse functions should provide the guidelines for the answer to the question of who provides? Churches should marshal their conceptions of the good and of human dignity as cultural resources that shape how we care for each other and how we provide the basic goods of life to which every human person as a creature of God is entitled. The religious concern with the poor and the stranger, therefore, can provide a cultural horizon that enables us to grasp the mutual respect every human deserves over against cultural stereotypes and prejudices. On the one hand, as communities of discourse about religious and moral traditions, churches have to be concerned about whether the use of money and law in a welfare society adequately secures that dignity. Does the current legislation and reform of social welfare, with its emphasis on the freedom and autonomy of work, achieve these goals by providing sufficient legal and financial resources to safeguard basic human dignity? On the other hand, those aspects of social welfare that require the development of motivation, character, and virtue both among the rich and the poor — are examples where the intersection between churches as voluntary organizations and the political organizations of society should work together. This is because churches have the ability to affect realms where law and money cannot adequately achieve such goals. Such activities are not simply activities of generosity but rather are integral to the well being of human persons, communities, and societies. In this way, the complementarity between justice and charity can be maintained in modern society. The classic motto *ubi justitia, ibi pax* (where justice exists, there peace exists) can be stated as: *ubi justitia, ibi caritas*. Where justice exists, there love exists!

Notes

1. George F. Will, *Statecraft as Soulcraft: What Government Does?* (New York: Simon and Schuster, 1983); and Peter L. Berger, and Richard John Neuhaus, *To Empower People: From State to Civil Society*. 2nd edition (Washington, D. C.: American Enterprise Press, 1996).

2. Gertrude Himmelfarb, *The Idea of Poverty: England in the Early Industrial Age* (New York: Random House, 1984).

3. Getrude Himmelfarb, "The Past and Future of Philanthropy," (http://www.ncpcr.org/report/himmel.html), p. 5.

4. Jane Addams, *Twenty Years at Hull-House* (New York: Macmillan, 1910).

5. See the analysis of this critique by Claufe Offe, *Contradictions of the Welfare State* (Cambridge: MIT Press, 1984), pp. 149–154.

6. Contesting this claim of the critics, Harold Wilensky writes "insofar as there is evidence of the effects of cash welfare benefits on the incentive to work, it shows little, if any, reduced motivation. . . ." *The Welfare State and Equality: Structural and Ideological Roots of Public Expenditures* (Berkeley: University of California Press, 1975), p. 108.

7. Charles Murray, *Losing Ground: American Social Policy* (New York: Basic Books, 1984).

8. For surveys of social welfare in the United States, see Walter I. Trattner, *From Poor Law to Welfare State: A History of Social Welfare in America.* 3rd edition (New York: Free Press, 1984); and Michael Katz, *In the Shadow of the Poorhouse: A Social History of Welfare in America* (New York: Basic Books, 1986).

9. Peter L. Berger and Richard John Neuhaus, *To Empower People: From State to Civil Society.* 2nd edition. (Washington, D.C.: American Enterprise Press, 1996).

10. Jürgen Habermas, "The New Obscurity: The Crisis of the Welfare State and the Exhaustion of Utopian Energies," in Jurgen Habermas, *The New Conservatism* (Cambridge: MIT Press, 1989), pp. 48–70.

11. See Nancy Frazer, "Women, Welfare, and the Politics of Need Interpretation," *Hypatia* 2, no. 1 (1987): 103–121. See also Jane Braaten, *Habermas's Critical Theory of Society* (Albany: SUNY, 1991), pp. 147–150; and Jürgen Habermas, *Between Facts and Norms: Contributions to a Discourse Theory of Law and Democracy* (Cambridge: MIT, 1996), pp. 420–21.

12. See Emil Brunner, *Justice and the Social Order* (New York: Harper, 1945), p. 127.

13. Anders Nygren, *Eros and Agape* (New York: Harper and Row, 1969). See also Soren Kierkegaard's division of types of Christian love in his *Works of Love* (Princeton: Princeton University Press, 1995). For a criticism of this distinction, see Catherine Osborne, *Eros Unveiled: Plato and the God of Love* (Oxford: Clarendon, 1994).

14. Albrecht Ritschl, "Theology and Metaphysics," in Albrecht Ritschl, *Three Essays* (Philadelphia: Fortress, 1972; original date 1881), pp. 151–217.

15. Gene Outka, *Agape* (New Haven: Yale University Press, 1972), p. 7. See the comments of Paul Ricoeur in "Love and Justice" in Paul Ricoeur, *Figuring the Sacred: Religion, Narrative, and Imagination* (Minneapolis: Fortress, 1995), p. 316.

16. Winthrop's praise of charity should be understood in the context of Puritan political ideas. For the full original text, see John Winthrop, "A Model of Christian Charity," in Edmund S. Morgan, ed., *Puritan Political Ideas: 1558–1784* (Indianapolis: Bobbs-Merrill Co., 1965), pp. 75–93.

17. Reinhold Niebuhr, "Love and Justice," in D. B. Robertson, ed., *Love and Justice: Selections from the Shorter Writings of Reinhold Niebuhr* (New York: World Publishing Company, 1957), p. 15.

18. Niebuhr, "Love and Justice," p. 26.

19. Quoted in Robert H. Bremner, *American Philanthropy* (Chicago: University of Chicago Press, 1960), p. 143.

20. See Robin W. Lovin, *Reinhold Niebuhr and Christian Realism* (New York: Cambridge University Press, 1995), pp. 191–232; and Paul Ramsey, "Love and Law," in Charles W. Kegley and Robert W. Bretall, eds., *Reinhold Niebuhr: His Religious, Social, and Political Thought* (New York: Macmillan, 1956), pp. 79–123.

21. Reinhold Niebuhr, *The Children of Light and the Children of Darkness* (New York: Charles Scribner's Sons, 1972).

22. Bill Kellerman, "Apologist of Power: The Long Shadow of Reinhold Niebuhr's Christian Realism," *Sojourners* 16 (March 1987): 15–20.

23. Francis Schüssler Fiorenza, "The Works of Mercy: Theological Perspectives" in Francis Eigo, ed., *The Works of Mercy* (Villanova, PA: Villanova University Press, 1991), pp. 31–71. This essay gives a more detailed survey of this history with reference to the considerable secondary literature on the history of charity and mercy in the practice of the Christian tradition.

24. For a survey of social welfare in the East, see Demetrios J. Constantelos, *Byzantine Philanthropy and Social Welfare* (New Rochelle, NY: Caratzas, 1991).

25. See Michel Mollat, *The Poor in the Middle Ages: An Essay in Social Theory* (New Haven: Yale University Press, 1986). See also Suzanne Roberts, "Contexts of Charity in the Middle Ages: Religious, Social, and Civic," in Jerome B. Schneewind, ed., *Giving: Western Ideas of Philanthropy* (Bloomington: Indiana, 1996), pp. 24–53.

26. See Fiorenza, "Works of Mercy," pp. 46–51, for the secondary literature at the turn of the century about this debate. A more recent presentation of the relation between the reformation and these initiatives, but not the debates is: Carter Lindberg, *Beyond Charity: Reformation Initiatives for the Poor* (Minneapolis: Fortress, 1993).

27. J.-Y. Calvez, and J. Perrin, *The Church and Social Justice: The Social Teachings of the Pope from Leo XIII to Pius XII* (Chicago: Henry Regnery, 1961). Joseph Gremillion, *The Gospel of Peace and Justice: Catholic Social Teaching Since Pope John* (Maryknoll: Orbis, 1976).

28. George F. Will, *Statecraft as Soulcraft: What Government Does?* (New York: Simon and Schuster, 1983).

29. See Gustavo Gutiérrez, "Option for the Poor," in Jon Sobrino and Ignacio Ellacuria, eds., *Systematic Theology: Perspectives from Liberation Theology* (Maryknoll, N.Y.: Orbis Books, 1996), pp. 22–37; and Leonardo Boff, Virgilio P. Elizondo, and Marcus Lefebure, ed., *Option for the Poor: Challenge to the Rich Countries* (Edinburgh: T. & T. Clark, 1986). For a survey, see Francis Schüssler Fiorenza, "Political Theology and Latin American Liberation Theologies, in James Livingston and Francis Schussler Fiorenza, et alia, *Modern Christian Thought*, vol 2. *The Twentieth Century* (Upper Saddle River, NJ.:Prentice Hall, 2000), pp. 273–308.

30. See John Paul II, *Sollicitudo Rei Socialis*, no. 42.

31. For an outstanding example of this emphasis on prudence in regard to issues of war, just war theory, and pacificism, see Richard M. Miller's argument in contrast to the positions of "realism" and "sectarianism" in Richard M. Miller, *Interpretations of Conflict* (Chicago: University of Chicago Press, 1991).

32. Francis Schüssler Fiorenza, "Theology: Tasks and Methods," in Francis Schüssler Fiorenza and John Galvin, eds., *Systematic Theology: Roman Catholic Perspectives* (Minneapolis: Fortress, 1991), pp. 3–80; and Francis Fiorenza, *Foundational Theology: Jesus and the Church* (New York: Crossroad, 1983), section IV deals with broad reflective equilibrium as a method within theology.

33. Niklas Luhmann, *The Differentiation of Society* (New York: Columbia University Press, 1982).

34. Niklas Luhmann, *Political Theory in the Welfare State* (Berlin: Walter de Gruyter, 1990).

35. The notion of inclusion is borrowed from Thomas H. Marshall, *Class Citizenship and Social Development* (Chicago: University of Chicago Press, 1977); and Talcott Parsons, *The Systems of Modern Societies* (Englewood Cliffs, NJ.: Prentice-Hall, 1971), pp. 11 and 92ff. (See also Kohn)

36. Luhmann, *Political Theory*, p. 35.

37. For a criticism of Luhmann's interpretation especially in relation to civic society, see Jean L. Cohen and Andrew Arato, *Civil Society and Political Theory* (Cambridge: MIT Press, 1992), pp. 299–341.

38. This view takes issue with the positions argued by Martha Derthik, *New Towns In-Town: Why a Federal Program Failed* (Washington, 1972); and Jeffrey L. Pressman and Aaron Wildavsky, *Implementation: How Great Expectations in Washington are Dashed in Oakland* (Berkeley: University of California Press, 1973).

39. See Norman Barry, *Welfare* (Minnesota: University of Minnesota Press, 1990), p. 2. Although much of the justification of welfare and the welfare society has been conceived of in terms of rights. Some have sought to justify welfare as expression of social solidarity. Welfare is the gift from the other rather than an entitlement, see Richard Morris Titmuss, *The Gift Relationship: From Human Blood to Social Policy* (London, Allen & Unwin, 1970).

40. John Rawls, *A Theory of Justice* (Cambridge: Harvard University Press, 1971).

41. Rawls, *A Theory of Justice*, p. 302.

42. Robert Nozick, *Anarchy, State, and Utopia* (New York: Basic Books, 1974).

43. He argues that "entitlements" cannot be built into Rawls's conception of the original position.

44. For an argument that Rawls is not as redistributive as Nozick claims, see Thomas W. Pogge, *Realizing Rawls* (Ithaca: Cornell University Press, 1989), p. 17–19.

45. Nozick, *Anarchy*, pp. 28–34.

46. Nozick, *Anarchy*, pp. 183–231.

47. Rawls pushes justice in an egalitarian direction, whereas Nozick develops an entitlement version. A similar contrast could be illustrated with regard Dworkin versus Hayek; see Ronald Dworkin, *Taking Rights Seriously* (Cambridge: Harvard University Press, 1977); and Ronald Dworkin, *A Matter of Principle* (Cambridge, Mass: Harvard University Press, 1985).

48. Martha Minow, *Making All the Difference: Inclusion, Exclusion, and American Law* (Ithaca: Cornell Press, 1990), p.154.

49. Jürgen Habermas, "Justice and Solidarity: On the Discussion Concerning 'Stage 6'," in Michael Kelly, *Hermeneutics and Critical Theory in Ethics and Politics* (Cambridge, MA: MIT Press), p. 47. See also Jürgen Habermas, "Morality and Ethical Life: Does Hegel's Critique of Kant Apply to Discourse Ethics?" in Jurgen Habermas, *Moral Consciousness and Communicative Action* (Cambridge: MIT Press, 1990).

50. Solidarity provides a third source of societal integration alongside of money and administrative power. See Habermas, *Between Facts and Norms*, pp. 448–449.

51. Habermas, "Justice and Solidarity," p. 47.

52. Habermas, *Between Facts and Norms*, chapters 8 and 9.

53. See Nikolaus Monzel, "Liebe als Sehbedingung der Gerechtigkeit," in Nikolaus Monzel, *Solidarität und Selbstverantwortung* (Munich: Kösel, 1959), pp. 33–71.

54. For the suggestion of the relation between Monzel and John Paul II, see Lothar Roos, "Gerechtigkeit oder Barmherzigkeit? Theorie der sozialen Gerechtigkeit als Bindsglied zwischen Katholischer Soziallehre und Caritas der Kirche," in Norbert Glatzel and Heinrich Pompey, eds., *Barmherzigkeit oder Gerechtigkeit? Zum Spannungsfeld von christlicher Sozialarbeit und christlicher Soziallehre* (Freiburg: Lambertus, 1991), pp. 38–59.

55. Lothar Roos points to a similar argument in John Paul II's Encyclical, *Dives in misericordia,* that love gives the vision to the deeper power in the human self in Roos, Gerechtigkeit oder Barmherzigkeit?" p. 46. The context of the arguments, however, differs. It argues that the power of charity counters the distortions of justice, as exemplified, in the Pope's view, by the Marxist advocacy of class struggle as a means for establishing justice.

56. Reinhold Niebuhr, *Faith and History* (New York: George Braziller, 1968), p. 190.

57. Francis Schussler Fiorenza, "Church as a Community of Interpretation" in Don S. Browning and Francis Schussler Fiorenza, eds., *Habermas, Modernity, and Public Theology* (New York: Crossroad, 1992).

58. Francis Schüssler Fiorenza, "Politische Theologie und liberale Gerechtigkeits-Konzeption," in Edward Schillebeeckx, ed., *Mystik und Politik. Johann Baptist Metz zu Ehren,* (Mainz: Matthias Grünewald, 1988), pp. 105–117.

59. Roos, "Gerechtigkeit oder Barmherzigkeit?," pp. 38–59, especially pp. 40–42. (See note 55).

60. Ibid., Lothar Roos points to article 154 of the Constitution of the Weimar Republic concerning the basic dignity.

61. Yeheskel Hasenfeld and Richard A. English, eds., *Human Service Organizations: A Book of Readings* (Ann Arbor: University of Michigan Press, 1974).

62. John Calvin, *Commentary on Genesis,* chapter 12, n. 7.

63. Martha C. Nussbaum, *Poetic Justice: The Literary Imagination and Public Life* (Boston: Beacon Press, 1995); and Richard Rorty, *Contingency, Irony, and Solidarity* (Cambridge; New York: Cambridge University Press, 1989). Neither, however, would give the same role to a discourse ethic as I do. See Martha C. Nussbaum's treatment of equity and mercy, in "Equity and Mercy," *Philosophy and Public Affairs* 22 (1993): 83–125; as well as the collection Martha C. Nussbaum and Amartya Sen, eds., *The Quality of Life* (Oxford: Clarendon, 1993).

64. For an excellent set of concrete reform suggestions that deal with the cultural as well as economic issues, see Mary Jo Bane and David T. Ellwood, *Welfare Realities: From Rhetoric to Reform* (Cambridge: Harvard University Press, 1994).

65. Richard J. Herrnstein and Charles Murray, *The Bell Curve: Intelligence and Class Structure in American Life* (New York: Free Press, 1994); and Charles Murray, *Losing Ground.*

66. Rawls, *Theory of Justice,* p. 192. "The love of mankind is more comprehensive than the sense of justice and prompts to acts of supererogation, whereas the latter does not."

67. Outka, *Agape.*

68. Paul Tillich, *Love, Power, and Justice* (New York: Oxford University Press, 1954), p. 84.

CHAPTER 4

Religious Ideas and Social Policy: Subsidiarity and Catholic Style of Ministry

J. Bryan Hehir

As a procedural principle, subsidiarity is conservative in political terms. But in the broader context of Catholic teaching, subsidiarity supports the engagement of all major social actors, including the state, in the obligatory task of meeting the basic rights of each person.

IN ADDRESSING THE THEMATIC CONCERNS OF THIS VOLUME, the role of religion in the renewal of American democracy, this chapter will focus on one religious tradition, Roman Catholicism, as a social actor in American society and polity. In other places, I have argued that religious traditions bring three resources to any society: ideas, institutions, and a community.[1] The way in which these three elements of a religious tradition are conceived, expressed, and related to secular discourse and civil polity varies substantially among the great religions of the world and even within the confines of Western Christianity. Hence it is necessary to sort out the different expressions of ideas, institutions, and community within each tradition. Religious traditions seek to interpret and provide meaning for personal and social experience; in this sense they shape an intellectual tradition. Among traditions, differentiation is evident in terms of the range and scope of the intellectual content of a belief system, in terms of the importance given to the role of ideas within the religious community, and in the emphasis placed on sharing this system of meaning with the wider society in which believers live and work. Similarly, on the institutional axis, one can compare among traditions the importance given to the establishment of social institutions as an expression of a religious vision, and the degree to which these institutions are seen as contributing to the welfare of the wider secular society. Finally, there are multiple variations concerning the way in which religious communities interpret the meaning of citizenship in society, the manner in which religious conviction is related to societal responsibility, and the expectation of whether religious and social roles can be harmonized, should be kept separate, or should be understood as fundamentally conflictual.

In assessing the potential of the Catholic Church in the United States to contribute intellectually and institutionally to social policy, this essay begins with the attention given during the 1990s to a principle of Catholic social ethics, the idea of subsidiarity. For much of the twentieth century the concept was used only in the discourse of Catholic social teaching. Its appeal to and invocation by voices in the wider U.S. policy debate seems to lie in a mix of factors, some of them rooted in particular policy debates (how to design effective delivery of services in highly complex societies), some of them rooted in philosophical convictions (resistance to the growth of the welfare state), and some of them generated by an attempt to find concepts which liberals and conservatives can use to bridge ideological differences. In public debate the appeal to subsidiarity is often made by plucking the term out of the air and using it to judge existing social policy as deficient or defective, usually because it is too statist. The basic premise of this essay is that the concept of subsidiarity is one dimension of a broader social philosophy. More specifically, while the use of the idea is not intrinsically tied to the one religious tradition, an understanding of its status, meaning, and role within the Catholic tradition is conducive to its effective application in a more pluralistic context. The design of this chapter, therefore, is meant to facilitate the use of this principle of social philosophy for those who find it persuasive. Relying on the premise that religious traditions serve society through ideas, institutions, and a community, I will first describe the role and place of subsidiarity in Catholic theory; second, illustrate how it shapes the design and function of Catholic social institutions; and third, test the potential of the principle in the wider U.S. social-policy arena.

The Principle of Subsidiarity and Its Role in Catholic Social Theory

In his book, *Woodrow Wilson and the Progressive Era 1910–1917*, Arthur S. Link comments on the difficulty of maintaining a stable definition of terms like "progressive" and "liberal" in political philosophy and public discourse. Link's lament is simply a piece of a larger problem: how any intellectual tradition shares its vision and yet maintains some control over the way its ideas are received and used by others. The success of attracting the attention of others is in tension with the desire to maintain some consistency in the use of concepts and language. It is the tension one finds surrounding the principle of subsidiarity in Catholic social theory. In brief, that principle seeks to establish how the state should help other actors in a society achieve their legitimate purposes. For most of the last 60 years, the idea was invoked almost always within the context of

Catholic debate and writing. In the past decade it has entered a broader conversation. In Europe, Jacques Delors, the driving force in the move to create the European Union (EU), invoked the idea to assure European publics that "Brussels" did not intend to take over the domestic policies of member states in the union; subsidiarity suddenly became a term of art in various referenda about support for the EU. In the United States, advocates of "privatizing" social welfare policy in the name of either lower taxes or more effective policy have invoked subsidiarity as a legitimating principle of their proposals. A concept that for long has seemed arcane in content and vague in its implications has entered the most concrete debates on social policy. One can note the increased currency of the term, yet wonder whether it will lead either to the understanding of the idea or enhancement of the policies being proposed.

To test that question, the approach of this chapter uses a criterion drawn from biblical studies. In that arena we are told to look first at "the literal sense" of a text then to move to broader uses of a term or text in light of its literal sense. The literal sense of subsidiarity is found in the social encyclical tradition of Catholicism. That tradition, while rooted in a longer and wider history of social philosophy and theology shaped principally by Augustine, Aquinas, and the Spanish Scholastics (Vitoria and Suarez), is itself the product of the last century. The social encyclicals—papal teachings about the political, social, and economic order—were conceived and articulated in tension with the dominant socio-economic positions regnant in the twentieth-century, liberal capitalism and Marxist socialism.[2] The normative vision of Catholic teaching found both of these defective but on different grounds; the teaching itself was always clearer in its critique than it was in developing a constructive alternative. But the concept of subsidiarity was a dimension of a constructive vision of how to shape the social system. The goal here is to locate the subsidiarity principle in the wider architecture of Catholic ethics, to specify its content, and to suggest ways in which it can be usefully incorporated in social policy.

The principle of subsidiarity first appears in the encyclical letter of Pius XI entitled *Quadragesimo Anno* (1931). This was the second of the "social encyclicals" following upon Leo XIII's inauguration of the tradition with *Rerum Novarum* in 1891. In the intervening years "the social question," as Leo XIII called it, had become much more threatening and critical. Faced with a worldwide depression and dangerous ideological proposals to address it, Pius XI called in more explicit terms than his predecessor for a systematic "reconstruction" of the socio-economic order.[3] While the motivation and themes of *Quadragesimo Anno* were religious and philosophical, a distinguishing note of the document was its dependence on the fruits of social science. Pius XI exhibited a much sharper awareness than his predecessor of the structural character of modern industrial society. This structural sense advanced the encyclical tradition in its ability to identify and describe the macro-social injustices of the day. Pius XI was less convincing in his attempt to fashion a "Third Way" as a clear substitute for the dominant models of the day. Many commentators saw the pope's proposal as far too similar to corporatist conceptions of society. The original statement of subsidiarity arose in the context of Pius XI's attempt at a Third Way; one need not hold to his conclusion in order to understand and make use of subsidiarity. The principle appears in the encyclical's discussion of the appropriate role of the state in social policy. It is best to let the text speak for itself:

> Nevertheless, it is a fundamental principle of social philosophy, fixed and unchangeable, that one should not withdraw from individuals and commit to the community what they can accomplish by their own enterprise and industry. So, too, it is an injustice and at the same time a grave evil and a disturbance of right order to transfer to the larger and higher collectivity functions which can be performed and provided for by lesser and subordinate bodies. Inasmuch as every social activity should, by its very nature, prove a help to members of the body social, it should never destroy or absorb them.[4]

Both the word subsidiarity and its description in terms of "higher and lower" functions are awkward concepts, but the basic meaning or "literal sense" of the idea is clear enough. The principal use of the concept is to set proper limits on the state's role in society. In the continuous tension between freedom and order as concepts of social organization, subsidiarity's primary thrust is in support of freedom, preserving a sphere of free activity in the socio-economic order. The goal of subsidiarity, however, is to find an effective, harmonious balance in social policy, not to defend an absolute or even in-principled opposition to the role of the state. Again, the literal sense helps to illuminate the intent of the principle. In Latin, *subsidium* means help or aid; subsidiarity seeks to determine how the state should aid other actors in society to achieve their legitimate purposes. In the socio-economic order (as opposed to the responsibilities of defending society or legislating for it) the state is a second order agent; its role, as we shall see, is critical but should be exercised in relationship to other primary agents of socio-economic development.

Andrew Greeley has observed that, "The principle of 'subsidiary function' is perhaps the central theme of Catholic social theory."[5] I believe this assessment overstates the role of subsidiarity; the principle is a distinguishing characteristic of Catholic social ethics, but it must be understood as part of a broader moral framework where it plays a supporting role. As its definition implies, subsidiarity is a procedural principle, and its meaning relies in part on a wider substantive social vision.

Presuppositions of Solidarity

Part of the problem with Andrew Greeley's assertion is that it bypasses or is silent about the foundation and structure of the social tradition which has produced the idea of subsidiarity. The basis of the tradition is a philosophical anthropology which defines the human person as both sacred and social, then plays out the implications of this polarity.[6] The sacredness of the person is more appropriate to a theological conception of the human, but its philosophical transposition affirms the dignity of each person. Investing each person with dignity establishes the basis for a spectrum of human rights, moral claims to a range of spiritual and temporal goods which protect and promote the humanity of the person. The philosophical (or theological) claims about the unique status of the person do not lead, however, to an individualistic understanding of human nature.

The other pole of the description, the social nature of the person, is equally constitutive. The person requires a multiplicity of communities to achieve and sustain full human development. Foundational communities include the family, civil society, and the entire human community. Intermediary associations cut across these three basic communities and fill out the fabric of social existence. The three basic communities are the context in which the relationship of human rights and corresponding human duties determine the map of our moral life. The clearest statement in Catholic teaching of the interplay between the sacred and social dimensions of human personality, and the way in which the two structure a view of society is the 1963 encyclical of Pope John XXIII, *Pacem In Terris*. The four central chapters of the letter move from interpersonal relations, through a discussion of citizen-state relations on to state-state relations and finally to a conception of the international system. Subsidiarity is a second-order principle which makes sense only in light of this larger framework; it is a procedural guideline not an independent substantive concept.

The valuable guidance which subsidiarity offers, however, can be articulated only in light of a prior discussion of the normative responsibilities of the state. During the welfare reform debate, and in other social policy debates in the United States, the contrasting positions often are cast in the terms of the *size* of the state or its *intrusiveness* or its undisciplined *expansion*. There is a place for consideration of the operational efficiency of the state which can usefully invoke ideas about the size and scope of the state. But the tradition that coined the subsidiarity principle understood the size and scope issues in light of a definition of the nature of the state and its multiple moral responsibilities. Some of the articulations of this tradition go to great lengths to set it off and over against the philosophy of liberalism and the liberal state. There are real and important substantive differences between the social philosophy of Catholicism and liberalism. Contemporary discussions between liberal and communitarian conceptions of society open an arena in which Catholic social thought should be able to make a contribution.[7] In the process, however, the Catholic-liberal differences should not be pushed too far; there is common ground as well as contrasting positions in this argument. Politically, Catholic teaching has demonstrably learned from liberalism and incorporated themes about human rights and pluralism into its teaching at the Second Vatican Council. Economically, the debate is still very much in process, but its contours include both confirmation of some liberal themes and a critique of aspects of modern capitalism. Culturally, ideas about autonomy, as they shape views on sexuality, abortion, artistic expression, and associated themes, highlight greater opposition of the Catholic and liberal traditions than either politics or economics do. Cutting through all three areas, however, is the conception of the state. In the U.S. political debate, conservative commentators and politicians stress the identification of subsidiarity and a constrained role for the state. It may be the case that the less known about the principle the more attractive it appears. Abstracted from the broader fabric of Catholic teaching, the principle carries a more conservative tone than its history, content, or evolution supports. Some attention to these three dimensions is needed.

The Struggle Over the State

Subsidiarity is a relatively recent addition to Catholic social theory. It emerged as one dimension of a broader, longer process of development encompassing the last two centuries of Catholic social teaching. Subsidiarity's role lies in the arena of socio-economic policy; but in the development of the theory it appears as a secondary consideration, subordinate to the struggle in Catholic theology about the political-cultural-religious role of the state.

The struggle presents a contrasting image of the political process which marked social policy in liberal democratic societies. In those societies the process involved beginning with a limited state and gradually developing a broader role for the state in social policy and legislation. The philosophical-theological argument in Catholic theology from the mid-nineteenth to the mid-twentieth century was about shrinking the state. The focus of the debate was not socio-economic policy but the role of government in the political-cultural order of society, particularly as it bore upon religious freedom.[8] The organic theory of society, joined to the concept of the common good, yielded a teleological argument about the state's role which gave it sweeping responsibilities to monitor and direct the moral and religious character of civil society. The nineteenth-century theological arguments (rooted in the teaching of Popes Gregory XVI and Leo XII) made it virtually impossible for Catholicism either to support the right of religious freedom or to address the fact of religious and moral pluralism in the debate on social policy.

To identify but not detail a long, conflicted narrative, it was the efforts of Pius XII, John XXIII and the American Jesuit John Courtney Murray that recast the arguments about the state in such a way that Vatican II could both endorse the right of religious liberty and engage pluralist democracies in a positive collaborative dialogue. Central to this effort was the endorsement of what Murray called the "constitutional state" of the Western liberal tradition and the move away from the contrasting conception of the "ethical state" with its comprehensive responsibility for religious-cultural issues. In his historical narrative describing how this transition occurred, Murray specifies the socio-economic teaching of Leo XIII and Pius XI as the initial point of divergence from the ethical to the constitutional notion of the state's role in society. Subsidiarity fits into this process of development. It does set limits to the state's role, but it does so from a starting point of a conception of state power that gave it *primary* responsibility for the achievement of the common good. Contemporary conservative discourse *begins* with a highly restricted conception of the state's social role and then seeks to use subsidiarity to maintain or even tighten these restrictions. But the background from which the principle emerged began with a quite positive conception of the state's role, and then sought to assess how that conception should function vis-à-vis socio-economic policy.

The Evolution of the Principle

It is not only the history of the principle of subsidiarity that induces caution in determining its view of the state; it is also the moral logic of the principle in its original formulation and its development in the broader context of Catholic social policy over the last 60 years. Even in its original formulation, the determination of where responsibility for meeting the basic socio-economic needs of the person should be located was dependent upon a criterion of effectiveness and capability. Subsidiarity's basic message is, do not move to the state *first* in addressing socio-economic needs. It is an argument for freedom in society and a pluralistic structure of power as the guiding norm for social policy. But failure of "lesser" agencies or actors to meet basic human needs returns the argument to the state as the ultimate guarantor of the common good. To use a contemporary example, access to basic health care is a right in Catholic social teaching; this moral claim does not pre-determine who has the duty to satisfy the right; what it does do is to include the right to health care in the fabric of the common good. This means that some part of the society must respond to a universal right of the citizenry. The logic of subsidiarity would begin the policy argument with "lesser agencies", like the health care profession as a whole. Only if such a response fails to meet the right of each person would the argument move upward to the state. But it *would move* in that direction if the alternative is to leave a basic right unfulfilled. As a procedural principle, subsidiarity is conservative in American political terms; but in the broader context of substantive justice claims in Catholic teaching, subsidiarity supports the engagement of all major social actors, including the state, in the obligatory task of meeting the basic rights of each person in the society.

The historical development of Catholic social theory since the 1930s reinforces the notion that an adequate account of subsidiarity cannot simply cite its 1931 definition, but must relate it to other themes in the broader moral vision of the social teaching. There have been two developments in the last 60 years which bear directly upon the interpretation of subsidiarity; the first in John XXIII's encyclical *Mater et Magistra* (1961) and the second in John Paul II's teaching on solidarity as a social norm.

Thirty years after Pius XI introduced the principle of subsidiarity in Catholic teaching, John XXIII returned to its meaning in a section of *Mater et Magistra* entitled "Private Initiative and State Intervention in Economic Life." As every pope does when he is about to alter the teaching of a predecessor, John XXIII begins by reaffirming the value of the principle. His dominant concern, however, is to highlight the changing character of social life in which the principle functions. The change is introduced under the rubric of increasing "socialization", which John XXIII describes in this fashion:

> One of the principal characteristics of our time is the multiplication of social relationships, that is, a daily more complex interdependence of citizens, introducing into their lives and activities many and varied forms of associations, recognized for the most part in private and even in public law. This tendency seemingly stems from a number of factors operative in the present era, among which are technical and scientific progress, greater productive efficiency, and higher standard of living among citizens.[9]

The dynamic of socialization arises from the quest to fulfill basic human rights and it often generates public intervention in social and economic life. John XXIII cites the possible danger of increased regulation and erosion of freedom, but his dominant judgment is that if public authorities have "a correct understanding of the common good," the balance between subsidiarity and socialization can be struck. This, in turn, provides hope that together they "will lead to an appropriate structuring of the human community."[10]

The direction of the pope's thought is clear but a more structural analysis of how subsidiarity and socialization should relate is in order. As commentary, to which I shall return below, I submit that the effect of *Mater et Magistra* is to provide two poles of judgement to assess the appropriate role of the state and other actors in shaping social policy. The subsidiarity pole remains a restraint on early state intervention, but the dynamic of socialization describes objective conditions which can be invoked to legitimate an expansive policy by the state in meeting socio-economic needs. The presumption of restraint can be overridden by demonstrating how unmet rights or needs require state action.

John Paul II has made clear, in light of his social philosophy and his personal experience, that he supports the principle of subsidiarity and the freedom of initiative which it protects. Indeed in contrast to his immediate predecessors, he has been explicitly critical of aspects of the welfare state in the advanced industrial societies and he has explicitly commended a "right of economic initiative" in socioeconomic policy.[11] At the same time, however, a major characteristic of the social teaching of John Paul II is his support for the principle of solidarity. He describes solidarity as a needed virtue today, analogous to the Christian understanding of charity.[12] The principle of solidarity should apply not only in interpersonal relations and national policy but at the level of international relations as well. Rather than a prescriptive principle defining specific obligations in the style of distributive justice, solidarity is a personal and social sense of obligation for the vulnerable in society. It establishes the foundation of moral (and religious) obligations to others while the principles of social and distributive justice, along with the substantive demands of human rights, specify and concretize these obligations. In referring to the role of solidarity as a basis of social relationships, John Paul II cites what he calls an "elementary principle of sound political obligation, namely, the more that individuals are defenseless within a given society, the more they require the care and concern of others, and in particular the intervention of governmental authority."[13]

The papal teaching since 1931 sustains but modifies the original understanding of subsidiarity. How to describe the contemporary understanding of the term? In my view we are left with a triad of different but complementary concepts, all of which should be located within an understanding of the common good. The common good is the central organizing idea in the Catholic social system. The duties of diverse actors in society are defined in terms of the needs of the common good. The concept is rooted in the social nature of the person; it asserts that, because we are social and interdependent as human beings, it is essential to the welfare of society that a material and spiritual context be created so that each person in society can pursue and attain his/her personal good. The content of the common good includes both values and institutions; in the first instance it is derived from the values associated with basic human rights claims. John XXIII argued in *Pacem In Terris* that the common good is best preserved when a social system defends the rights of each person and facilitates the fulfillment of duties toward others.[14] Institutionally the requirements of the common good define in broad outline the duties of the state and other key social actors, including public and private institutions. To invoke the earlier discussion of this chapter, the process of "shrinking the state" in Catholic social theory led to a differentiation of duties. The social teaching of Leo XIII, reflecting an inherited tradition, simply identified the state as the agent responsible for guaranteeing the common good. Contemporary Catholic teaching asserts a set of essential tasks for the state but also establishes limits on state action and identifies other actors—voluntary associations, professional groups, and trade unions—as essential contributors to the common good.[15] The state's role is unique but not exhaustive in pursuit of the common good. When a spectrum of agents responsible for the common good is identified, then the concepts of solidarity, socialization, and subsidiarity come into play with the objective of structuring relationships and guiding social policy.

The chronological order in which these terms entered papal social teaching was subsidiarity, socialization, and then solidarity. Conceptually, I believe the order should be reversed. Solidarity is a substantive moral concept, rooted, like the common good, in the social nature of the person. It seeks to move beyond a descriptive account of human interdependence to assert a bond of moral obligation or duty existing among persons at every level of human society. The general affirmation of solidarity does not descend to the particular duties implied by it. These are determined by a combination of human rights claims and the several principles of justice which Catholic teaching has developed from the work of Aristotle and Thomas Aquinas. Since solidarity and its duties extend from interpersonal relationships through international relations, it is useful to invoke Aquinas's delineation of an "order of charity," which prescribes a method of setting priorities, based on relationships (family, state, world), among the imperatives of solidarity. We have obligations to all, but not the same obligations.

Socialization, unlike solidarity, does not assert a moral claim; it is a descriptive term identifying growing levels of complexity in modern society which have moral consequences. The foremost of these, as articulated by John XXIII, is the need to consider on a selective, case-determined basis, a greater role for the state in meeting human rights claims of citizens. As a descriptive term, socialization does not have the standing of either solidarity or subsidiarity, both of which carry normative content. But John XXIII and his successors, as well as analysts of the social teaching, have invoked socialization to justify a reinterpretation of the role of subsidiarity.

The reinterpretation maintains subsidiarity as a key functional principle in Catholic social teaching and continues to give it primacy as a norm for assessing the appropriate role for the state and its relationships to other social institutions. But the character of socialization and its impact on the rights and duties of individuals provides a rationale for overriding the limit subsidiarity places on the state. To concretize this shift, it could be said that the rights and needs of the person define the core of the common good, that solidarity calls both individuals and institutions to meet the needs of others, that subsidiarity directs social policy to engage non-state actors first in responding to social needs, but subsidiarity also justifies moving to the state as the final guarantor of basic human rights (political and socio-economic) in society. This contextualized understanding of subsidiarity provides a guide for Catholic institutions as social actors and provides a norm for social policy on multiple levels.

Subsidiarity and Catholic Social Institutions

Subsidiarity, therefore, is designed to produce a pluralist structure of power in society; while acknowledging and endorsing the unique role of the state in society, subsidiarity seeks to engage the potential and the responsibility of other actors. In this sense the principle is about social space, not only for individuals but particularly for other institutions and groups beyond the state. While subsidiarity is proposed as a norm for social policy applicable throughout the society, it has a specific relationship to Catholic social institutions. Catholicism had been identified with a range of social institutions for centuries prior to the appearance of subsidiarity in its social teaching, but it is appropriate and useful to examine these institutions as an expression of subsidiarity. As independent nongovernmental institutions, they pursue activities that are complementary to the state but distinct from it. Particularly in the context of U.S. society and culture, the interplay between the norm which is taught and the social institutions which are sustained is clear. The institutions rely on the norm and offer examples of how it is fulfilled. They do so not only in terms of social service, but in terms of advocacy in the policy process.

The institutional character of Catholicism is noted by all analysts. In the United States the number and scope of institutions is the most extensive of any local church (i.e., a church within a nation). The most recent statistics list the following totals:[16]

Hospitals and Health Care Centers: 1,115
Schools (Elementary and High): 8,453
Catholic Charities Agencies: 1,400

While there is a basis for referring to this network of educational, social service, and health care institutes as the Catholic social system, the term system conveys a sense of greater centralization, internal integration, and unity of policy vision than the present configuration has achieved. While there is a way in which all of these institutions are sponsored by the Catholic Church in the United States, the patterns of financial support, the daily operating responsibilities and the channels of authority are quite diverse. Some institutions like elementary schools are directly related to parishes, others, like Catholic Charities, are directly tied to the bishop of their diocese. But there is a national office of Catholic Charities U.S.A. that is not under any single bishop and which generates an activist policy agenda. Health care institutions continue to have a relationship to a sponsoring religious community, but principal control has moved to lay boards of trustees. Most pertinent for the interests of this project is the relative lack of strategic planning across institutions in a way that would more accurately convey the sense of a system at work. Nonetheless, these institutions do identify their work as an extension of the ministry of the wider Church, are influenced by Catholic social teaching, and are recognized in the civil community as a religiously based institutional presence in society.

It is possible, in my judgment, to distinguish two phases in the historical development of how these institutions have understood their role in American society. From the mid-nineteenth to mid-twentieth century, Catholic institutions were a parallel presence to existing social institutions. From schools through hospitals to social services, institutions were created, staffed, and supported to serve an immigrant community which often lived at the edge of American society and culture. In addition to the fact that little or no public funding was available, theological reasons supported a separate social system. A pervasive fear existed that public systems of education threatened the transmission of faith, and that health care systems did not share Catholic positions on several issues of health care. The parallel social system was founded on shared values, staffed overwhelmingly by Catholics, and focused on the needs of the Catholic population. Two events—one secular, the other ecclesial—changed the character of Catholic social institutions. The first was the New Deal and its legacy. Samuel

Beer has argued that the New Deal was more than an avalanche of new programs; it was also "a state of mind, an outlook on politics and government, a public philosophy."[17] He described that philosophy as "federal activism," convinced of the need for national programs and for the federal government to administer them. It was the long-term consequences of this philosophy which ultimately led to extensive engagement between Catholic health and social service agencies and the federal government. From the Hill-Burton Act for hospital construction through Medicare and Medicaid, as well as a host of feeding, child care, and family support programs, Catholic social agencies expanded their activities and their constituency. The second change was not financial or bureaucratic but theological and pastoral. The Second Vatican Council called the Church to see itself as a "sacrament of unity" in society, and it defined as an essential role for the Church the protection of the dignity of the human person. These themes and others like them provided a more expansive foundation for the Church's social ministry. It was not to be seen as an extension of the "real work" of the Church (preaching and sacramental ministry), nor was it to be focused only on Catholics. The council's theology envisioned advocacy for social justice and direct service to those in need as the work of the Kingdom of God, an essential requirement for the Church.

The combined effect of these sacral and secular events transformed the social ministry from the establishment of a parallel social system to an effort to penetrate, collaborate with and transform existing social policies and programs so that the hungry would be fed, the poor empowered, the sick healed, and the vulnerable protected. Even when the broader public debate turned skeptical or hostile to public and private efforts to address issues of injustice, poverty and discrimination, a consensus existed in Catholic leadership that return to the parallel model was neither possible nor desirable.

Catholic social institutions illustrate the meaning of the principle of subsidiarity; they constitute a distinct, independent network of institutions, separate from the state but capable of both engaging collaboratively with it and setting limits on its reach. These institutions are, of course, not unique; they are part of a fabric of voluntary associations woven through the American social system. In some form all of these "subsidiary" institutions collaborate with but also limit and redesign the logic of the state and the market in American culture and society. Much of what religiously based institutions do is identical with their counterpart, nonprofit voluntary associations. But within Catholic institutions, at least, certain questions keep surfacing about their nature, function, and role. Having moved away from the parallel presence model, these institutions must continually address three issues: collaboration, identity, and the specific difference test.

Collaboration

This question focuses on the relationship of church-based social agencies with the government (although there are now similar questions arising from relationships with corporations and other for-profit institutions). A major distinction here, of course, is between health care, social service, and higher education on one hand, and Catholic elementary and high schools on the other. The latter receive no direct federal funding, so the collaboration issues are not central for them. The collaboration debate in the 1990s involves two quite distinct arguments. One arises from the political arena where advocates of privatization seek either to return all responsibility for the poor to private charity (without substantial government participation) or to direct whatever government funding exists through private institutions, with religiously based institutions usually given high priority. Catholic responses to this debate (again not unique among major religious communities) have been made at two levels. First, to assert that religious providers of social service are not capable of meeting all the needs which exist even with generous government assistance. Second, to assert even more strongly—that the privatization model amounts to the federal government forsaking its obligatory role to contribute to the common good, precisely in terms of the needs of the poor and vulnerable. This argument assumes that a "good society" is not one where the political authority of society is disengaged from those most in need. To repeat a statement of John Paul II cited above, it is an "elementary principle of sound political organization: that those in need require the care and concern of others and in particular of governmental authority."[18]

The other side of the collaboration debate arises from within the Catholic community itself; in 1996 a senior Vatican official, Archbishop Paul Cordes, raised questions about the amount of assistance which one U.S. Catholic agency, Catholic Relief Services, received from government funds. This argument has also been reflected in the views of some lay Catholics in the United States involving Catholic Charities. The thrust of the critique is that simply the amount of money involved introduces a threatening ambiguity for the Catholic character of these agencies.[19] Two responses can be made to this position.

First, there is in this argument a tone that does not correspond to the Catholic social style of ministry. That style affirms the value of the human, has a positive conception of the role of the state in society (based in Aquinas's revision of Augustine's conception of the state), and envisions *both* church and state existing under an obligation to address in systematic fashion problems of poverty and injustice (as highlighted in recent Catholic teaching on "the option for the poor"). While maintaining a distinction based on nature, function, and purpose between church and state, the Catholic style is to seek systematic cooperation and collaboration between these institutions wherever possible. Illustrations as diverse as the Vatican diplomatic corps and a local pastor's leveraging of the city council testify to the pervasiveness of this style of ministry. In short, arguments that collaboration, measured in quantitative terms, should be taken as signs of corruption of the Church's ministry constitute a dubious basis for discussion. They bear the burden of truth over against a much more ancient "tradition."

Second, while resisting the assumption that extensive collaboration equals distortion of religious ministry, a better statement of the case would acknowledge that collaboration, like all relationships and especially those involving power and public purposes, requires sophisticated moral standards and constant use of casuistry or case analysis. Here one shifts the ground of debate from ecclesiology (which relationships is it appropriate for the Church to engage in) to ethics (how to define, structure, and judge complex relationships). There are continuing problems of *how* church agencies should relate to public policies. In the health care field, a range of bioethical issues are evident from genetics through abortion to proposals about assisted suicide. As evident in the health care debate of the early 1990s, proposals for increased involvement of the state in health care (often supported by Catholic social teaching) can intensify the problems posed by bioethical issues.

In the area of social service, the post-welfare reform era poses choices about how religiously based social agencies will relate to a system whose inception they opposed. In Maryland a group of religious providers initially argued against assuming the "fill the gap" position which they saw the state assigning to private charities. Again, the Catholic style will tilt against this kind of absolutist approach in the face of a policy which is defective. But further questions arise: proposals to have church agencies "take over" the local administration of welfare are not simply issues of "how much" can we do, but what kind of specific responsibilities should a church assume. Again, the casuistry here is constant; specific needs can justify choices in a given area, which it may not be good policy for the Church to use on a national basis. From bioethics to soup kitchens, collaboration requires moral principles.

Identity

As observed above, the collaboration debate had its proximate roots in the New Deal legacy of activist federal funding of social programs, including funding Catholic agencies. The identity debate has its proximate origins in Vatican II's call for the Church to enter more expansively into the culture and society it serves. Thirty years after Catholic institutions in the United States aggressively accepted the conciliar mandate, there is a pervasive review of the record going on across Catholic institutions. Charles Curran has summarized the agenda of the identity debate:

> The discussion of Catholic identity logically involves three questions: Is it possible for such institutions to be Catholic today? Given existing priorities and parameters, should such Catholic structures exist? What does Catholic identity mean in these institutions today and what means should be taken to ensure their identity?[20]

In a project devoted to the role of religion in American democracy, these questions may appear excessively introverted. They are cited here to indicate that for a large religious institution with substantive ties to the wider social system, the policy debate can never remain purely external—about strategy and tactics, programs, and contracts. As Peter Frumkin elaborates in Chapter 8, issues about the institution's original purpose and its motivation to engage the wider society, and about how its pluralistic commitments and inner theological coherence are held together, inevitably come to the surface. To illustrate the significance of the debate, the extreme case is useful: there are arguments made that essentially say that the Church should withdraw from or limit specific ministries and commitments rather than blur or distort the religious-moral vision which initially generated the ministry. In the 1990s, arguments like that were heard on Catholic university campuses, in health care institutions, and in the social service world.

The identity debate does have core questions as Curran indicated, but it plays out differently for distinct institutions. In higher education the debate is about ideas and authority, such as the relationship of academic freedom and authoritative Catholic teaching or the composition of the faculty and student body. There is also concern about how significantly Catholic social teaching is addressed in business schools and in the teaching of church-state issues in law schools or that of bioethics in medical schools. In brief, do Georgetown, Notre Dame, or Boston College address the intersection of normative and empirical discourse differently than Harvard, Princeton, or Michigan? Should they? What should be similar and what should be distinctive in their scholarship and teaching?

In health care the identity debate ranges across issues of mergers, the market approach to health care and methods of medical care. In this setting, the questions are more specific than in the university setting and the pressure of financial survival looms more vividly. In an era of consolidation of heath care providers, choices about mergers raise issues of the morality of the market (when a basic human goal is at stake) and of life-giving and death-dealing actions in a way which merger-makers are ill equipped to even define much less decide. In health care, the identity debate rather quickly gets to institutional survival and at what moral price.

There is more breathing space for social service institutions, but they have their own problems. A penetrating presence envelops agencies in a maze of contracts, grants, legal reporting requirements, and procedures which are often not value-free. Beyond this context, Catholic Charities today serve a highly diverse public and do so through a professional staff which is as religiously pluralistic as American society. Questions of institutional policy and personal conscience (of the professional or the person being served) arise in a range of areas like religious education and foster care, contraception and teen pregnancy and ministry to gay and lesbian communities. Catholic social agencies today find themselves in identity questions vis-à-vis governmental contracts and in internal debates about institutional ethics and personal convictions.

Specific Difference Test

This awkward phrase refers to a question that is asked at times in the Catholic social system and should be asked all the time by religiously based social institutions. The question is what is the particular—specifically different—contribution that these institutions can make within the broader social system. Behind the question lies the premise that the religious communities have distinctive obligations, arising from their structure of belief and worship, to respond to the needs of the poor and the vulnerable, to oppose injustice and to contribute to the common good. It is assumed that these obligations exist whether the state and/or other institutions are working effectively on these questions or not. In other words, no other institution can substitute for the fulfillment of this obligation. In Christian theology, the legacy of the prophets, the ministry of Jesus and the mandate of the Epistle of James converge on the theme: authentic faith must reach out to those in need.

At the same time, the fulfillment of this mandate should use the best social science resources available to determine what effective response to the neighbor in need requires. The specific difference test means that the religious institutions should try not to duplicate efforts and should be particularly attentive to where the hidden or ignored gaps in the social system are. They may be glaringly evident or they may be subtlety concealed. In either case the freedom which these institutions have to move across the social system should be utilized—not just "to do something" but to act systematically in light of a sound awareness of what is being done well and what is not.

The point seems so clear as to be banal. But its fulfillment is less than linear. On the one hand, some religious traditions do not conceive of their social role in a collaborative model with public programs. Hence, assessing the latter and then seeking to complement them may be an alien idea. For some, the primacy of charitable endeavors is always superior to "bureaucratic tax-supported" (i.e., coerced) programs. Hence, there is almost a competitive model assumed from the beginning between public and religious forms of response to poverty and injustice. (It should be noted that this perspective is not confined to politically conservative religious perspectives; Dorothy Day had little use for the New Deal legacy.) Theological conviction may prevent systematic collaboration of religious actors and public programs.

On the other hand, institutional interest may be a major obstacle in using the specific difference test. This is the vulnerability of large institutionally supported programs like those found in the Catholic system. Once a large investment is made in a ministry, it is not simple or attractive to think about withdrawal or a major shift of emphasis and programs. Catholic health care institutions face this question today. While I strongly support a continued Catholic institutional presence in health care, including sustaining Catholic hospitals, it is also clear that we may now be contributing to the glut of hospital beds in some areas without a clear sense that we meet the specific difference principle, i.e., that no one else will fill the function the Catholic system is now performing.

A final complexity, however, is that it is often not crystal clear when social needs are being adequately met by other institutions. In the 1960s, many in the Catholic community were imbued with the conviction that sustained the Great

Society programs and were inclined to use the specific difference principle like a scythe, dispensing with Catholic institutions lest they be redundant or competitive with rationalized, large-scale public policy initiatives. One does not have to be in the chorus of the Great Society's critics to recognize that today a more modest sense of what is possible through public programs produces a welcome opportunity for the specific capabilities of religiously based social initiatives. To have dismantled them in the 1960s would have left us poorer as a society in this decade. This judgement does not invalidate the specific difference test; it simply illustrates the complexity of the questions posed.

Subsidiarity and Social Policy

A characteristic of Catholic social policy is that most of its ideas and principles are consciously designed to be usable and available to individuals, groups and societies beyond the boundary of the church or faith community. Subsidiarity, taken by itself, carries no theological content. Thus far, however, this chapter has emphasized the way in which the concept functions within a Catholic framework of ideas and institutions. Precisely because the principle of subsidiarity has been traditionally intended to be used in the wider society, some attention should be given here to its potential in policy discourse.

Perhaps the way into the discussion is to recall Daniel Bell's often used dictum that the pervasive policy challenge today, domestically and internationally, is that "the national state has become too small for the big problems in life, and too big for the small problems."[21] Bell's dictum reflects two empirical themes that have accompanied the changing understanding of subsidiarity in Catholic teaching over the last 60 years. The first is growing political and economic interdependence at the global level, and the second is socialization as a defining phenomenon of the national life of the advanced industrial democracies. Faced with these two phenomena, there is a place, I think, for subsidiarity to function "above" the state for the large problems and "between" the bureaucratic state and the small problems it must address. To illustrate the potential of subsidiarity (but hardly to analyze it) I will seek to relate it to (1) the fact of globalization; (2) the concept of civil society; and (3) the realm of the sacred.

Subsidiarity and Globalization

In the 1970s, Robert Keohane and Joseph Nye both challenged and changed (to a degree) the analysis of world politics by tracing the impact of interdependence on the politics of states and their societies. As they point out in a recent article, one way to think about globalization is that it is an intensification of interdependence.[22] Other literature reflects both a narrow and a broad definition of the phenomenon. In its most specific sense, globalization is captured by the definition proposed by the International Monetary Fund (IMF): "Globalization refers to the growing economic interdependence of countries worldwide through the increasing volume and variety of cross-border transactions in goods and services and international capital flows, and also through the more rapid and widespread diffusion of technology."[23]

While it is clear that globalization is driven by a combination of technology, communication systems, and economic ties, the impact of globalization reaches into broader dimensions of world affairs, including culture, politics and even military questions. To exemplify the relationship of subsidiarity and globalization I will focus on socio-economic issues. Bell's statement, made two decades before the term globalization had currency, focuses attention on the institutions needed to cope with both interdependence and globalization. The standard unit of analysis for international relations for four centuries has been the state. The work of Keohane and Nye thirty years ago and the analysis of globalization today both emphasize that, while the state is still the foundation of world politics, it now fits within a framework of forces and relationships which deny it unfettered control or uncontested status. The state by itself cannot direct or manage globalization. The second level of institutional activity is the structures created after World War II, designed to address what has now become a reality: a global economy and a world market. Both of these institutions—the state and international organizations like the IMF, the World Bank and the family of United Nations institutions—must in turn deal with the primary driving force of globalization, private corporate and financial institutions responsible for productivity, innovation and investment in the global market. Most of the scholarly literature on globalization is devoted to how these institutional levels of world politics interact, how they all shape and are shaped by the forces of globalization, and what impact the phenomenon has on global wealth and power.

The normative questions are not necessarily captured by, and certainly not exhausted by, these dense empirical debates. The intersection of the empirical and normative issues is highlighted by syndicated columnist E.J. Dionne in the *Washington Post*: "The issue has never been whether we will have a global economy. The argument is over what rules should govern it, who will make them and whether policies pushed by the IMF, the World Bank and comparable institutions help or hinder the spread of prosperity to those who have the least. The debates are at least as much about values as they are about economics."[24]

None of the existing institutions seem to be responding effectively to these normative questions. Bell's critique of the nation state points many toward multilateral institutional agencies, which clearly should be part of the solution. The paradox of the present, however, is that these institutions are under severe critique from those who look to them for assistance. The critique highlights the gap between a broadly shared intellectual consensus about economic growth and global integration and the political resistance found among many who must live with the immediate impact of globalization. There is no question about its creation of wealth in the aggregate, but there is debate about its distributional effects, its dynamic, and its governance.

The subsidiarity principle, in the face of states, international institutions, and private actors, points to the need for structures and institutions that can provide affected populations within states with a voice and an influence to mediate the impact of these macro-institutions on their lives. The state in developing societies is often not regarded as trustworthy or effective, and international institutions, however much needed, are seen as unaccountable to any constituency beyond the most powerful states. Effective governance will always need both states and multilateral organizations, but subsidiarity points beyond both, to the need for a network of institutions parallel to states (beneath or above them) which affected populations can access and which are capable of exercising influence in the development and implementation of policies shaping global integration. To some degree the rapid growth and influence of nongovernmental organizations provides a beginning or a foundation for what is needed. But they presently do not have the structure or the status to meet the need. The design, legitimacy, and effectiveness of such institutions pose enormous problems. But the present arrangements of both policy and institutions are plagued by issues of legitimacy and effectiveness as well as by the moral costs suffered by those populations for whom globalization has not yet delivered its undoubted benefits and who have neither voice nor vote to reshape its dynamic.

Subsidiarity and Civil Society

Where does the subsidiarity principle fit with the renewed interest in civil society, a topic reflected throughout this volume? There are several sources to the civil society debate, among them the second half of Daniel Bell's description of the state. The emphasis here falls on the bureaucratic state which is too large to address effectively basic human needs in a humane way. A policy vision based on universal principles mediated through the modern bureaucratic state is surely essential for post-industrial societies, but in the eyes of many liberals and conservatives seems to fall short in several areas of family policy, social policy and health policy. In addition, the civil society debate goes beyond effective delivery of services; it extends to the fabric of social and moral values, which are either in deep dispute or perceived to be in decline in American society. Ultimately discussions of civil society reach the very definition of citizenship in a democratic state.

The multidimensional nature of the civil society discussion provides a natural opening for subsidiarity. The principle, as we have seen, has both empirical and normative dimensions. It fits securely in a debate which cuts across these lines. Some appeals to civil society are narrowly confined to more efficient and effective social policy. While the objective is clearly a major challenge, many are convinced that the broader contours of the civil society discussion—its appeal to values, standards of civic engagement and openness to religious institutions—holds its richest promise. Subsidiarity can enhance both sides of this discussion; it does seek optimum coordination of multiple institutions and organizations in a society, but it pursues this objective in light of a broader fabric of normative premises.

To revert again to illustrative indications of how subsidiarity relates to the ideal civil society, I will stay in the realm of social policy. In this context civil society seeks to preserve space distinct from the state or the market but not in isolation from them. The conviction which drives the civil society debate is that this sector can be effective in shaping both the state and the market in ways which meet the demands of effectiveness, equity and justice.

In defining these relationships subsidiarity's contribution points to three ideas: limits, gaps and choices. The conservative function of subsidiarity does coincide with the concerns of those who seek institutional limits on the social role of the state. As this chapter has tried to illustrate, convergence of interest often is not rooted in a shared social vision; some voices calling for limits have a conception of the state which the tradition sustaining subsidiarity would reject. But practical convergence is possible because subsidiarity does seek to protect freedom of social space. It resists a "statist" conception of social order.

Setting limits is one side of subsidiarity; filling gaps is equally constitutive of subsidiarity's legacy. The principle seeks to empower "lower" or "lesser" actors in social policy. Subsidiarity seeks an effective state not simply a limited state. Precisely because its role is to point toward coordinated action in support of the common good, subsidiarity must continually call for responses to unmet human needs. There is not contradiction between support for subsidiarity and commitment to activist state policy. The principle will encourage initiatives by "lesser" agents to respond to human need, but such initiatives may well require new commitments by the state to be effective.

Beyond limits and gaps lies a realm of creative choice. The debate about whether to emphasize limits or gaps reflects the liberal-conservative arguments in American politics; in both uses of subsidiarity the choices lie at the margins of existing policy. Because the choices are marginal does not make them insignificant, as the welfare and health care debates of the 1990s illustrate. Incremental change in either direction can mean substantial fiscal, tax, and social policy changes in the U.S. political and economic system. Beyond marginal choices, however, lies a potentially different use of subsidiarity. The civil society discussion in the United States does not sound or look revolutionary; it is a reformist argument but one driven by a conviction that neither the state nor the market adequately serves its constituency today. It is not the case that either is radically failing; the point of the civil society discussion focuses upon "adequately". To parse this critique of what would constitute a more adequate social policy moves the discussion beyond marginal choices.

Michael Walzer, in a review of the variety of positions in the civil society discussion, has written that "The associational life of civil society is the actual ground where all versions of the good are tested. . . ."[25] This kind of conversation is broader, wider, less empirically specific than the intense left-right arguments about choices at the margin of policy. It assumes that Bell is correct about a state too large for some critical problems; it also assumes that post-industrial societies generate social problems not adequately captured in debates about the welfare state or the market as effective methods of addressing human needs. In the effort to expand the public argument to the level of testing "the good life" and the institutions needed to sustain it for all in society, subsidiarity has a role to play. It is particularly in this kind of broader discussion that the premises of subsidiarity—its relationship to the other concepts in Catholic social teaching—will be particularly significant. Arguments about the good life, and by extension the good society (its values, institutions and policies), often are regarded as too expansive or value-laden for the choices at the margin of policy. Even then, subsidiarity will not be well used if detached from a wider policy vision. But the realm of creative choice, beyond the boundaries of specific policies cannot be addressed without some substantive philosophical vision. Subsidiarity is most at home in this kind of discussion.

Subsidiarity and the Sacred

In addition to setting limits on the "privatization thesis" in contemporary policy debates, the subsidiarity principle is also a hedge against the "secularization thesis", i.e., arguments which seek implicitly or explicitly to keep religiously based social initiatives purely private, without government support and without public policy significance. These two ideas—privatization and secularization—often join voices on the political right and left in a common conclusion drawn from starkly different premises.

The right's case that private charity is morally superior to public policy and that religious programs provide better quality of service is one half of the conclusion. The other is the concern of some voices on the left who seek to keep religious activity private lest it corrupt a certain vision of constitutional neutrality. Together, in spite of themselves, they consign the role of religion to a marginal status in the life of society. Both are willing on occasion to praise the role, but both want it securely in the private sphere.

In its specific content subsidiarity does not address the conclusion; it seeks a pluralist structure of power in society without addressing the issue of the character of intermediary actors between citizens and the state. Once again, however, if seen in its original setting, subsidiarity arises from a social theory which *assumes* the public role of religious institutions without specifying the constitutional structure in which this public role is played. The assumptions are grounded at a far deeper level than the subsidiarity principle. John Courtney Murray once described the premises of Catholic social theory in terms of three distinctions:[26] at the ontological level, between the sacred and secular as basic categories of social existence; at the constitutional level, between society and the state; and at the ethical level, between common good and public order. The terms are interrelated. First, there must be in the fundamental organization of society space for the sacral dimension of human existence, space for religious expression in worship, teaching and social witness. Second, the space within which the religious dimension takes shape is society, beyond the state and not dependent on the state for its right to exist or the definition of its role. Third, the pursuit of the common good is the task for the whole society; the state has a unique responsibility for public order (which includes guaranteeing basic standards of social justice; here the state is the court of last resort). Subsidiarity is invoked to help define the shaping of society and to allocate responsibilities in pursuing the common good. But it comes to this task with the presupposition that religion has public space in the society, and therefore will be part of the structured relationship needed among several institutions and communities to pursue the common good. The precise role of religious communities will vary with what the needs of the common good are, and with an assessment of which institutions are best equipped to respond to diverse needs.

These usually unarticulated foundations of the subsidiarity principle run counter to both the privatization and the secularization positions. The opposition is deeply rooted. The anthropology of the person, identified earlier as the cornerstone of the Catholic social vision, intrinsically links the spiritual and the material. Because the person is a unity of both, the structure and organization of society must accommodate both: here lies the sacral/secular distinction in the orders of human existence. Because the sacral or spiritual dimension is essential for the person, it must be guaranteed social space. The preservation of social space for the sacred in turn requires a public, institutional order to protect the sacral against secular incursion and to provide the sacral with the potential for public engagement in society. This conception of secular-sacral is quite compatible with a constitutional separation of religion and the state. But it is not compatible with a purely private definition of religion—in its personal or institutional dimensions.

To oppose the secularization thesis does not result in any support for the privatization proposal. The kind of vigorous opposition to the social role of the state which is often evident in the privatization case is not what animates Catholic theory. The specific and essential role given the state in the protection and promotion of the common good guarantees it a significant social role in response to human needs.

Subsidiarity is less than a total vision of society or social policy. One needs to construct a broader fabric around it so that it can play its crucial role in the ordering of social institutions. That role yields a social vision which seeks to preserve freedom and to provide space for private initiatives and institutions, yet do so in a way which guarantees that the basic needs of the person, every person, are met and satisfied.

Notes

1. J.Bryan Hehir, *The Church and Politics: Twenty Five Years After Vatican II's Church in the Modern World* (The XI Moreau Lecture), King's College, Wilkes-Barre, PA, 1990.

2. For a historical-analytical synthesis of Catholic social theory, see David Hollenbach, *Claims in Conflict: Retrieving and Renewing the Catholic Human Rights Tradition* (New York: Paulist Press, 1979); also Charles Curran and Richard A. McCormick, eds., *Readings in Moral Theology No. 5: Official Catholic Social Teaching* (New York: Paulist Press, 1986).

3. William Ferree, *Introduction to Social Justice* (Dayton, OH: Marianist Publications, 1947), pp. 14–15.

4. Pius XI, *Quadragesimo Anno* (#79) in David O'Brien and Thomas Shannon, eds, *Catholic Social Thought: The Documentary Heritage* (Maryknoll, NY: Orbis Books, 1992), p.60.

5. Andrew Greeley, *The Catholic Myth: The Behavior and Beliefs of American Catholics* (New York: Scribner's Sons, 1990), p. 301.

6. The philosophical argument about human dignity is best exemplified in John XXIII's *Pacem in Terris* (1963); the theological argument is found in Vatican II's, *Gaudium et Spes* (1965) and in numerous places in the teachings of John Paul II.

7. The standard point of reference for the Catholic-Liberal discussion in American Catholicism remains the work of John Courtney Murray, S.J., *We Hold These Truths: Catholic Reflections on the American Proposition* (New York: Sheed and Ward, 1960); J. Leon Hooper, ed., *Religious Liberty: Catholic Struggles With Pluralism* (Louisville, KY: Westminster/John Knox Press, 1993); more recently, see Joseph A. Komonchak, "Vatican II and the Encounter Between Catholicism and Liberalism" in R.Bruce Douglass and David Hollenbach, eds., *Catholicism and Liberalism: Contributions to American Public Philosophy* (Cambridge, England: Cambridge University Press, 1994), pp. 19–44; 76–99.

8. John Courtney Murray, "The Problem of Religious Freedom," *Theological Studies* 25 (1964): 503–575.

9. John XXIII, *Mater et Magistra* (#59) in O'Brien and Shannon, *Catholic Social Thought*, p. 93.

10. John XXIII, *Mater et Magistra* (#65; #67), in O'Brien and Shannon, *Catholic Social Thought*, pp. 94–95.

11. John Paul II, *Centesimus Annus* (#48), and *Sollicitudo Rei Socialis* (#15) in O'Brien and Shannon, *Catholic Social Thought*, pp. 403, 476.

12. John Paul II defines solidarity as "a firm and persevering determination to commit oneself to the common good; that is to say to the good of all and of each individual, because we are all really responsible for all," *Sollicitudo Rei Socialis* (#38), in O'Brien and Shannon, *Catholic Social Thought*, p. 421.

13. John Paul II, *Centesimus Annus* (#10), in O'Brien and Shannon, *Catholic Social Thought*, p. 446.

14. John XXIII, *Pacem In Terris* (#60) in O'Brien and Shannon, *Catholic Social Thought*, p. 141.

15. Murray, "The Problem of Religious Freedom," 537–538.

16. P.J. Kennedy and Sons, *The Official Catholic Directory 1999* (New Providence, NJ: P.J. Kennedy and Sons, 1999), p. 2189; Dorothy M. Brown and Elizabeth McKeown, *The Poor Belong to Us: Catholic Charities and American Welfare* (Cambridge, MA: Harvard University Press, 1997), p. 197.

17. Samuel H. Beer, "In Search of a Public Philosophy," in Anthony King, ed., *The New American Political System* (Washington, D.C.: American Enterprise Institute, 1978), p. 5.

18. John Paul II, *Centesimus Annus* (#10), in O'Brien and Shannon, *Catholic Social Thought*, p. 446.

19. Archbishop Paul Josef Cordes, *Christian Charity and Its Distinguishing Character;* Address at the XXII Plenary Assembly of the Pontifical Council Cor Unum (April 16–19, 1997), pp. 4–5 (Xerox text).

20. Charles E. Curran, "The Catholic Identity of Catholic Institutions," *Theological Studies* 58 (1997): 91.

21. Daniel Bell, *The Winding Passage: Sociological Essays and Journeys* (New Brunswick, NJ: Transaction Publishers, 1991), p. 225.

22. Robert O. Keohane and Joseph S. Nye, *Power and Interdependence: World Politics in Transition* (Boston: Little, Brown and Co., 1977); Robert O. Keohane, and Joseph S. Nye, "Globalization: What's New? What's Not (and So What?)," *Foreign Policy* 118 (Spring 2000): 105.

23. Staff of the International Monetary Fund, *World Economic Outlook May 1997* (Washington, D.C.: International Monetary Fund, 1997), p. 45.

24. E.J. Dionne, "Valid Questions on the New Economy," *Washington Post*, April 14, 2000.

25. Michael Walzer, "The Idea of Civil Society: A Path to Social Reconstruction," in E.J. Dionne, ed., *Community Works: The Revival of Civil Society in America* (Washington, D.C.: Brookings Institution, 1998), p. 132.

26. Murray, "The Problem of Religious Freedom," 520.

CHAPTER 5

Where Religion and Public Values Meet: Who Will Contest?

Brent B. Coffin

Justice as participation requires personal responsibility that is proportional to the privileges and resources of citizens. The privileged are proportionally obligated to assure that all citizens enjoy the distributive conditions of justice and to act preferentially with those who are being excluded from community life.

PARTNERSHIPS FOR SOCIAL WELFARE ARE IMPORTANT for all Americans; they are especially important for the poor. At stake is whether all persons and groups are able to flourish in good times and have security against severe hardship in bad times, and, even more urgently, whether the most vulnerable Americans share in the good times and survive the devastating consequences of hard times. This being the case, we would expect public debates about social welfare to address more than the social-safety net for those at the very bottom of society. Our debates should be about the more inclusive questions of poverty *and* wealth, the responsibility of the poor to help themselves *and* the obligation of the prosperous to help others, the safety net at the bottom of society *and* the range of economic inequality among fellow citizens who, with them, make up a single democratic society.

Unfortunately, such has not been the case. American public debates about social provision have been framed largely in terms of welfare reform. Unlike partnerships for social welfare, which are about all of us, welfare reform is about them. Its animating question is not how all American families are able to manage working, caring for children and elderly, and staying active in religious and civic communities. Welfare reform is driven by the question of what legislators will do about "the underclass"—those who have stopped playing by the rules and stopped achieving, presumably unlike the rest of us. We may thus wonder if those unfortunate and often misunderstood words of Jesus from the Gospel of St. Luke, the poor you will always have with you, have come to include the political corollary, so, too, the welfare reform debate.

Why this perennial focus? As the welfare system has grown, some have suggested its periodic reform provides a public drama to manifest and reinforce a moral order.[1] The drama displays those fundamental boundaries separating the working from the nonworking, the deserving from the undeserving, we who are entitled to assistance in times of need from those who must learn to take responsibility for themselves. As society undergoes profound changes—in areas from gender roles and employment security to civic engagement and trust in government—many Americans feel a need to clarify the nation's shared moral values and to promote their observance. This no doubt was a driving force behind the historic 1996 welfare legislation as suggested by its title, "The Personal Responsibility and Work Opportunity Reconciliation Act."

In actuality, the welfare reform debate has proven to be something quite different than a public ritual displaying the nation's moral order. The intense public anger and political rewards generated by the welfare reform debate make sense only if we see it as an arena where fundamentally different perspectives are contesting the public values that should guide American institutions and policies as they undergo extraordinary changes.[2] A decade before the 1996 legislation ended welfare as we knew it, a number of thoughtful social observers foresaw the emergence of a new consensus on the public values. That hope carried over into the first two years of the Clinton Administration. However, the welfare bill that the president signed in his second administration reflected a tectonic shift in politics that occurred in the1994 congressional elections. The hope for a new consensus in social policy heralded at the beginning of the 1990s had become shattered.

The fact that decentralized welfare reform was carried out amidst the nation's longest sustained period of economic growth has obscured the battle over the public values guiding social welfare policies. However, as economic conditions put reforms to the test of time, the battle over what values should guide social welfare will also continue. What voices will contest them, and how will they do so?

In this chapter I argue that religious congregations generate two kinds of influences on public values: they shape the kind of persons who bear them and the kind of values that are born. After a general normative account of how communities do so, I caution against asserting religious values directly in public debates. Substantively, I argue that religious practices cultivate an understanding of persons as participants who value membership, contribution, and transformative interaction; such values can be articulated in a corresponding political view of justice as participation. Finally, I turn to the welfare reform debate to illustrate how justice as participation reformulates core public values in order to debate, not welfare, but social provision, what all of us owe one another as democratic citizens.

Private Preferences and Public Values

Considerable attention has been paid to the influence of individualism in American society. In their book *Habits of the Heart*, Robert Bellah and his colleagues identify two forms. Utilitarian individualism is the doctrine that persons are motivated by basic appetites and fears to maximizing their acquisition of resources; society in this view arises "from a contract that individuals enter into only to advance their self-interest." A second form, expressive individualism, "holds that each person has a unique core of feeling and intuition that should unfold or be expressed if individuality is to be realized."[3] While the second emerged historically as a protest against the first, the two kinds of individualism have become mutually reinforcing. In a market society, the acquisition of wealth allows individuals to buy the positional goods and expressive lifestyles that demonstrate their individuality.[4]

If individualism is the dominant ethic in American society, two consequences may follow for the prospect of shared public values, especially values mandating stronger partnerships for social welfare. First, men and women adhering to individualism may find it difficult to sustain strong and inclusive communities. If these are necessary to cultivate such non-individualistic values as compassion and social solidarity, it may be the case that persons in an individualistic society become less and less able to practice those values. They may gradually lose the moral language to imagine and debate the requirements of a democratic society based on social provisions for all citizens. A liberal democracy may thus sow the seeds of its own demise. Its citizens may pursue the *pluribus* of self-interest, but no longer pursue the *unum* of a common good upon which self-interest depends—what the Constitution refers to as "We the people" endeavoring "to form a more perfect union."[5] Americans may well have become so individualistic, warns Bellah, that "[just] when we are moving to an ever greater validation of the sacredness of the individual person, our capacity to imagine a social fabric that would hold individuals together is vanishing."[6]

Individualism may carry a second consequence—one residing less in the character of persons as bearers of values, but rather in the public values *per se*. Individualism may have the effect of dissolving public values into private preferences. Hence, one citizen may have a preference for feeding the hungry, while another for conspicuous consumption; but neither has the right to impose one's preference on another. As public values dissolve into private preferences, they may still hold meaning for individual actors and influence choices. But what is radically altered is the moral space between individuals. Public values constitute a shared moral space in which diverse citizens are able to call upon a useable past and debate a more desirable future.[7] Individualism collapses this domain of public moral space into mutually unaccountable cells of private preference, disconnected from shared narrative and impervious to ethical evaluation. Private preferences allow only the technical assessment of aggregating individual choices into market shares.[8]

The dissolution of public values can leave citizens unable to make sense of their deeply felt moral attitudes toward others. Religious citizens, for example, are taught by their traditions to care for "the alien, the orphan, and the widow."[9] They are also told in other public contexts, however, that such duties are simply matters of taste, and that to express them publicly is to mix religion and politics.[10] Thus, while religious traditions provide a comprehensive vision of reality in which human beings are connected in mutual obligation, such visions themselves may dissolve in a highly individualistic market society. Religious teachings become private beliefs, and moral obligations become private spiritualities, as epitomized by the young woman named Sheila in *Habits of the Heart* who described her religion as "Sheilaism."

Is American society as individualistic as Bellah and others fear?[11] With some trepidation, I would venture to say no. The consequences of individualism must be assessed along side the evidence that Americans continue to be a nation of joiners.[12] Particularly noteworthy, though often overlooked, is the fact that a great deal of joining occurs in religious congregations. There are over 350,000 such congregations in the United States.[13] Including all forms, "religious organizations constitute the third largest subsector of the U.S. nonprofit world, behind health and education. Just over 50 percent of U.S. adults report household contributions to their church or synagogue, representing 60 to 65 percent of total household giving."[14]

Religious Participation and Public Values

How do religious congregations influence the way American citizens understand public values? Most analysts approach this question at the *individual level,* assessing how particular kinds of religious affiliation may affect particular social or political behaviors. In contrast, I propose to focus, not on individuals as the unit of analysis, but on congregations *per se.* How do religious congregations influence the identity of religious citizens as bearers of public values, and how do they influence the character public values themselves? Without denying the enormous variation among religious congregations, I propose to answer this question with a general description of the patterns and processes that occur across a wide range of religious communities.

Religious congregations are public meeting places where people gather to encounter one another and Other through practices that enable them to interpret their personal and collective experience in light of transcendent reality.[15] The distinctive practices of religious congregations range between two poles: symbolic actions, such as sacraments, prayers, corporate silence, and hymn singing; and pragmatic actions, such as stewardship campaigns, soup kitchens, and providing space to community groups. Importantly, these two poles are never entirely separate; each is always embedded in the other. For example, hymn singing is a symbolic activity in which congregants express their faith in God. But hymn singing also transmits moral instruction and enhances bonds of mutual trust and cooperation. Similarly, when congregants work with Habitat for Humanity, they engage in the pragmatic activity of building an affordable new home; yet their pragmatic activity is symbolically imbued with "a theology of the hammer."[16]

The symbolic-pragmatic practices of religious congregations thus generate a distinctive cultural environment in which participants continually interpret their personal and collective experience in light of transcendent reality.

The interpretive process is invariably shaped by a congregation's religious tradition—its understanding of the divine, community, and institutions.[17] While generalizations are hazardous, the primary interpretive languages used in congregations are typically the narrative, prophetic, and ethical discourses of distinct religious traditions. Moreover, the interpretive process typically informs "the heart" as well as "the mind" of participants by evoking sentiments of awe, gratitude, humility, courage, and hope. At the same time, the process transmits cognitive understandings of the nature of persons, the character of goodness and evil, the conditions and prospects for human society, the nature of God or ultimate reality. In short, religious congregations are public meeting spaces where participants engage in pragmatic and symbolic practices that enable them to interpret their individual and collective experience in the light of what philosopher Charles Taylor terms an "horizon of strong evaluation."[18]

How do the interpretive practices inform the self-understanding of religious citizens as bearers of public values? They do so, I would suggest, by fostering a fundamental self-understanding of persons as participants.[19] Note that the idea of "participation" has a dual meaning: "the *act* of participating"; and "the *state* of being related to a larger whole."[20] It refers both to what members of congregations *do* and to who they *are*.

This dual meaning is perhaps best illustrated by the most defining activity of congregations—public worship. In worship congregants literally "take part" in a symbol-laden drama. Each member is asked to exercise his or her abilities to play a part that blends memory, movement, emotion, internal reflection, vocal expression, corporate ritual, and spontaneity. The purpose of this "taking part" is not merely to render a formal performance of the drama as has been done in the past. It is to make the drama "come alive" as a formative encounter of others and Other.

What I especially want to note in this general description is that each member's "taking part" is possible because it occurs in relation to larger wholes: other members, trained leaders, the memory of those who have gone before, or those gathered in other places. Each participant's creative part-taking is partially constitutive of the larger wholes. But equally, those larger wholes are partially constitutive of the person taking part. Such persons do not experience themselves simply as self-interested individuals. The fundamental self-understanding cultivated through religious practices is that of human beings interacting as parts of larger wholes; enabled and impaired by the conditions of the participation; subjects who interpret their individual and collective experience in light of the transcendent.[21]

If this is something of how religious congregations influence persons as bearers of values, is it possible to generalize across the enormous variation in faith communities about the values *per se* that are cultivated in religious practices? I suggest there are three fundamental values widely transmitted in and through religious congregations; I will term them membership, contribution, and transformative interaction.

Membership is a fundamental value transmitted through religious participation. There are, of course, many kinds of membership, because there are many kinds of communities to which persons belong, and membership in one community may be defined by very different criteria of access and exclusion than membership in another. Nevertheless, as Michael Walzer argues regarding political communities:

> The primary good that we distribute to one another is membership in some human community. And what we do with regard to membership structures all other distributive choices: it determines with whom we make those choices, from whom we require obedience and collect taxes, and to whom we allocate good and services. . . . Admissions and exclusion are at the core of communal interdependence. They suggest the deepest meaning of self-determination. Without them, there could not be *communities of character*, historically stable, ongoing associations of men and women with some special commitment to one another and some special sense of their common life.[22]

These features apply to the membership of religious communities as well. But the practices of religious communities, to a degree that theorists of secularization have found baffling, often cultivate the value of membership in the deeper sense of "belonging." Religious participants may very well not only affiliate with their chosen denomination. They may come to experience a deeper sense of human community through their encounters with others. Moreover, they may experience themselves as belonging to an horizon of strong evaluation disclosed in and through that community, as they encounter not only others but Other.[23]

The value of membership is fundamental in the sense that it not only designates what individuals seek to acquire for themselves, but who they are and how they value themselves in relation to others. In this self-understanding, persons "*are* parts of more inclusive wholes, and in the condition of interdependence with them. This is the case of ourselves as members of families and as professional persons in institutions; is the case of the institutions and communities in which we participate as they are interrelated to other institutions and communities; it is the case of our species within the ecosphere we inhabit."[24]

Furthermore, the value of membership is fundamental in that it situates persons in relation to the prior conditions that both enable and impair their capacities to act and contribute. Again, in this self-understanding, "we *are* sustained and impaired by other persons, by the social institutions of which we are a part, by the vitality or poverty of our culture, and by the ordering of the natural world. Our individual autonomy, the extent to which we can be self-legislating, *is* of limited scope. Both our powers as participants and the issues of how to use those powers *are* framed in large measure by our contemporary interdependence."[25]

When the prior conditions of persons-as-participants are severely limited—for example, when women are denied leadership positions—they are impaired from developing their full capacities and their communities are deprived of their full contributions. Conversely, when persons-as-participants are situated in strongly enabling conditions, otherwise disadvantaged groups are able to develop participatory skills and capacities that defy their subordinated status in the dominant society.[26] It was no coincidence that civil rights marches often began with preaching, singing, and praying in black churches, where African-Americans who suffered racial degradation enacted and experienced their equality before God in order to defy the racist practices of the dominant society. Thus, congregations are public places where men and women learn to value membership and belonging as part of who they *are* and what they *do*.

Secondly, religious congregations widely transmit the value of *contribution*. Religious congregants typically do not understand themselves to be merely the "products" of their churches, synagogues or mosques. Participants ". . . are not mere spectators, nor do they simply react. . . . They have capacities for innovation, intervention, and intentional action that do affect courses of events and states of affairs."[27] This crucial feature of religious participation is deeply rooted in the American constitutional separation of church and state. In the world of voluntary associations, individuals must commit and recommit themselves to sustain their membership in religious and other organizations. And as religious congregations constantly adapt to their changing social environments, their survival and flourishing depends, quite literally, on their ability to inspire the contributive motivation and capacity of members through vibrant interpretive practices. Thus, as men and women encounter others and Other in symbolic-pragmatic activities, they are often transmitting the fundamental value of contribution. And, as with membership, this value is not simply a good to be acquired. It is a good that informs who people *are* in their relation to one another. Persons-as-participants have a fundamental self-understanding that they help to sustain, and to reform, the larger wholes to which they belong by virtue of their contributions.

Finally, a third value is widely cultivated in religious congregations that I term transformative interaction. As persons experience the formative values of belonging and contributing, a dynamic process of interaction is taking place that itself alters the self-understanding of participants. Alterations may be predictable or unexpected; formulaic or iconoclastic, gradual or dramatic; gratifying or painful. In any case, the claim I am proposing is that religious participation entails patterns of interaction which may enlarge individual and collective self-understanding, and that such alteration is itself a fundamental value being transmitted through religious practices.[28]

One kind of transformative interaction occurs as men and women experience the transcendent afresh in their encounters. As the horizon of strong evaluation is encountered once again, whether in the symbolic activity of worship or the pragmatic activity of building a house, persons-as-participants recognize or remember themselves to be situated differently. They recognize or remember that they are not only members of an organization, but persons who belong to God's covenant; not only individual actors, but responsible actors who contribute or fail to contribute to a moral community; not only individuals who act on self-interest, but subjects whose self-interest is enlarged by virtue of being connected to the well-being of others. As sociologist Nancy Ammerman affirms, "Congregations are not just places to be reminded of what one ought to do. They are spaces where 'ought' is put into cosmic perspective. . . . We expect to meet God—at least on occasion—when we go to church or synagogue or mosque."[29]

Another kind of transformative interaction occurs when religious participants encounter their "nearby neighbors" in ways that allow interpersonal recognition to occur. In this alteration, the perception of nearby neighbors shifts from the "general other" to the "particular other."[30] The isolation of nominal or instrumental affiliation changes into communities that develop a narrative of shared suffering, purpose and hope.

Still a third kind of transformative interaction occurs as congregants purposefully act to encounter their "far-away neighbors." Neighbors may be "far-away" ideologically, geographically, racially, or socio-economically.[31] When persons-as-participants engage in encounters with those who they understand to be radically other—perhaps not even full members of the human community—they may enlarge their capacities to value far-away neighbors as equals and fellow members of the moral and political community. In such transformative interactions, the primary alteration does not reside in far-away neighbors, that is, in changing their character or their behavior, as is assumed in the framework of "welfare reform." It resides primarily in participants themselves who undergo an enlargement of their horizon of strong evaluation as it expands to include persons and groups who deserve equal regard as members of one's moral community. It is this practical enlargement in the self-understanding of diverse citizens that is the spiritual condition for the renewal of democracy and advancing a system of just social provision for all citizens. As Theda Skocpol argues so persuasively in Chapter One of this volume, the historic contribution of religious and secular voluntary associations has been to cultivate precisely this transformative enlargement of persons from isolated to connected citizens who understand themselves as parts of larger civic communities and movements bridging the boundaries of region, class, and even race.

Without denying their immense variations, I thus wish to propose that religious congregations merit careful attention and study in and of themselves, because their practices widely influence who citizens are as bearers of values and the kinds of values they bear as they engage in different organizations. Congregations widely cultivate a fundamental self-understanding of persons-as-participants-religious citizens who understand themselves to be interacting as parts of larger wholes; enabled and impaired by the conditions of their membership; subjects who continually interpret their individual and collective experiences as they undergo interactions that can alter and even transform their self-understanding. In the patterns and process of participation, the substantive values widely transmitted—membership, contribution and transformative interaction—are fundamental because they are not merely goods to be acquired; they are resources that inform the kinds of participants they are, how they value their relation as parts to larger wholes, and therefore what kinds of actions they are willing to undertake.

Religious Values and Political Justice

It might seem logical at this point to turn to the debate over welfare and social provision, and to demonstrate how religious values directly apply to it. However, this direct application leads to conceptual confusion and a practical misuse of religious values. It invites the conceptual confusion of asserting public religious values as politically normative claims. In contrast to private preferences that assert no moral obligations between individuals, religious values are genuinely public. They inform who persons are as value bearers, and they inform the kinds of values by which such persons orient themselves. Furthermore, they are public to the degree that persons exercising them do so not just in religious organizations but in the other organizations where they participate as well. However, while belonging to what John Rawls terms the background culture, religious values do not exercise direct authority in the political culture.[32] In the political arena, all citizens must be accorded equal regard, and none may privilege their particular religious doctrine of the values that constitute political justice. The values of political justice, therefore, must be articulated independently and in a manner accessible to all citizens—those who share one's religion, practice a different faith, or derive their values from nonreligious sources altogether.

Direct application of religious values to politics furthers a dangerous misunderstanding of the authority moral claims exercise in complex policy debates. Moral values are necessary, indeed inescapable, for policy deliberations to occur; but they are neither sufficient nor does their authority trump other forms of authority. As Charles Curran has argued, public ethical discourse requires multiple levels of authority: a fundamental perspective on human flourishing; a second level concerning the nature of persons, their dispositions, virtues and capabilities; a third level identifying the relevant norms and principles for making decisions; and a fourth level that combines available knowledge and prudential judgement in identifying the best course of action amidst the inevitable limitations and trade-offs of human decision making.[33] Attempts to directly relate religious values to policy options almost invariably collapse these levels of ethical discourse, and in so doing invest particular norms, factual analysis, or prudential judgements with the full authority of a fundamental religious vision. The politicization of religion runs the danger of betraying religious values and prophetic vision; the sacralization of politics runs the danger of eroding the civility and sustainability of democratic deliberation over imperfect solutions and limited aims. Thus, while religion generates genuinely public values for the reasons I have argued, those values must be mediated by more accessible conceptions of justice to properly inform democratic politics.

Justice as Participation

Because persons are participants, they require "justice as participation." Moral theologian David Hollenbach finds this conception in the Catholic bishops' pastoral letter on the American economy, *Economic Justice for All*. To explicate it, Hollenbach does not consider the problem that, at the level of parishes and congregations, many religious citizens move between the irreconcilable moral frameworks of communitarian religious values of dignity and solidarity on the one hand, and, on the other, an entitlement view of justice devoted to personal liberty and a minimal state.[34] Instead he contrasts the bishops' moral and political vision with the egalitarian theories of John Rawls and Michael Walzer. In Rawls's justice-as-fairness, he finds "a vision of a tolerant society that respects freedom and wants to aid those in need as long as this aid is compatible with the freedom of people to disagree about their personal definition of happiness." From the bishops' perspective, however, justice-as-fairness is not enough, and thus Hollenbach turns to Walzer's communitarian view of justice for a second point of comparison.

Walzer, too, wants to respect differences. But his definition of the differences that count is quite different from Rawls's. Walzer knows that people do not achieve happiness or full lives apart from friendships, kinship, and many other particular nonuniversal relationships. But note: for Walzer, *relationship* is key. Who is in positive relationship with me determines to whom I have certain obligations of justice. And the *kind* of obligation I have depends on the *kind* of relationship it is: political, familial, economic, ecclesial, and so forth. The key to Walzer's argument about the unity among different spheres of justice is his concept of membership.[35]

Membership for Walzer redefines how we think about justice. Fairness is not simply a matter of what kind of good a community distributes and the size of the portions each receives. "More basic than arguments about the relative portions is the one about who should be at the table in the first place. . . . In short, who is a member of the club to which the standard of justice is to apply?" This, according to Hollenbach, is the fundamental issue at stake in justice as participation.

> To be a person is to be a member of society, active within it in many ways through diverse sets of relationships. The key question that the bishops would place on the national agenda rests on the premise that the meaning of justice rises from this link between personhood and social participation. "'*Basis justice' [state the bishops] demands the establishment of minimum levels of participation in the life of the human community for all persons.* The ultimate injustice is for a person or group to be actively treated or passively abandoned as if they were nonmembers of the human race."[36]

Accordingly, as religious persons come to understand themselves as participants, their thick religious values may be articulated in the political arena as a vision of justice as participation. Such justice is guided by three related principles. Since *membership* in democratic polity is the fundamental good of persons-as-participants, the *distributive principle* requires that all citizens be provided with sufficient resources and opportunities to develop their capabilities to function well as contributing members in family, work, and civic life. What we must distribute to one another is more than purely material resources such as minimal income or food stamps. It includes participatory opportunities such as quality education, safe neighborhoods, and work opportunities. The distributive requirement of just participation thus goes beyond a *minimal floor* of resources and opportunities provided by a "social safety net." It rises to a level of resources and opportunities sufficient for all persons to develop their capabilities to function well as participants.[37]

Since persons are participants who sustain and reform the larger wholes to which they belong by their contributions, the *contributive principle* of just participation requires that all persons function by contributing to their civic-political community. The contributive principle applies to all able-bodied members of society by requiring them to meet common obligations such as obeying the law, gaining an education, and supporting their dependent children. Because of the prior obligation to ensure all persons sufficient resources and opportunities, greater contributions are required of those who are able, and the range of acceptable inequality will be limited accordingly.

Finally, the *transformative principle* recognizes that persons and institutions are continually in danger of contracting and excluding persons and groups, thereby perpetuating the fundamental injustice of rending them nonpersons in the democratic community. Persons as participants, therefore, bear a special and preferential obligation to recognize those who are in danger of being excluded and to seek ways to enlarge their genuine social and economic participation.

What We Owe One Another

How does this moral perspective enable us to consider what we owe one another as citizens of American democracy? In this section I illustrate justice as participation by applying it to the welfare reform debate. From this perspective, I describe how three influential policy scholars have each contested public values at the heart of the debate, evaluate how they did so, and suggest how these values should be reformulated to move us beyond the welfare reform framework to a broader debate over social provision. Two of the values are stated in the title of the 1996 legislation—"personal responsibility" and "work opportunity." To these I add a third, social solidarity, since future deliberations about what we owe one another in the vast *pluribus* of our differences requires the moral *unum* of "we the people."

Work Opportunity. Americans believe in "work opportunity"—both words together, not one or the other. When there is no opportunity, we do not require work. When there is not a willingness to work, we do not feel obligated to provide opportunity. As Judith Shklar states:

> During the Great Depression the unemployed workers of America still regarded both their lack of income and their need to rely on some form of assistance as a shameful loss of independence and beneath the dignity of a citizen. By now unemployment is recognized as a social misfortune rather than a disgrace, but long-term welfare dependence is not seen in that light at all. To be on welfare is to lose one's independence and to be treated as less than a full member of society. In effect, the people who belong to the underclass are not quite citizens.[38]

The contest over what we mean by work opportunity, and whether its moral obligations are being met in real circumstances, has long been at the heart of the welfare debate. And few have been more probing in their analysis of work and welfare than Francis Fox Piven and Richard Cloward. In their influential 1971 book *Regulating the Poor,* Piven and Cloward argue the welfare system regulates the poor in the interests of elites. Starting with the Great Depression, elites have been willing to expand social programs and benefits in times of high unemployment and unrest to maintain social stability. However, this stabilization function invariably gives way to a work enforcement function in subsequent periods. During episodes of welfare reform, political and economic elites tighten social welfare regulations, reduce rolls, and curb benefits. While couched in high moral purpose, the work enforcement cycle actually functions to serve elite interests by curbing public spending, expanding use of private sector contractors, enlarging the labor pool for undesirable jobs, restraining wage growth, and reinforcing a Victorian doctrine of work as intrinsically noble. According to Piven and Cloward, therefore, the welfare system serves the "work opportunity" interests of the privileged, not the poor. Thus, in hard times the welfare system functions to silence social unrest and political demands for change. In good times it functions to force relatively powerless and disadvantaged citizens to chose between the hardship of working poverty and the humiliation of welfare poverty. Those who remain "on the dole" must endure a social standing "so degrading and punitive as to instill in the laboring masses a fear of the fate that awaits them should they relax into beggary and pauperism. To demean and punish those who do not work is to exalt by contrast even the meanest labor at the meanest wages."[39] In other words, welfare advances the "work opportunity" interests of the powerful, not the poor.

How are we to assess this critical view of work opportunity? From the standpoint of justice as participation, it has strong validity in several respects. As participants, all persons are impaired and enabled by the prior conditions of the larger wholes of which they are parts. Descriptively as well as morally, therefore, it is invalid to separate "work" and "opportunity," and to implement policies that mandate the first but do not assure the second. This, I would argue, is precisely what occurred in the 1996 welfare legislation.[40] The Personal Responsibility and Work Opportunity Act terminated the nation's 61-year-old federal entitlement to welfare, replacing it with Temporary Assistance to Needy Families. Through block grants for states to pursue their own initiatives, TANF enforced child support; required most able-bodied adults to undertake work activity within a maximum of two years; and imposed a life-time limit for federally-funded assistance of five years. But under TANF there were neither federal nor mandatory state guarantees to provide work to persons leaving public assistance who could not find a private sector job. Nor were there guarantees that working would enable parents to support families above the poverty line. As Mary Jo Bane discusses in Chapter Twelve, welfare reform has turned many welfare poor into working poor.[41]

Moreover, justice as participation reformulates Piven and Cloward's critique of work opportunity beyond the welfare framework. Its distributive principle has priority over the other two guiding principles. It stipulates that the necessary conditions enabling persons to participate be met first, so they are able to contribute responsibly and to enlarge spheres of participation with those who are excluded. Specifically, when the opportunity to work is assured to disadvantaged citizens (the distributive principle), then working may be fairly required of them (the contributive principle). While asserting the first, it is the contributive requirement that Piven and Cloward fail to address. Due to deficiencies in their moral framework, they view work almost exclusively as exploited paid labor producing surplus wealth for managing and governing elites. While this assessment all too often has validity, nevertheless work holds deeply positive meanings for most Americans. It provides a means for self-realization, a venue for social relations, the material resources to meet physical and emotional needs, resources to exercise a voice in politics and culture, and opportunities to contribute to human society.[42] All these valences inform the value of work as it is understood among the diverse citizens of American democracy. When opportunity is assured, work is a condition for our being citizens in good standing.

What do we owe one another regarding work opportunity? For justice as participation, we expect and require able-bodied citizens to work to contribute to the larger wholes of family and community by working. And because meeting this obligation depends on the prior obligation of opportunity, we owe one another the guaranteed right to earn a living. How we specify and enforce this right is an open-ended question. What cannot be left open is that citizens in a just democracy provide one another the right to earn a living as the condition of their participation. As Shklar writes: "It is not a right to self-respect, but a right not to be deprived of one's standing as a citizen that is at stake here. And the minimal political obligation must be the creation of paying jobs geographically close to the unemployed and offering them a legally set minimum wage and chance to advance."[43]

Personal Responsibility. Not surprisingly, personal responsibility is firmly lodged in the 1996 welfare legislation. This has long been one of the central tenets of the American moral compact, as Hugo Helco observes: "The overwhelming preference [among Americans] is for neither indiscriminate help nor laissez faire approaches that abandon people to their fate but rather an emphasis on policies to *support*—and not replace—people's taking responsibility for themselves and for those dependent upon them."[44]

When the over-stated hopes of the War on Poverty gave way to stagflation and welfare conundrums in the 1970s and 1980s, personal responsibility eclipsed the Great Society as the dominant motif in the welfare debate. And few were more influential in contesting its meaning in the welfare debate than Charles Murray.

Murray's 1984 book, *Losing Ground,* came to be regarded as the bible of the Reagan Administration. The book, copies of which sat on the desk of numerous public officials, provided the rationale for social welfare retrenchment. Burgeoning social welfare spending, according to Murray, had been more than ineffective in reducing net poverty; it was the primary cause of chronic poverty and welfare dependence. Social engineers had waged war on poverty, but they generated a system of perverse incentives and unintended consequences. Welfare programs, rather than helping the poor out of poverty, rewarded them for staying in it, and thereby fostered social behaviors of nonwork, out-of-wedlock births, dropping out of school, and crime. If the welfare system was causing these trends, curbing them called for nothing less than "scrapping the entire federal welfare and income-support structure for working-aged persons, including AFDC, Medicaid, Food Stamps. . . . It would leave the working-aged person with no recourse whatsoever except the job market, family members, friends, and public or private locally funded services."[45] It is important to recognize that Murray's attack on welfare became the bible of neo-conservatives because it argued the case on both empirical *and* moral grounds; central to both was Murray's understanding of personal responsibility. How then did he contest this public value, and how should it be reformulated beyond welfare reform?

I have argued that persons are participants-subjects profoundly enabled and impaired by the prior wholes of which they are parts. In sharp contrast Murray posits human beings to be atomistic individuals unencumbered by race, gender or social environment; and this premise undergirds both his social science and moral reasoning. The premise that all persons are essentially the same, namely rational individuals acting to maximize utilities of income and social status, allows Murray to undertake a purportedly objective social scientific inquiry. He claims to objectively demonstrate that social welfare spending caused the social deviance of those who are "black and poor," while at the same time disavowing racial and class bias.[46] Morally, if there is blame to be assigned, Murray argues it should go to the social engineers who built the welfare system and offered incentives for individuals to engage in socially destructive behaviors.

The atomistic view of human nature takes on fuller form when Murray moves from supposedly objective empirical analysis to policy prescriptions. While all persons are rational utility maximizers, human nature has two fundamentally different forms—what Murray calls "public man" and "private man." "Public man" is a self-interested actor who forms factions to use the power of government. Invariably, government welfare programs yield net harm, because they use state power to interject incentives that distort the free exercise of personal responsibility. In contrast, "private man" ideally pursues self-interest under the conditions of the pristine market where each individual is rewarded or penalized on the basis of his contributions. The private market thus performs a quasi-redemptive function, cultivating what Murray calls "man-as-he-would-be-if-he-realized-his-essential-nature"—a good society in which personal responsibility governs each person's actions and determines his or her life outcomes. Such a society cannot assure the full participation of all citizens, and it should not. "In our social triage, the decision is left up to the patient. . . . The patient always has the right to fail. Society always has the right to let him."[47]

This portrait of a second influential policy scholar illustrates how public policy debates are about how we construct a useable past and imagine a desirable future. Embedded in each of these constructs are fundamental beliefs regarding human nature, society and justice. Moreover, this portrait illustrates the high stakes of the contest we are waging. Murray and other contestants are not merely appealing to fixed public values and norms such as "personal responsibility." They are battling to control the meaning and practical authority of shared public values by locating them in a particular horizon of strong evaluation. Ironically, by anchoring personal responsibility in a libertarian, anti-state horizon, Murray provided a logical justification for moral irresponsibility among democratic citizens. "And so," writes Michael Walzer, "an insidious myth is born which holds that the remaining exclusions are no longer unjust, that they are instead the unexpected product of justice itself. Excluded men and women get what they deserve, or what they have chosen, or they are victims of bad luck; no one else is responsible for their fate."[48]

Despite this flawed rationale for public indifference, personal responsibility can neither be ignored or jettisoned. Deeply embedded in American political culture, it must be contested and reformulated in a different horizon, one consistent with other deeply held values. Otherwise, personal responsibility will continue to be deployed in the framework of welfare reform, where it focuses on disadvantaged men and women—the so-called underclass—rather than helping us to understand what we all owe one another as democratic citizens. Justice as participation does so by taking into account the social conditions and relationships that enable persons to develop their capacities to respond as members of a moral community. Just as work cannot be expected without the right to earn a living, so personal responsibility depends on distributive conditions of just opportunity, and transformative social interactions that enable marginalized persons and groups to participate in the economic and social life of their communities. Because justice as participation requires distributive and transformative responsibilities of citizens, all of us are expected to adhere to norms of responsibility, but not equally.

Recast as justice as participation, personal responsibility moves from a welfare framework and informs a debate over social provision in two important respects. First, it challenges and undermines the deep-seated moral logic of a two-tier system characterizing American social welfare from its inception with the Social Security Act of 1935.[49] In that system, low-income elderly Americans benefit from substantial, redistributive income transfers and are accorded social respect as full citizens; low-income families with dependent children receive lower, in-kind benefits and are denied social respect as full citizens. Underlying this two-tier system is the moral presumption—often fostered by liberals who fear to "blame the victims"—that some "kinds of persons" cannot be expected to abide by norms of personal responsibility that expected of others. Justice as participation presupposes that all persons are to be regarded as co-participants worthy of distributive justice; and all participants are expected to contribute responsibly to sustaining their families and civic communities. Truly disadvantaged citizens are rightly expected and required to obey the law, stay in school, pursue job training, support and nurture their children, and be involved in community life. Suspending norms of personal responsibility for some is not a refusal to "blame the victims;" it perpetuates a profound pattern of exclusion.[50] And it does great disservice to the vast majority of disadvantaged men and women who know personal responsibility is not a class privilege.

In addition, justice as participation reformulates personal responsibility for social provision beyond the minimalist requirement it exercises in a welfare framework. In that terrain it functions as a simple equality of moral responsibility, a minimal set of requirements beyond which citizens are free to maximize their private interests.[51] Justice as participation requires personal responsibility that is proportional to the privileges and resources citizens have by virtue of their participation in democratic society. The privileged are proportionally obligated to assure that all citizens enjoy the distributive conditions of justice. They are proportionally obligated to act preferentially with those individuals and groups being excluded from community life. How they do so allows for a wide ranging debate about the appropriate standards and most effective institutions. But a society where the privileged ignore their proportional responsibility lacks the moral basis to require personal responsibility of the least advantaged citizens. "[When] a [person] has had a great deal given him on trust, even more will be expected of him."[52]

Social Solidarity. This brings us to the third value—and the thought of a third policy scholar—in this brief reprise of the welfare debate. Social solidarity is the only one not stated in the title of the 1996 welfare law, an omission that is no oversight. In a culture of ethical individualism and growing distrust of government, Americans find it difficult to articulate convictions of social solidarity. Yet they are not absent. They are symbolically expressed in our public rituals, cultivated in communities, and provide an essential moral underpinning for progressive social policy. Our social solidarity constitutes the moral "we" that allows us to ask what we owe one another.

A decade before the 1996 welfare act, thoughtful social observers foresaw the emergence of a new consensus on public values, one that could strengthen social solidarity. The Family Support Act of 1988 was seen as a harbinger of the new consensus. Passed by a Democratic Congress and signed by a conservative president, the act required all states to establish mandatory welfare-to-work programs under Job Opportunities and Basic Skills Training (JOBS). In addition to education and training, JOBS required states to provide welfare recipients with child care subsidies and Medicaid coverage for one year after exiting welfare for employment. The moral underpinning of the family support law was a renewed social contract. Americans would enhance their support to low-income families on welfare; those families, in turn, would be obligated to work and strive for economic independence. The legislation kindled a hope among public policy scholars that they might clarify these mutual and reciprocal responsibilities, and identify policy strategies to promote them in actual practice. David Ellwood was among those who took up the challenge in his influential 1988 book, *Poor Support*.[53]

Ellwood argues that effective social policy must build on and advance our fundamental American values: autonomy of the individual, the virtue of work, primacy of the family, and desire for and sense of community.[54] Above all, however, Ellwood seeks to build on and advance the value of social solidarity. This purpose is reflected in the subtitle of his book: *Poverty in the American Family*. The term "family" is key to the author's moral vision and policy prescriptions. For Ellwood, the term "family" refers to a fundamental social unit, made up of parents or caregivers and their children—yet a social unit that must be understood in its diverse forms and settings. In contrast to Murray, Ellwood thus analyzes a variety of *families*—two-parent, single-parent, and those living in urban ghettos. At the same time, the telling feature of Ellwood's moral vision is his use of this term in the singular—"the American family." In this sense, it refers to the single political and moral community of the nation, a community which has a number of its family social units continuing to live in poverty. "Family", therefore, is a root metaphor for a normative vision with a double reference—to a diversity of sociological units and to a national political-moral community.

This double entendre of family compasses another tension, this between two senses of community. Ellwood's empirical description of families in *Poor Support* portrays *actual communities*—parents and children functioning under the hardships of poverty and social disorganization. On the other hand, the single political-moral entity of the nation represents *an ideal community*—one that, by providing the just conditions that make mutual responsibility genuinely possible, enables families to overcome their poverty. Implicit in this ideal, moreover, is a normative ideal of families as fundamental and indispensable social units whose purposes cannot be assumed by public institutions. Thus, the moral argument in *Poor Support* is formulated not only in terms of the dual reference of "family" but also in terms of the two senses of "community." If the American moral community will live up to its ideal responsibilities, it will enable suffering, at-risk families to live up to their ideal responsibilities as working and nurturing primary communities.[55]

What understanding of justice informs the two spheres of community? It is one of mutual responsibility with guaranteed membership in civic-political community. Mutual responsibility: all able-bodied adults are to be held to reasonable levels of personal responsibility—such as work, caring for dependent children, paying child support—and such contributions must be enforced by effective public policies. Mutual responsibility: an enlarged moral sphere extending to the nation in which "those who play by the rules do not loose the game." Importantly, a defining feature of civic liberal justice is to assign priority to distributive justice, while linking this priority to the claims of contributive justice. States Ellwood: "Ultimately, there ought to be some expectation that people will provide for themselves through work. Such an expectation is fair if (and only if) sufficient supplemental assistance is in place so that people need not work more than is "reasonable" and if the government ensures that last-resort jobs are available for people who have used up their transitional assistance."[56]

In contrast to Murray's pristine marketplace, Ellwood argues that most welfare recipients want to work; and when they do so, most are thrown back onto welfare. What amounts to a heroic challenge for two-parent, middle-income families is a near impossibility for poor families. When the poor play by the rules and leave welfare for work, they find themselves unable to nurture their children out of poverty. To remedy this tragic exclusion, Ellwood proposes to strengthen the family-support structure America provides; and, within that structure, to promote personal responsibility and work. Specifically, he advocates that the failed welfare system be abolished and replaced with a federally-guaranteed program of transitional assistance for needy families requiring able-bodied adults to work after two years. A new structure of opportunity would advance the public values of security, responsibility, family, and social solidarity.

According to justice as participation, Ellwood's civic liberalism admirably seeks to advance social solidarity. It does so by rejecting Murray's libertarian distortion of persons as atomistic individuals unaffected by race, class and social conditions; and the neo-Marxist distortion of Piven and Cloward that reduces persons into the products of social and economic structures. It more closely recognizes persons as participants, impaired and enabled by their communities, agents who contribute to larger wholes. One "whole" is our democratic moral community, "*the* American family," where it is a moral scandal to exclude members by providing them "poor support." Another "whole" is our particular families and communities neighborhoods—those headed by single parents balancing work and nurture of children; others headed by two parents who also endeavor to balance work, family and community; and still others locked in urban ghettos where these responsibilities become extraordinarily difficult to sustain. As participants we are all civically and politically situated, impaired and enabled by the wholes to which we belong. What we owe one another, therefore, is the distributive justice that enables all families to participate economically and socially and, as well, the contributive justice by which citizens sustain and change their communities in proportion to their resources and privilege.

While morally compelling, Ellwood's civic liberalism proved to be unduly optimistic. The welfare reform legislation written in the first Clinton Administration took seriously the distributive justice requirement of strengthening family support and assuring work opportunity; in turn, it proposed to strengthen the contributive requirement that welfare recipients would exit within two years for available jobs. However, following the 1994 elections, President Clinton's political promise to "end welfare as we know it" was torn from its civic liberal moorings. With minor exceptions, the revised legislation mandated greater personal responsibility in the form of paid work, but failed to mandate the structures needed to guarantee work and to guarantee those who work will not be poor.[57] In other words, the 1996 welfare act sought to advance work but not the right to earn a living, the responsibility of the poor but not the proportionally greater responsibility of the privileged. The Personal Responsibility and Work Opportunity Act of 1996 was lacking social solidarity.

Communities of Moral Dialogue

Public values are never a fixed overlapping consensus. In a democratic society they are being contested continually. Proponents endeavor to claim our shared values by defining their meaning and moral logic according to their understanding of who we are as persons and citizens, and thus what we owe one another. Moreover, the contest is waged in many arenas. The state is the final guarantor of distributive justice; all citizens are proportionally responsible for contributive justice; and nonprofit organizations, religious and secular, are probably the most dynamic agents of transformative interactions. Yet all these dimensions are being contested in the practices of religious communities where citizens gather to interpret their individual and collective experiences in light of the transcendent.

Accordingly, I have proposed that we understand religious congregations more accurately as public places where men and women engage in very particular practices that inform the kinds of persons they are and the values they bring to their varied roles. Through these practices, I have suggested that persons widely understand themselves neither as atomistic individuals nor social products but as participants. As participants, our self-interest is informed by the desire to contribute what we are uniquely able to sustain and to alter the larger wholes of which we are parts. We are enabled to do so by the prior conditions that permit us to develop and flourish, or impair us from doing so. And our participation continually requires the enlarging of the interpretive horizons in which we recognize ourselves to be in relationship with others and thus able to imagine what we owe one another.

In proposing this normative account, I raised several cautions. Though public, our religious values do not directly provide political norms of justice. They must be articulated in corresponding views of justice, appropriate for deliberation among diverse citizens each of whom is due equal regard, and they must be tested in the practical contest over public values and policies. Justice as participation is one such perspective. I have argued that it enables us to reformulate the core public values of work opportunity, personal responsibility, and social solidarity beyond the framework of welfare reform. We owe one another more than we have delivered: the obligation to work *and* the guaranteed right to earn a living; the obligation of the disadvantaged to contribute to their families and communities *and* the far greater responsibility of the prosperous to assure just participation. In the language of the 1996 welfare bill: personal responsibility and work opportunity, but *also* the social solidarity to engage with those who are being excluded.

What I have not argued is that religious communities equally inform the values of their members, nor that all religious values effectively promote justice as participation. Sectarian religious communities may very well reject my argument that religious values obligate men and women to work for the participation of all citizens in democracy society. Assimilated religious communities may lack the capacity and inclination to transmit fundamental religious values that inform civic engagement. I believe, however, that many congregations have the capacity to be communities of moral dialogue where members articulate their deepest religious values in word and deed, enlarge their solidarity with neighbors near and far, and find the moral resources to contest what we owe one another.

Notes

1. See Frances Fox Piven and Richard Cloward, *Regulating the Poor: The Functions of Public Welfare*, updated edition (New York: Vintage Books, 1993), pp. 395ff.

2. For a discussion of public concepts as contested, see Jane Mansbridge, "On the Contested Nature of the Public Good," in Walter W. Powell and Elisabeth S. Clemens, eds., *Private Action and the Public Good* (New Haven: Yale University Press, 1998), pp. 3–19.

3. Robert Bellah et al., *Habits of the Heart: Individualism and Commitment in American Life* (Berkeley: University of California Press, 1985), pp. 333–36.

4. See Robert H. Frank, *Luxury Fever: Why Money Fails to Satisfy in an Era of Excess* (New York: The Free Press, 1999).

5. See Michael Sandel, *Democracy's Discontent: America in Search of a Public Philosophy* (Cambridge, MA: Belknap Press, 1996).

6. Robert Bellah, "Is There a Common American Culture?" *Journal of the American Academy of Religion* 661(3) (Fall 1998): 622.

7. See, for example, Jennifer Hochschild's probing study, *Facing Up to the American Dream: Race, Class and the Soul of the Nation* (Princeton: Princeton University Press, 1996).

8. See Amartya Sen, *Development as Freedom* (New York: Alfred A. Knopf, 1999), pp. 54–86.

9. For example, Deuteronomy 24:19: "When you reap the harvest in our field and forget a swathe, do not go back to pick it up; it shall be left for the alien, the orphan, and the widow, in order that the Lord your God may bless you in all that your undertake."

10. For an insightful analysis of the trivialization of religious belief, see Stephen L. Carter, *The Culture of Disbelief: How American Law and Politics Trivialize Religious Devotion* (New York: Basic Books, 1993).

11. For a more positive interpretation of individualism, in a culture of spiritual questing, see Wade Clark Roof, *Spiritual Marketplace: Baby Boomers and the Remaking of American Religion* (Princeton: Princeton University Press, 1999), pp. 145–52.

12. See Robert Wuthnow, *Loose Connections: Joining Together in America's Fragmented Communities* (Cambridge: Harvard University Press, 1998).

13. John McCarthy and Jim Castelli, "Religion-Sponsored Social Service Providers: The Not-So-Independent Sector," (The Aspen Institute, Working Paper Series, 1997), p. 11.

14. Mark Chaves, "The Religious Ethic and the Spirit of Nonprofit Entrepreneurship," in Walter Powell and Elisabeth Clemens, eds., *Private Action and the Public Good* (New Haven: Yale University Press, 1998), p. 48.

15. For a valuable discussion of this paradigm in the sociology of congregations, see Martin E. Marty, "Public and Private: Congregation as Meeting Place," in James P. Wind and James W. Lewis, eds., *American Congregations, Volume 2: New Perspectives in the Study of Congregations* (Chicago: University of Chicago Press, 1994), pp. 133–66.

16. Millard Fuller, Founder and President of Habitat for Humanity, has written a book titled, *The Theology of the Hammer* (Macon, Georgia: Smyth and Helwys Publishing, Inc., 1994).

17. There are enormous variations among the 350,000 congregations in the United States, reflecting such variables as religious tradition, geographic region, immediate social ecology, demographic changes, leadership, and many others. Any attempt to construct a typology of religious congregations—much less a general religious or sociological theory—runs a danger of distorting more than it reveals.

18. Charles Taylor, *Sources of the Self: The Making of the Modern Identity* (Cambridge: Harvard University Press, 1993), pp. 25–52.

19. For the normative understanding of persons-as-participants, I am deeply indebted to James M. Gustafson. See, in particular, his *Ethics from a Theocentric Perspective: Ethics and Theology, vol.* 2 (Chicago: University of Chicago Press, 1984), pp. 1–22.

20. *Merriam Webster's Collegiate Dictionary*, tenth edition (Springfield, MA: Merriam-Webster, Inc., 1993), p. 847 (italics added).

21. For a discussion of transcendence as theological metaphor, see Eugene B. Borowitz, *Renewing the Covenant: A Theology for the Postmodern Jew* (New York: The Jewish Publication Society, 1991), pp. 95–117.

22. Michael Walzer, *Spheres of Justice: A Defense of Pluralism and Equality* (New York: Basic Books, 1983), pp. 31, 62.

23. In another context, this general description will be developed in terms of how Christian, Jewish and Muslim religious communities engage in their *particular* interpretive practices in order to transmit the general values I am proposing.

24. Gustafson, *Ethics from a Theocentric Perspective, vol.* 2, pp. 279–80; See also Sen, *Development as Freedom*, pp. 189–203.

25. Gustafson, *Ethics from a Theocentric Perspective, vol.2*, p. 284. This feature is elaborated in Anthony Giddens, *Social Theory and Modern Sociology* (Oxford: Polity Press, 1987).

26. See Sidney Verba et al., *Voice and Equality: Civic Voluntarism in American Politics* (Cambridge: Harvard University Press, 1995).

27. Gustafson, *Ethics in a Theocentric Perspective, Vol.* 2, p. 13.

28. At the risk of overstatement, people voluntarily gather in the public places of their churches, synagogues or mosques, purposefully to encounter others and Other, because they seek to be altered in some way by their encounters of the sacred. See Robert

Wuthnow, *Producing the Sacred: An Essay on Public Religion* (Chicago: University of Illinois Press, 1994), pp. 40–67.

29. Nancy Ammerman, *Congregation and Community* (New Jersey: Rutgers University Press, 1987), p. 368.

30. For an analysis of the ethics of the concrete and generalized other, see Seyla Benhabib, *Situating the Self: Gender, Community and Postmodernism in Contemporary Ethics* (New York: Routledge, 1992), pp. 148–177.

31. Arguably, in a market based culture of achievement, all neighbors may become "far away" as each strives for comparative advantage. Thus, one way the market culture can invade and enervate communities of faith is to prevent men and women from disclosing their suffering to one another, and thus experiencing transformative alteration from isolation to community.

32. "Comprehensive doctrines of all kinds—religious, philosophical, and moral—belong to what we may call the 'background culture' of civil society. This is the culture of the social, not of the political." John Rawls, *Political Liberalism* (New York: Columbia University Press, 1993), p. 14.

33. Charles E. Curran, "Relating Religious-Ethical Inquiry to Economic Policy," in Thomas Gannon, S.J., ed., *The Catholic Challenge to the American Economy* (New York: Macmillian Publishing Co., 1987), p. 48–53.

34. For example, Robert Nozick, *Anarchy, State, and Utopia* (New York: Basic Books, 1974). This conception underlies Charles Murray's view of welfare reform taken up in the next section.

35. David Hollenbach, S.J., "Justice as Participation: Public Moral Discourse and the U.S. Economy," in Charles Reynolds and Ralph Norman, eds., *Community in America: The Challenge of Habits of the Heart* (Berkeley: University of California Press, 1988), p. 225.

36. Ibid., p. 227.

37. See Martha Nussbaum, *Women and Human Development: The Capabilities Approach* (Cambridge: Cambridge University Press, 2000), pp. 12–15, 70–86.

38. Judith N. Shklar, *American Citizenship: The Quest for Inclusion* (Cambridge: Harvard University Press, 1991), p. 22.

39. Piven and Cloward, *Regulating the Poor*, p. 395. Piven and Cloward proposed increasing welfare roles as a strategy for realizing a larger social welfare aim: "to whip out poverty by establishing a guaranteed annual income." Indeed, a wide range of policy scholars shared that goal in the 1960s. Even so, the Nixon Administration's Family Assistance Plan, a quite modest program of guaranteed minimum income, met with defeat in 1972.

40. In the first Clinton Administration, the Work and Responsibility Act of 1994 would have required most healthy adults to work after two years, enforced child support, and held teen mothers more accountable for their personal and family development. In turn, public employment would have been provided when private jobs were not available; and an expanded earned income tax credit and universal health care could have helped low-wage workers to rise out of poverty. See David Ellwood, "Welfare Reform as I Knew It," 23–4; and "Work Responsibility Act of 1994: Detailed Summary" (unpublished document of the Department of Health and Human Services).

41. For a probing analysis of both, see Kathryn Edin and Laura Lein, *Making Ends Meet: How Single Mothers Survive Welfare and Low-Wage Work* (New York: Russell Sage Foundation, 1997).

42. Alan Wolfe, "The Moral Meaning of Work," The American Prospect, (September/October 1997): 82–90.

43. Shklar, *American Citizenship*, pp. 100–01. See also Robert M. Solow, *Work and Welfare* (Princeton: Princeton University Press, 1998); and William Julius Wilson, *When Work Disappears: The World of the New Urban Poor* (New York: Alfred A. Knopf, 1996).

44. Hugo Helco, "The Political Foundations of Antipoverty Policy," in Sheldon H. Danziger and Daniel H. Weinberg, eds., *Fighting Poverty* (Cambridge, MA: Harvard University Press, 1986), p. 330.

45. Charles Murray, *Losing Ground: American Social Policy, 1950–1980* (New York: Basic Books, 1984), p. 228.

46. Ibid., p. 51.

47. Ibid., p. 180.

48. Michael Walzer, "Exclusion, Injustice and Democracy," *Dissent* (Winter 1993): 56–7.

49. Paul Peterson, "An Immodest Proposal," *Daedalus: Journal of the American Academy of Arts and Sciences*, vol. 121 (4) (Fall 1992): 151–74.

50. See Walzer, *Spheres of Justice*, pp. 91–3.

51. This normative position is exemplified in Lawrence Mead, *Beyond Entitlement: The Social Obligations of Citizenship* (New York: The Free Press, 1986).

52. Gospel of Luke 12:48b (*The Jerusalem Bible*).

53. For the sake of full disclosure, David Ellwood was a member of the faculty committee for my doctoral dissertation, "A View from Below: Justice in the American Welfare Reform Debate" (Harvard University, 1997).

54. David T. Ellwood, *Poor Support: Poverty in the American Family* (New York: Basic Books, 1988), p. 16.

55. For a discussion of the dual sense of "community" in political discourse, see Elizabeth Frazer and Nicola Lacey, *The Politics of Community: A Feminist Critique of the Liberal-Communitarian Debate* (Toronto: University of Toronto Press, 1993), pp. 153ff.

56. Ellwood, *Poor Support*, 13.

57. David Ellwood, "Welfare As I Knew It," *The American Prospect*, no. 26 (May-June 1996).

PART THREE

Partnerships, Strategies and Inescapable Dilemmas

CHAPTER 6

Choice or Commonality: Welfare and Schooling After the Welfare State

Martha Minow[1]

Mixing public and private cooperation while pursuing some limits on the partnerships involving religion could promote mutual aid but also preserve the distinct contributions each kind of entity makes to the needs of the poor, of children, and of the larger society.

IT IS PROBABLY INEVITABLE THAT SIMPLE SOLUTIONS to hard problems attract attention and support. Even when the simple solutions fail, they continue to frame debates about what to do next.

Simple solutions dominate two hot policy issues. For the public schools the solution is "choice." For the failure of public assistance, the solution is time limits to get people off of it—and direct those who temporarily need it to private support, notably through religious groups. For these and a variety of ailments in liberal secular society, the solution is more religion and less constitutional worry about separating church and state. Both come together in the idea of vouchers for schooling and welfare. State monies are to be distributed in the form of vouchers allowing individuals to select private providers that are likely to be religious. Such choices permit pluralism and competition. Yet they also risk shrinking the sense of "we" to whom anyone in the country feels connected or responsible.

The turn to vouchers paradoxically reflects both the triumph of the market as the preferred mode for social organization—and resistance to the market

[1]A version of this article was presented as the Brainerd Currie Lecture, Duke Law School, Feb. 18, 1999 and appears at 49 Duke L. J. 493 (1999). I thank Dean Gamm for the invitation and members of the Duke Law School community for engaged questions and comments, as well as members of the Harvard Divinity School Seminar on Democratic Revival, Jenny Mansbridge, Ronald Dworkin, Frank Michelman, Tom Nagel, Avi Soifer, David Wilkins, David Wong, Larry Blum, Rick Weissbourd, and Larry Sager for valuable discussions and comments. Thanks to Andrew Varcoe, Catherine Claypoole, Nina Wang, and Jean Chang for research assistance, and to Laurie Corzett for help in producing the manuscript.

mounted especially by people based in particular religious traditions. After exploring this paradoxical development, I offer both legal and policy analyses which suggest that school vouchers are probably constitutional but also troubling as policy, while welfare vouchers raise more thorny constitutional problems but could be good policy. I then compare vouchers with an array of even more simplistic alternatives for social provision, and conclude that vouchers are better in their capacity to promote pluralism and to foster complex partnerships between private groups and federal and state governments. Vouchers would be even better, however, if they were designed more explicitly to advance pluralism and social cohesion while sustaining and enlarging the settings of public discussions about how this society should meet the needs of poor people and all children. More access to more private options framed by public guarantees would improve voucher proposals in both constitutional and policy terms.

These brief ideas animate my effort: we, in this diverse nation, should resist the temptation to reach for simplicity. We should cultivate appreciation for deliberately complex solutions to honor our many purposes. For example, we should enhance both individual freedom and also social solidarity. No one can make it all alone through life, and no group ever sustains itself without support or respect from the larger polity. We need plural communities, institutions, and structures; we also need the larger public framework devoted to that plurality and to individuals who may, but also may not, be comfortably situated within a caring community. How we respond to seemingly appealing slogans today will affect the very material and spirit we have to address these complex needs in the future.

The Moment

Across the globe, as well as in the United States, we are witnessing a tidal change in the role of governments in providing for basic human needs. Western democracies, including our own, are backing away from the social welfare state created through democratic politics. To produce stable currencies and promising postures in the global economic markets, Canada and countries across Europe are cutting back on social welfare guarantees. Here in the United States, devolution of governmental responsibility to the states is part of a larger withdrawal of federal commitment. The most vivid example is the elimination of the entitlement to economic relief for the poor that the New Deal established. Formerly socialist countries are also cutting back on social guarantees ranging from childcare to police; now, in Russia, for example, you must arrange for your own.

The metaphor and reality of economic markets drive the movement of persons as well as capital. The vivid phrase, "creative destruction," captures both features of the growth and change that markets promote. Markets, or more accurately, the actions people take in their name, rip from their moorings any social, political, or cultural practices that stand in the way of free markets and individual consumer choice. Instead, the new ideal for children's schooling seems to be maximal individual choice for students and parents over what kind and what specific school to select. The dream of a common school, joining children from all classes, races, and backgrounds, is in grave jeopardy.

Magnet and charter schools inside the public system accord even students in the public system choices beyond the neighborhood school. Public schools systems experiment with parental choice of particular school buildings and programs for their children. Public tax credits and vouchers stretch this expanding arena of choice even farther so that even students whose own families lack sufficient resources to opt out of the public system could do so. With legislation for vouchers, scholarships, or tax credits to enable the selection of private schools pending in many states, and lawsuits challenging such plans pending in several states, we are in the midst of a major public revision of state subsidies for choice in the context of schooling.

Booming enrollments in religiously-affiliated private schools demonstrate both disillusionment with public schools and growing desires among many parents to foster the moral, disciplinary, or group identity aspects of their children's education.[1] Although little discussed, the disillusionment with public schools is occurring just about the same time that they have fully taken on the task of educating all children, including those with disabilities and limited English proficiency, and those who are non-citizens, homeless, or migrants. The rush of leaders toward choice proposals both within and beyond public schools may in no small way respond to the ambitious and troubled diversity in public school enrollments. Choice rhetoric also seems to offer ways to cut through public bureaucracies. Here, choice seems the answer for parents and children who feel that they have had no control over what happens in schools. As education becomes ever more central to economic opportunity and job security, increasing parental choice seems a vital way to manage anxieties about children's futures and frustration with sclerotic state and local bureaucracies. As with economic enterprises, the idea goes, competition and consumer sovereignty make change and produce improvement, even at the price of some failures.

Yet, some of the support for "choice" in schooling precisely comes from critics of market values and the secular, competitive world they seem to produce. Large support for vouchers comes from particular religious groups and religious individuals to enlarge the role of religion in the public square. Public schools are castigated for abandoning values and the task of socializing children into a world of obligations, not just self-interest. In the same way, secular social services seem wanting. Religious charity, to some, seems preferable to public welfare for meeting the needs of the poor. Religiously infused arguments against a public welfare program include several strands.

Critics from what are called "faith-based communities"[2] argue that bureaucratic public programs fail to respect the individuality of people in need. They fail to afford a moral frame or encourage responsible behavior. They fail to forge social connections both for those who are most isolated and despised and those who are relatively comfortable and privileged. Religiously motivated arguments animate the campaigns for vouchers and tax credits to assist parochial school enrollments. Religious values can also be deployed to challenge the encroaching market and commercialization of everyday life. Whatever the tensions among each of the varied strands, they share an assertion that religiously informed viewpoints belong in political debate and in public decision making. That assertion contravenes theories and practices sharply demarking public life from the worlds of religious belief and practice.

At the same time, spokespersons associated with both the right and left wings in American politics urge efforts to strengthen civil society, the institutions, associations, and practices that occupy realms between individuals and the state.

They tell us that we need more than purely liberal relations between individuals and the state, and more than individuals and the market if a vital democracy is to endure. Robert Putnam's work is among the most renowned in such calls for enlarging settings where people engage in mutual aid and mutual recreation apart from either the market or the polity.[3] Both Republican and Democratic leaders have urged greater reliance on nonprofit organizations and community groups to meet the needs of vulnerable and at-risk groups through means other than big government.

Yet this call for more is often coupled with policies of less. Hence, the federal government ends the welfare entitlement and local communities reject levies to maintain or build new schools. This is the context for the voucher movements in both schooling and welfare.

Vouchers seem the perfect meeting ground for both market believers and market critics. In the school context in particular, they also seem to unite suburban middle-class parents with inner city working-class parents who each seek more choice and control over the very different educational options existing for their children. In the welfare context, they unite free market true believers with religious traditionalists. Would vouchers enabling individuals to purchase private religious schooling and social welfare services harmfully blur the boundaries between the public and private spheres? Would they offer more people exits from common life into private sectors divided by religion, race, and/or class? Would increasing activity by religious groups in schooling children and in providing food, shelter, childcare, job-training, counseling, and treatment in necessarily sectarian settings so alter the nation's fabric as to shrink what is public? Would it alienate those who differ from the religious affiliations of growing schools and service providers?

The first response to such questions, as previous contributors in this volume have noted, must be that public and private, secular and religious, already blur and blend across the United States. Private organizations, with religiously affiliated ones prominent among them, already play major roles in the provision of schooling, food, shelter, and social welfare services, as well as health care. Often such private organizations work closely with the state through contracts, reimbursement from public third-party payers, other material assistance, and referrals.

Consider, for example, the roles played by Catholic Charities and Catholic schools especially in urban areas across the country. Local parishes have provided schools and assistance to the poor with no public support (beyond tax exemption) since colonial times. Changing demographic patterns and the policies launched by the second Vatican Council from 1962 to 1965 promoted a deliberate shift in Church-run services and schools. Rather than focus exclusively on serving Catholics, the services and schools were called to respond to the diverse populations in need and to work to advance a human society directly and by modeling human cooperation for the common good.[4] And for many working class people, even many non-Catholics, Catholic schools have afforded avenues for educational advancement, moral development, and order in the midst of urban decay. Public school systems implicitly depend on the existence of Catholic schools to accommodate children otherwise eligible for public schooling, depending upon the particular surges and declines in school-aged enrollments. A recent book argues that Catholic schools actually better foster human cooperation than do the public schools, which were founded in the common school movement for that very purpose. The authors argue that Catholic schools do this job because they are devoted to the purpose of promoting human cooperation for the common human good, and they ground their work in a moral base with experienced teachers, communal organization, and a capacity to engage teachers and students.[5]

In the contexts of child protective services and foster care, the functional and financial ties between religiously based programs and public commitments are even tighter. Catholic agencies receive contracts from municipalities to provide child protective services and foster care, job training and drug counseling services, food pantries and homeless shelters. Catholic hospitals serve Medicare and Medicaid patients. Heads of public departments and agencies regularly rely on programs created and run by Catholic agencies (as well as programs created and run by other religious groups) in order to provide responses to human needs as authorized by their public mandates.

Against this factual backdrop emerge questions that would be better framed in terms of the allocation of responsibilities in a world that mixes public and private, rather than in terms of where to place walls of separation between public and private, church and state. Indeed, most helpful would be ways to conceive of partnerships and coordination to enhance the actual delivery of services, the respect for human individuality and group affiliations summarized by the ideal of pluralism, and an enlargement of intellectual and moral resources to deal with the potentially destructive features of global markets. Perhaps religious groups—and other private groups—can do better at social provision than can public bodies. In the current moment of welfare's demise and chronic urban school crises, however, most notable is the commitment of religious groups to do it at all. That said, experiments with plural views of social provision should not obscure the larger issue of responsibility. What matters is not just who delivers schooling or aid to the destitute, but who is responsible to see that it is done. Religious groups enact one vision of responsibility, but the bankruptcies of so many Catholic schools and agencies give some clue as to why they cannot accept ultimate responsibility. Some form of shared responsibility seems both most practical and most fitting.

We can contrast school and welfare vouchers with simpler alternatives that do not imagine shared responsibility or partnerships joining federal, state, and local governments and public and private bodies.

Simple Alternatives

Consider three starkly stated alternatives for organizing social resources to meet the needs of dependents, whether poor or children:

1) each "community" is responsible for "its own";
2) the largest unit of public authority—typically, the national government—is responsible;
3) no one, or no one outside the immediate family, is responsible.

The first alternative admittedly presents definitional problems: what is a "community" and who constitutes "its own"? A community could be defined in geographic terms, or in terms of social networks, or in terms of an affiliation with a shared religious, ethnic, or ideological experience or commitment. So a society could organize its response to dependents by directing that each municipality is responsible for its dependent residents, or each religious group should fulfill the basic needs for adults and children who are affiliated with the religion, and provide education for the children of co-religionists. There can be a combination of these geographic and sub-group notions, as the Catholic and Mormon Churches pursue through systems of parishes. But even aside from these crucial definitional problems, this alternative reflects two deeply problematic assumptions.

Declaring that each community will take care of its own rests on the two assumptions: a) all comparable communities—whether geographic, religious, ethnic, or otherwise constituted—will perform the same roles toward dependents; and b) there will be no people left out of the pattern—no people who will fall outside the "our own" of some community. As an empirical matter, these assumptions are simply not accurate. Abundant historical examples illustrate failed public efforts to require each community to care for its own.

The English Poor Laws embraced the principle of local responsibility for the poor. The 1662 amendment to these laws not only designed a period of residence as a requirement for receiving assistance, but also directed the return of a newcomer even if he did not apply for assistance.[6] In the American colonies, Plymouth copied the English Poor laws and in 1642 ruled that each town must support its own indigents. Later, Plymouth colony adopted strict residency requirements, and prohibited people from bringing into town anyone liable to become a public charge absent consent from public officials; ship captains were charged with any expenses arising from passengers landing in Plymouth who became needy and also had to return such passengers to their place of origin.[7] Similar rules were adopted elsewhere in New England and in the Northwest Territories in 1795.[8]

One historian notes how growing geographic mobility created difficulties in implementing the traditional principle that each community was responsible for its own poor.[9] Each town relied on a notion of "inhabitancy" rather than residence and used a system of "warning out" individuals lacking inhabitancy to lay the basis for removing them from the town if they became public charges. "The harshness of a warning out system was presumably mitigated by the fact that some town somewhere would have to take in and care for the transient poor; by definition everyone had an inhabitancy somewhere, no matter how many towns from which an individual had been warned out. The problem was that inhabitancy might be virtually undiscoverable, particularly in a situation where there was no incentive for a town to volunteer itself as a poor person's home."[10] Even a person who lived for 20 years in a town could be warned out and sent from her home when she became destitute.

Perhaps in response to such problems during the 18th century, especially in emerging cities, religious and ethnic groups organized charity to support primarily, if not exclusively, their own members. The model of caring for the community's own persisted, but the unit for community here was religious or ethnic or in some cases occupational, rather than secular and governmental. Catholic charities emerged both to fulfill a religious duty and as a form of mutual self-help against a difficult and potentially hostile larger world, consistent with the efforts by other immigrant groups to form social and fraternal mutual aid societies.[11] Catholic hospitals, agencies, and schools paralleled public hospitals, agencies, and schools. Private organizations also worked cooperatively with towns and counties on issues of relief.[12] These religiously based efforts never reached the needs of all members of each group, much less those who lacked sufficiently organized and well-resourced affiliations. By the end of the 19th century, reformers criticized reliance on a system of local charity because it defeated a principle of public responsibility and prevented the achievement of minimum standards.[13]

As public programs developed in the 20th century to meet the needs of indigents grew into partnerships between state and federal governments, so did the efforts by localities and states to set minimum residency requirements as a condition for eligibility. The U.S. Supreme Court in turn set limitations on such residency requirements in the name of the right to travel. In *Shapiro v. Thompson*, the Court rejected a one-year residency requirement imposed by local governments to deter the in-migration of indigents.[14] (Though it is important to note here that abolition of the welfare program itself would have been constitutional.) Similarly, in the 1999 *Saenz v. Roe* decision, the Court rejected California's effort to limit public assistance for new residents to the level the individual would have received in the state of his prior residence.[15]

The U.S. Supreme Court has approved the use of local residency requirements to determine eligibility for public education because they serve each state's interest in assuring that only state residents take advantage of state educational services.[16] The courts have struggled over how to handle the residency issue for children who are homeless.[17] In addition, localities typically have the authority to set the tax rates used to finance public schools, which produces variations in the per-pupil expenditures across communities.[18] This profiles another way for local communities to express their commitment to take care of their own children, but not others.

In contrast, the Court has rejected U.S. citizenship requirements that limit eligibility for certain programs. A plurality of the Supreme Court justices (four out of nine) joined the 1982 controlling opinion in *Plyer v. Doe*, which held that Texas could not deny public education to school-age children who are not citizens or legally admitted aliens.[19] The justices reasoned that the state lacked any rational basis for discriminating on the basis of citizenship status given the children were not to blame for their presence in the United States and given the importance of education to assuring their economic self sufficiency. A federal district court relied on *Plyer* when it considered challenges to Proposition 187, California's voter initiative denying public education to undocumented immigrant children. The court rejected substantial portions of the proposition as unconstitutional and then approved an agreement between the state of California and civil rights groups to drop remaining portions of the suit.[20]

Thus, despite traditional uses of local towns and states as units of the primary responsibility for poor people and local school districts as the measure for educating children, grass-roots advocacy and public officials have marshaled federal statutes and constitutional law to set limits on the power of the localities and states to exclude individuals on the basis of residency or duration of residency. Even though voters periodically revive the model of each community caring for its own, this model conflicts with hard-won and by now settled interpretations of the Constitution's guarantees of equal protection of the laws, due process, and freedom to travel.

The second simple alternative locates responsibility for the poor and for educating youth in the public rather than the private sector, and also pins the ultimate duty on the federal government. This alternative does not require the federal government to create and operate by itself social welfare agencies, schools, food pantries, and the like. It only demands that the federal government and universally applicable national laws set and guarantee the provision. Thus, the federal government can ensure performance of the responsibility for social provision and education through directives, contracts, or cooperative relationships with state and local governments, religious groups, and other private entities.[21] A paradigmatic example here is the federally administered and federal-based entitlement program, Social Security. The recent elimination of an enforceable federal entitlement to public assistance signals rejection of federal responsibility to provide for the poor.

This country, unlike others, has repeatedly rejected federal responsibility for children's education.[22] The federal government does help subsidize public education with specially targeted monies to assist programs for children in poverty and children with special educational needs. The Supreme Court has commanded equal availability of public education where a state has chosen to provide it. Yet the responsibility for education is maintained at the state and local levels with the result of real disparities in expenditure, quality, and opportunity both within and across the states. Some state constitutions do assure public provision of education for children, and school finance litigation over the past several decades has produced court orders specifying in some states a right to an effective or adequate education. Given the reliance of such suits on particular state constitutional commitments, however, no uniformity has emerged across the nation. For both basic financial support and schooling, the democratic and constitutional processes in the country repeatedly reject social provision at a national level as unworkable and undesirable.

The third alternative leaves care for poor people and education for children to the voluntary actions of individuals. If no one provides, there is no public or private norm of judgment to find the results unacceptable, even though observers might find them unfortunate. In the absence of relevant public or private responses, this model is the only resort.

The third alternative may not seem relevant, however, to the context of schooling in industrialized countries like the United States that have adopted compulsory schooling laws. In the United States, each state has adopted compulsory school laws and most state constitutions include a provision assuring children some kind of access to basic education. Therefore, by law, the polity has designated public responsibility for provision of education at least through high school. The remaining domain of private family responsibility in our system includes parental prerogatives to select private, including religious, schools, subject to the family's ability to pay or obtain scholarships, and parental duties to supervise children's educational experiences, including homework.

Yet there is a respect in which the third alternative could become a salient feature of American education. As schooling moves more into a competitive model either within the public system or across public and private options, parents are given greater responsibility to select the school for their children. As a result, children will become increasingly dependent upon their parents or guardians to exercise informed choices. The quality control for education then will be shifted at least partially from the public sector to individual parents. Where parents or guardians lack ability, motivation, or knowledge to fulfill that function—and leave their children in substandard public school settings—the third model becomes potentially germane.[23] "Choice" could be coupled with communal or federal obligations, but the theory and reality of this option are not the same. In a world of insufficient numbers of quality schools, inadequate information about the stakes and alternatives, and large numbers of people unable to work the choice system, choice means not only choice for some and not others. It means the needs of some children, but not others, will be met, based on their or their parents' abilities.

Advocates of school choice claim that over time, the bad schools themselves will have to close; bad options ultimately will disappear; and competition will favor those schools that deliver better results. It remains to be seen, however, how the system will work out a timely, practical mechanism for identifying and shutting down "failing" schools before their students have lost meaningful chances to receive educations elsewhere.[24] Vouchers may instead make liberty the only value, and in practice, liberty only for some. Vouchers combined with state or federal standards, however, could begin to propel equality of opportunity as well as liberty, quality as well as choice, and central responsibility as a paradoxical correlate of local control.

As this brief discussion indicates, our nation has rightly resisted each of the simple models. We have embraced more complex solutions that combine notions of each community caring for its own, through local government and private activities, with national standards and sometimes national guarantees. The voucher proposals for schooling and for charitable choice at least have the potential to foster combinations of religious and secular providers in a general scheme of social provision. Public dollars can be accompanied by at least some basic public standards to protect against the abandonment of each person and family to be left always to provide for themselves.

This political moment holds rich promise for re-invigorated public conversation about and commitment to meeting human needs as federal governmental commitments decline. Religious and other private groups have always helped to meet basic human needs of people at the economic margins for food and shelter while developing some of the best schools for children. In the current moment of welfare's reform and chronic urban school crises, what is most notable is the commitment of religious groups to stay engaged with social provision. But religious groups cannot fill in the holes of a shredded public safety net; nor can they build the capacity to educate all American children—if we would even want that. Religious provision can never substitute for secular alternatives or by themselves ensure public norms of equality and fairness.

No practical and yet coherent conception of social provision can proceed without facing the further constraints of American law. Most adept at liberty, American law has some experience pressing for equality, and at resolving tensions between the two through both public and private structures of plurality.

Laws

At least one legal constraint sets limits on social provision in the United States. The role of religious organizations and religiously affiliated services must not either amount to a governmental establishment of religion or a burden on individuals' free exercise of religion. The Constitution's First Amendment expresses these joint commitments to ensure no governmental law establishing religion and no governmental law prohibiting the free exercise of religion.

Interpreting the religion clauses requires addressing quite a different world than the one the framers knew. Justice William J. Brennan emphasized in 1963 that the current national "religious composition makes us a vastly more diverse people than were our forefathers. They knew differences chiefly among Protestant sects. Today the Nation is far more heterogeneous religiously. In the face of such profound changes, practices which may have been objectionable to no one in the time of Jefferson and Madison may today be highly offensive to many persons, the deeply devout and the nonbelievers alike."[25] Blatant governmental regulation of religion is unlikely today, yet the complex network of state and federal laws still carry potential for adversely affecting religious exercise and for preferring some religions or religion generally.

Interpreting the religion clauses has proved truly vexing for courts, legislatures, and commentators. Are there two clauses with independent meaning, or should the two clauses be read to modify one another? Restrictions on establishing religion could easily collide with assurances permitting the free exercise of religion. If a state cannot close schools and businesses on Sundays or Good Friday for fear of establishing Christianity as an official or preferred religion, that burdens individuals' abilities to observe their sabbath and their holy days. If the state cannot exempt a synagogue from city historic preservation codes, then public rules may infringe on a religious group's self-government. If a public school denies funding and space to an Islamic student group while granting resources to a stress-reduction meditation group, it prefers one group while burdening another. How should such collisions be treated under the law? Does the ban against establishment guard against government preference for any one religion, or for religion per se, as opposed to the secular? These questions remain open in contemporary jurisprudence, with clues provided only in the particular judgments of the courts, themselves often marked by sharply divided panels of judges. Simple guides, or tests, either fail to answer hard questions or else prove manipulable and unpredictable. Alternatives proposed by individual justices and scholars fail to secure widespread support or decide hard cases.

Predicting the Supreme Court's interpretation of the religion clauses is especially difficult in this moment. Nonetheless, I here engage in prediction about potential challenges to public subsidies for private religious schooling and governmental partnerships with private religious groups in the provision of welfare assistance.

Doctrinal Framework

Despite its common use, the phrase "separation of church and state" actually has no relevance to the task of constitutional interpretation.[26] The phrase does not appear in the Constitution, nor does it well summarize the complex case law implementing the ban against governmental establishment of religion and the guarantee of religious free exercise. The much-battered doctrinal test developed by the Supreme Court to deal with risks of governmental establishment of religion concedes that absolute separation between the state and religious entities is not the goal.[27] *Lemon v. Kurtzman* calls for determining whether the law or governmental action under question 1) has a secular purpose; 2) has primary effects that neither advance nor inhibit religion, and 3) does not excessively entangle the government with religion. Note how this last prong admits that entanglement of some sort is not only permitted, but contemplated. At least five members of the Court think this test should be replaced, and it has not supplied the basis for rejecting a law in over 10 years. The trend, if anything, is toward less stringent demands for separation than *Lemon* implied.[28] For example, in a remarkable decision in 1997, the Court reconsidered and reversed its prior rejection of the use of federal categorical funds to serve on the site of a religious school any children otherwise eligible for federal services.[29]

The Court has not yet, however, rejected the *Lemon* test nor approved an alternative single doctrinal framework. Justice Sandra Day O'Connor has proposed an alternative inquiry into whether the state's action could be viewed objectively as an endorsement of religion.[30] Others emphasize the constitution's purpose in preventing social or political division due to religious differences,[31] or in ensuring governmental neutrality toward religion.[32]

As for free exercise of religion, the Court's trend has been to shield government action that is couched in a general form against challenges that seek to frame such action as a burden on the free exercise rights of minority religious groups. At the same time, a majority on the Court favors loosening up previous restrictions on public funding where religious adherents seek public benefits available to others, in the name of preventing discrimination on the basis of religion. Several Supreme Court justices make central to an Establishment Clause challenge assessment of potential coercion of the individual in the realm of religious belief or practice while others reject this approach.[33]

More probative at this point than any simple verbal formulation of the guiding principles for judgment are the actual actions taken by the Court in recent years. The Court has rejected as unconstitutional schemes that delegate a state function to a religious group. Thus, in *Larkin v. Grendel's Den, Inc.*, the Court struck as unconstitutional a statute granting churches and schools the power to veto the grant of liquor licenses to restaurants within 500 feet of the church or school buildings.[34] In a more tortured opinion in *Board of Education of Kiryas Joel Village School District v. Grumet*, the Court forbade New York from drawing school district lines to encompass only members of a particular religious group.[35]

For years, beyond this no-delegation doctrine, no discernible pattern appeared in the Supreme Court's decisions affecting public financial support for any activities related to private parochial schooling. A particular tangle of cases approves some kinds of tax assistance and reimbursements for parochial school tuition while disapproving others.[36] A scheme that neutrally provides governmental assistance to a broad spectrum of citizens is more acceptable than one that assists only some parents or only parents pursuing sectarian schools.[37] Public support for textbooks used by students regardless of their attendance at public or private schools passed constitutional muster. Public funds may also support transportation of children to parochial schools. Yet a state cannot supplement the salaries of teachers at nonpublic schools to approximate the salaries of public school teachers. Full-time public employees may not provide remedial or accelerated instruction, counseling, testing, and services to students on the site of parochial schools. But public employees may provide remedial instruction and counseling to nonpublic school children on sites away from the nonpublic school.

The Supreme Court inclines toward more leniency, permitting state financial assistance to students in parochial schools. It also emphasizes the significance of the private choice of parents and students that severs any prohibited connection between the public funds and the religious institution. Thus, recently the Court has ruled that, through generally applicable financial aid programs, a state may pay a blind student's tuition at a sectarian theological institution, because the public funds are paid directly to the student who then transmits them to the educational institution of his or her choice.[38] Public provision of a sign language interpreter in a pervasively sectarian school does not violate the Establishment Clause.[39] A state may allow taxpayers to deduct from their state income tax certain expenses incurred in providing nonpublic education for their children, despite objections that this provision had the effect of advancing the sectarian aims of nonpublic schools. Federal funds to assist students with disabilities, students from low-income communities, and students identified as presenting special risks of school failure may be used on the site of religious schools where these monies are distributed through a public agency to the eligible students, regardless of where the students choose to attend school.[40] And monies generally available to support student speech on the campus of public universities must be available to support a religious speech.[41]

Similarly, federal monies generally available to public and private organizations as grants to assist counseling and research in the area of premarital adolescent sexual relations can be obtained by religious organizations. Yet in the case challenging this scheme, *Bowen v. Kendrick*, the Court remanded for a factual finding about the actual uses of the monies, and warned of potential unconstitutionality if the funds assisted "pervasively sectarian" institutions or paid for "specifically religious activity in an otherwise substantially secular setting."

Applications

Recent Supreme Court decisions suggest that government programs allowing public funds to pay for religious school tuition will survive constitutional challenge, while government efforts to share or turn over responsibilities in the welfare area to religious entities may be found constitutionally defective.

School-Choice Programs. Vouchers and other methods designed to direct public funds to expand educational opportunities for children in religious settings include tax deductions, tax breaks on education savings plans, publicly funded scholarships, and vouchers. All of these divert public funds to private schools.[42] The vast majority of private schools are religiously affiliated. Hence, these mechanisms raise potentially impermissible entanglements between religion and the state.

Some recent cases highlight this issue. The Cleveland City School District case arose when the federal district court found the quality of the public schools so poor that it ordered the state to take them over. In response, the state initiated a scholarship program to permit students to attend neighboring public schools and registered private schools.[43] Some 80 percent of the registered private schools for the 1996–97 school year were sectarian; no neighboring public school districts participated. A taxpayer group filed suit alleging that the program violates both federal and state constitutions, and the state court of appeals agreed.[44]

The Ohio Supreme Court, however, ruled that the school voucher program did not violate the Establishment Clause, except where selection criteria gave priority to students whose parents belonged to the religious group supporting the sectarian school.[45] Finding these selection criteria severable from the statutory scheme, the court rejected the remaining federal constitutional challenges, while at the same time ruling that the statute violated the "one subject per statute" requirement in the state constitution. This technical problem was fixed by the legislature in 1999. On August 25, 1999, a federal district court enjoined the voucher program on Establishment Clause grounds. After waves of public concern over halting a school program just as the school year was starting, the district court stayed its order as to already-enrolled students.[46]

The Milwaukee Parental Choice Program, initiated in 1989, was amended in 1995 to allow up to 15 percent of the low-income students in that city's public system to attend private, including sectarian, schools. Those schools must agree to follow guidelines against discrimination and promoting health and safety. Approximately 84 percent of the pupils attending Milwaukee private schools prior to the implementation of the plan attended religious schools. A state trial court enjoined its implementation; the Wisconsin Supreme Court upheld its constitutionality even though religious schools are the likely beneficiary of most of the public funds. When the United States Supreme Court later declined to review this decision, it appeared to signal a green light for such experiments at the state level without giving explicit federal constitutional approval.[47]

The Vermont Supreme Court found a defect in the Chittenden town plan to pay the tuition of resident children to attend a nearby Catholic academy. The Court relied on a state constitutional provision forbidding state support of religious worship.[48]

Given these developments, I predict the courts will assess potential constitutional challenges by looking to the chain of choicemaking. If the actual decision to spend the governmental money—obtained through tax breaks, scholarships, or vouchers—is made by the private individuals, such as parents and students—the public measures can plausibly be understood as enhancing private choices rather than establishing religion through governmental means. Using the *Lemon v. Kurtzman* test, the purpose of promoting parental choice to improve education is secular, the effect arguably is to enhance competition and therefore overall educational quality, and entanglement between church and state can be minimized if funds simply pass from state to parents and then to private schools. Moreover, if this chance for parental choice is afforded to all parents, it avoids the appearance of favoring only some.[49] The legal system comfortably adopts the view that parental choice avoids state action in other contexts. A parental decision to refuse medical treatment for a child who is hospitalized does not trigger public obligations on the hospital to ensure care because the treatment decision is made by the parents.

Indeed, if a state authorizes any school vouchers permitting private election of private schools, the current Court's concern to protect religious adherents against discrimination in public programs probably would lead it to require such programs to extend to religious schools. Otherwise, those parents who would prefer religious schools could plausibly claim a burden on their free exercise of religion, or else a kind of discrimination that might even violate the equal protection clause. Crucial here, though, is the retention of public and nonsectarian schools as alternatives. The very success of parochial schools no doubt has something to do with their ability to select and exclude; their constitutionality depends on the presence of genuine alternatives.[50]

The constitutional challenge most likely to succeed would attack the way in which a voucher plan is carried out rather than its design. If all or most of the vouchers are used to select religious schools, especially if those religious schools are largely or exclusively of one denomination, perhaps the law could be challenged in an "as applied" fashion. Discerning such effects would require a factual finding about the actual operations of the scheme, and yearly monitoring. The Supreme Court has emphasized that "We would be loath to adopt a rule grounding the constitutionality of a facially neutral law on annual reports reciting the extent to which various classes of private citizens claimed benefits under the law."[51] Mere disparities in the numbers of private schools receiving vouchers that are religious and the numbers that are not would not convince at least some members of the Supreme Court that an Establishment Clause problem has arisen. Indeed, a majority of the Court signed onto the view that any unequal effect of a public program assisting private school choice "can fairly be regarded as a rough return for the benefits . . . provided to the state and all taxpayers by parents sending their children to parochial schools."[52] So long as a public, nonreligious option remains available, private schools and assistance to them seem compatible with the Court's emerging treatment of religion; the sheer existence of private religious schools remains itself a constitutionally protected option for parents who choose them.[53]

Absent a successful constitutional challenge, we are left with debates over policy. My own qualms about school vouchers and public funds for private scholarships must be seen to reflect my own strong regret over the dimming fate of the dream of the common school. The common school was supposed to afford children from all walks of life equal opportunities and a shared experience, even if it is a shared experience to regard with unhappiness in later life. The policy of the common school has been followed, as ever, much in the breach. Failures (and perceived failures) of so many public schools to afford genuine chances for education especially in large urban districts make the turn toward competition in the school world a plausible if not urgent public policy development.[54]

Yet, as a purely policy matter, it would be an enormous mistake to imagine that parochial schools, or for that matter, school choice, can solve the problems of schooling for America's children. It is impossible to disentangle the parochial school successes in retaining children from at-risk backgrounds and generating good test scores from the schools' abilities to exclude or expel troublesome students or from the involvement of the parents who select such schools. The faith that competition itself will elevate the quality of all schools has yet to be demonstrated by any system that has adopted charter schools or magnet schools. Increasingly, even those "public" choice options will include schools run under contract by private, and often untested, management. The deep problems of public education in America parallel closely longstanding and complex problems in families, communities, and skewed economic opportunity structures. The immediate consequence of school choice programs most likely leaves the most vulnerable children from the least engaged and put-together families in the worst schools. The solution of school choice—inside public systems or crossing over to private ones—is worth exploring but only as one of many strategies to improve the real opportunities for all children.

"Charitable Choice." The charitable choice provision of the Personal Responsibility and Work Opportunity Reconciliation Act of 1996, otherwise known as the welfare reform, is more vulnerable to a constitutional challenge on Establishment Clause grounds and yet, in my view, less troubling on policy grounds. The provision, known as Section 104, authorizes states to pay religious agencies directly to provide welfare services and to pay vouchers to individual aid recipients. The vouchers are then to be redeemed for services from religious agencies without impairing the religious character of such agencies and without diminishing the religious freedom of the beneficiaries.[55] Indeed, charitable choice obliges any state that chooses it to involve independent-sector providers of social services. These in turn are to include religious providers, and the state must not interfere with the religious expression and identity of the providers. Congress extended the provision to Head Start and other federal programs.[56]

The provision was hardly discussed in Congress or in public and media debates that were occupied with other provisions of the welfare reform.[57] The charitable choice element was sponsored by Sen. John Ashcroft. It is part of a broader vision he advances for expanding the role of religion in the nation, and perhaps as an opening launch in a presidential bid.[58]

Prior to this reform, states and localities, often with federal funds, routinely contracted with Catholic Charities, Jewish welfare leagues, and other religious counterparts, to provide much if not most of the state child welfare services and other human services. Previous practices depart from the charitable choice vision in three important ways. First, it extends the public-private partnership across the range of public benefits, not only social services. The Act extends the connection between states and religious entities to stipends of state welfare. It applies to temporary public assistance and also potentially to Food Stamps, Medicaid, and Supplementary Security Income, to the extent that they can be implemented by the states through purchase of services and voucher arrangements.[59]

Allocating basic public aid through religions organizations could have the appearance of advancing religion in contravention of one element of the *Lemon v. Kurtzman* test for Establishment Clause violations, or else appear to endorse religion, contrary to Justice O'Connor's articulation of the constitutional concern. If the state retains any ongoing supervision of the program, it could also pose problems under the entanglement prong of the doctrinal test announced in *Lemon*. Further, it is possible, although far from obvious, that courts would find individuals seeking temporary public assistance, food stamps, and emergency medical and disability assistance vulnerable to coercion prohibited under the free exercise clause.

Secondly, the Act permits state contracts with, and use of vouchers by, not only religiously affiliated services providers, but also pervasively sectarian institutions, including churches. This means that public funds will directly support religious organizations and religious messages. The Act's inclusion of even pervasively religious organizations, not merely the social service office across the street from the church but the church itself, does tighten the link between the public and the religious more than past public funding of religiously-provided human services. The law specifies that states cannot exclude religious organizations, not just their service arms, from a vouchers program that turns to any private providers. It also protects the religious character of the faith-based organizations obtaining state contracts or receiving vouchers. These organizations are exempted from Title VII's ban on religious discrimination in hiring and are permitted to maintain their art, symbols, scripture or other symbols that are associated with religious identity.[60]

Indeed, their pervasive religious character is precisely what commends such organizations to many advocates of the welfare reform.[61] One defense was inspired by Marvin Olaksy, author of The Tragedy of American Compassion. He called for the replacement of welfare because the governmental displacement of religious charities undermines the spiritual and moral capacities of individuals. More practically, he and others argue, religious groups do better than government with meeting the needs of the poor, persons with addictions and drug problems, and teenagers at risk of pregnancy. Spiritual renewal can be as or more important than meeting material need. Provision of care for the most vulnerable should not be passed through the cold bureaucratic indifference of state sponsored programs but through the face-to-face exchanges of a moral community. Then care is spiritual and moral as well as physical. Ideally the provision of care by religious groups adds moral dimensions of expected responsibility, hope, and the relationships within which people can feel the pressure to change. John DiIulio puts a similar case about services for children; he emphasizes that children are in need not of services, but of caring adults in their lives.[62]

According to advocates, religious organizations are the alternative to government in the welfare business because governmental material aid fails and may actually harm by causing self-defeating behavior for those who become dependent. Religious organizations can offer ongoing interaction connecting independent and dependent individuals, especially modeled by evangelical social ministries.

In these respects, the Act departs not only from prior statutory frameworks, but also from the guidelines used by the Supreme Court in *Bowen v. Kendrick* for challenges to federal grants programs as they are implemented. The Court remanded that case to the trial court to review the constitutionality of the Adolescent Family Life Act. The Supreme Court directed the trial court to assess whether the federal grants flowed under the Act to religiously affiliated institutions that are pervasively sectarian. Perhaps, today, the Court would not be so concerned with public funds flowing to a pervasively sectarian institution, but such a conclusion would be a departure from pre-existing decisions.[63]

Finally, the Act's voucher option opens up avenues for federal aid to worship activities and to proselytizing. The Act specifies that "No funds provided directly to institutions or organizations to provide services and administer programs [under the charitable choice provision] shall be expended for sectarian worship, instruction, or proselytization."[64] This provision notably uses the term "directly" in its prohibition, leaving open the indirect use of vouchers held by individuals to fund services that include sectarian worship, instruction, or proselytization.[65] Indeed, foreclosing these options vitiates the very argument for the special promise of religious-based social provision.

As in the earlier analysis of school vouchers, the intercession of private choice could well immunize such expenditures from an Establishment Clause challenge. Just as the child whose parents use a voucher to select a parochial school exercises a private choice and does not effect a governmental promotion or endorsement of religion, an individual recipient of a voucher for temporary financial assistance who elects to redeem it at a local church expresses a personal, not a governmental, choice. The individual, then, could choose a program that includes prayer, for example, as part of the contact with the participating nonpublic agency.

Yet three serious problems could render even the voucher scheme unconstitutional. First, unlike in the schools context, a state could turn the entire charitable responsibility over to private, religious organizations, leaving no secular option. The statute requires states to provide an alternative to an individual who objects to a particular provider but does not require preservation of a purely secular or governmental option. This makes an important difference whether we use the *Lemon* test, Justice O'Connor's concern about the appearance of governmental endorsement of religion, or the more general constitutional guard against political divisiveness along religious lines; the government should not eliminate a secular option for the distribution of human necessities such as food and shelter. The presence of a secular and public option preserves governmental neutrality and nonsectarian alternatives for individuals who could feel pressured otherwise toward a religious alternative they do not want.

Second, the sheer fact that the arena for public support is subsistence aid renders questionable any assertion that recipients can engage in free, autonomous choices. Coercion or undue burden on their religious beliefs, or non-beliefs, may indeed arise where the only local provider authorized to accept vouchers is a pervasively religious organization of a particular denomination. The option of another provider that is more remote is often not a real option to a poor person who lacks transportation and childcare. Placing the burden on the recipient to object also neglects the vulnerabilities of someone who is destitute and seeking aid.

Third, and most serious, charitable choice could be even more vulnerable than school vouchers to a challenge to the statute on the grounds that its foreseeable impact on religion makes the intention of the framers suspect. If, in practice, the framework will promote only one religion, or even religious organizations to the exclusion of nonreligious ones, under *Bowen v. Kendrick*, the Court could find the provision an impermissible establishment of religion. An "as applied" challenge could well find constitutional defects.

No one yet knows for certain how the charitable choice provision will work in practice, but there is good evidence already that only a limited number of religious organizations are agreeing to participate. Leaders of religious groups themselves are divided over whether to support or seek involvement in the charitable choice provisions. Some conclude that the larger welfare reform is immoral. Some resist the implication that the religious communities can cover the cutbacks, and cite their already overburdened shelters and soup kitchens as reasons to refuse even pretending to bail out the government. Some see no need to participate; others view collaboration with the government as self-defeating or dangerous to their own practices. As a result, there may be a notable discrepancy in the identities of religious groups that do seek participation. An "as applied" challenge could then be mounted to demonstrate an unacceptable pattern of support for only one religion or a select set.

Initial statements of views about charitable choice make this possibility quite likely. The National Association of Evangelicals endorses charitable choice.[66] But Southern Baptist Christian Life President Richard D. Land, in contrast, counsels against participation because their mission could be corrupted by taking public monies.[67] Similarly, others warn that government involvement jeopardizes the independence of a religious organization or the religious commitment to serve as advocates for the poor.[68] The Baptist Joint Committee on Public Affairs opposes the charitable choice provision as unconstitutional.[69] Rev. Fred Kammer, President of Catholic Charities, U.S.A., suggests that the charitable choice provision would help Catholic Charities in its work but would otherwise not further mix church and state.[70] Some conservative Christian groups emphasize that their success depends on resisting public monies. Thus, there are particular, predictable religious groups that will participate, and others that will not. An "as applied" challenge might soon be able to demonstrate a pattern of support for only one or a select set of religions, and even a foreseeable pattern of this nature.

Ironically, Marvin Olaksy, whose work is often cited by supporters of charitable choice, himself urges church groups to resist the temptation of the money and to refuse to partner with the states. He writes that only God can help reform the vulnerable; and church groups should resist the temptation to take any public money that would forbid such action.[71] Olasky apparently thinks the Act did not go so far as to entrust the welfare and social services task to religious groups because the Act specifies that its funds must not be used directly in supporting worship and proselytizing. Yet if vouchers that are received by individuals escape scrutiny for establishment problems, Olasky is wrong to be so worried. On the other hand, if the voucher device leads a state exclusively to pursue Olasky's vision of a religious response to indigency, constitutional concerns would be severe.

The drafters of the charitable choice provision showed more concern about at least appearing to protect the religious freedom of individuals eligible for aid. The statute prohibits discrimination against beneficiaries on the basis of religion;[72] it also calls upon the states to accommodate an individual who objects to the religious character of the organization from which the individual receives benefits under the Act.[73] Notably, however, nothing in the Act requires states to notify applicants of such a right to objection. The absence of a statutory duty to tell applicants of their option to object the services provided by a religious organization reduces the likelihood of such objections by economically and psychologically vulnerable people. The vulnerability of applicants in need of financial assistance could profoundly affect their ability or willingness to object to the provision of aid through a particular religious organization. Litigation can test the definition of a reasonable time for provision of an alternative, and potentially also challenges on grounds of coercion.

More basically, the statute on its face could be challenged as delegation of state functions to religious groups. This objection could well fail, given the power retained by states under the statute to choose which contracting partners and organizations to designate voucher recipients. Yet, if a state chooses to turn all of its welfare activities over to one religious organization, it could amount to a delegation of state functions to a religious organization. This the Supreme Court has rejected in *Grendel's Den,* and Justice Souter pursued this analysis in a portion of his opinion, joined by four others on the Court, in *Kiryas Joel.*[74]

Consider these scenarios that could unfold as charitable choice is implemented in the states:

1) The only local provider of services is a single religious organization, which requires participation in religious activity;
2) The only local provider of services is a single religious organization which does not require participation in religious activity but such activities pervade every contact with the organization;
3) To comply with the statutory requirement of an alternative provider within a reasonable time after an applicant's objection, the state contracts with other providers but they are not located in the same town;
4) A single mother who has left her home with her two preschool children due to fears of domestic violence arrives at the local church, which has the city contract for providing temporary assistance, and is too afraid to object to the religious character of the services.

In each of these scenarios of services governed by contracts between the state and the religious organization, a plausible if not powerful Establishment Clause defect could arise. If instead, in each instance, an individual recipient presents a voucher to independent providers, the constitutional analysis may afford more latitude but the effects could well be the same. Different scenarios—in which vouchers help to generate a range of religious and nonreligious alternatives for meeting human needs in different settings—could emerge, yet the states could well conclude that these would also be less potentially efficient and easy to administer.

If charitable choice implies a simple solution of turning all public duties in a state over to religious organizations, it is unwise, unworkable, and probably unconstitutional. Yet, as a matter of policy, partnerships between governments and religious organizations hold genuine possibility of better responses to human needs.

Retaining public limitations and ensuring options equivalent in value and access to the ones sponsored by religious organizations will be crucial for accountability and individual liberty. Properly retained as a method for promoting pluralism, vouchers that are framed in terms of genuinely accessible alternatives and coupled with public standards of equality and quality look better than even cruder, simpler solutions.

Closing Thoughts

If the government becomes involved in promoting a particular religion, and religion in general, though, there are risks of the kind of entanglement between religion and government that can endanger both.

The remedy for the risks, I believe, is a vigorous pluralism that promotes individual freedom, equality, and mutual respect among different groups. Pluralism must make room for religiously affiliated schools, social services, and providers of basic human needs but also for nonreligious schools, social services, and providers of basic human needs. This kind of pluralism should guard against the governmental establishment of religion and preserve individuals' free exercise of religion; it should also afford resources for critiquing and monitoring state alliances with global market forces. A robust independent sector and vibrant religious communities thus are worthwhile not only for their own purposes, and not only for the immediate good they do for others, but also in nurturing normative centers where people can articulate values potentially at odds with this global moment.[75] Mixing public and private cooperation while pursuing some limits on the partnerships involving religion could promote mutual aid but also preserve the distinct contributions each kind of entity makes to the needs of the poor, of children, and of the larger society.

Another way to put the point turns to Michael Ignatieff's elegant book, *The Needs of Strangers,* which captures two crucial yet potentially conflicting insights for societies that mean to be democratic, pluralist, and decent. The first may seem simply a Fourth of July statement. But he is right to note that "[w]e need justice, we need liberty, and we need as much solidarity as can be reconciled with justice and liberty."[76] Nations such as ours rightly endorse and celebrate liberty and justice as primary to human society. Rights for individuals afford chances to break away from inherited social stations as well as opportunities to challenge exclusions and degradations based on religion, race, or other traits. Liberty and equality should guide political structure. This includes religious liberty and freedom from discrimination on the basis of religious affiliation—or non-affiliation. Alternatives that subordinate such liberty and equality to solidarity, or any other purpose, are worse and undesirable. Social solidarity too often comes at the price of foreshortened liberty, equality, and justice for the variety of distinct human beings. Even were it possible to arrange a world in which "each community cared for its own," the enforcement required would constrain individuals intolerably. Therefore, only the forms of social solidarity compatible with these watchwords should be promoted in constitutional democracies.

Yet here is Ignatieff's important, additional insight: "It is because money cannot buy the human gestures which confer respect, nor rights guarantee them as entitlements, that any decent society requires a public discourse about the needs of the human person."[77] The welfare state practices that many democracies produce have been demeaning and inadequate; too many public schools across the nation deserve the same adjectives. Neither money nor entitlements administered by a bureaucratic state can guarantee the basic human needs for respect, care, connection, or genuine opportunity to flourish. Placing not only ultimate but also primary responsibility for those in need with the national government is highly unlikely to fulfill this insight. Nor, of course, would abandoning any idea of public responsibility for those in need outside the individual or immediate family. It is important to resist the faulty assumption that local, private, including religious initiatives can or always will afford the human gestures that confer respect and also the basic social provision that is necessary for the destitute to survive. Choice might help improve schools and services, but not if exchanged for the norm of equal regard.

The movements for school choice and for charitable choice admirably reflect the belief that we can and therefore must make better schools available to more children and more meaningful public assistance paired with community ties. These movements also embody fair criticisms of the public bureaucracies that have made too many schools and too many social service programs dehumanizing and incompetent. Yet the value of general rules to guide local schools and human services should not be ignored.

Even with the best motivation, private groups, including religious groups, can demonstrate biases against individuals or members of other groups. They can perpetuate longstanding lines of exclusion or degradation on the basis of race, or gender, or religion. They can leave untouched or exacerbate legacies of intergroup conflict and stigmatized group memberships. They can fail to build sufficient capacity to reach all with comparable needs. More basically, beyond including private religious groups as options in the delivery of education and human services, the shift to choice may come to mean shedding public responsibility for social provision. This would be a costly change, potentially devastating to the very fabric of the society. Even individually attractive choices cannot add up to a shared context for pursuing the common good. Without that shared context, there is no setting for debating what everyone deserves, no method for ensuring that choices are real for everyone, and no coordination of information and accountability standards that no private individuals or groups can ensure.

The push to use public dollars to pay for private and religious schools poses a double challenge to the shared context that connects private and public lives. Although the commitment to pluralism, religious freedom, and parental rights has long ensured parents the authority to opt-out of the common public schools, that option has remained until now just that: an option, leaving in place public schooling as the norm.[78] Only the public schools received direct public support, although nonprofit private schools remain eligible for the more modest assistance of tax exemption and incidental aid for transportation and books. The current choice movement calls for directing the funds set aside by the society to educate youth away from the public system. Channeled by parents to a variety of schools of their own choice, the funds may not violate the existing constitutional scruples against direct public aid to religious schools. Yet this very channeling dismantles the idea of a common school, open to all, capable of integrating students from a variety of backgrounds, and committed to inculcating a shared American tradition. However elusive that ideal has been, given racial and class segregation and implicit preferences for some version of the American tradition over others, the ideal itself has both symbolized and fertilized the shared context that binds diverse Americans together. Without that ideal, the prospects for common language and for a public domain where citizens grapple to frame the common good become more difficult.

The injection of private religious options in the delivery of human services is in many ways less worrisome perhaps because even food and shelter, job training and drug treatment do not hold the place of civic and cultural meaning that schooling does. Here the risk lies more in unwitting, or witting, exclusions and coercions, violative of the freedoms that have imbued the nation's ideals.

Recognizing the power of arguments for school choice and charitable choice, and believing in the need for experiments where so many prior efforts have failed so many people in need, I do not think that constitutional law should prevent initiatives in these directions. Yet the details would profoundly influence the prospects for commonality, respect across different groups, and inclusion. So although this cuts against the spirit of most arguments for school choice and charitable choice, four kinds of federal and state regulations should frame any options that become eligible for public funds in the contexts of schooling and welfare reform.

First, no private school or program should be eligible for payment through public dollars or vouchers if it excludes individuals on the basis of race, ethnicity, or nationality.[79] Second, any religious school receiving public funds or vouchers must engage in educational programming to address the legacies of intergroup hatred and conflict and to promote tolerance and respect across religious, racial, and ethnic groups. Such programs should include in-class curricula but even more importantly extracurricular music, sports, and other activities directly connecting the students with students from other schools outside the school's own religious denomination. Here it would be important that students from different schools joined in the same teams, orchestras, and theatre groups—not merely participating in opposing or competing groups—so that students actually have the chance to work together on common projects, and get to know one another in that context.[80] These are small steps to mitigate the challenge to the ideal of the common school posed by the use of public dollars to support private and religious schools. Third, neither charitable choice nor voucher school programs should be allowed to eliminate a genuinely accessible and attractive secular option for people who do not want to work with a religious provider of services or schooling. Fourth, all participating programs and schools must supply comparable information to watchdog and public groups to permit comparisons of their operations and outcomes. Some private religious providers may find these conditions too intrusive or onerous. But then they can opt out of participation. These requirements may seem large but they offer a minimal guard against segregated self-confirming enclaves and the erosion of a public space necessary to a complex, pluralistic society.

None of these requirements tell the private group how to run; they simply identify basic criteria for eligibility. Would such requirements be politically feasible?[81] If adopted, would they be administrable? These are fair questions that I hope would be aired and addressed in a broad public debate about how to arrange for social provision in a pluralist society committed to tolerance, liberty, and equality. That debate could, and should, be informed by the failure of simple solutions and the efficacy of complex ones.

Initiatives that do seem to work are complex mixtures of public and private, federal and local, professional and lay, legal and cultural resources. Consider, for example, Head Start. A federal program with roots in the religious activism of communities of Southern women, Head Start has always combined federal and local norms and people. Mandated roles for parental involvement make Head Start an unusual, but intriguing example of the way national law can structure gestures, and more, of respect for those who otherwise are constructed as the needy. Public and private agencies collaborate in training, delivery of services, and evaluation. There is nothing simple about it. Another example is the Indianapolis Front Porch Alliance.[82] The City, led by a Republican mayor, works with community organizations and religious congregations to create a kind of "civic switchboard connecting private and appropriate public resources with grassroots leaders" to meet community needs while helping to shape values, instill hope, and honor virtue.[83] The public role involves monetary support and symbolic endorsement as well as matchmaking and information sharing. The community organizations and religious groups do not only meet the needs of those they see and identify on their own; the government does not displace these local and rooted sources of authority and commitment.

There is some comfort, perhaps, in the messy realities that defy simple models.[84] Ours is not a nation that has ever or foreseeably would abandon the complex mix of public and private, religious and secular, local and regional, state and federal authority, responsibility, and community. In responding to the poor and in educating children, ours is a complex and untidy system. America is both plural and united. Can this untidiness be preserved alongside commitments to justice, liberty, and as much solidarity as is compatible with them? Can our traditional pluralism be strengthened by collective discussions of human need? The public square should be filled with boisterous, conflicting views about how to address these questions. It should also sustain and deepen the commitment to enlarge the "we," the sense of who is in this life together, who is within the ambit of concern and community of participants. Ensuring this is the challenge of the current moment.

Notes

1. Although there are expansive claims made on behalf of private, and especially religious schools, see, e.g., James S. Coleman, Thomas Hoffer, and Sally Kilmore, *High School Achievement* (Basic Books: New York 1982); John E. Chubb and Terry M. Moe, *Politics, Markets, and America's Schools* (Brookings: Washington 1990); it is impossible thus far to separate their apparent successes in retaining enrollments and boosting academic performance from the self-selection of families and the private schools' abilities to refuse and to expel troublesome students. See Arthur S. Goldberger and Glen G. Cain, "The Causal Analysis of Cognitive Outcomes in the Coleman Hoffer and Kilgore Report," *Sociology of Education* 55 (April –June 1982): 103–22; Douglas J. Wilms, "Catholic School Effects on Academic Achievement: New Evidence from the High School and Beyond Follow-up Study," *Sociology of Education* 58 (1985): 98–114.

2. This phrase is meant by its users to be inclusive, and yet it often seems divisive to those whose religions do not place faith at the center and to those who do not identify primarily or at all as members of a religious community.

3. Robert Putnam, "Bowling Alone: America's Declining Social Capital," *Journal of Democracy* 6 (1995): 65- 6; Robert Putnam, "Tuning In, Tuning Out: The Strange Disappearance of Social Capital in America," *28 PS: Political Science & Policy* (1995): 664, 677. For critiques, see Michael Schudson, *The Good Citizen: A History of American Life* (Free Press: New York 1998); Richard L. Hasen, "Symposium: Law, Economic, and Norms: Voting Without Law?" *University of Pennsylvania Law Review* 144 (1996): 2135, 2155; Katha Politt, "For Whom the Ball Rolls," *Nation* (April 15, 1996): 9.

4. See Anthony S. Bryk, Valerie E. Lee and Peter B. Holland, *Catholic Schools and the Common Good* (Harvard University Press: Cambridge 1993), pp. 1–11, 33–54.

5. Ibid., pp. 11, 327.

6. June Axinn and Herman Levin, *Social Welfare: A History of the American Response to Need* 2nd edition (Harper & Row: New York 1982), pp. 15–6.

7. Lucy Komisar, *Down and Out in the USA: A History of Public Welfare* Revised Edition (Franklin Watts: New York 1977), pp. 14–5; Marcus Wilson Jernegan, *Laboring and Dependent Classes in Colonial America 1607–1783* (Greenwood Press: Westport CT. 1931, 1971, 1980), p. 194.

8. Sydney Lens, *Poverty: America's Enduring Paradox: A History of the Richest Nation's Unwon War* (New York: Thomas Y. Crowell Co. 1969), p. 38; Komisar, *Down and Out*, p. 17.

9. Hendrik Hartog, "The Public Law of a County Court: Judicial Government in Eighteenth Century Massachusetts," *American Journal of Legal History* 20 (1976): 282, 292–3.

10. Ibid., 293.

11. Michael B. Katz, *In the Shadow of the Poorhouse: A Social History of Welfare in America* (Basic Books: New York 1986), pp. 59, 62.

12. Howard Gensler, ed.,. *The American Welfare System: Origins, Structure, and Effects* (Praeger: Westport Ct. 1996), p. 98.

13. Edith Abbott, *Public Assistance Vol. 1: American Principles and Policies* (University of Chicago Press: Chicago 1940), pp. 509–511.

14. 349 U.S. 618 (1969).

15. 119 S.Ct. 1518 (1999).

16. *Martinez v. Bynum,* 461 U.S. 321 (1983). See *Israel S. v. Board of Education of Oak Park and River Forest High School District 200,* 235 Ill. App.34d 652, 601 N.E.2d 1264 (Ill.App. 1992).

17. The federal district court in the District of Columbia found no claim under the Stewart B. McKinney Homeless Assistance Act to permit homeless children to enroll in schools connected with their prior residences, *Lampkin v. District of Columbia,* 1992 U.S. Dist. LEXIS 8049 (D.D.C. June 9, 1992). The appellate court reversed, finding such an enforceable right, *Lampkin v. District of Columbia,* 27 F.3d 605 (1994), cert. denied, 513 U.S. 1016 (1994), and the district court on remand enjoined the District to provide educational services including transportation, *Lampkin v. District of Columbia,* 879 F.Supp. 116 (D.D.C.1995). But the District of Columbia subsequently withdrew from the McKinney Act Education Program, which led to a dissolution of the court's injunction. *Lampkin v. District of Columbia* 886 F.Supp. 56 (1995).

18. See generally Molly S. McUsic, *The Law's Role in the Distribution of Education: The Promises and Pitfalls of School Finance Litigation,* in Jay P. Heubert ed., *Law and School Reform: Six Strategies for Promoting Educational Equity* (New Haven: Yale University Press, 1999), pp. 88–159.

19. 457 U.S. 202 (1982).

20. See *League of United Latin American Citizens et al. v. Wilson,* 997 F.Supp. 1244 (C.D. Cal. 1997), aff'd in part on other grounds and dismissed in part on other grounds, 131 F.3d 1297 (9th Cir. 1997); "California Measure Found Unconstitutional," Facts on File, P. 944 D3 (Dec. 25, 1997). The federal judge further ruled that Prop. 187 cannot stand in the face of the Personal Responsibility and Work Opportunity Reconciliation Act of 1996, which demonstrates the federal occupation of the domain of immigrant access to public benefits. 908 F.Supp., at 876; Patrick J. McDonnell, "Prop. 187 Found Unconstitutional By Federal Judge," *Los Angeles Times,* November 15, 1997. See also Tom Harrigan, "Judge Oks Agreement Ending Attempts to Revive Prop. 187," *San Diego Union-Tribune,* September 14, 1999.

21. See, e.g., June Axinn and Herman Levin, *Social Welfare: A History of the American Response to Need* 2nd edition (New York: Harper and Row, 1982), pp. 175–209.

22. San *Antonio Ind. School Dist. v. Rodriguez,* 411 U.S. 1 (1973).

23. See Note, "The Limits of Choice: School Choice Reform and State Constitutional Guarantees of Educational Quality," *Harvard Law Review* 109 (1996): 2002–3. See also Joseph G. Weeres and Bruce Cooper, *Public Choice Perspectives on Urban Schools,* in James V. Cibulka, Rodney J. Reed & Kenneth K. Wong eds., *The Politics of Urban Education in the United States* (Washington: Falmer Press, 1992), pp. 57, 67.

24. See Note, "The Hazards of Making Public Schooling a Private Business," *Harvard Law Review* 112 (1999): 665 (arguing for standards-based reform rather than privatization).

25. *School District of Abington Township v. Schempp,* 374 U.S. 203, 240–1 (Brennan, J., concurring).

26. Thomas Jefferson is usually cited as the author of the notion that the First Amendment was intended to create a "wall of separation between church and State." See *Everson v. Board of Educ.* 330 U.S. 1, 16 (1947). The Court itself has reasoned that total separation is not required nor even possible, *Lynch v. Donnelly*, 465 U.S. 668, 672–73 (1984); *Committee for Pub. Educ. & Religious Liberty v. Nyquist*, 413 U.S. 756, 760 (1973); *Lemon v. Kurtzman*, 403 U.S. 602, 614 (1971).

27. See Ronald F. Thiemann, *Religion in Public Life: A Dilemma for Democracy* (Washington, D.C.: Georgetown University Press, 1996), p. 42–66; Laura Underkuffler-Freund, "The Separation of the Religious and the Secular: A Foundational Challenge to First Amendment Theory," *William and Mary Law Review* 36 (1995): 837–988.

28. In recent opinions, some justices invoke *Lemon*; others seek to replace it; and Justice O'Connor resists the notion of any "grand unified theories" where bedrock principles collide. See *Rosenberger v. Rector*, 515 U.S. 819, 852 (O'Connor, J., concurring). Yet Justice O'Connor has led the Court toward another touch-stone—if not test—for analyzing Establishment Clause claims. This is an inquiry into whether the government's action would be viewed by an objective observer as an endorsement of religion or of a particular religion. See, e.g., *Capitol Square Review and Advisory Board v. Pinette*, 515 U.S. 753, 772–83 (O'Connor , J., concurring).

29. *Agostini v. Felton*, 521 U.S. 203 (1997)(overruling *Aguilar v. Felton* and *School Dist. of Grand Rapids v. Ball* in relevant part).

30. *Wallace v. Jaffree*, 472 U.S. 38, 69 (O'Connor, J., concurring).

31. *Bowen v. Kendrick*, 487 U.S. 589 (1988)(Rehnquist, C.J., for the Court).

32. See Carl H. Esbeck, "A Constitutional Case for Governmental Cooperation with Faith-Based Social Service Providers," *Emory Law Journal* 46: 1. For a critique of this view as inadequately attentive to separationist concerns, see Douglas Laycock, "The Underlying Unity of Separation and Neutrality," *Emory Law Journal* 46: 43.

33. Compare *Allegheny v. American Civil Liberties Union*, 492 U.S. 573 (1989)(Kennedy, J., joined by White, J., Scalia, J., and Rehnquist, C.J.)(emphasizing importance of coercion) and *Lee v. Weisman*, 505 U.S. 577 (1992)(same) with Ibid., pp. 627–28 (O'Connor, J., concurring in part and concurring in the judgment) and Ibid., p. 650, n.6 (Stevens, J., concurring in part and dissenting in part). Free exercise of religion may be burdened even by indirect coercion, *Lyng v. Northwest Indian Cemetery Protective Ass'n*, 485 U.S. 439, 450 (1988), but there may be no constitutional violation if the government's requirements are generally applicable, as with a general criminal prohibition. *Employment Division, Department of Human Resources of Oregon v. Smith*, 494 U.S. 872 (1990).

34. *Larkin v. Grendel's Den*, 459 U.S. 116 (1982).

35. 512 U.S. 687 (1994).

36. Thus, the Court has summarily affirmed several cases in which lower courts rejected tax credits or deductions to assist nonpublic school parents. See *Kosydar v. Wolman*, 353 F.Supp. 744 (S.D. Ohio 1972), aff'd sub nom. *Grit v. Wolman*, 413 U.S. 901 (1973); *Public Funds for Public Schools of New Jersey v. Byrne*, 590 F.2d 514 (3rd Cir. 1979), aff'd sub nom. *Beggans v. Public Funds for Public Schools of New Jersey*, 442 U.S. 907 (1979). In a full opinion, the Court rejected federal tuition grant and tax benefit program for low-income parents because of no effective means to guarantee the state aid would be used exclusively for secular, neutral, and nonideological purposes. *Committee for Public Education v. Nyquist*, 413 U.S. 756 (1973). The Court emphasized that "the fact that aid is disbursed to parents rather than to the schools is only one among many factors to be considered." Ibid., p. 781. In a subsequent case, the Court approved a state provision allowing parents to deduct from their state income taxes certain expenses relating to transportation, tuition,

and textbooks in support of their children's schooling. *Mueller v. Allen,* 463 U.S. 388 (1983). The Court did try to explain the difference between this scheme and ones it had found unacceptable in terms of its availability to parents who send their children to public school as well as those who choose private schools. Ibid., pp. 397–9.

37. *Mueller,* 413 U.S., at 397–99; *Committee for Public Education v. Nyquist,* 413 U.S. 756 (1973).

38. *Witters v. Washington Dept. of Services for Blind,* 474 U.S. 481 (1986). The Court restated and reaffirmed this view of the case recently in explaining that "any money that ultimately went to religious institutions did so 'only as a result of the genuinely independent and private choices of' individuals." *Agostini,* 117 S.Ct. 1997, *2011–2012 (quoting *Witters,* 474 U.S., at 487).

39. *Zobrest v. Catalina Foothills Sch. Dist,* 113 S.Ct. 2462 (1993).

40. Again, in *Agostini,* the presence of state-supported assistance in a sectarian school resulted from a private decision by individual parents rather than state decisionmaking because the assistance followed the child and the child attended the school by parental choice. 117 S.Ct. 1997, 2012. "[A]ny money that ultimately went to religious institutions did so 'only as a result of the genuinely independent and private choices of individuals'" and could not be attributed to state decisionmaking, 138 L.Ed.2d 391, 415–16 (quoting *Committee for Public Ed. and Religious Liberty v. Nyquist,* 413 U.S. 756, 782–83 n.38 (1973).

41. *Rosenberger v. Rector and Visitors of the University of Virginia,* 515 U.S. 819, 840 (1995). The Court did emphasize that the funds there at issue came from a student activity fee, not from a general tax, and refrained from extending its analysis to expenditure from a general tax fund. Ibid., pp. 840–41.

42. It is a matter of some dispute whether tax deductions and tax credits amount to public funds or instead preservation of private funds, but in a strict economic sense, they deduct monies that otherwise would be collected and put into the public fisc. See *Texas Monthly v. Bullock,* 515 U.S. 819, 899 (1989)(plurality opinion, announcing judgment of the court). Some, taking the private funds perspective, argue that parents who send their children to parochial schools are unfairly forced to pay tuition twice; once through taxes that only support public schools, and once to the parochial schools. The central defect with this argument is that not only parents of school-aged children are taxed to support public schools because public schools are a public good, investing in the education of the next generation on the premise that the results will make everyone better off. A contrasting and more powerful argument can be made that provision of a voucher program that covers private but not religious schools risks invidious discrimination against those who would choose religious schools.

43. The program provides a maximum of $2500 for tuition (90% of tuition for those with family income that is not more than twice the federal poverty level, and 75% of tuition for others). *Simmons-Harris v. Goff,* 1997 Ohio App. LEXIS 1766 at *4, 1997 WL 217583 at *1.

44. *Simmons-Harris v. Goff,* 1997 WL 217583 (Ohio App. 10 Dist. May 1, 1997), discretional appeals and cross-appeals allowed, 684 N.E.2d 705, Table (Ohio 1997).

45. See *Goff,* 711 N.E.2d at 210.

46. 6 See *Simmons-Harris v. Zelman,* Nos. 1:99 CV 1740, 1:99 CV 1818, 1999 WL 669222, at *2 (N.D. Ohio Aug. 27, 1999).

47. *Jackson v. Benson,* 578 N.W.2d 602 (Wis. 1998), cert. denied, 119 S.Ct. 466 (1998).

48. *Chittenden Town Sch. Dist. V. Vermont Dep't of Educ.,* No. 97–275, 1999 WL 378244 (Vt. June 11, 1999).

49. See *Mueller v. Allen*, 463 U.S. 388 (1983)(approving tax deduction for educational purposes in part because of its availability to all parents).

50. See Isaac Kramnick and R. Laurence Moore, "Can the Churches Save the Cities?: Faith-Based Services and the Constitution," *The American Prospect* (Nov.-Dec. 1997): 47–53.

51. *Mueller*, 463 U.S., p. 401; see also *Agostini*, 138 L.Ed.2d, p. 418 ("Nor are we willing to conclude that the constitutionality of an aid program depends on the number of sectarian schools students who happen to receive the otherwise neutral aid").

52. *Mueller*, 463 U.S., p. 402.

53. *Pierce v. Society of Sisters*, 268 U.S. 510 (1925).

54. See, e.g., "Organisation for Economic Co-Operation and Development," *OECD Economic Surveys: United States* 52 (November 1993); Eric Hanuschek et al., *Making Schools Work: Improving Performance and Controlling Costs* (Washington: Brookings Institute 1994), pp. xvii-xviii; Carnegie Corporation of New York, *Years of Promise: A Comprehensive Learning Strategy for America's Children* (1997).

55. Personal Responsibility and Work Opportunity Reconciliation Act of 1996, Pub. L. No. 104–193, 110 Stat. 2105 (1996). The charitable choice provision is codified at 42 U.S.C. section 604(a). Primarily sponsored by Senator John Ashcroft, the charitable choice provision "is intended to encourage faith-based service providers to cooperate with public welfare programs by ensuring that they will not have to attenuate or abandon their religious character or style of service." Stanley W. Carlson-Thies, "'Don't Look to Us': The Negative Responses of Churches to Welfare Reform," *Notre Dame Journal of Law, Ethics & Public Policy* 11 (1997): 667, 672–3 (1997). Carlson-Thies continues with a statement identifying an additional feature of the statute that could lead to legal challenge: "All federal welfare funds block-granted to the states must be expended in accordance with the charitable choice rules, even in states with constitutional barriers to the expenditure of public funds by sectarian organizations," Ibid., 673. This last element imposes the federal statute even upon states with contrary state constitutional provisions, and could pose a special problem if funds are commingled. Section 104 (K) of Public Law 104–193 tries to manage the conflict by noting that "Nothing in this section shall be construed to preempt any provision of a State constitution or State statute that prohibits or restricts the expenditure of State Funds in or by religious organizations." This covers only state, and not federal funds. Currently, at least 27 states prohibit taxpayers' funds from going to any religious organization. Chris Collins, State Officials Will Soon Find Themselves Central in the Legal Debate Over Roles of Church, State, Gannett, News Service (Dec. 24, 1997). The Supreme Court's Decision in *Rosenberger v. Rector* suggests, however, a willingness to impose a federal standard on a state with such a ban.

56. See Public Law 10–285; 112 Stat. 2702, Oct. 27, 1998. President Clinton apparently believes that the act excludes pervasively sectarian institutions while Senator Ashcroft, its chief sponsor, has the opposite view. Compare Statement by the President On Signing the Community Opportunities, Accountability and Training and Educational Services Act of 1998, Federal Document Clearing House Transcript, Oct. 27, 1998 with Sen. Ashcroft, Charitable Choice, 144 *Congressional Review* S 12686, No. 150. Ashcroft also seeks legislation to expand the charitable choice concept to other social services such as housing, juvenile services, and substance abuse programs. Ashcroft Would Expand 'Charitable Choice' to Help Needy Escape Poverty (Feb. 3, 1999), http://www.senate.gov/~ashcroft/pressf.htm (visited Feb. 10, 1999).

57. The drafter was Professor Carl Esbeck. See Sam Walker, "'Faith-Based' Welfare Reform," *Christian Science Monitor* (April 22, 1997): 1; Kathy Lally, "Unlikely Alliance Aids Poor," *Baltimore Sun*, Feb. 17, 1997.

58. With Senators J.C. Watts and James Talent, Senator Ashcroft has also introduced legislation entitled, "Saving Our Children: The American Community Renewal Act," which would afford economic aid to communities while requiring the adoption of school choice plans including private and religious schools. Carlson-Thies, "Don't Look to Us", 673.

59. A Guide to Charitable Choice, http://cpjustice.org/~cpjustice/Cguide/ccqanda.html (visited Feb. 10, 1999). The Guide was sponsored by The Center for Public Justice and the Christian Legal Society's Center for Law and Religious Freedom.

60. Section 104(d)(2). The Act allows separate accounting procedures for the portion applied to the services paid by federal block grants and thereby shields the rest of the private organization's financial records from public review. Section 104 (h)(2)(Limited audit).

61. See "Ashcroft Applauds D.C.'s Use of Private Organizations in Making Welfare Work," News Release (November 12, 1998), http://www.senate.gov/~ashcroft/pressf.htm (visited February 10, 1999).

62. Interview with "Jim Wallis: With Unconditional Love—Criminologist John Di-Iulio," *Sojourners Magazine*, http://www.sojourners.com?soj970910.html (visited February 10,1999).

63. In *Bowen v. Kendrick*, Justice Kennedy's concurrence, joined by Justice Scalia, emphasized that the provision of funds to a pervasively sectarian institution would not in itself constitute a violation of the Establishment Clause; "[t]he question in an as-applied challenge is not whether the entity is of a religious character, but how it spends its grant." 487 U.S., pp. 624–25. In contrast, Justice O'Connor's concurring opinion announced that "any use of public funds to promote religious doctrines" would be unconstitutional. 487 U.S., p. 623.

64. The word "directly" appears in section 104(j): "No funds provided directly to institutions or organizations to provide services and administer programs under subsection (a)(1)(A) shall be expended for sectarian worship, instruction, or proselytization." 42 U.S.C. 604a(j)(1998).

65. A Guide to Charitable Choice, http://cpjustice.org/~cpjustice/Cguide/ccqanda.html#intro (visited February 10, 1999).

66. "Heeding the Call of the Poor: Let the Church Be the Church," A Resolution Adopted by the 55th Annual Meeting of the National Association of Evangelicals, http://www.nae.net/resolutions/poor.html (visited February 10, 1999.)

67. "'Charitable Choice' Entangles Church and State, Say Ethicists," Reporter-Interactive-news, *Baptist Press*, (August 29, 1996), http://www.umr.org/htfoxhen.htm (visited February 10, 1999); http://www.baptist press.org?Archive/BaptistPress/view.cgi?file=19960802html (visited February 10, 1999). The commission recently changed its name to Ethics & Religious Liberty Commission. Randy Frame, "God in a Box?" *Christianity Today* (April 7, 1997), quotes the general counsel of the Baptist Joint Committee as opposing charitable choice. See http://www.christianity.net/ct/7T4/7T4046.html (visited February 10, 1999).

68. See *Stephen V. Monsma*, When Sacred and Secular Mix: Religious Nonprofit Organizations and Public Money 81–99, 128–29, 154–61 (1997); Carlton-Thies, "Don't Look to Us", 11.

69. See Resolution on the Charitable Choice Provision in the New Welfare Act (October 8, 1996), http://www.erols.com/bhcpa/timely/charchc.html.

70. National Public Radio, Morning Edition (September 6, 1996).

71. See Marvin Olasky, "Holes in the Soul Matter as Much as Dollars," *USA Today*, February 15, 1996. See also Robyn Blumer, "Choose to Rescind Charitable Choice," http://www.aclufl.org/r-chr.htm (visited February 19, 1999) (quoting Olasky).

72. Section 104(g).

73. Section 104(e)(1).

74. 459 U.S. 116, 122–27 (1982); 512 U.S. 687, 696–702 (1994)(Souter, J., joined by Blackmun, Stevens, and Ginsburg, JJ.). See also id., at 706, 709–10 (opinion for the court)(citing unconstitutional delegation as one ground for the Court's rejection of the legislative scheme).

75. *Cf.* Robert Cover, "Nomos and Narrative," *Harvard Law Review* 97 (1983): 4 (small normative communities compete with the state).

76. Michael Ignatieff, *The Needs of Strangers* (New York: Viking, 1985), p. 141.

77. Ibid., p. 13.

78. See *Wisconsin v. Yoder*, 406 U.S. 205 (1972); *Pierce v. Society of Sisters*, 268 U.S. 510 (1925); *Meyer v. Nebraska*, 262 U.S. 390 (1923). Even the parental right to opt-out of public education has limits "if it appears that parental decisions will jeopardize the health or safety of the child, or have a potential for significant social burdens." *Wisconsin v. Yoder*, pp. 233–34.

79. Given ongoing study about the value of same-sex education, same-sex job training programs, same-sex drug and alcohol treatment programs, and services tailored for individuals with particular disabilities, I would not be ready to ban exclusion on the basis of gender and disability by particular programs if the system as a whole ensures comparable opportunities for all (including curricular quality and athletic opportunities). However, this requires the maintenance of some system-level analysis and evaluation rather than simple reliance on a marketplace.

80. See generally Martha Minow, *Not Only for Myself: Identity, Politics, and the Law* (New York: New Press, 1997), pp. 128–131 (reviewing research about such integrative programs).

81. Many of the religious groups most likely to participate in charitable choice and in the running of schools will resist regulations that seem to bring the government inside their worlds; the stifling, bureaucratic qualities of regulation are precisely what seem to argue for the use of alternatives to meet human needs. Yet if public dollars are at stake, public values should frame the outer bounds of their use; those organizations that refuse nondiscrimination, participation in district-wide activities, and sharing information can certainly choose not to accept the public dollars. It is worth noting that public solicitude for religious activities can be expressed in different degrees. Direct contractual relationships create more mutual involvement than do vouchers. Tax-exempt status is less direct support than contracts and vouchers—but even tax-exempt status can, and should be, denied where the religious entity violates norms central to national norms. See Bob Jones University v. United States, 461 U.S. 574 (1983)(approving Internal Revenue Service decision to deny tax-exempt status to private school engaging in racial discrimination). And an entity may be denied tax-exempt status but still be permitted to operate free from criminal ban.

82. Stephen Goldsmith, "Sources of Strength in Community," *The Indianapolis Star* (May 27, 1998); see http://www.IndyGov. org/mayor/fpa/essay527.htm (visited February 11, 1999). See also David Holmstrom, "Front Porch Alliance Fosters Church-City Cooperation," *The Christian Science Monitor* (May 13, 1998); and Jo Loconte, "The Bully and the Pulpit: A new model for church-state partnerships," *Policy Review: The Journal of American Citizenship* (Nov./Dec. 1998): 28.

83. Goldsmith, "Sources of Strength."

84. Cf. Mary Ann Glendon, "Knowing the Universal Declaration of Human Rights," *Notre Dame Law Review* 73 (1998): 1153, 1176(admiring sculpture by Arnaldo Pomodoro, located by U.N. building, depicting cracked globe with another, cracked sphere emerging from inside as a metaphor for the dynamism, potency and emergent probabilities of politics guided by principles to which people of vastly different backgrounds can appeal).

CHAPTER 7

Doing Whose Work? Faith-Based Organizations And Government Partnerships

Anna Greenberg

It is not the moment to take government out of the business of caring for our nation's social and economic welfare. If there is an economic downturn, it is realistic to assume we can rely on religious organizations to cope with wide scale homelessness, joblessness and poverty?

NONPROFITS HAVE A VENERABLE HISTORY of social service delivery and partnership with government to tackle thorny social and economic problems. Since the 19th century, as Theda Skocpol notes, "Voluntary civic federations have both pressured for the creation of public social programs and worked in partnership with government to administer and expand such programs after they were established."[1] What is new in the current political climate is that policy makers at every level of government are calling congregations and religious groups to take on these responsibilities, privileging religious models and local responses over centralized, bureaucratic solutions.[2] Moreover, religious leaders and communities are increasingly formulating social welfare innovations and policy through formal institutionalized channels, rather than merely pressing authorities for funding or political change.

For many, the most appealing aspect of this trend is the reliance on solutions conceived at the local level by community based groups. These solutions are understood to be more effective and efficient than "top down," government social policy and more responsive to individual needs. The connection of religious values and a faith commitment to service delivery, it is contended, is central to the effectiveness of this community-based model. Legislators and bureaucratic actors have responded in kind, creating special offices, grant programs, and partnerships, as well as initiating legislative challenges to restrictions on public funding of religious organizations.

Yet as commentators champion the efforts of religious communities, little is known about the scale of faith-based public/private partnerships underlying the social safety net. In fact, congregations and small religious groups, as distinct from national denominational charities or nonprofits, are highly unlikely to receive any public funding for their social service delivery. Their work is almost completely funded by member donations and conceived of independently from government. To date, the Charitable Choice provisions in the Personal Responsibility and Work Opportunity Reconciliation Act of 1996 have not significantly increased public funding for faith-based institutions to deliver welfare services and only cover a fraction of the kinds of services faith-based organizations provide. Charitable Choice, however, has led to an increase in the voluntary, unfunded partnerships of congregations with government to address the needs of the poor. These partnerships are often part of a coordinated community response that includes other nonprofits and the business community.

There is currently, therefore, a disparity between the appeal to faith communities to respond to problems like poverty, homelessness, juvenile crime, and substance abuse, and the ability or inclination of those communities to accept government funding for such efforts. Further, significant political, material and even religious constraints continue to prevent congregations and sectarian groups from applying for public funding and participating in government programs. Any wish to evaluate the desirability, effectiveness, and efficiency of faith-based service delivery must first grapple with the ambiguity of the legal and political environment, as well as the legitimate trepidation of members of faith communities.

In this chapter, I describe the kinds of social service programs and public funding available to congregations in the post-welfare reform environment, carefully distinguishing between congregations and national denominational charities, which are the traditional providers of faith-based services. I discuss the way states and local communities have responded to innovations in federal and state approaches to welfare reform. Finally, I briefly describe the constraints on congregational involvement in social service delivery. I argue that targeting the faith community to aid in efforts to address our nation's social ills must proceed with caution. In an uncertain economic, political and legal environment, we cannot afford to eliminate the role of the state in caring for our poor and disadvantaged.

Government Funding and Religious Partnerships

Public funding of the nonprofit world to take on social and economic problems is not a new phenomenon.[3] Beginning in the 19th century and in earnest since the late 1960s, government agencies have contracted with private providers to supply social services in the areas of health, welfare, education, and the like. Salamon estimates that by 1980, "40 percent of the funds spent by federal, state, and local government in the United States for a broad range of human service activities supported service delivery by nonprofit organizations."[4] Faith-based organizations ranging from national denominational charities to special purpose groups to congregations deliver a significant share of these services.[5]

Castelli and McCarthy calculate that the large religious charities, such as Catholic Charities USA and the Salvation Army, serve over 60 million people.[6] These organizations receive a substantial amount of their revenue from government sources, mainly contracts for service. For instance, in 1996, Catholic Charities USA received $1.3 billion or 64 percent its total income, the Salvation Army received $245 million or 16 percent of its total income and the YMCA received $203 million or 8 percent of its total income from government sources.[7] According to the *NonProfit Times*, Lutheran Social Ministries no longer qualifies for the *NPT 100*, a list of the nation's biggest nonprofit organizations, because it receives 92 percent of its revenue from the government.[8]

This receipt of public funds by national denominational charities is consistent with accepted legal interpretation of the Establishment Clause in the U.S. Constitution.[9] The guidelines developed in *Lemon v. Kurtzman* (1971) permit public funding of faith-based service delivery as long as (1) the legislation establishing a program does not have a religious purpose; (2) the primary intention is not to advance religion; and (3) there is no "excessive administrative entanglement" between religious organizations and government agencies.[10] Monsma argues these guidelines rest upon the ability of sectarian organizations to separate their sacred and secular missions (at least on paper), as large denominational charities have ostensibly been able to do.[11]

In the current political environment, however, a new orientation toward the faith community's participation in the social safety net has emerged. First, consistent with the popularity of devolution strategies, policy makers are championing the role of congregations and small religious groups in generating innovative, locally-based solutions to poverty and other social problems.[12] Conservative thinkers, for instance, share the belief that government efforts to end poverty have failed, or more perversely, have even created incentives that tend to keep the poor in a dependent relationship with the state.[13] Welfare reform, and other initiatives like the "Project for the Renewal of America,"[14] offer an opportunity to undo the "accumulated damage of a quarter-century" of government programs by substituting direct service responsive to particular community needs.[15] On the Left, the criticism of government is more muted, nevertheless support for faith based solutions is predicated on the greater "effectiveness" of local solutions. As Al From, the President of the Democratic Leadership Council puts it: "The reality is that in today's age, bureaucratic structures don't work very well. . . . Solutions have to be honed for each community and each neighborhood. Local institutions are the best to do that; often the best local institution is the church."[16]

Second, policy makers and religious leaders increasingly argue that what they describe as the effectiveness of faith-based social service delivery is linked to the individual experience of faith. President Clinton, praising the work of Rev. Eugene Rivers, the founder of the Azusa Christian Community in Boston and a co-founder of Boston's prominent Ten Point Coalition,[17] with endangered black youth, cites the healing effects of prayer: "He has gotten to know some of

Boston's most troubled children, welcoming them to his parish, Baker House, offering them counseling, recreation and an occasional pizza party; *introducing children who have known nothing but chaos at home to the serenity of prayer.*"[18]

Jim Wallis, editor of *Sojourners Magazine* and organizer of Call to Renewal, calls these intervention efforts "kid-by-kid and block-by-block redemption programs."[19] The effectiveness of faith, for many, is linked to the way it alters the behavior of poor people or welfare recipients. Senator John Ashcroft, the champion of Charitable Choice, for instance, argued from the floor of the Senate that religiously inspired charity "address[es] the deeper needs of people—by instilling hope and values which help change behavior and attitudes."[20]

Both of these arguments—that local faith based communities are more effective than government and that faith exerts a transformative effect on the disadvantaged—have made their way into presidential debates. In a 2000 campaign speech, Vice President Al Gore speech declared his support for Charitable Choice, arguing that religious communities better understand local circumstances and treat people in pain as human beings, not merely as clients with case numbers. Faith, moreover, helps distressed individuals confront personal challenges because it provides "inner discipline" and sustains a commitment to clean living: "There is a reason faith-based approaches have shown special promise with challenges such as drug addiction, youth violence and homelessness. Overcoming these problems takes something more than money or assistance—it requires an inner discipline and courage, deep within the individual. I believe that faith in itself is sometimes essential to spark a personal transformation—and to keep that person from falling back into addiction, delinquency, or dependency."[21]

Similarly, George W. Bush invokes his strong record of support for Charitable Choice initiatives as governor of Texas, asserting that resources should flow directly to "the people serving their neighborhoods" rather than to state agencies. He believes this, in part, because government cannot deliver social services with a "heart," as religious organization do: "We found that government can spend money, but it can't put hope in our hearts or a sense of purpose in our lives. This is done by churches and synagogues and mosques and charities that warm the cold of life. A quiet river of goodness and kindness that cuts through stone."[22]

Policy analysts today also emphasize local, government-supported faith-based responses to poverty and other community needs, as opposed to the more traditional service delivery by large nonprofit religious charities. Since the mid–1990s, policy makers have responded with a number of bureaucratic and legislative initiatives designed to support these kinds of local partnerships. First, federal agencies, such as the Department of Housing and Urban Development, are developing programs and expanding eligibility for grants awarded to faith-based groups. Second, the Charitable Choice provisions of the welfare reform act have loosened the restrictions on government funding of religious groups to deliver a limited range of welfare services. Third, at the state and local level, faith-based organizations, religious leaders, government officials, business groups and other nonprofits are forming funded and unfunded coalitions to fight crime, build housing for low-income people, help people make the transition from welfare to work, and provide a host of other community services.

Federal Initiatives

Bureaucratic Response[23]

Policy makers across different federal agencies are interested in communities of faith in social service delivery. At present, faith-based organizations can and do receive monies from federal agencies, but the funding mechanisms are quite complex. Some agencies have designated special programs and offices to help increase religious group participation in public/private partnerships. Most frequently, faith-based organizations are one of many nonprofits that government agencies permit to apply for grant money directly or via block grants to state governments.

The Department of Housing and Urban Development, or HUD, has made the most significant outreach efforts to faith-based communities.[24] Under the auspices of the Center for Community and Interfaith Partnerships, HUD is holding regional conferences "to focus, integrate and intensify HUD's involvement with faith- and community- and faith-based organizations in an effort to maximize the use and impact of our mutual resources in building strong communities."[25] HUD offers faith-based organizations opportunities to apply for grants directly from HUD and its area offices; it also permits eligible candidates to apply for funding from state, county, and local government and housing authorities under their block grant programs such as the Community Development Block Grants. The HUD center's most recent newsletter notes that the federal budget for FY2001 includes $20 million for competitive grants and targeted technical assistance to develop affordable housing and economic development.[26]

Under HUD's broad mandate, faith-based organizations can offer transitional housing to the homeless, develop youth programs and drug prevention programs, and offer housing assistance and counseling.[27] They can also enter into creative partnerships with government and other nonprofits to build or rehabilitate low-income housing. For example, in 1994, the city government of Augusta, Georgia, and the Antioch Ministries, Inc. (the nonprofit branch of Antioch Baptist Church) used $700,000 from the federal agency's Home Investment Partnership Program to convert 11 duplexes into 16 units of housing for very low and low income residents of their community.[28] Antioch Ministries, Inc. worked closely with Augusta's neighborhood development department, the Augusta Housing Authority and local banks and businesses to identify housing needs and eligible residents, as well as fund the rehabilitation.

In 1998, the Department of Justice launched a "values based crime prevention initiative," awarding grants totaling $2.2 million to 16 local Weed and Seed programs. This initiative, which employs the existing Weed and Seed structure of 178 local community steering committees, funds activities "such as mentoring, school violence prevention, job training, mediation, gun abatement, and substance abuse prevention."[29] Clergy and other religious leaders play a central role in these committees, often serving as the chairperson, making decisions about the priorities of the program, and funding recipients.[30]

Some federal agencies lack dedicated offices or programs, but make religious organizations eligible for funding for various programs in other ways. For instance, the Department of Agriculture encourages church groups and other faith-based organizations to participate in its "food recovery and gleaning" program, which distributes salvaged surplus food from farms, grocery stores, and the like.[31] Under the Community Food Projects Competition, faith-based organizations are also eligible to apply for grants to create programs to help meet the nutritional needs of poor people. The Department of Education allows congregations to participate in its Partnership for Family Involvement in Education, a program which channels parents, kids, and volunteers into activities like after-school programs and tutoring.[32] Religious institutions with 501(c)(3) status can sponsor projects in low income communities with AmeriCorps*VISTA volunteers through the AmeriCorps program.[33]

Charitable Choice

The legislative response to this emphasis on localism and the centrality of a faith commitment is realized in the 1996 landmark welfare legislation. This act converts welfare or Aid to Families with Dependent Children into block grants (Temporary Assistance for Needy Families or TANF) with fairly flexible implementation guidelines.[34] The legislation also includes the Charitable Choice provision, which allows religious institutions such as churches or synagogues to enter into contracts or voucher programs with states, allowing them to deliver welfare services without compromising their religious mission. Faith-based providers, under this statute, can direct "'the definition, development, practice and expression' of their religious convictions," though they cannot require beneficiaries to participate in religious activities or use federal funds to support such activities.[35]

The Charitable Choice clause in the 1996 legislation broadens the existing opportunities for faith-based organizations to participate in government partnerships in the delivery of social services. It should be noted, however, that this expansion stems from a loosening of the legal restrictions on funding such organizations, rather than an increase in appropriations for welfare programs. Under these guidelines, faith-based organizations can either accept vouchers from welfare recipients or enter into contracts with state government to deliver welfare services; relevant welfare funds include TANF, and in all likelihood, food stamps, Medicaid and Supplemental Security Insurance.[36]

While the bulk of the TANF money is distributed at the state level, there are discretionary grant programs available under TANF and administered directly by the Department of Health and Human Services and the Department of Labor. For instance, the Welfare-to-Work[37] Competitive Grants administered by the department are available to community based organizations to provide job training to

TANF recipients. In the first round of awards, Bethel New Life of Chicago, whose partners include Lutheran Family Mission and Gateway Foundation, received $2.7 million to develop a "holistic approach to leveraging resources from within the community to provide employment assistance to eligible, hard-to-employ residents."[38] In the third round of awards, St. John the Baptist Church, a Roman Catholic parish in Brooklyn, N.Y., and North Brooklyn Coalition for Welfare Reform and Economic Development received $2.9 million to work on English proficiency to help move welfare recipients into unsubsidized employment.[39] In July 1998, HHS announced its own demonstration grant program tied into the Welfare-to-Work program to provide "local seed money" to communities and organizations providing job training to hard-to-employ welfare recipients. The funding announcement explains that priority will be given to organizations coordinating with "public, private, nonprofit, community and faith-based organizations and businesses" in the local community.

To consider the full scope of potential partnerships between faith communities and government, therefore, in building a social safety net requires thinking more broadly than just welfare reform. In fact, the programs covered by Charitable Choice represent only one form of government funding for FBOs' participation in the delivery of social services; these partnerships extend to housing, crime prevention, childcare, substance abuse, education, and health promotion. More importantly, the distribution and implementation of these federal programs are almost universally directed at the state and local community level. It is up to each state and local community to decide if, and in what manner, to respond to these relatively new opportunities to expand the participation of faith communities.

State and Local Response

States and local communities have been the leaders in forging creative partnerships between faith communities and government to build the social safety net. In fact, their involvement appears to have either predated or developed simultaneously with Charitable Choice, though barring anecdotal evidence, it is extremely difficult to gauge the scale of this engagement. The response of policy makers across states and localities is contingent on a variety of factors that make it difficult to generalize about the nature of government and faith-based partnerships. These factors can range from the local political culture to the current structure of the welfare apparatus to the organization of the religious community to the ideological inclinations of policy makers.

As with national debates, support for faith-based partnerships at the state and local is bipartisan. At the state level, Republican and conservative lawmakers are comfortable with devolution of government services and the freedom welfare reform affords them to innovate. In fact, the only states to officially adopt Charitable Choice boast Republican governors (Oregon considered the policy change during their 2000 legislative session). Texas instituted Charitable Choice early, building their model on the work of the Texas Comptroller's office (see below). In 1999, Arizona adopted Charitable Choice, while Virginia and Oregon established task forces to study the policy innovation. In early 2000, Charitable Choice legislation was pending in Florida and Michigan.

Much of the local innovation occurs in urban areas, particularly cities with sizable minority populations. This trend is not surprising given the challenges cities face with respect to anti-poverty polices; as many scholars note, local government often lacks the resources to engage in serious redistribution of wealth to its poorer citizens and often rely on coalitions with nonprofits and businesses to deliver services.[40] These partnerships allow city government to address social and economic ills without raising taxes or cutting important services such as police protection or garbage pickup. The political alliances between Democratic mayors and black and Catholic churches, especially in America's largest cities, facilitate these partnerships.[41]

There are two important ways in which faith-based organizations support the social safety net locally. First, block grants are distributed at the state and local level, with a substantial portion of this funding targeted at religious charities. The national denominational charities, such as Catholic Charities and Lutheran Social Services, generally distribute services through contracts with state and local agencies. For instance, Catholic Charities of the Archdiocese of San Francisco runs 37 programs at 24 sites with services for homeless families, people with HIV or AIDS, and the elderly. Fifty-three percent of its total resources come from government sources, including $8 million from San Francisco's city government.[42] These local efforts by denominational charities are generally secular in nature and a majority of their beneficiaries are not part of their faith community. Catholic Charities of the Archdiocese of Boston, for example, reports that in 1996 only 36 percent of its clients identified themselves as Catholic.[43]

Second, a more limited amount of government funding is targeted at congregations and sectarian religious groups. This funding comes from the federal, state, or local discretionary grant programs and block grants monies distributed by local agencies. These funds nearly universally require churches to have 501(c)(3) or Community Development Corporation status, except for services covered by Charitable Choice. Congregations will usually enter into partnerships with other nonprofits to develop coordinated community responses to particular problems such as lack of affordable housing. Faith-based organizations are more likely to receive grant money when they cultivate coalitions, even if they are legally eligible alone. In fact, a major function of the Office for Community and Interfaith Partnerships within HUD is to assist smaller religious groups to develop grant proposals and work with other groups to enhance their ability to receive funding.[44]

Some recent state and local initiatives include:

- In New Jersey, Governor Christine Todd Whitman announced a $5 million program, the "Faith-Based Community Development Initiative," in her 1999 budget proposal. The Department of Community

Affairs will work directly with faith-based, urban community development corporations to "revitalize their neighborhoods."[45]

- In Indiana, the Front Porch Alliance (FPA), launched by former Indianapolis mayor Steven Goldsmith, is designed to bring together "values-shaping institutions" to collectively address community needs. In 1998, faith-based organizations, with help from the FPA, received modest funds from the city and more substantial income from federal sources to develop youth programs and convert dilapidated housing into a drug treatment centers.[46]
- In Michigan, the state's welfare reform initiative, To Strengthen Michigan's Families, began an experiment with a program called Project Zero. Under Project Zero, the state partners with nonprofits to mentor welfare recipients to move to unsubsidized work. In 1997, Michigan's Family Independence Agency contracted with Samaritan Ministries, a local social service ministry, to develop support systems and mentoring programs using volunteers from local churches.[47]

Other states and cities have adopted more modest programs or merely included faith-based organizations among the groups eligible to participate in government initiatives. For example, in 1999, the Illinois Department of Human Services awarded $5 million to community groups participating in Teen R.E.A.C.H., a program aimed at keeping kids in school, and preventing juvenile crime, drug abuse and teenage pregnancy. Churches are among the groups eligible to apply.[48] In Chicago, religious organizations are eligible to participate in the abandoned-lot project run by HUD; the project's work included rehabilitating housing for senior citizens. Chicago's Board of Education awards funds to churches to provide after school programs for neighborhood kids.

While in principle Charitable Choice allows churches to enter into direct contractual relationships with government or serve as a location for redemption of welfare vouchers, as I noted earlier, few states have taken advantage of the provision.[49] The pilot programs that do exist tend to rely on unfunded relationships between government agencies and congregations. For example, the leading models, Mississippi's Faith and Families and Texas's Family PathFinders, rest on the voluntary adoption of welfare families by local congregations or religious groups.

In 1995, Mississippi Governor Kirk Fordice introduced Faith and Families, a program where congregations voluntarily "adopt" welfare families to help them with "counseling, child care, transportation, or help with resume writing or job interviewing skills."[50] According to Therese Love, the program has 850 congregations working with 1,088 families and has helped 286 former welfare recipients find employment.[51] And in Texas in 1995, State Comptroller John Sharp introduced the Family Pathfinders program, modeled on Mississippi's Faith and Families initiative.[52] The program, along with the Texas Department of Human Services and Texas Workforce Commission, matches welfare recipients looking for work with religious institutions and other community groups, which provide supportive services like job training and daycare. A program newsletter reported in 1998 that 400 families have been "matched" with community groups.[53]

Other states and counties have followed suit. Some counties in North Carolina, for instance, allow congregations to voluntarily take on welfare families, even matching them by religious denomination.[54] In Alabama, a coalition of congregations assists the Montgomery County Department of Human Resources through their program Caring Congregations, but only receives government funds for their substance abuse program.[55] In Anne Arundel County, Maryland, congregations can volunteer through the county's Community Directed Assistance Program to administer welfare recipient's benefits.[56] Congregations that enroll in this program receive up to six months of welfare benefits, which they spend on behalf of the recipient on "supportive services, financial and job counseling and related help."[57]

Congregational Response

A majority of congregations in the United States provide social services, ranging from independently sponsored activities to denominationally affiliated programs to partnerships with other nonprofit organizations. According to the Independent Sector, an advocacy organization devoted to the nonprofit sector, the overwhelming majority of congregations in the United States offer some sort of social service or program; in their 1993 survey, 92 percent of congregations reported engaging in an activity related to human services or welfare. Most frequently these programs take the form of family counseling or youth activities (between 71–73 percent). Many fewer reported providing demanding services such as running a food pantry (50 percent), shelters for the homeless (39 percent), affordable housing development (20 percent), or after school programs (18 percent).[58] The 1997 Sacred Places Study of 111 historic congregations in six U.S. cities found that 93 percent offered some social service including food pantries (60 percent), clothing closets (53 percent), recreational programs for teens (46 percent), recreational programs for children (42 percent), and soup kitchens (41 percent).[59]

A more recent study conducted by sociologist Mark Chaves shows that the level of congregational service delivery is lower and less intensive than these other surveys suggest. In his survey,[60] only 57 percent of congregations report participating in service delivery projects; the bulk of these efforts meet the immediate needs of individuals, for instance, through food and clothing programs. When congregations participate in programs, they tend to work in partnership with other nonprofits as opposed to supporting independent, resource intensive projects or programs. These findings suggest that America's congregations rarely sponsor the sorts of programs that would support systematic intervention with welfare recipients or wide scale economic redevelopment. As Chaves concludes, it is foolhardy to expect congregations to take on the challenges presented by welfare reform's Charitable Choice provisions:

> Although a majority of congregations participate in or support social service activity at some level, only a small minority of congregations participate extensively in such activities either by operating their own projects or programs, by having a staff person devote at least 25 percent of work time to these activities, or by spending large amounts of money in supporting these activities. . . . *Expecting congregations to operate social service programs in large numbers is unrealistic since most do not currently run such programs* (emphasis added).[61]

Congregations and small religious groups receive minimal levels of government funding for the service delivery they do engage in. Their participation in public/private partnerships and receipt of funding is dwarfed by the national denominational charities. The limited scope of funding is confirmed by the Independent Sector data, which shows that less than 1 percent of the congregations in their sample receive any government contributions or program revenue.[62] Only 2 percent of the congregations surveyed even participate in "a joint venture with a government organization."[63] Chaves reports slightly higher numbers, with 3 percent of congregations receiving government funding.

The black church is somewhat more likely to be involved in public/private partnerships. A recent survey of African American churches in Washington, D.C. finds that less than 5 percent of black churches receive any form of government support.[64] A larger study by Lincoln and Mamiya of urban and rural African American churches, shows that between 6 and 7 percent of black churches "participate in any governmental program for which [they] receive funding".[65] Regardless of race or religious tradition, however, the vast majority of congregational revenue in the United States comes from individual donations and denominational coffers, not directly from the government.[66]

There are important reasons why congregations receive so little money from the government. Despite increasingly legal flexibility, significant restrictions still limit the ability of congregations or sectarian organizations to apply for and receive government funds. Charitable Choice only covers certain social services; the remaining programs still require faith-based organizations to have 501(c)(3) or Community Development Corporation status, or at least non-profit partners. Efforts are underway to broaden the scope of Charitable Choice. A central component of presidential candidate Governor George W. Bush's policy proposals, for example, loosens restrictions on ability of government to award federal dollars to religious organizations. He proposes, for example, recognizing "alternative licensing regimes," which would deem religious training an alternative to other professional training.[67]

In the 105th and 106th Congresses, Senator John Ashcroft of Missouri introduced the Charitable Choice Expansion legislation that would "apply to programs such as housing, substance abuse prevention and treatment, juvenile services, seniors' services, the Community Development Block Grant, the Community Services Block Grant, the Social Services Block Grant, abstinence education, and child welfare service."[68] In effect, this initiative would allow congregations to provide any services for which states contract with private providers, with the exception of most education programs. A variety of bills pending in the House and Senate include similar provisions. For example, a juvenile justice bill introduced by Senator Orrin Hatch and a youth drug treatment bill introduced by Senator Jack Reed include the identical Charitable Choice language found in welfare reform legislation.[69]

Given that congregations do not receive much government money or enter into direct contractual relationships to deliver services in the same way larger institutions like Catholic Charities do, it is important to consider their informal relationships with government and partnerships with other nonprofits. State and local innovations in welfare reform, such as Family Pathfinders and Faith and Families, are built upon voluntary and informal relationships between local agencies, nonprofits, businesses, and congregations. As policy makers respond to the challenges of welfare reform, they are institutionalizing their relationships with religious communities and awarding religious leaders important advisory roles. In Texas, a task force including prominent members of the clergy developed the *Faith in Action* plan, which was introduced into the state legislature by Governor Bush. In Sacramento County, California, the Department of Human Assistance actively seeks the participation of the Interfaith Service Bureau's welfare reform task force.[70] Ministers advise the Human Services Planning Committee in Hamilton County, Ohio, which is "guiding the county's welfare reform plan."[71] The Department of Social Services in Durham, North Carolina, hired a Baptist minister to link welfare recipients with local congregations.[72] In Fairfax County, Virginia, a coalition was formed between religious congregations, nonprofits, the Fairfax County Board of Supervisors and the county Department of Family Services called Faith Communities in Action. The leadership of this group rotates between government officials and the faith community. In San Diego County, California, the Department of Social Services created a program called All Congregations Together to assist with welfare reform efforts — complete with a desk in the lobby of the welfare office.[73]

Faith-Based Initiatives—A Cautionary Tale

The question remains, why don't more congregations and small religious groups take advantage of recent legislative and bureaucratic innovation in faith-based partnerships? There are a number of important factors related to mission, capacity, and politics that explain the reluctance of congregations and faith communities to engage in public/private partnerships. These constraints introduce a cautionary note against an unreflective and enthusiastic embrace of faith-based service delivery funded by the state.

Mission-Related Constraints

There are a number of religious leaders and groups on the right and the left who believe that these sorts of government partnerships are inappropriate for religious institutions. Many worry that the entanglement with the government will divert congregations from the more explicitly religious aspects of their mission. What makes faith-based social service delivery special, they argue, is its connection with spiritual values and commitment to religion. Charitable Choice relaxes restrictions on the institutional expression of religious belief, but it forbids proselytizing or sectarian worship. This constraint may rob religious groups of what makes them most effective.[74] Moreover, others such as Rev. Stephen Burger, the leader of International Union of Gospel Missions, express concern that religious groups risk lawsuits if they accept government funds, precisely because religious conversion and instruction are intertwined with effective service delivery.[75]

There is an important demographic here issue as well. The fastest growing religious groups in the United States, white evangelical Protestants, are the least likely to take advantage of Charitable Choice. In the early 20th century, the evangelical community embraced the Social Gospel and progressive politics, believing that Christians had an obligation to create "heaven on earth" by meeting the needs of the poor and improving working conditions for the laboring classes. After the split between modernists and traditionalists, evangelical Protestants retreated from social involvement, concentrating energies on building organizational infrastructure and evangelical outreach.[76] Today, conservative Christians are more committed to pursuing missionary work and evangelizing than intervening directly on behalf of the poor. In fact, Wuthnow argues that "evangelism and social justice" have become the "polar positions around which religious conservatives and religious liberals increasingly identified themselves."[77] The National Congregations Study confirms this trend. The survey shows that nearly half of liberal and moderate Protestant congregations and Catholic parishes are willing to apply for government funds, compared to only 28 percent of conservative denominations.

Material Constraints

Many congregations lack the material and professional capacity to participate in burdensome social service programs. The most important predictor of participation in social service delivery is size; larger congregations have the financial resources and membership base required to staff food pantries, job training programs and after school programs, as well as adopt welfare families. But according to the Independent Sector survey, 72 percent of congregations in the United States have 400 members or less and 20 percent have less than 100 members on their rolls.[78] A majority of these smaller congregations do not provide social services and many congregations cannot serve the populations that already rely on them. For instance, in an Urban Institute study of congregations in Washington, D.C. and surrounding suburbs, a majority of congregations believe that they do not have adequate facilities, staff or volunteers, nor the ability to raise additional funds to meet increased demand.[79]

Many of the legislative proposals to expand Charitable Choice address challenging societal problems, particularly substance abuse and juvenile crime, which require significant training and medical support structures. It is not clear that clergy or lay people have the appropriate skills or resources to help substance abusers or counsel children. Eligibility for non-Charitable Choice programs, moreover, requires technical expertise and sophistication to meet the federal requirements, in particular, acquiring nonprofit status, assembling the proper board of directors, separating government funds from congregational monies, and complying with federal employment and safety laws.

Political and Legal Constraints

There are serious political and legal concerns about Charitable Choice. First, some of the religious groups most concerned with care for the poor believe that Charitable Choice represents an abdication of government responsibility for social welfare. For instance, Catholic Charities USA elected not to support an ecumenical statement endorsing Charitable Choice because it "will not add any money for new or innovative services to benefit the poor."[80] Rev. Fred Kammer, the head of Catholic Charities, notes that it will be fiscally impossible for America's religious institutions to fill in the gaps as the federal government cuts funding for social services.[81] The United Church of Christ's Welfare Working Group (with the Children's Defense Fund) opposes welfare reform, noting that faith based organizations that cannot keep pace with the needs of the people removed from the welfare rolls.[82]

There are ongoing legal controversies associated with Charitable Choice and its expansion. Despite consensus among various religious groups on the left and on the right concerning the desirability of faith-based service delivery, there are important groups that oppose contracting with sectarian organizations. The Working Group for Religious Freedom in Social Services, a coalition of religious groups and other organizations including the American Civil Liberties Union, opposed the American Community Renewal Act, which would allow congregations to receive public funds to provide mental health and substance abuse services, on the grounds that it violates both the Establishment Clause and the religious liberty of participants.[83] Americans United for the Separation of Church and State has opposed Charitable Choice and its expansion precisely because, it contends, the provision violates the Establishment Clause, which forbids state-supported religion. In light of this opposition, Charitable Choice will almost certainly face legal challenges as particularly as more states adopt the provisions.

Conclusion

It is not the moment to take government out of the business of caring for our nation's social and economic welfare. There is little hard evidence that faith based communities do a better job than government at solving our society's social and economic problems, despite the hopeful claims of proponents of public/private partnerships. There are important constraints on the resources and capacity of congregations to take on complex and demanding social service projects. Legal concerns abound about the ability of religious institutions to separate the sacred from the secular. Finally, it is not clear how much of this innovation is a luxury afforded by a booming economy. If there is an economic downturn, it is realistic to assume we can rely on our religious organizations to cope with the wide scale homelessness, joblessness, and poverty?

At the same time, we should embrace what is best about religious organizations. Our nation's religious institutions hold a deep theological commitment to care for the poor, and they frequently have structures in place, particularly through their denominational charities, to help meet the immediate needs of people in their communities. Churches, synagogues, and mosques create an important public space where community groups such as civic associations, community policing programs, and Alcoholics Anonymous congregate to address communal and individual needs. They also anchor neighborhoods undergoing changes, facilitating the integration of new residents and immigrants and preserving economic stability.[84] Local religious leaders understand the particular challenges facing their members and neighbors, perhaps better than impersonal bureaucrats do. The challenge, therefore, is to figure out how to support the good works of congregations without compromising their integrity or corrupting their mission, violating the principle of separation of church and state or allowing the state to abdicate responsibility for the poor.

Notes

1. Theda Skocpol, "Unravelling from Above," *American Prospect* 25 (1996): 22. Also see Ronald Thieman, "Who Ought to Provide? Government and Faith-based Organizations, " this volume.

2. Jim Castelli, "Faith-based Non-Profits," Policy Report No. 27 (Washington: Progressive Policy Institute 1997).

3. Steven Rathgeb Smith and Michael Lipsky, *Non Profits for Hire: The Welfare State in the Age of Contracting* (Cambridge: Harvard University Press, 1993); Lester M. Salamon, "The Marketization of Welfare: Changing Nonprofit and For-profit Roles in the American Welfare State," *Social Service Review* 67 (1993): 18.

4. Salamon, "The Marketization of Welfare," 19.

5. Stephen V. Monsma, *When Sacred and Secular Mix* (Lanham: Rowman & Littlefield Publishers, Inc., 1996).

6. The authors, however, do not clearly indicate what time period these estimates cover. The estimates are based on the self-report of the Salvation Army, Catholic Charities USA, the Evangelical Lutheran Church in America, the Lutheran Church-Missouri Synod, the YMCA, the YWCA and the International Union of Gospel Missions. John McCarthy and Jim Castelli, *Religion-Sponsored Social Service Providers: The Not-So-Independent Sector*, Working Paper Series (Washington: The Aspen Institute, 1998).

7. Paul Clolery, "Total Raised by Elite 100 Include Two $2 Billion Organizations and Four Generating at Least $1 Billion," *NonProfit Times* (1997): 37.

8. William Tucker, "Sweet Charity," *The American Spectator* 28 (1995): 38.

9. See, however, Martha Minow, "Welfare and Schooling After the Fall of the Welfare States: Who is Home in the Public Square," this volume. Minow argues that there may be important ways Charitable Choice violate the Lemon test and decisions in more recent cases, like *Bowen v. Kendrick* (1988).

10. Carl H. Esbeck, "A Constitutional Case for Government Cooperation with Faith-Based Service Providers," *Emory Law Journal* 46 (1997): 13–14.

11. Monsma, *When Sacred and Secular Mix*, pp. 30–31, 114ff.

12. Support for devolution and local innovation is not new, of course. For instance, see David Osborne, *Laboratories of Democracy* (Cambridge: Harvard Business School Press, 1990).

13. Stanley W. Carlson-Thies, "'Don't Look to Us': The Negative Responses of the Churches to Welfare Reform," *Notre Dame Journal of Law, Ethics & Public Policy* 11 (1997): 669–700.

14. Senator Dan Coats conceived of "Project for American Renewal" in 1996. It consisted of 19 legislative proposals, with a tax credit for charitable donations aimed at alleviating poverty as its centerpiece. He developed this proposal, in part, in response to the "failed government experiment" with social policy. He "calls it the 'promotion and privatization of compassion,' based on an assumption privately funded and community-based charity gradually would replace most but not all government-run welfare. It would stress personal responsibility, discipline and spiritual values. . . ." Helen Dewar, "Coats Seeks to Warm GOP Image Through 'Poverty Tax Credit' Plan," *The Washington Post* 25 February 1996.

15. William J. Bennett and John DiIulio, "What Good Is Government," *Commentary* 5 (1997).

16. Quoted in James W. Bronsnan, "Gore Seeks Faith, Government Union," *The Arizona Republic,* May 24 1999.

17. Reverend Eugene Rivers is the founder of the Azusa Christian Community, a Pentecostal community in Boston. In 1995, he opened the Ella J. Baker House in the Four Corners Neighborhood in Dorchester. The Baker House activists engage in "faith-based" intervention in the neighborhood, providing space for sports and job training, among other activities. He also is a co-founder of the Ten Point Coalition, which works with the Boston Police Department to address juvenile crime in the neighborhood. See Michael Jonas, "The Street Ministers," *CommonWealth* 4 (1999): 36–45.

18. "Remarks by the President at Crime Prevention Event," Office of the Press Secretary, White House, July 28, 1998.

19. Jim Wallis, "The Church Steps Forward," *Sojourners Magazine* 26 (1997): 7–9.

20. *Congressional Record,* 105th Cong., 2d sess., 1998, 144, 56: S4534-S4535.

21. "Remarks as prepared for delivery by Vice President Al Gore on the Role of Faith Based Organizations," *www.algore2000. . . speeches/speeches_faith_052499.html,* May 24, 1999.

22. Governor George W. Bush, "Duty of Hope," *http://www.georgewbush.com/speeches/faith/dutyofhope.asp,* July 22, 1999.

23. These programs represent only a fraction of the funding that sustains faith-based social service delivery. Even before the introduction of the Charitable Choice provisions in the 1996 welfare reform package, the bulk of the financial support for faith-based social service came in the form of block grants to state governments. Block grants mainly

from the Department of Health and Human Services (HHS), such as Social Services Block Grants and Community Services Block Grants, support a range of faith-based services in low-income communities and populations. For instance, most local Catholic Charities agencies receive Social Services Block Grants, mainly for support for abused children, adoption services, and day care. Catholic Charities USA, "Catholic Charities USA, Coalition of Groups Speak out for Social Services Block Grant," *www.catholiccharitiesusa.org/061698.html.*

24. In 1997, Housing Secretary Andrew Cuomo created a special office, called the Center for Community and Interfaith Partnerships, designed to increase the participation of the faith community in HUD initiatives. It is headed by a Catholic priest, Father Joseph Hacala.

25. US Department of Housing and Urban Development, "Commitment to Justice: Creative Partnerships to Renew our Hope in Communities," *http://www.hud.gov/cdc/commjust.html#further.*

26. US Department of Housing and Urban Development, "Proposed Budget includes $20 Million for Community and Faith Baed Groups," *Building Communities Together,* Volume 2, Issue 2 *http://www.hud.gov/cdc/febblast.pdf.*

27. "Faith Communities and Community Building," Department of Housing and Urban Development, www.hud.gov/faith1.html, January 22, 1998.

28. "Blue Ribbon Practices in Community Development," Department of Housing and Urban Development, www.hud.gov/ptw/docs/ga07.html. The Home Investment Partnerships Program is the largest federal block grant to states and local governments to create affordable housing.

29. "President Announces New Funds for Values-Based Efforts to Prevent Youth Violence," Press Release, Department of Justice, July 22, 1998, www.ojp.usdoj.gov. This program was modeled after the work of Eugene Rivers's Ten Point Coalition. He attended the press conference with the President, though Boston was not one of the communities that received money from the Justice Department.

30. Interview with Steve Rickman, Executive Director of the Weed and Seed program, telephone conversation with author, September 29, 1998.

31. "USDA Gleaning and Food Recovery," U.S. Department of Agriculture, *www.usda.gov/fcs/glean.html.*

32. Though there is no funding attached to this program. "Religious Groups," Department of Education, www.ed.gov/PFIE/religiou.html, June 16, 1998.

33. "The AmeriCorps Home Page," Corporation for National Service, *www.cns.gov/americorps/index.html.*

34. For instance, a state government can even choose to divert some TANF funding for other uses. David A. Super, Sharon Parrott, Susan Steinmetz, and Cindy Mann, "The New Welfare Law – Summary, Center on Budget and Policy Priorities," Center on Budget and Policy Priorities, www. cbpp.org/WCNSUM.HTM, August 13, 1996.

35. "A Guide of Charitable Choice," The Center for Public Justice, www.cpjustice.org/~cpjustice/Cguide/Guide.html, 1997.

36. Ibid.

37. Welfare-to-Work was allocated 3 billion dollars in the 1997 Balanced Budget Act. The DOL provides oversight, but it will be distributed through Private Industry Councils (PICs) to local communities. Vice President Al Gore is spearheading the "Welfare-to-Work Coalition," a coalition of civic groups interested in exploring how to employ people

making the transition off welfare to unsubsidized work. "Clinton-Gore Accomplishments Reforming Welfare," *http://www.whitehouse.gov/WH/Welfare/Accomp.html.*

38. Bethel New Life, Inc. is a Community Development Corporation. The other FBO awarded funds was Catholic Charities of Albuquerque New Mexico. "Welfare to Work, Competitive Grants," U.S. Department of Labor, wtw.doleta.gov/documents/commsumm.html, May 27, 1998.

39. U. S. Department of Labor, "Welfare to Work: Round Three Competitive Grant Summaries" *http://wtw.doleta.gov/competitive/round3/summaries.htm#ny–6.*

40. Paul E. Peterson, *City Limits* (Chicago: University of Chicago Press, 1981); Clarence N. Stone, *Regime Politics* (Lawrence: University of Kansas Press, 1989).

41. Fred Harris, *Something Within* (New York: Oxford University Press, 1999); Anna Greenberg, *Divine Inspiration: Faith, Congregations and American Politics,* unpublished book manuscript, 2000.

42. Don Lattin, "A Look at Religious Charities' Missions in San Francisco" *The San Francisco Chronicle,* September 15, 1998.

43. "Who We Serve," Catholic Charities Archdioceses of Boston, *www.ccab.org/WhoWeServe.cfm.*

44. Interview with Father Joseph Hacala, Director of the Center for Community and Interfaith Partnerships, phone conversation with author, October 2, 1998.

45. "Initiatives," Office of the Governor, www.state.nj.us/governor/init_life.html.

46. "Front Porch Alliance," City of Indianapolis, *www.indygov.org/mayor/fpa/index.html.*

47. Dana Milbank, "In God's Name: Michigan Now Relies on Chuches to Help People Leave Welfare," *Wall Street Journal,* March 17, 1997, A1; State of Michigan, Family Independence Agency, "Project Zero", www.mfia.state.mi.us/PROJZERO/pzintro.

48. "State Program Offers Alternatives for Young People at Risk for Substance Abuse and other Problems," Illinois Department of Human Services, *www.state.il.gov/agency/dhs/reach.html.*

49. Texas has officially adopted Charitable Choice, but the program has not yet been implemented, except on a voluntary basis. In 1996, Governor George Bush created a "Faith-Based Task Force," comprised of 16 members of the clergy and "volunteer leaders," to explore obstacles to the participation of the faith community in service delivery and other programs. *Faith in Action,* the task force's report, made a series of recommendations including adoption of Charitable Choice, congregational involvement in healthcare, crime and drug use prevention, childcare and counseling and self-help.

50. Jim Castelli, "Faith-Based Social Services."; Jim Yardley, "Focus on Overhauling Welfare" *The Atlanta Journal Constitution,* April 30, 1996.

51. Interview with Theresa Love, Mississippi Governor's Office, phone conversation with Brian Welch, September 30, 1998.

52. "Lighting the Path," Office of Comptroller of Public Accounts, *www.window.state.tx.us./comptrol/fampath/light.html.*

53. "Family Pathfinders News," Office of Comptroller of Public Accounts, www.window.state.tx.us/comptrol/fampath/path9809.html, Summer 1998.

54. Ronnie Glassberg, "County Looks to the Churches for Help," *The Herald Sun* (Durham, N.C.), July 22, 1998.

55. Mike Cason, "Churches Open to Expanding Outreach," *The Montgomery Advertiser,* January 10, 1998.

56. Kathy Lally, "Unlikely Alliance Aids Poor," *The Baltimore Sun*, February 17, 1997.

57. Jessica Yates, "Partnership with the Faith Community in Welfare Reform," Welfare Information Network, March 1998, www.welfareinfo.org/faith.

58. The Independent Sector, working with the Gallup Organization, regularly conducts a survey of American congregations. The 1993 questionnaire was mailed to 1,003 congregations, yielding a sample size of 727 congregations. The sample was a representative sample compiled from telephone directors, and excluded denominational organizations, religious charities, or religiously owned institutions such as schools or hospitals. Clearly there are number of sources of bias in the sample, particularly that many congregations are not found in phone books (e.g., storefront churches) or change their contact information. Results reported in *From Belief to Commitment* (Washington, DC: Independent Sector, 1993).

59. Diane Cohen and A. Robert Jaegger, "Sacred Places at Risk," (Philadelphia: Partners for Sacred Places, 1997). Mark Chaves, however, notes that these congregational surveys suffer from inflated reports of activities because they heavily weight larger congregations in their samples. His survey based on a representative sample of U.S. congregations shows significantly lower number of congregations, though still a majority (57 percent), offering some sort of social service ("Congregations' Social Service Activities," *The Urban Institute*, Policy Brief No. 6, December 1999).

60. Mark Chaves, working with the National Opinion Research Center (NORC), conducted the National Congregations Study. The sample is drawn from responses from NORC's General Social Survey, which enabled Chaves to compile a representative sample that includes congregations missed by surveys such as the work of the Independent Sector. The sample size is 1,236 congregations (interviews conducted with religious leaders), with a response rate of 80 percent. See Mark Chaves, et al., "The National Congregations Study: Background Methods, and Selected Results," *Journal for the Scientific Study of Religion* 38 (1999): 458–476.

61. Chaves, "Congregations' Social Service Activities."

62. *From Belief to Commitment*, p. 73.

63. Ibid., p. 97.

64. Elizabeth T. Boris, "Services and Capacity of Religious Congregations in the Washington, DC Metropolitan Area," (*The Urban Institute*, January 1997).

65. Lincoln and Mamiya's results are based on a survey of 1895 urban clergy from 2,150 urban churches and 363 rural clergy from 619 churches. The participants were drawn from the seven major black denominations using regional subsets to generate a national sample. See C. Eric Lincoln and Lawrence H. Mamiya, *The Black Church in the African American Experience* (Durham: Duke University Press, 1990).

66. *From Belief to Commitment*, p. 80.

67. George W. Bush, "George W. Bush Eliminating Barriers to Faith Based Action," *www.georgewbush.com/issues/domestic/faith/barriers.asp*, August 2, 1999.

68. "The Charitable Choice Expansion Act of 1998 – Bill Summary," July 7, 1998 (Photocopy).

69. Americans United for Separation of Church and State, "Charitable Choice," *www.au.org/cc-leg.html*.

70. Jan Ferris, "Churches Enlisted in Welfare Reform," *Sacramento Bee*, November 4, 1997. Apparently the local Industrial Areas Foundation organization, the Sacramento Valley Organizing Community was active in demanding inclusion in county welfare re-

form efforts. Don Lattin, "On the Crusade's Front Lines," *The San Francisco Chronicle,* September 16, 1998.

71. Julie Irwin, "Church Groups Urged to Seek States' Aid," *The Cincinnati Enquirer,* December 17, 1997.

72. Ronnie Glassberg, "County Looks to Churches for Help," *The Herald Sun* (Durham, N.C.), July 22, 1998.

73. "Faith-Based Involvement," The Welfare Information Network, *www.welfare-info.org/faithbase.html.*

74. See Joe Loconte, "Qualms about Alms: The 7 Deadly Sins of Government Funding," *Policy Review* 82 (1997).

75. "IUGM & the New Welfare Reform Bill," International Union of Gospel Missions, *www.iugm.org/welfare/wel-bill.html.*

76. This battle was most famously played out in the Scopes Monkey Trials in 1925, when William Jennings Bryant took a school teacher from Dayton, Ohio, to court for teaching the theory of evolution and lost in a humiliating defeat. See Martin Riesebrodt, *Pious Passions* (Berkeley: University of California Press, 1993).

77. Robert Wuthnow, *The Restructuring of American Religion* (Princeton: Princeton University Press, 1988).

78. *From Belief to Commitment,* p. 7.

79. Boris, "Services and Capacity of Religious Congregations in the Washington, DC Metropolitan Area."

80. "Issue Brief: Charitable Choice," Catholic Charities USA, February 1998 (Photocopy).

81. Joseph P. Shapiro, "Can Churches Save America?" *U.S. News and World Report,* September 9, 1996.

82. United Church of Christ Welfare Working Group, "Synod Calls for Action to Repair Serious Flaws in Welfare Reform", *www.uccwelfareworking*group.com.

83. Members include: American Civil Liberties Union, American Counseling Association, American Federation of State, County and Municipal Employees, American Jewish Committee, American Jewish Congress, Americans United for Separation of Church and State, Anti-Defamation League, Baptist Joint Committee on Public Affairs, Catholics for a Free Choice, Central Conference of American Rabbis, CHILD Inc., Friends Committee on National Legislation, General Board of Church and Society, United Methodist Church, General Conference of Seventh Day Adventists, Legal Action Center, National Association of Alcoholism & Drug Abuse Counselors, National Council of Jewish Women, National Jewish Community Relations Advisory Council, NOW Legal Defense and Education Fund, People for the American Way Action Fund, Presbyterian Church (U.S.A.), Washington Office, The Rabbinical Assembly, Union of American Hebrew Congregations, Unitarian Universalist Association, United Church of Christ, Office for Church in Society, Women's American Ort and The Workmen's Circle. *www.aclu.org/congress/l042597a.html*

84. Greenberg, *Divine Inspiration.*

CHAPTER 8

After Partnership: Rethinking Public-Nonprofit Relations

Peter Frumkin

Public management of the delivery of services by the nonprofit sector should move toward strategies that promote more autonomy for faith-based nonprofits and that support independent and pluralistic nonprofit initiatives.

THE NONPROFIT AND PUBLIC SECTORS have frequently been described as collaborators or partners in public service, sharing a common commitment to meeting community needs[1]. However, as the nonprofit sector has grown in size and as many organizations have begun to compete for public funds, the sector's fundamental orientation to service through voluntary action has been in the midst of radical reinvention. In an increasingly competitive environment, many nonprofits have been forced to go to great lengths to secure public funds, sometimes modifying their missions and changing their operations in order to survive financially[2]. As a consequence of the growing financial pressures within the nonprofit sector, the character of public-nonprofit relations has clearly changed, and this has in turn called into question the adequacy of the dominant "partnership" model.

The increasing role of the nonprofit sector in the delivery of publicly funded services has also created new challenges for the field of public management.[3] Chief among these is how public managers can best negotiate the real tensions that now characterize this complex relationship, especially when faith-based nonprofits are involved. Rather than working toward tighter oversight and more programmatic control, I will argue, public management should move in the opposite direction toward strategies that promote more sectoral autonomy and, in the process, support independent and pluralistic nonprofit initiatives. Such an approach entails rethinking what accountability means and how oversight should be exercised when public and nonprofit sectors interact. Several significant obstacles stand in the way of such a strategic reorientation, including the enduring influence and intuitive appeal of the partnership perspective.

This chapter begins by reviewing the origins of the partnership perspective and its flaws in light of more recent research. I then discuss developments within neo-institutional theory that are relevant to the question of what happens when nonprofit organizations come to depend increasingly on public funds. Finally, I sketch the outline of a new approach to managing public-nonprofit relations that I call "pluralistic autonomy." Throughout, my goal is to raise new questions about an area of public management that will only increase in importance and visibility as the role of the nonprofit sector in delivering government-funded services grows.

The Triumph of Partnership in the First Wave of Research

The nonprofit sector today encompasses close to 2 million organizations, including 501(c)(3) nonprofits (organized for religious, educational, charitable, and scientific purposes) and a host of other types of nonprofits, such as business leagues, chambers of commerce, social and recreational clubs, civic leagues, and labor associations.[4] Of the more than half million 501(c)(3) charitable nonprofits, only about 125,000 organizations have gross receipts of over $25,000.[5] Although many smaller, community-based nonprofits aspire to secure public funding, they often face serious managerial and political obstacles to that goal. By contrast, a relatively select group of large social-service and health nonprofits have long received the bulk of public funding, and it is this group of organizations that lies at the center of the growing debate over the impact of financial ties between nonprofit organizations and government.

Today, most scholars interested in the study of public policy implementation are aware of the important role that nonprofit organizations play in the delivery of human services. This awareness is in no small part due to a first major wave of research on nonprofit organizations during the late 1970s and early 1980s that charted the theory[6] and scope[7] of the nonprofit sector. This early research on the growth of the American nonprofit sector produced two important findings. The first was that the nonprofit sector had become by the late 1970s the principal vehicle for the delivery of government financed human services. The second was that government had also quietly become the main source of nonprofit human service agency finance.[8] Much of the early research trod lightly around the question of the quality of government-nonprofit relations. Instead, the focus was on developing a new body of descriptive data that tracked the way that many nonprofit organizations, particularly those delivering health and social services, were coming to depend on government funds for an increasingly large part of their budgets. Beyond measuring this development, the relationship between government and nonprofits was thought to be best characterized as a mutually supportive and equal partnership, one in which the two parties collaboratively pursued public ends.

A key figure in the early theorizing about public-nonprofit relations was Lester Salamon. Through a series of important contributions in the 1980s, Salamon developed the argument that the nonprofit sector is not—and probably was never well suited to be—the "independent sector" in either financial or programmatic terms: "In short, for all its strengths, the voluntary sector has a number of inherent weaknesses as a mechanism for responding to the human service needs of an advanced industrial society. It is limited in its ability to generate an adequate level of resources, is vulnerable to particularism and the favoritism of the wealthy, is prone to self-defeating paternalism, and has at times been associated with amateur, as opposed to professional, forms of care."[9]

These problems were not unmanageable in Salamon's view. By joining with government to form a partnership in public service, the nonprofit sector could fulfill its mission of delivering needed services. Salamon argued that in areas where the nonprofit sector may lack the ability to attract substantial financial resources, regulate the way care is provided, and aspire toward universal provision, the public sector could readily provide assistance.

> The voluntary sector's weaknesses correspond well with government's strengths, and vice versa. Potentially, at least, government is in a position to generate a more reliable stream of resources, to set priorities on the basis of a democratic political process instead of the wishes of the wealthy, to offset part of the paternalism of the charitable system by making access to care a right instead of a privilege, and to improve the quality of care by instituting quality-control standards.[10]

The result of this partnership is what Salamon termed "third-party government," one in which government funds, collaborates and works through the nonprofit sector in the delivery of human services.

Salamon was clearly aware of the potential problems that his partnership model might generate and he correctly located three fundamental threats to nonprofits brought on by government funding: (1) loss of nonprofit autonomy and independence; (2) "vendorism" or distortion of the agency missions in pursuit of available government funding; and (3) bureaucratization or over-professionalization leading to a loss of flexibility and diversity in program design. After identifying these three important threats to nonprofits, Salamon dismissed them—even though he noted that at the time of his writing in 1987 there was little systematic data available about the effect of government funds on nonprofits. Citing one author in 1975 who commented that no real data was available about the effects of government contracts on nonprofit organizations, Salamon concluded: "Clearly, dangers to agency independence, pursuit of agency purposes, and internal management style may result from involvement with public programs, but these dangers do not appear to be so severe as to argue for dismantling the partnership that has been created."[11] Over the past decade, the idea of a public-nonprofit "partnership in service" has proven extremely popular and gained widespread currency particularly among advocates for the sector.

New Research and New Conflicts

Since the time that early research first drew attention to the important role public funding plays in supporting nonprofit organizations, a second wave of research has dramatically cast in doubt the early optimism about the consequences of the nonprofit sector's growing dependence on public funds. Taken together, this research[12] challenges quite directly earlier analyses of the threats to nonprofits posed by increasing government contracting relations. In fact, this new wave of research on public-nonprofit relations has located time and time again substantial tension and loss of autonomy within nonprofit organizations as a result of a dependence on government contracts.

After tracking the financial health of community organizations in Chicago over time, nonprofit scholar Gronbjerg found that government contracts did indeed threaten agency autonomy and lead to bureaucratization: "The external control and lack of discretion that characterize government grants and contracts limit the range of internal management decisions that recipient organizations can make. These features have direct and immediate management implications for nonprofits."[13] Many of the nonprofits in the Chicago study assigned dedicated staff to each government contract for compliance and reporting reasons. As a result, many nonprofit organizations developed "very complex organizational structures, which largely parallel their public funding streams."[14] Moreover, when asked to compare a variety of funding sources, including government, individual donations, corporate and foundation grants, federated gifts, and fees for service, nonprofit organizations found government grants to be the least flexible, the most difficult to administer and account for, the least reliable over time, and the least sensitive to mission and program priorities.[15] Some nonprofit organizations even reported they no longer pursued public funds because of the threat it posed to their long-term independence. In many ways, Gronbjerg's study of Chicago nonprofits develops the best and clearest evidence of the impact public funding can have on nonprofit organizations, evidence that challenges early thinking about a public-nonprofit partnership.

A second blow to early optimism about public funding of nonprofit organizations can be found in the work of Susan Bernstein,[16] which focused on managers of human services agencies in New York. Through detailed interviews, Bernstein concluded that nonprofit agencies are forced to play a perverse game involving proposal writing, reporting, and financial planning that bears little connection to the reality of their daily professional lives. Bernstein catalogs in detail the way nonprofit organizations suffer from excessive auditing, fluctuating public sector budgets, and multiple reporting requirements to federal, state, and city agencies. What is particularly striking about Bernstein's approach is that it captures well the mutual dependence—codependence, one is tempted to call it—that the public-nonprofit relationship can create. On the one hand, public sector funders put pressure on nonprofits by threatening to withdraw funding when programs are not designed to their liking. On the other hand, nonprofits are led sometimes to form coalitions to put pressure on government to increase funding of their particular area of interest. Throughout Bernstein's book, the voices of embattled nonprofit managers create a vivid first-hand account that contradicts earlier hopes for a fundamental compatibility between public and nonprofit sectors.

Steven Smith and Michael Lipsky[17] provide a third and telling rebuttal to early minimizing of the threats to nonprofits posed by public funding. Smith and Lipsky argue that the evidence is that government contracting has led indeed to the bureaucratization of many nonprofits. To receive public funds, nonprofit organizations are led to introduce professional staff into their organizations to both administer the new public programs and comply with the terms of the contract:

> To obtain a government contract, nonprofit agencies often must agree to professional staffing levels. Even if the agency considers that professional staffing is desirable, this requirement frequently represents an important shift in the orientation of the organization. . . . When nonprofit organizations accept government funds, they often agree to serve clients that are needier than those the organization had previously served. To provide for these clients adequately, nonprofit organizations broaden the qualifications of their staff, adding salary expenses which may or may not be paid by government.[18]

Smith and Lipsky go on to discuss how government contracting has sometimes led nonprofits to compromise their missions in order to hold onto to their government contracts. They note that this trend poses a real threat to the long-term diversity of the sector and to its ability to serve as a laboratory of innovation and experimentation. The end result has been at times quite unexpected: Smith and Lipsky point out how many radical community-based organizations in the 1960s have been transformed into docile, homogenized, publicly-supported social service bureaucracies—a process driven by years of dependence on government grants.[19]

Beyond the sobering findings of recent research on public-nonprofit contracting, two other developments call into question the continuing optimism about public-nonprofit relations. First, for there to be a true partnership between government and nonprofits, there must be a relative balance in power between the sectors. However, as the data on the sector's explosive growth abundantly illustrated, the number of nonprofit organizations has been increasing substantially over the past decade.[20] With more nonprofits competing for what have become in some areas increasingly scarce public funds, it is now clear that increased competition among nonprofits has made it harder for nonprofit organizations to achieve an equal partnership with government. Government agencies disbursing funds have been able to be increasingly selective and demanding in their awarding of contracts to nonprofits. Under-financed and duplicative nonprofit organizations have had to contend with the inability of government (and private funders) to finance the growth of the sector. One consequence of this development has been the rise in nonprofit bankruptcies and closings.[21]

A second problem with the idea of collaborative inter-sector partnership is more significant: Little attention has been paid to the different values and operating principles of nonprofits and government agencies. Far from heading toward a seamless partnership, the two sectors have experienced severe tensions that have only risen over the past decade, particularly as many faith-based nonprofit organizations have developed contractual relationships with government for the provision of human services. There is fast growing disjunction between public sector values (e.g., accountability, equity, and universalism) and the values of a growing number of nonprofit organizations, particularly those that are faith based. Thus, in addition to the problems of independence, vendorism, and excess professionalization that have been confirmed in recent research, a fourth type of conflict appears to be emerging, one related to the distinctive moral and religious values that guide and animate so many nonprofit organizations. Two recent controversies over values illustrate this emerging challenge to the idea of a frictionless public-nonprofit partnership.

Two Recent Controversies

In February 1997, the city of San Francisco had a major and highly charged confrontation with Catholic Charities, the area's largest nonprofit provider of children's services. The city's new domestic partnership law required all contractors to provide benefits to domestic partners. Not surprisingly, Catholic Charities, which receives annually over $5 million in local social service contracts, strenuously objected. A highly charged exchange soon ensued, pitting a city's "public policy" against the charity's "private values." At one point, Archbishop Levada threatened to sue the city, arguing that recognizing domestic partnerships would violate the church's ethical and religious beliefs: "I am against government forcing church agencies to comply with laws that run counter to their religious principles," Lavada said.[22] The conflict highlighted the size and significance of the church-state relationship and the fact that some nonprofit organizations that deliver social services hold private beliefs that may conflict with public policies. Contracting with the state may also limit religious freedoms, the archbishop noted: "I believe the ordinance imposes an unconstitutional condition on the recognized right of a religiously affiliated organization such as Catholic Charities to contract with the government for the secular services it offers to clients, while managing its internal operations in a manner consistent with its religious principles."[23]

Complicating matters further was the fact that Catholic Charities was about to open Leland House, a 45-unit residential community for people with disabling HIV, which was funded by $4.5 million in local, state and federal funds. Critics of the archbishop soon attacked him for not immediately complying with the city's ordinance since Catholic Charities had the status of a nonprofit service organization, not a religious entity or church. The archbishop responded that "religious agencies are entitled to contract with the government to serve the poor. This is our city, too. Catholics are not outside the city. We are part of the city."[24] The conflict was ultimately resolved after Mayor Willie Brown, the archbishop, and four members of the Board of Supervisors agreed to a solution of sorts. Without using the words "domestic partners," the group settled on the following language: "An employee may designate a legally domiciled member of the employee's household as being eligible for spousal equivalent benefits."[25] This meant that Catholic Charities would extend benefits, but do so in a way that would include an employee's brother, sister, mother, father, or gay lover. The church was thus led to adopt an awkward, compromised policy in order to retain its city contracts, which accounted for 40 percent of its local budget.

In New York, a conflict of a somewhat different sort recently erupted between the city's government and a coalition of 68 churches and social service agencies. This time the issue was the implementation of the city's new welfare to work policies. The clergy members and nonprofit leaders announced that they would not take part in the new program because it was akin to slavery. They objected to the city's requirement of work in exchange for welfare benefits because it would force many to abandon school, push down wages of city workers, provide no possibility of advancement, and require work in difficult conditions. Unlike the San Francisco case, which turned on the narrow provisions of an ordinance, the New York case illustrates a broader conflict between public and nonprofit agencies.

Few accomplishments were more important to New York's Mayor Rudolph Guiliani than the changes he implemented in the city's welfare programs. Adding new screening procedures and a tough new work requirement reduced the rolls by over 285,000 and placed thousands of individuals in community service positions with nonprofit and city agencies.[26] However, for the coalition of community and religious leaders, the program was a "a moral disaster"[27] from the start since it did not meet the criteria of justice and fairness. The program forced community college students out of school into dead-end jobs and made work a requirement for those who faced multiple barriers to ever finding permanent positions. Most importantly for church leaders, the work program was completely unacceptable because it represented a "public humiliation" and a "moral spectacle, akin to the Puritans' practice of exhibiting 'sinners' in stocks in the village common."[28] An "implementation boycott" was thus organized and carried out as a way of signaling the gulf between public policy and the values of nonprofit and religious groups. The confrontation between New York City and its community and religious leaders starkly highlighted a broadening and deepening disjunction between public and nonprofit values.

Many other "value" conflicts between the sectors have emerged in recent years in fields ranging from education (vouchers for religious schools) to arts (public funding of controversial artists) to health care (public policy allowing for-profit conversions of charity hospitals run by religious orders). In addition to values, of course, conflicts between government and nonprofit organizations have continued to arise from a variety of other issues, including financial control, program design, and compliance costs. The first wave of research never adequately confronted just how easily nonprofit needs and public purposes can come to be at odds with one another when funds flow between the sectors. As conflicts between sectors have arisen, however, the need for a new paradigm for public-nonprofit relations has grown even more pressing.

New Challenges for Public Managers

Over the past decade, new studies of nonprofit organizations and management have sought to redress some of the shortcomings of the early research. Looking at the broader implications of the shift of responsibility for the delivery of services, this research has largely focused on the policy implications of growing government-nonprofit relations and on the consequences for nonprofit organizations of the new contracting regime.[29] The focus on nonprofit policy has, however, obscured somewhat the need for new thinking about the practice of public management. Not enough work has been done to think through *in practice* how public managers can best structure their relationship with nonprofit service providers in light of the changes that are transforming the welfare state and the nonprofit sector. What is needed is a more explicitly normative theory of public management that builds on the recent scholarship that has called into question the partnership paradigm. As they develop contracting relations with nonprofit service providers, all public managers must at least consider the following questions:

- How should the need for accountability be weighed against the need to give nonprofits freedom and flexibility in program design and implementation?
- If preserving the independence of recipient organizations is an important goal, what strategies should public managers adopt when working with nonprofit mangers?

The fact that these two basic questions have yet to be systematically addressed by researchers points toward the lasting power and influence of the still dominant partnership perspective: It is difficult to ask tough evaluative and normative questions about nonprofit performance if the boundaries between sectors are blurred and every program or contract is portrayed as public service. Over the past two decades, the partnership perspective has actually come to have a clear bias in favor of nonprofits, granting these private organizations legitimacy by virtue of their association with public purposes. In this sense, the powerful assumptions inherent in the partnership perspective have shielded the nonprofit sector from real critical analysis. Moreover, the favorable bias implicit in the notion of a public-nonprofit partnership has contributed to a sense that research on nonprofits has been too closely aligned with advocacy on behalf of the financial needs of the sector, which has in turn contributed to the relatively low status of nonprofit studies within the disciplines.[30]

Instead of seeking to blur the lines between sectors for all the wrong reasons, I believe that a new, more detached perspective on public-nonprofit relations is needed—one that preserves some of the boundaries between sectors, that gives nonprofits as much freedom as possible, and that makes broad, multi-dimensional appraisals of their performance easier. Rather than see the nonprofit sector as the faithful servant of the public sector, which helps executes its ideas and programs, scholars and practitioners must start to take more seriously the unique visions, values, and commitments that animate the nonprofit sector itself. Challenging the dominant paradigm of partnership and collaboration has at least one important consequence: It requires developing new strategies for managing public-nonprofit relations that promote and preserve truly independent and eclectic nonprofit approaches to service delivery. This means developing public management strategies that take full advantage of the distinctive features of nonprofit organizations. Where is one to look for a theoretical foundation and rationale for such an approach? Recent developments in organization theory provide a good starting point.

Looking to Neo-Institutional Theory

Institutional theories of organizations provide a complex and penetrating perspective on organizational structure and development.[31] In its broadest sense, the new institutionalism argues that organizations are driven by outside pressures to legitimize their work, professionalize the workplace, and copy what other organizations are doing. With its emphasis on legitimacy, satisficing behavior, and symbols, institutionalism represents a major departure from rival approaches such rational action theory, transaction costs economics, and resource dependence theory. Neo-institutionalism has particular relevance to nonprofit organizations because of its emphasis on the role funding, regulation, and accrediting play in shaping the operations of organizations. Once new practices emerge in a few organizations working in a common area or field, these "ways of doing things" spread among similar organizations, as the desire to fit in and avoid further conflict with the environment increases. The pressure to conform to external constituencies and the need for legitimacy ultimately are what theorists believe lead to institutional isomorphism within fields. The kind of homogenization that neo-institutionalists describe would be an especially dangerous development in the case of the nonprofit sector, because the sector's diversity and its expressive—not just instrumental—dimension have been seen as important virtues and rationales for the sector's existence.[32] The neo-institutional perspective on organizational development leads, I believe, to a clear set of public management precepts to guide interactions with nonprofit organizations. Before detailing these precepts, it is useful to briefly review the central concepts underlying the neo-institutional approach to organizational analysis.

In its simplest terms, neo-institutionalism has sought to defeat the old assumption that an organization's internal structure efficiently matches its function or mission. In the place of this assumption, a new perspective on organizations emerges in which structure is decoupled from work activity, where roles, myths, and ceremonies emerge and spread within organizational fields. Organizations are no longer seen as pioneering innovators and efficiency maximizers, but instead as legitimacy-seeking conformists that are on the look-out for rationalized institutional rules within given domains of work activity, which can eventually be incorporated as structural elements within organizations. In short, as rationalized institutional myths emerge about effective practices, organizations are drawn to these myths and adopt them as a way of building legitimacy and securing resources.[33] Although rationalized myths can be spread through dense relational networks among organizations, they may receive an impetus from legal mandates in the external funding or regulatory environment.

Accordingly, the theory predicts that practices may appear and gain acceptance in the nonprofit sector because of perceived expectations of public authorities. As external funding pressures increase, neo-institutionalists hypothesize that nonprofit organizations will respond by adopting increasing levels of institutionalized rules and procedures. Since most nonprofit service providers, particularly those working in the social service and health arenas, depend heavily on public sector funding, these predictions are particularly germane to our understanding of the dynamics of public-nonprofit relations.

What exactly are the processes that lead to convergence and homogeneity? Paul DiMaggio and Walter Powell[34] identify three forces driving institutionalization: (1) coercive isomorphism that stems from political influence and the need for legitimacy; (2) "mimetic" isomorphism resulting from standard responses to uncertainty; and (3) normative isomorphism associated with professionalization. DiMaggio and Powell emphasize that these three mechanisms can overlap and intermingle, but they tend to derive from different conditions. At an analytic level, only coercive isomorphism is linked to the environment surrounding the organizational field. Mimetic, or imitative, and normative processes are internal to the field and help explain the spread of roles and structures.

Neo-institutional theory thus predicts that when nonprofit organizations are subjected to external scrutiny, evaluation, and regulation, they tend to react defensively and gravitate toward isomorphic transformation. As the pressures from the outside grow, organizations will be led to find ways to either diffuse or eliminate this pressure by changing their practices. One of the easiest ways to change is to adopt those routines and structures that are defined by law or government agencies as legitimate. To do so may ensure nonprofit survival by minimizing conflict. Building on a range of case studies focusing on art museums,[35] private foundations,[36] public-health charities,[37] theaters[38] and community colleges,[39] neo-institutionalism has slowly emerged as a key perspective not just on organizational change but on nonprofit organizations in particular. Since nonprofit organizations are particularly sensitive to funding and regulatory pressure, it is only natural that an important part of the substantive work within neo-institutionalism has been focused on these organizations.

Implications for Public Management

While neo-institutional theory is a powerful analytic tool to study organizational change, it has not yet led to an explicit management theory. Drawing on the core concepts of the theory, I want to sketch the outline a neo-institutional approach to managing public-nonprofit relations that aims for what I will term "pluralistic autonomy" as its cornerstone. At its core, this approach recognizes the need to create space between the sectors as a buffer against isomorphism and the new forces driving bureaucratization, and as a critical means for protecting the autonomy of nonprofit activity. Key elements of this strategy must include:

- an understanding of the role nonprofits can play as a vast and diverse set of laboratories for policy experimentation.
- an appreciation of the power differential between public managers and nonprofit managers—and its real potential for distorting nonprofit behavior.
- a new approach to accountability focused on outcomes as a means of both measuring performance and, more importantly, protecting the autonomy of recipient organizations.
- a conscious effort to reward nonprofits that express their values and missions through programmatic innovations.
- a willingness to think systematically about how to avoid conveying assumptions and excessively narrow standards to nonprofit managers.
- a contracting system that is designed to encourage nonprofits to take chances and experiment with programs.
- an extreme vigilance against stimulating mimetic, normative, or coercive isomorphism as a result of oversight and contracting relations.
- a commitment to pluralism within the nonprofit sector as both a good in itself and a critical guarantor of the sector's independence.

With their orientation toward the needs of nonprofit organizations, these principles constitute an admittedly unorthodox approach to public management. To be sure, strategies for fostering innovation[40] and arguments for outcome-based funding[41] have been gaining popularity in recent years. However, both of these strategies have largely been conceived as ways of bringing change to public sector organizations with the goal of increasing their performance. The principles of pluralistic autonomy and neo-institutional public management—though they express an interest in innovation and outcomes—have a completely different logic and purpose underlying them. Instead of focusing on innovation and accountability as a means toward the narrow end of improving performance, these goals are ultimately justified as a means toward the broader end of protecting the autonomy of nonprofit recipient organizations. Thus, above and beyond increasing the ability of nonprofits to perform well under the terms of specific contracts, public managers must look after the autonomy needs of nonprofits so that they can continue to express through their programs a variety of missions and values.

The nonprofit sector has never been an eager partner with government,[42] though it has come to accept public funds out of financial necessity. Rather than exploit the power that comes with controlling funds, public managers should consider loosening their grip on nonprofits and see the long-term value of preserving a truly independent and flexible nonprofit sector. Anchored in a commitment to the autonomy and distinctiveness of the sectors and a belief in pluralism in program implementation, the management principles described here represent one possible alternative to the growing trend toward greater public control and oversight of nonprofit service providers. To counter this trend it is imperative to reframe the debate over public-nonprofit management and to suggest strategies that might reverse the trends that threaten the long-term autonomy of nonprofit organizations.

Emerging Strategies

What exactly would it mean pursue pluralistic autonomy and to manage as a neo-institutionalist? What would be an example of such an approach? A new contracting system in Oklahoma and a set of recently enacted laws in Texas governing welfare contracting present intriguing glimpses at what this approach might entail in practice. In both cases, the state wrestled with the issue of balancing the need for public accountability with the desire of nonprofits for autonomy. In the Oklahoma case, the result was a flexible contracting system that focuses on outcomes not processes. In Texas, the result was a law that opened welfare contracting up to faith-based organizations and set in place safeguards to preserve the distinctive character of these groups during the contracting process.

Like many other public agencies, the Oklahoma Department of Rehabilitation Services (DRS) used for many years a typical fee-for-service payment system when dealing with nonprofit service providers. Under this contracting regime, the state paid for services mostly through hourly rates for services, a process that created some perverse incentives. Nonprofits were rewarded for the time they spent with clients and not for the speed or effectiveness with which they helped clients reach independence. In short, "hourly billing amounts had an inverse relationship to customer service."[43] The system also put a huge administrative and accounting burden on nonprofits.

To address both the needs of clients and service providers, Oklahoma instituted a "milestone payment system" that keyed financial payment to outcomes rather than processes. For rehabilitation services, this meant that each service provider would provide a bid geared to outcomes, one that would allow substantial latitude on how to achieve each milestone. Today, all of Oklahoma's mental health and developmental disability service providers work on milestone contracts. How does this process work in practice?

> An example of outcomes defined for the Milestones project is a six milestone payment structure: (1) Determination of Consumer Needs—10 percent of bid; (2) Vocational Preparation Completion—10 percent of bid; (3) Job Placement—10 percent of bid; (4) 4 weeks job retention—20 percent of bid; (5) Job Stabilization—20 percent of bid; and (6) Consumer Rehabilitated (Stabilization +90 days)—30 percent of bid. Each milestone definition includes quality outcome indicators which must be accomplished for payment to be made.[44]

The milestone system contrasts clearly with both lump-sum grantmaking and fee-for-service contracting. The former, while giving nonprofits plenty of freedom, does not include incentives for nonprofits to achieve specific outcomes. The latter, while encouraging nonprofits to provide the services specifically detailed in the contract, does not ensure that service providers will achieve the specified outcomes because payment is based only on the mere delivery of services. The milestone approach thus has at least two closely related advantages of interest to neo-institutionalists: It includes incentives to achieve broad programmatic results and it avoids setting up a system that privileges certain narrow processes.

The end result of this contracting system is "the creation of a self-regulating, customer focused, outcome driven service delivery system" that eliminates the negative incentives inherent in hourly billing. Oklahoma also reports that the move to outcome based payments in its milestone system has reduced administrative work of first line staff, freeing up work time that can be directed toward providing customer services rather than filling out billing forms:

> When hourly rates are the basis of payment, the process of documenting increments and categories of services provided must be meticulously tracked. Our service vendors had as many as 10,000 data entry screens to complete each month to insure payment for every increment of service time. It was then necessary for the counselor approving the vendor's claim to spend an inordinate amount of time reading each bit of documentation to determine whether service was 'billable'

> under our system. Now, time formerly devoted to detailed documentation is redirected toward accomplishing the outcome for the consumer. The only information which must be documented . . . is the proof that outcome was achieved. This reduced the data entry screens to be completed from as many as 10,000 to less than 100 per month. This results in over 10 percent of vendor staff time being re-channeled from record keeping to direct customer services."[45]

By focusing on outcome milestones, the state also notes that it was also able to reduce the need for regulation and oversight of service providers. This meets another objective of the neo-institutional approach outlined earlier: the creation of a looser regulatory environment that allows nonprofits room to experiment while holding them accountable for outcomes.

Reducing paperwork and regulations is an important part of protecting nonprofit independence, but it is not the only part. To be truly successful, any turn toward outcomes must be part of larger commitment to building a system that allows room for -- and even encourages—nonprofits to draw on a range of values, commitments, and programmatic methods in pursuit of public goals. The outcomes that are chosen must encourage nonprofits to strive for innovative routes to the specified ends. If they are serious about protecting nonprofit independence, public managers administering outcome contracts must be ready to both validate and reward the full range of instrumental and expressive outcomes that nonprofit organizations generate. This will require a commitment to building performance measures that reflect an understanding of the complex mix of outcomes that nonprofit service providers deliver.

Even though the idea of outcome-based funding has been discussed in the literature for some time,[46] only a few other states, such as Missouri and Hawaii, have begun experimenting on a limited basis with multiple milestone funding systems. By focusing on outcomes and not outputs, by respecting the need of nonprofits for autonomy, and by reducing the need for paperwork and oversight, the Oklahoma milestone contracting system conforms, at least in some important respects, with the principles of pluralistic autonomy in public-nonprofit relations.

The state of Texas has taken a different approach than Oklahoma to improving public-nonprofit relations, one that focuses more on the "values" or expressive dimension of nonprofit organizations. Reacting to a key provision in the new federal welfare reform law, Texas has worked to limit the burdens that public agencies can impose on faith-based nonprofit service providers. After establishing a Task Force on Faith-Based Community Service Groups to investigate how to enforce the "charitable choice" provision of the Personal Responsibility and Work Opportunity Act of 1996, Gov. George W. Bush signed a set of bills formally recognizing the importance of values in the delivery of government-funded social services. Compared to Oklahoma's milestone system, Texas' approach to welfare contracting presents a different—though equally important—side to seeking pluralistic autonomy in the management public-nonprofit relations.

What exactly is the "charitable choice" provision of the welfare reform bill? Inserted by Senator John Ashcroft of Missouri, the provision empowers states to utilize faith-based social service agencies on the same basis as secular agencies in all anti-poverty initiatives. Moreover, the provision clearly states that religious providers need not cleanse their programs in order to qualify for and obtain contracts. The "charitable choice" provision explicitly provides that:

- States may provide welfare services via contracts with religious groups, and/or give beneficiaries vouchers redeemable with such groups.
- Religious groups may participate "on the same basis as any other non-governmental provider without impairing the religious character of such organizations, and without diminishing the religious freedom of beneficiaries of assistance."
- States may not discriminate against a religious provider "on the basis that the organization has a religious character."[47]

Although the federal law has clear provisions protecting faith-based organizations, the real challenge for states lies in fashioning contracting systems that comply with the spirit of the new law. The challenge faced by the Texas task force was thus to develop specific guidelines and contracting rules for the state which breathe life in the "charitable choice" provision of the federal legislation.

After reviewing contracting practices in numerous areas of human services, the report of the Texas task force notes the inherent tension between accountability and autonomy that arises when public and nonprofit sectors interact: "Religious charities need to recognize, though, that where they receive direct public money, public accountability must follow. *The challenge is this: how to fashion reasonable oversight while respecting the charity's religious identity and without corrupting and secularizing its work.*"[48] The specific proposals offered by the task force were eventually written into four bills that were signed into law by Bush on June 12, 1997.

The first bill exempts non-medical faith-based drug and alcohol treatment programs and counselors from state regulation and licensing. Although they cannot offer detoxification and medical services, these providers were made eligible for state counseling contracts. The second bill permits child-care and child-placing agencies to be accredited by private sector entities instead of the state. The goal was to encourage churches and other religious organizations to offer child care and foster care programs without worrying about state regulation. The third bill was a legislative resolution encouraging the Texas Board of Criminal Justice and other state agencies to use faith-based programs to help criminal offenders and those who are at-risk of becoming criminal offenders turn their lives around. Finally, the fourth bill shields from legal liability those who donate medical equipment and medial supplies to non-profit medical providers for use in providing free or reduced cost health care.

Speaking at the signing of these bills, the governor said of the child care provisions included in the law: "This legislation says that churches and synagogues that want to provide help to children can do so without losing their soul or the religious nature of their mission."[49] Texas's other efforts to bring faith-based organizations into welfare reform efforts, the criminal justice system, and rehabilitation services signal an important new philosophy of managing public-nonprofit relations. Rather than seek a deep and overlapping partnership, Texas has decided to fashion a more formal relationship, one which gives faith-based nonprofits relief from as much oversight and regulation as is compatible with the reasonable accountability needs of government.

Although there are substantial differences between the Oklahoma contracting system and the Texas initiative, both efforts contain at least a piece of the broader neo-institutional agenda for public management aimed at bolstering the autonomy of nonprofit organizations. Oklahoma's milestone system emphasizes outcomes with the goal of reducing reporting requirements and, more importantly, protecting agency autonomy. Texas's new law opens public funding to a much broader array of nonprofit visions and values. Hopefully, these two pioneering efforts to address the special needs of nonprofit organizations will shape the way other states manage public-nonprofit interactions and slowly move us closer to a comprehensive neo-institutional approach to public management. The two experiments also demonstrate that managing this complex inter-sector relationship will require an appreciation of both the role values play in nonprofit activity and the need of nonprofits for autonomy in the design of programs and delivery of services.

Conclusion

As public managers begin to reassess the terms of their interaction with nonprofit organizations, the rhetoric of partnership will only get in the way of critical and realistic appraisals of this complex relationship. Bound closely to advocacy efforts within the sector, some of the early nonprofit scholarship failed to ask hard normative questions about the place of nonprofits in society. Assuming that nonprofits could and should perform public purposes, the idea that there was something distinctive about the nonprofit sector was ultimately lost in the rush for public funds and arguments supporting this new funding stream. By failing to appreciate the way private visions and values animate nonprofit activity, the partnership perspective has ended up impoverishing our understanding of the distinctive character of nonprofit organizations and their unique role in a democracy.

Instead of embracing a partnership that exists in words only, nonprofits have the greatest chance of maximizing their impact by acting as independent innovators and by bringing new ideas and approaches to long-standing problems. Free from the pressures of public opinion, nonprofits should seize upon their special status to lead society toward new solutions to social problems. A first step is rejecting the vision of nonprofits as passive vessels through which government-defined purposes can be conveniently pursued. The question of nonprofit independence is not one that requires more descriptive data or advocacy on behalf of the sector's financial needs. Rather it requires serious thought about the underlying rationale for having a nonprofit sector.

Thus, at the heart of the debate over the partnership model is a fundamental question of how independent the nonprofit sector *should* be. While the advocates of partnership frequently point to the large amount of public funds that now flow through the nonprofit sector as "evidence" that the partnership is here to stay no matter its consequences, this descriptive claim avoids the important normative issues that surround the evolution of public-nonprofit contracting relations. Researchers who dare to point out problems in the partnership model are often dismissed as clinging to a "mythology of a nonprofit sector operating in splendid isolation and supported only by private giving."[50] Unfortunately, by consistently confusing a normative argument with a descriptive one, the advocates of "partnership" have yet to engage the "values" critique on its own normative terms.

The argument for protecting the independence of nonprofits as a channel for the expression of a diversity of private values and visions is clear enough. It posits the view that nonprofit organizations are important because they provide a unique channel for individuals to pursue innovative, iconoclastic and value-driven solutions to social problems. The early scholarship, however, never articulated a convincing normative theory in support of their descriptive conclusions. In the absence of such an argument, nonprofit organizations simply appear desirable because they provide a new, more neutral vehicle through which new public spending programs can usefully be channeled. This kind of tactical political argument is, however, hardly the basis on which to build both a positive and a normative theory of nonprofit activity.

In the end, the first wave of research on nonprofit organizations was based on a flawed vision of public-nonprofit relations, one that lacked an appreciation of the tensions inherent in the contracting regime. As a consequence of the dominance of the partnership perspective on public nonprofit relations, the fundamental "values" differences between the sectors have been downplayed by appeals to a shared concern for public service. In place of a longing for a close and collaborative relationship that no longer exists, I have argued that we need to recognize the fundamental conflicts that are now beginning to characterize this complex relationship. More importantly, we need to build a public management style for the future that gives nonprofit organizations as much independence as possible while meeting the accountability needs of the public sector. As long as large amounts of public funds continue to flow into the nonprofit sector, elaborating more fully a neo-institutional theory of public management that includes a coherent defense of "pluralistic autonomy" will remain a pressing task. It will also constitute the critical next step toward replacing the metaphor of partnership with real practices that will allow nonprofit organizations to achieve their unique potential.

Notes

1. Lester M. Salamon and Alan J. Abramson, *Partners in Public Service: Government Nonprofit Relations in the Modern Welfare State* (Baltimore: Johns Hopkins University Press, 1995); Ralph M. Kramer, *Voluntary Agencies in the Welfare State* (Berkeley, CA: University of California Press, 1981); Benjamin Gidron, Ralph M. Kramer, and Lester M. Salamon, "Introduction," in Benjamin Gidron, ed., *Government and the Third Sector: Emerging Relationships in Welfare States*(San Francisco: Jossey-Bass, 1992).

2. Susan Bernstein, *Managing Contracted Services in the Nonprofit Agency* (Philadelphia: Temple University Press, 1991); Kirsten A. Gronbjerg, *Understanding Nonprofit Funding: Managing Revenues in Social Service and Community Development Agencies* (San Francisco: Jossey-Bass Publishers, 1993); Steven Rathgeb Smith and Michael Lipsky, *Nonprofits for Hire: The Welfare State in the Age of Contracting* (Cambridge: Harvard University Press, 1993).

3. Judith R. Saidel, "Resource Interdependence: The Relationship Between State Agencies and Nonprofit Organizations," *Public Administration Review* 51 (1991): 543–551; H. Brinton Milward and Keith G. Provan, "The Hollow State: Private Provision of Public Services," in Helen Ingram and Steven Rathgeb Smith, eds., *Public Policy for Democracy*, (Washington, D.C.: Brookings, 1993).

4. Virginia Hodgkinson and Murray S. Weitzman, *Dimensions of the Independent Sector: A Statistical Profile* (Washington, D.C.: Independent Sector, 1986).

5. William G. Bowen, Thomas I. Nygren, Sarah E. Turner, and Elizabeth A. Duffy, *The Charitable Nonprofits* (San Francisco: Jossey-Bass, 1994).

6. Henry Hansmann, "The Role of Nonprofit Enterprise," *Yale Law Journal* 89 (1980): 835–98; Burton A. Weisbrod, *The Voluntary Nonprofit Sector* (Lexington, MA: Heath, 1977); Lester M. Salamon and Alan J. Abramson, "Of Market Failure, Voluntary Failure, and Third party Government: The Theory of Government-Nonprofit Relations in the Modern Welfare State," *Journal of Voluntary Action Research* 16 (1987): 29–49.

7. Virginia Hodgkinson and Murray S. Weitzman, *Dimensions of the Independent Sector: A Statistical Profile* (Washington, D.C.: Independent Sector, 1986). Lester M. Salamon and Alan J. Abramson, *The Federal Budget and the Nonprofit Sector*, (Washington, D.C.: Urban Institute Press, 1982).

8. Lester M. Salamon and Alan J. Abramson, "The Invisible Partnership: Government and the Nonprofit Sector," *Bell Atlantic Quarterly* 1 (1984); Lester M. Salamon and Alan J. Abramson, *Partners in Public Service: Government Nonprofit Relations in the Modern Welfare State* (Baltimore: Johns Hopkins University Press, 1995).

9. Lester M. Salamon and Alan J. Abramson, "Of Market Failure, Voluntary Failure, and Third Party Government: The Theory of Government-Nonprofit Relations in the Modern Welfare State," *Journal of Voluntary Action Research* 16 (1987), 29–49.

10. Lester M. Salamon and Alan J. Abramson, "Of Market Failure, Voluntary Failure, and Third Party Government," 49.

11. Lester M. Salamon and Alan J. Abramson, "Partners in Public Service: The Scope and Theory of Government-Nonprofit Relations," in Walter W. Powell, ed., *The Nonprofit Sector: A Research Handbook*(New Haven: Yale University Press, 1987), pp. 115–6.

12. Susan Bernstein, *Managing Contracted Services in the Nonprofit Agency* (Philadelphia: Temple University Press, 1991); Kirsten A. Gronbjerg, *Understanding Nonprofit Funding: Managing Revenues in Social Service and Community Development Agencies* (San Francisco: Jossey-Bass Publishers, 1993); Steven Rathgeb Smith and Michael Lipsky, *Nonprofits for Hire: The Welfare State in the Age of Contracting* (Cambridge: Harvard University Press, 1993).

13. Kirsten A. Gronbjerg, *Understanding Nonprofit Funding: Managing Revenues in Social Service and Community Development Agencies* (San Francisco: Jossey-Bass Publishers, 1993), p. 193.

14. Ibid., p. 193.

15. Ibid., p. 183.

16. Susan Bernstein, *Managing Contracted Services in the Nonprofit Agency* (Philadelphia: Temple University Press, 1991).

17. Steven Rathgeb Smith and Michael Lipsky, *Nonprofits for Hire: The Welfare State in the Age of Contracting* (Cambridge: Harvard University Press, 1993).

18. Ibid., p. 105.

19. Ibid., pp. 134–44.

20. Virginia Hodgkinson and Murray S. Weitzman, *Dimensions of the Independent Sector: A Statistical Profile* (Washington, D.C.: Independent Sector, 1986).

21. Woods Bowman, *Bankruptcy as a Management Tool for Financially Distressed Nonprofits,* Working Paper, Graduate Program in Public Services Management, DePaul University, 1997; Mark Hager, Joseph Galaskiewicz, Wolfgang Bielefeld, and Joel Pins, "Tales from the Grave: Organizations' Account of their Own Demise," *American Behavioral Scientist* 38 (8): 975–94.

22. Tim Golden, "Opposition in San Francisco to Policy on Unmarried Partners," *The New York Times,* February 6, 1997.

23. Michael Prince, "New York Eyes Partner Mandate: Councilman Seeks to Copy Controversial San Francisco Rule," *Business Insurance,* February 10, 1997.

24. Don Lattin, "S.F. Archbishop Insists He's Not Anti-Gay," *The San Francisco Chronicle,* February 4, 1997.

25. Torri Minton, "S.F Archbishop Agrees to Discuss Partners Policy," *The San Francisco Chronicle,* February 7, 1997.

26. Steven Greenhouse, "Nonprofit and Religious Groups to Fight Workfare in New York," *The New York Times,* July 24, 1997.

27. Peter Laarman, *Sojourners Magazine* (September-October 1998): 4.

28. Ibid., 4.

29. H. Brinton Milward and Keith Provan, "The Hollow State: Private Provision of Public Services," in Helen Ingram and Steven Rathgeb Smith, eds., *Public Policy for Democracy* (Washington, D.C.: Brookings, 1993).

30. Peter Dobkin Hall, *Inventing the Nonprofit Sector and Other Essays on Philanthropy, Voluntarism and Nonprofit Organizations* (Baltimore, MD: Johns Hopkins University, 1992), pp. 221–255; Peter Dobkin Hall, "No One Best Way: Teaching and Research for Nonprofits in an Interdependent Society," *The Philanthropy Monthly* 29 (1996): 10.

31. Paul J. DiMaggio and Walter W. Powell, "The Iron cage Revisited: Institutional Isomorphism and Collective Rationality," in Paul J. DiMaggio and Walter W. Powell, eds., *The New Institutionalism in Organizational Analysis* (Chicago: University of Chicago Press, 1991); John W. Meyer and Brian Rowan, "Institutionalized Organized: Formal

Structure as Myth and Ceremony," in Paul J. DiMaggio and Walter W. Powell, eds., *The New Institutionalism in Organizational Analysis* (Chicago: University of Chicago Press, 1991); Lynne G. Zucker, "Institutional Theories of Organizations," *Annual Review of Sociology* 13 (1987): 443–64.

32. David E. Mason, *Leading and Managing the Expressive Dimension* (San Francisco: Jossey-Bass, 1996).

33. John W. Meyer and Brian Rowan, "Institutionalized Organized: Formal Structure as Myth and Ceremony," in Paul J. DiMaggio and Walter W. Powell, eds., *The New Institutionalism in Organizational Analysis*(Chicago: University of Chicago Press, 1991).

34. Paul J. DiMaggio and Walter W. Powell, "The Iron cage Revisited: Institutional Isomorphism and Collective Rationality," in Paul J. DiMaggio and Walter W. Powell, eds., *The New Institutionalism in Organizational Analysis* (Chicago: University of Chicago Press, 1991).

35. Paul J. DiMaggio, "Constructing an Organizational Field as a Professional Project: U.S. Art Museums, 1920–1940," in Paul J. DiMaggio and Walter W. Powell, eds., *The New Institutionalism in Organizational Analysis* (Chicago: University of Chicago Press, 1991).

36. Peter Frumkin, "Fidelity in Philanthropy: Two Challenges to Community Foundations," *Nonprofit Management and Leadership* 8 (1997): 65–76; Peter Frumkin, "Private Foundations as Public Institutions," in Ellen Condliffe Lagemann, ed., *Studying Philanthropic Foundations* (Bloomington: Indiana University Press, 1999); Peter Frumkin, "The Long Recoil from Regulation: Private Philanthropic Foundations and the Tax reform Act of 1969," *The American Review of Public Administration* 28 (1998): 266–286.

37. Soren Christensen and Jan Molin, "Origin and Transformation of Organizations: Institutional Analysis of the Danish Red Cross," in W. Richard Scott and Soren Christensen, eds., *The Institutional Construction of Organizations* (Thousand Oaks, CA: Sage, 1995).

38. Jan Mouritsen and Peter Skoerboek, "Civilization, Art and Accounting: The Royal Danish Theater – An Enterprise Straddling Two Institutions," in W. Richard Scott and Soren Christensen, eds., *The Institutional Construction of Organizations* (Thousand Oaks, CA: Sage, 1995).

39. Steven Brint and Jerome Karabel, "Institutional Origins and Transformations: The Case of Community Colleges," in Paul J. DiMaggio and Walter W. Powell, eds., *The New Institutionalism in Organizational Analysis* (Chicago: University of Chicago Press, 1991).

40. Alan A. Altshuler and Robert D. Behn, *Innovation in American Government* (Washington, D.C.: Brookings, 1997).

41. David Osborne and Ted Gaebler, *Reinventing Government* (New York: Penguin, 1993), pp. 138–65; Lisbeth B. Shore, *Common Purpose: Strengthening Families and Neighborhoods to Rebuild America* (New York: Doubleday, 1997), pp. 115–139.

42. Jennifer Wolch, *The Shadow State: Government and the Voluntary Sector in Transition* (New York: The Foundation Center, 1990); David Billis, "Planned Change in the Voluntary and Government Social Service Agencies," *Administration in Social Work*, 16 (1992): 29–45.

43. Oklahoma Department of Rehabilitative Services, *Innovations in American Government Semifinalist Application*,(1997), p. 1.

44. Ibid., p. 2.

45. Ibid., p. 4.

46. Harold S. Williams and Arthur Y. Webb and William J. Phillips, *Outcome Funding: A New Approach to Targeted Grantmaking* (Rensselaerville, NY: Rensselaerville Institute, 1995).

47. Governor's Advisory Task Force on Faith-Based Community Service Groups, *Faith in Action: A New Vision for Church-State Cooperation in Texas* (Austin, TX: Office of the Governor, 1997), p. 4.

48. Ibid., p. ix.

49. Office of the Governor, *Governor Bush Signs "Faith-Based" Bills to Expand Availability and Choice in Welfare-Related Services* (Austin, TX: Office of the Governor, 1997).

50. Lester M. Salamon and Alan J. Abramson, *Holding the Center: America's Nonprofit Sector at a Crossroads* (New York: The Nathan Cummings Foundation, 1997), p. 61.

CHAPTER 9

Beyond "Villages": New Community Building Strategies For Disadvantage Families

Richard Weissbourd

Disadvantaged children are living not just in one type but in many types of communities. We need far more complex models of community that recognize the great diversity in the living situations of disadvantaged families.

Americans are routinely told that the disintegration of communities has placed children in serious jeopardy. The unraveling of communities is seen as a root cause of rotting schools, rising crime, widespread drug abuse and pervasive alienation and anomie. Teenagers, it is said, lack role models and mentors, and children of all ages no longer grow up under the watchful eye of caring neighborhood adults who are themselves firmly tied to one another. Men especially are scarce. Because of increasing geographic mobility and greater anonymity among neighbors, many children, it is now commonly assumed, no longer grow up laced together with other neighborhood children. Moreover, these sorts of informal networks are no longer undergirded by the formal affiliations that families once maintained through neighborhood religious, political and social institutions. Some children have been placed in serious jeopardy and many children have lost a kind of paradise—sometimes the whole country seems to be mourning this drowned innocence—with large costs to them and to our culture. It is in part this sense of loss that has spawned a movement to retrieve this type of community, a kind of community embodied for some people in the commonplace proverb, "It takes a village to raise a child."

There is a great deal to commend this notion of community. These kinds of local communities have great advantages for many children and are vital to the well being of others. But some of this nostalgia for community is based on half-truths—and some is pure confection. While the image is that these neighborhood communities were once ubiquitous and are now scarce, the reality is that such communities were never typical. For various reasons, large numbers of American children have never planted deep roots in communities. For example, studies suggest that nineteenth century Americans were just as mobile as are twentieth century Americans.[1] Conversely, many neighborhood communities today, including some poor communities, clearly have large degrees of social cohesion and function like villages in important respects.

More important, these neighborhood communities in the past have hardly been frictionless for many families. For example, in every era and in every part of the country, local communities have not only included and supported some people, they have clearly isolated and scapegoated large numbers of vulnerable parents and children, especially members of religious, racial, and ethnic minorities.

Even if we could create communities across the country based on some exact model of an imagined "traditional" community, it would be unwise to try. We need, instead, new models of community, models that embrace many elements of "traditional" neighborhood communities but that also substantially depart from them. Religious institutions have a crucial role to play in creating these new types of communities. Creating these new models will be especially critical for disadvantaged children, whose welfare often depends more than better off children on a variety of types of support from outside their immediate family. In this chapter I describe the important benefits of cohesive neighborhood communities for disadvantaged children—especially poor children—but I also put forward ideas about new community structures and strategies that will be more responsive to these children's needs. I focus on the roles that both religious institutions and schools can play in developing these structures. I argue that to meet the needs of disadvantaged children, these institutions need to help build certain elements of neighborhood communities, especially lasting ties among children, among parents, and between children and community adults. They also need to take up other kinds of community-building strategies that are more in sync with two often-overlooked realities of disadvantaged children's current lives.

First, large numbers of children, especially disadvantaged children, are growing up in sealed neighborhood communities that are isolated from the social and economic mainstream, and faith-based institutions and schools need to find ways of giving both parents and children access to many different communities. For religious institutions, providing this access would means giving poor families greater access to better-off communities, something most religious communities do not currently do. Religious communities provide a wide array of services to poor families, but as Theda Skocpol points out in her introduction to this book, doing "for" is vastly different from "doing with"—providing opportunities for people of different classes to engage as equals. As Skocpol observes, the quest to provide these opportunities is not quixotic; there are examples of faith based associations in our history that have crossed deep ethnic and class divides.

Second, although geographic mobility is not a new feature of American life, millions of disadvantaged children are imperiled today because they move repeatedly during childhood. Seeking to recreate "traditional" communities will do little for these children. Religious institutions and schools need to take up new community structures and strategies to both reduce mobility and to deal with the toll taken by constant uprooting.

Finally, disadvantaged children are not living in one type of community but are living in many types of communities. We need far more complex models of community that recognize the great diversity in the current living situations of disadvantaged families, the great diversity in the preferred social arrangements of these families as well as the great diversity among individual families in terms of their community needs.

My observations about faith-based communities here are based in part on recent interviews with about two dozen leaders and members of faith-based communities in Boston, New York, and Chicago. Given the limits of this sample, these observations are only intended to be suggestive. My observations about schools are based in part on scores of interviews with children, parents and school staff that I have conducted in different parts of the country—including Little Rock, Boston and the Boston area, Baltimore, Chicago, and Seattle—over the last 12 years. While I purposefully sought to interview diverse families and schools, I certainly make no claim that these families or schools are representative of the full range of families and schools across the country.

The Advantages of Local, Cohesive Communities

Nostalgia for "traditional," local communities is largely based on several quite accurate perceptions about the importance of strong neighborhood ties for many children. Such communities, for example, often provide children an array of nearby, immediate role models and mentors. Watchful neighborhood adults can protect children from hazards and intruders, and every parent benefits from other nearby adults who can spell them and provide a safety net in times of crisis. Both parents and children can clearly become greatly attached to a place, to the physical spaces they occupy, attachments that easily and synergistically merge with the people with whom they share those spaces. There are, too, many tight-knit local communities in which a wide array of adults transmit to children consistent, important values, including principles of respect and fairness. Sociologist Frank Furstenberg describes an urban village in Philadelphia, for example, in which "[P]arents look to friends and neighbors to enforce prevailing community standards." These adults not only intervene when a child has transgressed; "negligent parents are severely chastised by their neighbors." Neighborhood activities are also structured so that adults and children, including adolescents, share in many activities, such as sports, and have frequent contact—there is a great deal of opportunity for moral socialization.[2] Neighborhoods with these types of social capital and social cohesion have many documented benefits for children, including lower rates of dropping out of school, drug abuse, violence, and other crimes.[3]

Moreover, there are great advantages to children in growing up with long and deep connections to other neighborhood children. Many children who have been abandoned or mistreated in one way or another by their parents come to rely on their friends for basic emotional and sometimes physical survival. Both the films *Stand By Me* and more recently *Good Will Hunting* depict children abused by their parents who are powerfully buoyed and healed by their deep friendships with other neighborhood children.

These aspects of villages are crucial to preserve, and there is much that many religious institutions and schools are currently doing to preserve them. Some schools are developing extensive community partnerships that place children in contact with nearby adults and increase these adults' sense of responsibility for neighborhood children. Schools across the country are providing a variety of school-based and school-linked social and health services for both parents and children—including full-service or "one-stop shopping" schools, which are designed in part to make schools the hub of the neighborhood, connecting nearby families both to the school and to one another. Good parent involvement programs in schools are not only designed to strengthen parents' ties with teachers but to strengthen their ties to other neighborhood parents.

In addition, many schools, partly in response to the perceived loss of traditional communities, have undertaken major structural reorganizations that seek to create "villages" within the school building. For example, some large high schools across the country are seeking to deepen and extend children's involvement with other children and adults by enabling children to spend the bulk of their day with the same group of teachers and students. Common strategies include clustering teachers and students, creating schools within schools or houses within schools and assigning children to advisors who meet with them once a week in small groups all four years. Multigrade classrooms, where children stay with the same teacher for two or even three years, enable teachers to develop stronger connections to children. "Newcomer schools"—schools for new immigrant children—which are now cropping up in Southern and Western states in particular, are designed as small villages that ease these children's entry into American life. Some schools are also quite consciously seeking to unite staff in sending consistent moral messages to children. As a principal of one of James Comer's model public schools in New Haven told me: "In here we all sing from the same hymn book, we all strike the same chord."

In many communities, religious institutions, far more than any other institution, are playing a critical role in tying neighborhood parents to one another and in creating strong, enduring connections both among children and between children and neighborhood adults. These institutions now commonly operate a wide array of social, academic, and recreational programs that join children in common activities and connect children to nearby adults. Religious institutions not only often offer food banks and clothing drives for neighborhood families but play critical roles in mediating problems among neighborhood parents and provide an array of support groups. Forty percent of people who describe themselves as participating in a self-help group report that their group meets at a church.[4] Religious institutions have become involved in the lives of troubled adolescents in particular—29 percent of congregations provide programs concerned with teen pregnancy, and violence prevention programs are common.[5] Twenty percent of religious institutions provide literacy or tutoring programs.[6] A wide array of faith-based communities has gone to significant lengths to connect teenagers to neighborhood adults informally or through formal mentoring programs. Some local religious institutions, like schools, are seeking to become "full-service" or "one-stop shopping" centers for neighborhood families. And many institutions strengthen and expand families' neighborhood ties by actively encouraging both parents and children to take up neighborhood causes. According to a survey by the Independent Sector, 45 percent of religious institutions have taken up community service or community development projects, although there is considerable variation in the extent to which different denominations take up this work.[7] The kinds of neighborhood social networks and social capital that children and parents develop through their churches has many positive influences on children, including bolstering children's resilience, their ability to weather hardship, as early as preschool.[8]

There are, to be sure, problems with these local community-building strategies, and there is much more that these institutions could do to build neighborhood ties. School-based services, for example, often never reach immigrant parents and other parents who are intimidated by or alienated from the school building, and many parents do not want the stigma and loss of privacy that comes with receiving a service at either their children's school or their church. Both faith-based and school-based services can reinforce a hierarchical division between those who provide and those in need, rather than creating mutually supportive and lasting relationships among neighborhood adults. Moreover, many religious institutions have become passive and disconnected from struggling neighborhood residents. A great deal of voluntary activity in churches is devoted to the maintenance and prosperity of the church itself as opposed to helping outsiders—nearly 60 percent of volunteering in evangelical churches involves this kind of maintenance.[9] Anecdotal evidence suggests that this was not always the case. A son of a minister in a low-income community in Detroit, for example, described to me how, 30 years ago, his father used to knock on the doors every Monday morning of those congregants who had failed to attend church the day before. Whether or not this practice was ever widespread, there was wide consensus among those I spoke with that this kind of practice is highly atypical now. Many faith-based communities may lack the financial resources to reach out to struggling residents. Another problem is that local churches that build neighborhood ties have been shutting down in recent years—at a slow but steady pace—in part, it appears, because they are losing congregants to larger churches which offer a much wider variety of services and programs: "It's Wall-Mart versus the corner grocery," a businessmen involved in the development of megachurches was quoted as saying in an article in *The Atlantic Monthly*, "It ain't a fair fight."[10]

The Importance of Participating in Multiple Communities

At the same time, a wide variety of schools and religious institutions are involved in various aspects of village creation, such as strengthening parents' ties to one another, children's ties to neighborhood adults and children's ties to one another. These aspects appear to be at least explicit purposes of a significant majority of schools and religious institutions across the country. The problem is that these efforts are often unresponsive to some of the most troubling difficulties of disadvantaged families. Perhaps most serious, while developing neighborhood ties is useful in places where parents are isolated and want more contact with their neighbors, it can be useless and even harmful in places where parents want less contact with their neighbors. Some parents do not want extensive involvement with their neighbors—they simply want one or two nearby friends—and many parents and children suffer the stresses and burdens not of isolation but of being dependent on relationships with neighbors that are stressful and burdensome.[11] While some urban villages are clearly large and diverse, many disadvantaged families also live in confined neighborhoods that seriously limit their social relationships. What these parents and children often need is not a tighter neighborhood social network, but some freedom from these relationships and access to a far wider and more diverse social network.

Low-income parents especially often find themselves trapped in small, isolated neighborhoods and dependent on neighborhood relationships that create stress. A study of 43 low-income women by psychologist Deborah Belle revealed that many low-income women depend on other nearby parents and adults when available for both emotional support and concrete assistance. Yet these relationships often drag them down and stir up anxiety and hostility. Some low-income women feel constantly burdened by neighborhood friends with illnesses or problems, such as a neighbor who drinks or is in constant financial crisis. Generosity for these women may have a zero-sum quality: to give something may be to suffer an acute loss to one's self or one's own children. Many of these women resent their lack of privacy and want more choice and diversity in their friendships.[12] Well-healed urbanites and suburbanites may lament the fragmented nature of their lives because their choices lead them to belong to many different communities—a work community, a health or social club, or a political organization—rather than to one seamless neighborhood community, but it is precisely these choices that low-income Americans lack. Toby Herr, the director of Project Match, a program for welfare recipients in Chicago, notes, "Many low-income mothers do not want more involvement with their neighbors. They want to meet other women and get involved with activities outside the projects. They might want to send their kids to a class downtown. They want the kinds of opportunities and communities that middle class people have." Not surprisingly, many low-income women, given an opening, opt out of these burdensome relationships or temper their dependence on neighborhood relationships and revitalize themselves through outside sources of emotional support provided through, for example, a workplace, a political organization, a support group, a cultural or recreational activity.[13]

Moreover, isolated communities cut parents off from crucial economic opportunities. Sociologist Mark Granovetter shows how people who are embedded in single, close communities can be seriously disadvantaged because their access to economic resources tends to be defined and bounded by the resources of their group. Granovetter makes the case for the "strength of weak ties"—ties to many different communities that generate economic opportunities.[14]

Many low-income parents, of course, do not live in sealed worlds, and many friendships among low-income women are clearly *not* overwhelmed by these burdens. Cultural difference in the purposes and patterns of social interaction is one of many factors shaping the degree to which low-income communities create friction for families. Low-income white parents, for example, appear to have more stressful relationships with neighbors than low-income black parents, in part because black parents tend to rely on more extensive, geographically dispersed kinship ties.[15] Yet across racial and ethnic groups large numbers of low-income parents are burdened by neighborhood ties.

Further, while these problems are more common in poor communities, these problems are certainly not confined to poor communities. To be sure, parents in middle-class neighborhoods are more likely to consider their ties to neighbors unstressful and helpful. In middle class neighborhoods, people tend to want their neighbors to be "friendly" but not "friends," and they can afford to maintain this distance—the greater resources of middle class families reduces their dependence on neighbors. Middle class parents tend to have far more latitude in determining when, how and with whom to associate among neighbors.

Yet the problems of ties among neighbors are also found in all sorts of communities where significant numbers of people are under stress—for example, in neighborhoods comprising large numbers of new immigrants, or on military bases where numerous families are missing a parent or must move repeatedly from base to base, or in towns whose economies depend on a single industry that is failing or threatened with closure. Many families are forced into affiliations with those with whom they feel little kinship or who violate their privacy. For countless parents, small towns can be airless and intolerant. Families can be bound to a neighborhood for racial, ethnic or religious reasons or because of work, yet feel little in common with or rub against their neighbors.

The reality is that while Americans value their neighborhood ties, they typically do not want to depend on their neighbors, and they want to choose both their neighbors and friends. Poverty is one of many circumstances that can curtail parents' choices. Every parent also needs to be able to regulate closeness and distance with other adults day to day, and this capacity for regulation can require delicate choreography. Poverty, among other circumstances, can impair this capacity for regulation. Unable to match their needs with the shape of their communities, large numbers of parents are isolated and many feel trapped by neighborhood ties that create stress.[16]

Many children, too, are endangered because they live in isolated neighborhoods that severely circumscribe their social relationships, and low-income children especially are often harmed because they are growing up in villages that provide them virtually no exposure to diverse social or economic worlds. It in not uncommon to find children in towns that border Boston who have never been in this city. Nor is it uncommon to find children who live in poor neighborhoods in Chicago who have never seen the lake or entered downtown, even though they live just several blocks away.

Living in small, sealed worlds hurts children in several respects. Children in these circumstances can be far more vulnerable because they are dependent on a single group of children for friendship. Children are more likely to be dragged into destruction by a clique or gang when the alternative is social isolation.[17] Children who entirely depend on one social group or clique are more vulnerable to its brutal qualities—to the competitiveness, scapegoating, narrow typecasting, and constant fencing in and out. While a great deal of attention has been given to the "loud" troubles of children in gangs, many children are endangered precisely because they do not fit into a gang or any other social group or because they are forced to play a narrow or demeaning role in these groups.[18] One child that I have been close to for many years moved into a new, largely middle class community where he was scorned both because of his social awkwardness and for being poor—derided as a "welly" because his mother was on welfare. Yet not being able to afford transportation or fees for various recreational and social activities in the surrounding area severely limited his access to other social groups. The harm done by this kind of peer rejection or marginalization can be serious, especially for children who already feel abandoned or rejected by their family. This kind of rejection can not only cause immediate agony but long term damage.[19]

Small, sealed communities also leave children far more exposed to the various problems of other children. In some communities, parents go to great lengths to shield their own children from other children who they consider inappropriate or dangerous.[20] One mother I spoke with wondered whether her own children were becoming frustrated and violent—fighting with each other and with other children—because they were forced into relationships with children whom they would otherwise avoid.

And many children clearly benefit from access to multiple communities. Emotional support from friends outside of school has been shown to be important to children's academic success.[21] Children often report a greater sense of self-worth in high school than in middle school because they are able to find a niche—a sports team, the chess club, a theatre group—amid a far more diverse array of peer groups.[22] There are, too, many benefits to adolescents especially in being able to float among diverse social groups. Psychoanalyst Erik Erikson underlined the importance of adolescents exploring various social roles and affiliations—"trying on" various identities, and research has underscored the importance of such exploration to identity development.[23] The wider the number of social groups a child is exposed to, the greater the prospects of that child consolidating an identity that merges what is best from his or her past with valued, worthy and attainable roles in his or her future.

Access to multiple, diverse communities has simply become vital to many children's ability to escape poverty. Much has been made of the fact that it is not only cognitive but social and emotional competencies that are key to job success, and that a mismatch sometimes exists between the kinds of social skills that children develop in some low-income communities and the kinds of skills that children need to function in more mainstream social and economic settings. A common example is that walking away from a fight can endanger a child in certain neighborhoods, while it is precisely walking away from a fight that may make it possible for a teenager to hold a job in a mainstream setting.[24] A critical, well-documented characteristic of resilient children is that they are able to navigate in these different worlds.[25] They are able to adapt successfully to mainstream mores and expectations without losing their capacity to navigate in their own world. Moreover, there are not, of course, only two worlds—a low-income world, largely comprised of children of color, and a mainstream world. Both of these worlds are themselves varied, and no precise boundary exists between them. In a society that is highly diverse in many respects, it has become increasingly important that children have the capacity to work effectively with many different kinds of people from many different worlds. In *Teaching the New Basic Skills,* Richard Murnane and Frank Levy document the importance, for example, of workers being able to solve problems in teams with people from many different backgrounds. This ability, Murnane and Levy argue, has become virtually a prerequisite for earning a middle class wage.[26]

Moreover, having access to many different communities is critical to children believing that they have a stake in the larger society, that they have some power to influence larger political and economic spheres. It is surely important for a child to have an identity as a resident of a tight-knit community like South Boston, say, but it is also critical for any kind of well-functioning democracy for children to see themselves as citizens of Boston and of the United States—to identify enough to at least vote, if not to be an advocate or agent of change. Yet to large numbers of children living in isolated communities, large political and economic institutions are incomprehensible and alien.

The problem is that most schools and religious institutions appear to be doing little to expand and diversify the communities available to low-income families. Many schools and religious institutions, to be sure, are already providing parents and children access to diverse communities. There are examples of schools across the country—regular public schools, magnet schools, charter schools, pilot schools, private schools—which provide parents and children access to a large and socially and economically diverse population, and many children have access to many communities because they attend large, diverse high schools or because they are involved in many types of extracurricular activities. While there are clearly complex benefits and costs to busing and school choice, one advantage of these initiatives is that they give children and parents access to a community outside of their neighborhood. There are also various school programs and projects that give marginalized children access to mainstream communities, placing children in internships with downtown businesses, for example, or enabling a child to shadow a mainstream employee for a week, or importing tutors and mentors from businesses and universities.

But giving children and parents access to diverse communities is clearly not on the agenda of most schools across the country. Large numbers of teachers and administrators feel that they have little influence over children's peer groups, especially in middle school and high school, and do little to assist children in gaining access to other communities or groups of children.[27] And at a time when urban schools are becoming increasingly economically segregated, it is the atypical school that works to give low-income children and other marginalized children access to diverse social and economic communities.

Efforts to connect children to other communities are also often brief and late in childhood—not nearly sufficient enough to enable children to develop meaningful relationships with children and adults outside their neighborhood or to develop more mainstream social skills. While some children create lasting ties to other communities through, for example, summer internships with businesses or through mentoring programs, there is a good deal of evidence that these relationships often do not take hold and do little to help children navigate in mainstream culture.[28] Serious efforts to expose children to other worlds need to begin far earlier in childhood, and these efforts need to be both deeper and more sustained.

Members of religious institutions typically see themselves as trying to cultivate diverse communities for parents and children. Church leaders I spoke with pointed out that there was nothing more central to their religion than reaching out to people with various needs and in various circumstances. Many large churches and the new megachurches—on some dimensions at least—are highly diverse. Some have become so large and diverse that they have created "cells"—small niches or villages of ten to fifteen people—often organized around a topic or theme, such as being a single parent. Congregants belong to a cell but also attend services with the entire church, so that families can feel both a sense of belonging to a small, tight-knit community and to a larger, more diverse community.[29] As sociologist Robert Wuthnow explains, this diversification is partly financially driven, helping religious organizations adapt to a "more competitive market situation."[30] There are, too, many examples of small churches that are vibrant and highly diverse.[31] Churchgoers, especially Protestants, also often become involved in a diverse array of civic communities and associations through their involvement in a religious institution, and develop civic skills, such as how to run meetings, that they utilize in diverse community settings.[32] Some churches are also involved in community organizing and political activity that exposes poor families to other worlds. A minister in one Chicago area church I spoke with quite actively engages poor children in political campaigns and voter registration drives and teaches them to interview, to debate and to speak in public in a quite explicit effort to give them the knowledge and skills they need to function in a wide variety of social and economic communities.

Yet there are a variety of factors that seriously limit the degree to which religious institutions expose families—especially poor families—to diverse communities. For one, religious institutions vary considerably in how they define diversity. While some churches, for example, give African American families access to diverse groups within the African-American community, those groups are very purposefully and exclusively African American, wanting in part to give African Americans a community where they don't have to deal with the tensions of interacting with white culture.[33] A higher percentage of African Americans attend church than any other large racial or ethnic group in the United States, and a large majority of these churches are either entirely, or almost entirely, comprised of African Americans.[34] Both race and ethnicity remain a very substantial boundary in most of American church life.[35] There are, of course, compelling arguments for maintaining racially and ethnically homogeneous faith-based communities, but these arguments need to be weighed against the potential downsides of these communities for some children and parents who never interact with other ethnic or racial worlds.

And the great majority of religious institutions do little in particular to give poor families access to other communities, especially diverse economic communities. According to all the congregants, leaders and religion observers that I spoke with, these institutions tend to be, and always have been, significantly stratified by economic class, and this stratification exists across race, ethnic, and denominational lines, with some variation. While residential economic segregation explains much of this segregation, church members and leaders cited many other reasons for this segregation, including the discomfort that many poor people feel attending churches where there are many markers of wealth—" the parking attendants, the usher at the door, the nice clothes everyone is wearing"—and the desire of many middle class congregants for shelter in their religious institutions from the troubles of the outside world. Further, the new megachurches are themselves comprised of few low-income families. While only a small fraction of churchgoers attend these megachurches—probably no more than 5 percent—these and other large churches appear to be siphoning affluent church members from local churches and increasing the number of local churches that have either folded or that are now comprised of almost entirely poor members.[36]

Finally, while many different kinds of religious institutions, both large and small, Christian and Jewish, have mobilized affluent volunteers to provide service to the poor in various capacities, these are very clearly what Skocpol describes as "doing for" relationships. These religious institutions have failed to build mutually supportive relationships between people of different economic classes. As a Chicago minister puts it, "Churches think like social services agencies. . . they are not about transforming social relationships."

While the barriers to economic integration are tall and wide, there are numerous examples of religious institutions that have successfully economically integrated. Those I interviewed pointed to a few principles and practices that appear to be key. Perhaps most important, economic integration usually did not come about by accident, it came about because of the extremely purposeful, determined efforts of a church leader. These leaders not only communicate to their congregations that this kind of diversity and commitment to social justice is central to their faith but have been highly vigilant about seizing opportunities to create economic diversity—one minister, for example, encourages women in the church-run homeless shelter to join the church choir. Sometimes these church leaders are "charismatic," but even more important appear to be a sensitivity to both the concerns of poor families and of more affluent families. The importance of attention to different styles of worship—especially to different tastes in music—came up over and over in my interviews. As one minister put it, "you have to know how long to keep [certain kinds of] music on to keep the poor families coming, and when to turn it off if you want to keep the doctors and lawyers coming." Some churches also attract economically diverse parents by offering activities and programs that are attractive to a wide range of children. Diverse ranges of parents first become interested in the church through their children's participation. Religious institutions as well as schools might also attract and maintain economic diversity by more consistently developing support groups around themes—such as parenting a disabled child—that are meaningful to parents in every economic situation.

Yet all this poses no small challenge for schools and religious institutions. Not only is the task of overcoming class barriers huge and complex, there is the danger that giving families access to multiple communities can ultimately be detrimental to their own neighborhoods. Parents who participate in many communities may turn away from the problems of their neighbors and the conflicts of their neighborhood relationships, and when large numbers of parents in a neighborhood spend large amounts of time outside of their neighborhood, it can be the beginning of neighborhood decline, depleting the social capital of a neighborhood and the power of neighborhoods parents to advocate effectively for change.[37] Schools and religious institutions need to find ways to serve the twin goals of giving parents and children resources and assistance so they can function effectively in the local community in which they are embedded and opportunities to belong to multiple communities.

Difficult as this challenge is, both religious institutions and schools seem like the right institutions to take it on. Both expanding and diversifying the community while undertaking the difficult of work of improving neighborhood ties and increasing neighborhood cohesion is entirely consistent with the mission of most faith-based communities. Maintaining ties and a sense of responsibility for neighbors who are laid low is hard and exacting, but it is precisely this commitment that is at the core of many theologies, and the effort required to stay in the fray of these relationships can surely be nurtured by a strong faith. The importance of strong faith is one reason religious institutions have tended to be more successful than other institutions in cultivating volunteers.[38] Good schools, too, are not about helping children flee conflict in their relationships: they underline the importance of children working out these conflicts while still seeking to expose children to a wide variety of other children and to diverse communities.

None of this work will be possible, however, until schools and religious institutions, as well as many other community agencies, recognize at the very least the value not only of strengthening neighborhood ties but also of giving poor families access to multiple communities.

Children and Geographic Mobility

> My mother was married to my father. After that my mother went away to New Jursey. There she found my new father. He took me to the age of 3. And then we came to New York. We lived in manhatin. And there they robed us. And then we moved to Stagg. There we had trouble with the landlord. we moved to Nicker Bocker. There we had to move because we had trouble with the water and the service. And from there we moved to Major. There we are having trouble with service and my father got in jail for a day. And there I stayed and went to school and hope that I'll never move.
>
> *Lorenzo, eight years old, diary excerpt.*[39]

Seeking to re-create "traditional" neighborhoods not only fails to expand and diversify the communities available to families, it fails families in another large respect: it does little by itself for the millions of children who, like Lorenzo, are forced to uproot many times during childhood. Although in the past many children migrated one or more times during childhood, family migration in the United States today is high: nearly 20 percent of families change residence every year.[40] Children in poor families in particular are driven from place to place by troubles similar to those that uprooted Lorenzo: a mother's remarriage, neighborhood crime, trouble with a landlord, a plumbing problem, a father's incarceration. I have spoken with mothers in homeless shelters who have moved up to ten times in their child's first five years of life. Children in poor families move about twice as often as children in other families, yet large numbers of families who move repeatedly are not poor.[41] Poor children are also more likely to cycle in and out of schools as well as child care situations as their mothers cycle on and off welfare and as their eligibility for child-care programs changes. In major urban areas, such as New York, Chicago, Boston, Los Angeles, between 20–30 percent of children change schools during the year. In a few schools in very low-income neighborhoods in Chicago, as many 80 percent of children change schools during the year.[42]

New community strategies are clearly needed for these children as well, given both their large numbers and the damage wrought by repeated moves. Although frequent moving has received far less attention than other childhood problems, such as violence and teen pregnancy, it may harm just as many children as these problems and is often connected to them.

While many children weather frequent moves unscathed, such frequent moves can harm them in various ways. Frequent moving often creates stresses on parents that impair parenting, disrupt the consistency and predictability that are so important to children, and hinder children's ability to draw support from friends and community adults. In many direct and indirect ways moving can also undermine children in school. Many children are unable to build skills and knowledge because they ricochet among schools that use different curriculums and teaching methods or because they do not stay at a school long enough to engage. At a school in Somerville, Massachusetts, a new fifth grade child spent his first few weeks with a coat over his head: It turned out that this was the fifteenth school he had attended in three years. As the school principal says, "His teacher is working hard to engage him, but he's sullen and apathetic. He probably knows he may leave again at any moment. You can't expect a child to feel secure or to get into the rhythm of a class who is always on the road." Further, records are often not transferred in a timely fashion, so a teacher may not even know if a new child has, for example, a learning disability.

When children move frequently, they also must rely far more on their parents and siblings. This can throw children back on their parents precisely when independence is important for development and thus exacerbate almost any kind of family problem. Moreover, mobile children often never overcome the wide range of troubles that require sustained attention by a health, social service, or mental health professional, and the gains that children make in dealing with problems are often swiftly undone. In Little Rock, I followed 12 children for three years who were identified as at-risk and who were receiving school-based services. By the third year, seven of these children had either changed schools or moved away from Little Rock.

Constant moving can destroy the stable neighborhood social networks that are so important to all neighborhood children, and the damage done as a result can be significant and lasting. The more children move, the more likely they are to suffer a wide range of health, learning, and emotional problems, even when poverty, ethnicity, marital status and a mother's education are taken into account.[43] Each move diminishes, for example, a child's chances of finishing school, on average, by 2.6 percent.[44]

The harm done by moving is often compounded because it is combined with other losses and hardships in children's lives, such as their parents' divorce or the sudden unemployment of a parent. The harm wrought by moving may also be greatly exacerbated when a parent is already stressed or depressed, and when other adults are moving frequently around children. For some children, adults are constantly appearing and evaporating. "Kids in the hallway stop me and ask, 'Where are you going next?'" a school principal laments. Turnover among day-care providers and teachers in many neighborhoods is especially high. The average center-based early education and care program suffers the loss of approximately 25 percent of its teachers every year.[45]

Sparing children the troubles of repeated moves clearly means dealing with huge and complex problems—including inadequate and unstable employment, family instability, poor schools—that commonly press families to pull up stakes. Yet schools and faith-based institutions can also take up more direct strategies that both reduce mobility and that allay the harm created by repeated moves.

With the exception of migrant education programs, schools across the country do little to help children weather mobility.[46] Yet a variety of strategies have proven useful. A few cities, including Seattle, have developed magnet schools specifically for highly mobile children, so that even when children change residences within the city they can stay in the same school. One school in Houston, Texas, has dramatically reduced mobility rates by hiring two social workers who mediate landlord-tenant difficulties and other problems that cause families to move, and other schools in Texas have developed full year schools with staggered schedules for children who regularly return to their country of origin for part of the year.

State and city education policies can also make a difference. While there are complex benefits and costs to creating educational standards in schools, creating uniform academic standards for all schools in a district or a state will reduce the discontinuities in mobile children's educational experience. The number of times children change schools can also be reduced by careful attention to school policies and school structure: some schools in Boston, for example, have two classrooms at one grade level and only one classroom at the next grade level, so half of the children at the earlier grade level are required to change schools.

Further, an individual school's attention and commitment to addressing this problem can be critical. Isabel Mendez, a Boston public school principal, recognizes that some children change schools repeatedly because their parents distrust schools, based on their own experience and the experience of their children. These parents are skittish: they push on to a new school the first time a problem crops up. Mendez and teachers at her school go out of their way to tell both children and parents that they are wanted, and they insist that parents work problems out. "We won't let kids feel that they have failed at another school," Mendez says. "We tell them and their parents, we're going to make it work here."

When children must move, there is a good deal that schools can do to ease their transitions, creating a culture, for one, that embraces new children and rooting out the many tacit, unseen ways in which schools and communities deny entry to or marginalize outsiders. Schools also need rituals for welcoming and parting with both children and parents.

Some religious institutions do help reduce mobility, because they deal regularly with housing problems as well as neighborhood problems and abrasions that cause families to relocate, and some religious institutions help families with the physical logistics of moves and in other ways reduce the stress of relocation. Many faith-based communities both now and in the past, of course, have gone to considerable lengths to embrace new immigrants. Like schools, though, religious institutions could do a great deal more—according to almost all the churchgoers and leaders I spoke with—to deal with the problems that force families to move, to welcome new members into their communities, to assure that mobile parents and children stay involved with church activities when they move somewhere nearby and to assist mobile families in both emotional and practical ways.

Developing More Effective Community Strategies

I have argued here that we need new community strategies that not only strengthen local neighborhoods but give poor children and other disadvantaged children access to many different communities and that respond to the damage done by repeated moves. New community strategies are also needed that are rooted in an understanding of the highly complex and diverse social networks of poor families. Inattention to these differences can doom social support interventions. [47]

Social networks vary widely in size, density, geographical dispersion, the degree of diversity of members, stability and their functions, among other dimensions, and these variations have powerful implications for school, church, and other community-based interventions. For example, increasing the homogeneity of social networks may be important for affirming and supporting members, but increasing the diversity of network members may be critical for participants' learning and changing. Reducing the dispersion of a social network may be critical for families with transportation problems or families who may need various forms of urgent assistance.[48] As I have noted, families vary considerably in the number of social networks they are involved in, both within their immediate neighborhood and more broadly, and the nature of these different networks has important implications for interventions. The work community, for example, is clearly an important community for large numbers of families—and will become an important community for an increasing number of low-income families who will be required to work in the next several years. Creating useful and meaningful social networks for parents may increasingly require shifting focus to the workplace.

These differences call for fashioning fine-grained community interventions based on careful attention to these many different dimensions of social support.

While those undertaking social support interventions—whether churches, schools or other community institutions—can usually not afford to engage in a complex mapping of neighborhood families' social networks, they can engage families more informally in describing their social networks and in crafting interventions, and they can at least roughly monitor the impact of their interventions on families' support networks. They can also seek to provide diverse opportunities for social support to accommodate families in diverse circumstances.

Conclusion

The road to translating popular, yet often fairly general, notions of social cohesion and social capital into effective interventions is not likely to be straight and narrow. The chance of success will be far greater, however, if these interventions are grounded in a firm understanding of the community circumstances of poor families. Minimally, it is crucial to recognize that poor children tend to be mobile, that they need both neighborhood ties and access to diverse communities, and that they are embedded in many different kinds of complex communities. Effectively responding to these facts of poor families' lives will not require retrieving old, familiar notions of community but rather being willing to take up community building strategies that are quite unfamiliar. Across the country, people are now calling for "restoring community institutions," yet simple restoration will not suffice. In some cases, we may need to conceive of religious institutions and schools that "look" quite different from current community institutions. Schools in the Southwest that are adapting to mobile children by making fundamental changes in their structure and curriculum are one example of this kind of shift. Needed at the heart of this change is the willingness to enable religious and other institutions to take their shape from neither nostalgic conceptions of community, nor from bureaucratic and funding mandates, but from close attention to the needs of disadvantaged families themselves. Perhaps then we will be one step closer toward developing more communities that protect and strengthen disadvantaged families, build on the substantial strengths of their neighborhoods and give them cause to celebrate their shared lives.

Notes

1. Mary Jo Bane, *Here to Stay: American Families in the Twentieth Century* (New York: Basic Books, 1976), p.59–62

2. Frank Furstenberg, "How Families Manage Risk and Opportunity in Dangerous Neighborhoods," in Willaim Julius Wilson, ed., *Sociology and the Public Agenda*, (Newbury Park, CA: Sage Publications, 1993).

3. See studies cited in Richard Putnam, "The Prosperous Community: Social Capital and Public Life," *The American Prospect* 13 (Spring 1993): 39.

4. Robert Wuthnow, *Sharing the Journey: Support Groups and America's New Quest for Community* (New York: The Free Press, 1994), p.114.

5. From the Independent Sector Survey—called "From Belief to Commitment"—cited in Ibid, p.114.

6. Robert Wuthnow, "Mobilizing Civic Engagement: The Changing Impact of Religious Involvement," Unpublished paper, Princeton University, p. 24.

7. Wuthnow, *Sharing the Journey*, p.114.

8. Desmond K. Runyan, et al, "Children who Prosper in Unfavorable Environments: The Relationship to Social Capital," *Pediatrics* 101 (January 1998): 12–9.

9. Wuthnow, "Mobilizing Civic Engagement," 20.

10. Charles Trueheart, "Welcome to the Next Church," *The Atlantic Monthly*, (August 1996): 47.

11. Ross Thompson, *Preventing Maltreatment Through Social Support: A Critical Analysis* (Thousand Oaks, CA: Sage Publications, 1995), p. 24–65.

12. Deborah Belle, "Social Ties and Social Support," in Deborah Belle, ed., *Lives in Stress: Women and Depression* (Beverly Hills, Ca: Sage Publishers, 1982), p. 133–144. See also Carol Stack, *All Our Kin: Strategies for Survival in a Black Community* (New York: Harper and Row, 1974); and Furstenberg, "How Families Manage Risk."

13. See Stack, *All Our Kin*; and Richard Weissbourd, *The Vulnerable Child: What Really Hurts America's Children and What We Can Do About It* (Reading, MA: Addison-Wesley, 1996), p.101.

14. Mark Granovetter, "The Strength of Weak Ties," *American Journal of Sociology* 78 (6) (July-November 1972): 1360–79.

15. Thompson, *Preventing Maltreatment*.

16. As sociologist Robert Wuthnow points out, many people opt for support groups (e.g., Bible Study Classes, Alcoholic Anonymous meetings, self-help groups) that serve individual aims and affirm the self yet, unlike tight-knit neighborhoods, make no lasting, onerous demands.

17. James, a child in the Henry Horner Homes project in Chicago described by Alex Kotlowitz in *There Are No Children Here* (New York: Doubleday, 1991), copes with a gang that dominates his social world by trying "to make as little friends as possible."

18. Weissbourd, *The Vulnerable Child*, chapter 5.

19. Jeffrey G. Parker, and Steven Asher, "Peer Relations and Later Personal Adjustment: Are Low-Accepted Children At-Risk?" *Psychological Bulletin* 102 (1987): 357–89. See also Michael Rutter, *Fifteen Thousand Hours* (Cambridge, MA: Harvard University Press, 1979).

20. Kotlowitz, *There Are No Children Here*. See also Furstenberg, "How Families Manage Risk"; and Weissbourd, *The Vulnerable Child*, p.104.

21. Richard Schmuck, "Some Aspects of Classroom School Climate," *Psychology in the Schools* 3 (1966): 59–65.

22. David Kinney, "From Nerds to Normal: The Recovery of Identity among Adolescents from Middle School to High School," *Sociology of Education* 66 (January 1993).

23. Erik Erikson, *Identity, Youth and Crisis* (New York: Norton, 1968). For research suggesting that this exploration is critical to identity development, see studies cited by Kinney, "From Nerds to Normal."

24. See, for example, James Comer, "Educating Poor Minority Children," *Scientific American* 259(5) (1988): 42–8.

25. "Community Ecology and Youth Resilience: A Report to the Annie E. Casey Foundation, Public/Private Ventures," (April 1994).

26. Richard Murnane, and Frank Levy, *Teaching the New Basic Skills* (New York: The Free Press, 1996).

27. This is based on my conversations with teachers, parents and students as well as on the prevalent view that adolescent peer groups are isolated worlds impervious to the influence of adults. See Weissbourd, *The Vulnerable Child*, chapter 5.

28. For a discussion of why mentoring relationships do not take hold, see Freedman, M. *The Kindness of Strangers*, San Francisco: Jossey-Bass, 1993.

29. See Trueheart, "Welcome to the Next Church."

30. Wuthnow, *Sharing the Journey*, p. 355.

31. J. Sexton, "A Visit from the Pope: The Faithful; Vibrant Parishes Find Strength in Diversity," *The New York Times*, October 3, 1995.

32. Wuthnow, "Mobilizing Civic Engagement," p. 15.

33. See, for example, Trueheart, "Welcome to the Next Church," 50.

34. "Emerging Trends," a publication of the Princeton Religion Research Center, Vol. 21, no. 5, ISSN 3567890–1.

35. An observation of church scholar Lyle Schaller as well as other church scholars with whom I spoke. Quoted in Trueheart, "Welcome to the Next Church," 50.

36. For portrait of economic composition of members of megachurches, see Trueheart, "Welcome to the Next Church."

37. See Furstenberg, "How Families Manage Risk."

38. Wuthnow, "Mobilizing Civic Engagement."

39. Stephen M. Joseph, *The Me Nobody Knows: Children's Voices from the Ghetto* (New York: Avon Books, 1969), p. 21.

40. "Geographical Mobility: March, 1992 to March, 1993," U.S. Census Bureau, Current Population Reports, Series P–20–481, table E., p. xv.

41. Arloc Sherman, *Wasting America's Future: The Children's Defense Fund Report on the Costs of Childhood Poverty* (Boston: Beacon Press, 1994), p.19. The 1989 American Housing Survey tabulations come from the Children's Defense Fund report.

42. These statistics were related to me by school district research personnel in each of the respective cities.

43. U.S. General Accounting Office Report, "Elementary School Children: Many Change Schools Frequently, Harming Their Education," (February 1994), GAO/HEHS–94–45.

44. Naomi Carol Goldstein, "Why Poverty is Bad for Children," Ph.D. Dissertation, Kennedy School of Government, Harvard University, 1991, p.120.

45. Ellen Eliason Kisker, "A Profile of Child Care Settings: Early Education and Care in 1990," prepared under contract for the U.S. Deptartment of Education (Princeton: Mathematica Policy Research, Inc.), p.146, table iv.14.

46. U.S. General Accounting Office Report, "Elementary School Children: Many Change Schools Frequently," p. 9.

47. Thompson, *Preventing Maltreatment Through Social Support.*

48. For a useful discussion on the dimensions and variations of social support and their implications for policy interventions, see Thompson, *Preventing Maltreatment Through Social Support.*

CHAPTER 10

"That's What I Growed Up Hearing": Race, Redemption and American Democracy

Lucie White

A social program like Head Start cannot promote the development of children, families, and communities unless it recognizes the overwhelming salience of race in the American experience.

Duke University, 1996

Along the way of life, someone must have sense enough and morality enough to cut off the chain of hate. . . . [1]

On April 3, 1996, two African-American women associated with a Head Start program in a rural county in the Piedmont of North Carolina accompanied me to Duke University to conduct a seminar on "Welfare Rights and Women's Rights." Project Head Start is the well-respected school-readiness and family-support program for low-income three and four year-old children that was established in 1964 by President Lyndon Johnson.[2] The seminar was part of a colloquium, "Think Globally, Act Locally: Women's Leadership and Grassroots Activism," sponsored by the Andrew W. Mellon Foundation and the Duke University of North Carolina Joint Center for Research on Women. It featured presentations by activists from regions with records of widespread human rights violation, including Rwanda, China, Zaire, Haiti, and South Africa.

The older of the two Head Start women, Sally Clemmons, had taught public school in the counties served by the Head Start program for 50 years before retiring. She was also the great-grandmother of a young girl enrolled in the Head Start program. The younger woman, Brenda Allen, had gone through the county's Head Start Program herself before returning there to work as a social services and parent involvement staff assistant. Ms. Clemmons began the presentation by presenting statistics about the racial composition of their home county's public school population. She reported that although 63 percent of the students in the county's public schools, only 19 percent of the teachers and 8 percent of the professional staff in the central office were African American. The rest were white.

Allen then continued the presentation. She reported that a few weeks earlier she had driven a van of four-year-old Head Start children 50 miles from the county's Head Start Center to the city of Greensboro, about 50 miles to the northwest, for their annual dental screenings. Greensboro was the site of the February 1960 sit-in at the Woolworth's lunch counter that is often said to have launched the Civil Rights Movement.[3] Allen, speaking in a strong, clear voice, explained that she had to drive the children all the way to Greensboro for their dental screenings because she could not locate a dentist in the program's home county who was willing to look inside the mouths of these black children.[4]

I first met Clemmons and Allen in the winter of 1992, while doing fieldwork for an ethnographic study of women's participation in Project Head Start.[5] I had been introduced to Head Start in the early 1980s, while working as a poverty lawyer. The program made a powerful impression on me. From my vantage point as a battle-weary welfare lawyer, Head Start seemed to be something more than a federal program that provided services—hot meals, health screenings, early education and care—to poor children. It was also a place where low-income women and men came together to create community and to participate in the program's governance. Indeed, in their ground-level culture, the Head Start centers in which I became involved as a young welfare lawyer felt like a cross between spiritual communities and democratically managed schools.

As a lawyer, I understood Head Start as a creature of public law: this place that so intrigued me would not have *been there* but for a dense framework of federal statutes, regulations, administrative guidelines, and funding formulas. Yet the thing that drew me to the program, particularly the quality of community that I sensed among Head Start women, did not seem to be programmed by this law. The qualities that the women said the program had nurtured and affirmed in them and their children seemed to be more imagined—or prayed for—than real. Head Start seemed to be as much a creation of the stories that they told to each other about it as a replicable intervention of state welfare policy *into* their lives.

In 1992, after I had become a law professor, I undertook a year-long ethnographic study of low-income women clients at two local Head Start sites, one in South Central Los Angeles, and the second at the North Carolina program with which Clemmons and Allen were affiliated, and in which I had been briefly involved a decade before. I undertook the project because of a concern that our programs of social provision rarely pay serious attention to the perspectives of the people and communities they serve. Head Start has been one of most successful of this nation's programs of social provision. By listening closely to Head Start clients, I sought to understand why they often hold that program in such high regard, at the same time that they typically describe other means-tested social programs as either demeaning to their dignity or irrelevant to their most basic human needs.

This chapter draws on my interviews with Jo Elaine B., an African-American parent in the North Carolina Head Start that I studied. Through a close reading these interviews, I seek to trace how Ms. B has "storied" her own life experience and how she has understood Head Start to figure in it. From this starting point, I contemplate why women like Ms. B. often feel such loyalty to Head Start, and then ask what wider lessons we might draw from Head Start's reputed "magic."

Ms. B's story shows that race division was an overwhelming force in her life. From childhood, racial animus repeatedly assaulted her dignity, provoking anger that she dared not express directly. Thus, she struggled against turning that anger inward, into feelings of humiliation, depression, and despair. In waging this internal struggle, Ms. B. drew strength from deeply held religious values. She worked hard to answer to a world that was fraught with race hatred with a life that was centered in care. At the same time that Ms. B. drew upon her faith to sustain her dignity in the face of repeated race injury, the Head Start program, at the grassroots level, had two distinctive features that worked to affirm the efforts of individual women like Ms. B. to survive, and indeed, to overcome, the race division that threatened their lives. The first of these two critical features of Head Start's local practice is a clear recognition that race still matters enormously in the lives of its people. The second is a subtle reliance, in the parent involvement programs that create a sense of community among Head Start clients, on activities like gospel singing and witnessing that are evocative of faith-based African-American practices for overcoming the destructive impact of race division on their human potential.

Listening closely to Ms. B.'s life story poses three hard questions to this nation's practices of social provision. First, should programs of social provision address race directly in their day-to-day work with clients? Second, can the values and practices of African-American faith communities help in that project? And third, can such spiritual practices be brought into programs of social provision without compromising pluralist value commitments or intruding on clients' cultural and religious autonomy?

Going Home

After my father died and I turned thirty, I decided to go back home. That was in 1982, just before the Reagan Congress made its first deep cuts in welfare. I got a job as the legal aid lawyer in a rural community about an hour's drive due south from Mebane. I worked with Della, who had grown up in the county and was trained as a legal secretary. Most of our work was with African-American women who had not been as lucky as Della, who had been blessed with good health, a good husband, and a steady job.

Della and I ran a no-nonsense, high-volume legal aid practice. We represented poor people in claims under the new public laws of social provision—AFDC, Medicaid, Food, Stamps, Section 8, and SSI. We called them poor laws, even though the best of them paid good money and had clear rules. Our objective was simple: we were out to maximize our clients' incomes. The work brought a certain satisfaction; the victories were often easy. We had learned to be quite shrewd at working the law.

The women that we worked with were grateful for the money, but they hated what we made them do to get it. They hated telling white folks that their children were bastards, or the toilet was backing up sewage and the rent wasn't paid. They hated telling white folks that they were too sick or too stupid to hold down a job. All of the hearing officers who heard these claims in the county were white. They were low-paid civil servants: many were going to night school to study business so they could get better jobs. I had learned how to win them over by getting my clients to tell their stories like pictures, right in the eye. The judge would invariably rule in the client's favor, without knowing *why* he had been moved. After they got their money from these kinds of hearings, women would curse "the welfare." They would say things like, "Why is the Man always nosing in your business," and, "Why does the welfare have to treat you like a dog."

Elaine Scarry has written about situations in which a dominant social group, insecure perhaps that its power is eroding, will make the people it seeks to keep down swear to their own incapacity to speak at all. She calls this kind of thing "unmaking"—the unmaking of the world.[6] The place that I had come home to had followed Jim Crow to the letter until just a decade earlier. The spirit of that order still hung in the poor laws that I was coaxing these women to use.[7] Gradually, I got sick of what they called "fair" hearings, and began to spend time at the Head Start Center in the building that had been town's all-black high school before the courts finally ordered the school board to close it down. The women I worked with seemed different when they were there. When they talked at my office about "the welfare," they always seemed rigid and sullen. At Head Start their bodies moved more freely.

For three decades, Head Start's reputation as successful—the crown jewel of the War on Poverty—has been secure, as much among the low-income women who use it, as among the politicians who fund it, and the wider publics who have repeatedly approved. At first, what I saw fit this simple picture. But as I got to know the program better, its contradictions started to jar me: an intimidating framework of administrative rules that had translated the monthly policy council sessions into odd rituals that seemed more like Quaker Meetings than "maximum feasible participation"; the teachers' defiant voices, demanding lockstep order from three- and four-year-old children; the children singing out their rote-learned letters, as bodies fidgeted on the floor; and the mothers' wistful judgments about the program's failures, judgments that showed how hope won't let go. What secrets, I wondered, about what is best, in this country, in the way of social welfare policy, might I learn by listening more closely to these women? A decade later I came back to the state with some funding and a tape recorder to pursue this question.

When I interviewed Jo Elaine B., she was living in a simple wood frame house not too far from the railroad, on a shady, sloping, raked dirt lot. I didn't find her house until my third try. First you had to take a sharp right off of the four-lane highway between Monroe and Wadesboro, near the Seven Eleven that lay in the trough of a hill that looked like the ocean. Then you had to cross the tracks and turn at the crossroads where the one-time train station, now used for feed storage, stood opposite the Methodist church. Then you had to follow the dirt road that ran beside the track for a couple of miles. On the afternoon I finally found her, the rain had turned that road's red clay pot holes into ponds for hatching tadpoles and mosquitoes, and the sidewalls of my rental car's tires were caked with mud.

This was the part of North Carolina's red clay region where you didn't want to be at this time of year, especially if you couldn't buckle your sandals because you had just gotten pregnant and your feet felt as swollen as your belly. It was too close to the sand hills; too far from the cool air of the mountains. Every day the weather would follow the same cycle. You could breathe all right in the morning, when the mist would rise from the grasses into the sky. But by midafternoon, the sun would thicken the air like gravy. On bad days the heat would settle like velvet, and the women at home with their children would turn on their fans, darken their sitting rooms, and watch TV. On good days, the wind would rise, and it would rain. These rains were hard and sudden, the kind that make you pull off the highway to avoid getting rear-ended by a long-haul truck. When the rain was over, steam would burn off the roadway, and the line where the road met the sky would shimmer like sand.

It was a decade since I had worked in the county for Legal Aid, and I felt like an outsider all over again: driving these roads in the hottest part of the year, trying to track down a list of fifteen Head Start women, more or less randomly chosen, who hadn't had the time or inclination to get involved in the program's parent activities. I was spending the month of August tracking down this list of women, to round out the picture I had gotten from the active parents I had interviewed at the Head Start center during the school year. I called those women the Boosters and the ones I was searching for now, like Jo Elaine B., the Disappeared. At my Legal Aid site, the Disappeared women were usually very young, with several babies and just as many problems—depression for sure, and usually a few other items from the standard list of underclass afflictions. Here in Carolina, the Disappeared were usually older country women, who were raising their kinfolks' babies and didn't have cars. Most, like Jo Elaine B., had spent their working lives in D.C. or Baltimore or New York.

These women lived in wooden shacks and mobile homes without mailboxes, on the dirt roads that spread out into the fields like the lines on the palm of your hand. A few miles to the east, in Sampson and Johnson Counties, these roads sheltered the camps for Haitian and Salvadoran migrants without papers, who had come north to pick peaches and sweet potatoes and apples in exchange for food. In this part of the Piedmont, the farm work was less labor intensive; the families that lived in the country took jobs in the nursing homes and chicken processing plants and fast food outlets when they could get them, and got money sent back from their children, and went on and off of disability and AFDC. I learned later that Jo Elaine B. paid her bills with the disability check that she got from having lupus, and the welfare check that she got for the child.

The front porch of her house, just big enough for a rocking chair, was propped up off the ground on red brick piers that looked like they were glued together with toothpaste. The no-nonsense floor plan reminded me of my LA bungalow: on one side was a sitting room and tiny kitchen; on the other were two bedrooms just large enough for a double bed and dresser, joined by a bath. The floor was papered with a sheet of green linoleum. The walls were papered with pictures: large families posed on sofas, babies of every complexion laid out on rugs, snapshots of schoolboys and soldiers, and full-body portraits of young women in choir robes and bridal gowns. On top of the TV were a dozen or so pictures of the same child who had answered the door.

She had on a bright cotton school dress, with matching ribbons in her hair. My field notes described her as "bright, outspoken, well mannered." She opened the door with a "sheet of newsprint paper on which she had laboriously written her name, and her numbers up to ten, with a thick pencil." I learned later that her name was Jennifer. Ms. B. was raising Jennifer. Her mother, Saline, had gone North when Jennifer was four months old. Jennifer had just completed a year at Head Start.

Jo Elaine B. was born on July 1, 1939; she was 53 years old when we talked. She had clear skin, large bones, and a deep voice. She welcomed me, offered tea, and assured me how pleased she was to talk with me for two successive afternoons. She was the kind of woman who would command your attention when she cleared her throat. Just as I turned on my tape recorder, she coughed up a thick wad of phlegm, spit into her handkerchief and left the room. Left alone on the love seat that matched the floor, I looked down at my silk pantsuit and muddy shoes. My belly felt leaden. In the silence, I started to count the pictures on the wall. When Ms. B. returned, I flicked the orange plastic pause button to restart my tape recorder and recited my often-repeated opening question:

Tell me about your mother's background.

It turned out that Jo Elaine B.'s people were different from many of the African-American families that lived in the county. They hadn't moved up from the cotton plantations when the railroads brought factories for textiles and cigarettes and furniture to the Carolina Piedmont after the Civil War. Rather, her people traced their lineage to the generations of Africans and Indians who had been raising corn and pigs, and birthing babies, and firing bricks, and milling lumber in that region for as long as Jo Elaine's grandmother could trace back in time.

LW: *Tell me what your mother was like. As a person, how would you describe her?*
JEB: *Old-fashioned*
LW: *What do you mean by old-fashioned?*
JEB: *Well, she was just set in her ways. She never wanted electricity. She wanted kerosene lamps. She used them for years. She didn't have modern stuff like automatic washers and appliances and electric can openers, and toasters. She just didn't go for anything like that. When the house got wired she never got an electric stove. She used a wood stove to cook, a stove that burned wood.*

Her grandmother took care of her and her sister while her mother worked as a maid.

LW: *Did your grandmother ever tell you anything about her own life?*
JEB: *She told me a little, but she didn't tell me much. Back then, all the people didn't talk about their lives, their childhood lives much.*
LW: *Why do you think they didn't do that?*
JEB: *Back then they would lead us off on the wrong direction. We asked the truth. We never got the truth.*[8]

"We asked the truth. We never got the truth." She spoke this line with an odd intonation that brought another passage, this one by Lillian Smith, to my mind:

> *If you could just keep from your children the things that must never be mentioned, all would be well! It was not evil but the knowledge of it that injured.*[9]

Smith was writing about her own mother's effort to shelter a white child from the evil that was all around her in the years before the Great Depression in the South. For girls like her, and me, the costs of not learning what must *never be mentioned* was merely psychic pain.

Over the year of fieldwork, I heard many stories about the nuance way of speaking that African-American elders taught their children at an early age. First the elder would answer the child's simple questions with riddles. Then she would teach the child to do the same. Then the elder would teach the child the art of speaking truth about important things through doubled statements that white people could never quite understand. Later on in our conversation, Ms. B. explained why this skill was so important.

LW: *Now at the time you were going to school, that was before the court had come in and integrated the schools . . . .*

She answered as predicted, and then went on.

JEB: *The schools weren't integrated because most of the white people around here were prejudiced.*
LW: *Were prejudiced?*
JEB: *Against blacks.*
LW: *How did they show that?*
JEB: *They showed it when you see them. They didn't want no parts of you, didn't want no conversation with you, didn't even want to be bothered with black people, period. White people call you Nigger. When you go uptown, they'll call you, "There come a Nigger. Oh Nigger, Nigger this," and "Oh, Nigger, Nigger that." Everywhere you go those white peoples around here called black children Nigger. You go uptown, it was Nigger, Nigger, Nigger, every time you stepped out of the house, and a white person, a white car see you, they will call you Nigger. In the stores they were much more hateful to black peoples than they was to whites. You could tell that they had something against us. You could feel it when you didn't see it. You felt funny and strange, like you were in the wrong place at the wrong time. I'm not supposed to be here, you know. Cuz I'm black and this here is these white people's place. I'm not supposed to be here. I couldn't understand why they could take my money, but they couldn't accept me. The color of my skin, it's not gonna rub off on you. It can't. . . . Yes, that's the way they acted. We were separate, and we had to keep to ourselves, because that's the way it was. . . . I remember hearing that in places, like in South Carolina, if a black person went there, the white people would kill them. If black people go there, the white people would kill them. That's what I growed up hearing.*[10]

As she spoke, her voice was slow and measured. She looked me, squarely but without accusation, in the eye.

I'm not supposed to be here, you know . . . I remember hearing about places . . . that if the black people go there, the white people would kill them . . . . That's what I growed up hearing.

Lillian Smith described this world from a white girl's perspective:

And because they did not believe things could change or that they should . . . they had to shut their minds against knowledge of what existed. They could not let their imaginations feel the sorrow of a colored mother whose child is shamed from birth, nor once look deep into poverty, nor once realize what they themselves had been deprived of. They could not have borne it. And because they could not let themselves know, they were terrified at a word, a suggestion, anything that caused them to feel deeply. It was as if one question asked aloud might, like a bulldozer, uproot their garden of fantasies and tear it out of time, leaving only naked bleeding reality to live with.[11]

* * *

For as long as Jo Elaine can remember, all of the women in her family—her grandmother, her mother, her sisters—took care of other people's needs. *My momma baby-sat, housekept, did domestic work out in the homes.*[12] Jo Elaine started caring for white folks when she was a child.

> *I would go out to a lady's house and help do stuff to her house—take her rugs out, dust a little bit in the house for her, little things like that. She'd pay us with apples. We'd take the apples home and tell our mother that the lady gave us apples instead of money. She'd make us go back and take the apples and tell her we wanted money.*[13]

Jo Elaine's grandmother kept her daughter's family together. Early on, she had saved up her wages from cleaning houses and doing laundry, so she could buy a five-acre farm, with a "*house and a garden, chickens, and pigs, and corn.*"[14]

Jo Elaine's memories of school were mostly bad. Even though all the children in her school were African American, as a country child, she was different:

> *I enjoyed staying home more than going to school, because of the kids picking at me so bad. I thought about quitting. I couldn't wear clothes like they was wearing, because their parents were making a lot of money, and my mother wasn't getting that kind of money, so I didn't wear as fine clothes as other kids. And they were picking at me and that's why I didn't want to go. They were mostly boys, but some girls too. Even once the teacher made a comment about my clothes. And I said, "You talk to my mother about that, because she told me to wear it." So he didn't say more.*[15]

Right about the time that Jo Elaine started grade school, her grandmother got too sick to keep on taking care of sick white people,[16] so Jo Elaine's mother had to quit her regular maid's job to look after her. On some days, though, she had to work a day job to get cash to pay the taxes on the farm. On those days, Jo Elaine or her sister would get to stay home from school to care for their grandmother.

> *She had to keep us out, because she had to work. Somebody had to work. My grandmother wasn't able to be left alone by herself. She would wander and get into things and try to cook, and stuff like that. We didn't want her to get hurt, and as long as somebody was home with her, we could talk her out of these things.*[17]

It was at that point in Jo Elaine's story that the family started to move. After her grandmother died, an aunt came from Charlotte to sell the farm to pay the taxes. After that, they lived in many different places. Sometimes they would live in run down rental housing in the colored sections of Wadesboro or Polkton or Monroe. Sometimes they would live in two- or three-room, concrete-block apartment units on dirt roads that cut off from the asphalt highway on the outskirts of town. Most of the time, though, they would live in sharecropper cabins, in the woods between the cotton fields that stretched south and east from the town, toward Peachland, and Charleston, and the outlying barrier islands, and into the sea.

> *We moved over there by the prison camp first, and left from there and went to a farm. And from the farm, we came back to Polkton. We didn't do any farming there. We lived in a house on the other side, up above Church Street. We were renting that house. We stayed about two or three years. I think I was about eight years old, nine, because I said I'm tired. I told my sister one day, "I'm tired of moving and then going to farms and farming. And then after we get through our farm we've got to help somebody else to pick cotton and chop cotton. I'm gonna run away and go back home and stay with my grandma."*

One of the worst things about the moving was the packing and unpacking. Another was the way that the moving kept her from feeling like she could make any choices about her life.

> *We moved so much every time you look around we were packing up moving. I didn't feel like moving so much, but it was my momma's decision. Children couldn't make no decisions. When they moved, we had to move with them. We didn't have no choice. Every time I get settled in one place I had to get up and move from one place to another. Just go somewhere and get a nice decent place to live and put your roots somewhere, where you can't—a rolling stone can't gather no moss, rolling all over the world. And going, every time you get settled here you gotta go. I didn't feel like going there. And that packing and moving, that's hard work.*[18]

Ms. B.'s words seemed to rake back and forth over the same ground.

> *We didn't have no choice. . . . If we didn't want to move, we still had to go . . . we still had to go . . . from one place to another . . . packing and moving. . . . Just go somewhere and get a nice decent place to live and put your roots somewhere, where you can't . . .*

You can't what? I wondered. She hadn't completed that sentence. . . . *rolling all over the world . . . packing and moving . . . you gotta go.* What would it have been like, I wondered, to have come of age as a woman on such shifting ground?

> *It is doubtful that slaves possessed an immunity that victims lack today . . . Historians need to heed the wisdom of psychologists and pursue the hidden truths of slavery. The task is essential, for our mental health as a society.*[19]

In her autobiographical novel, *Bastard out of Carolina,* Dorothy Allison writes about the childhood of a dirt poor white girl named Bone. Bone also hated to move:

Moving had no season, was all seasons, crossed time like a train with no schedule. We moved so often our mail never caught up with us, moved sometimes before we'd even gotten properly unpacked or I'd learned the names of all the teachers at my new school. Moving gave me a sense of time passing and everything sliding, as if nothing could be held on to anyway. It made me feel ghostly, unreal and unimportant, like a box that goes missing and then turns up but you realize you never needed anything in it anyway. . . . It got to where I hated moving worse than anything . . . One winter we spent three months staying over with Aunt Alma, who had bought a new house on no money down. None of us expected her to keep it, and the bank filed papers on it almost as soon as we'd arrived. Something happened to me, something I had never felt before and did not know how to fight. Anger hit me like a baseball coming hard and fast off a new bat. . . . The anger lifted in me and became rage.[20]

The next thing recounted by Bone, the young heroine of Allison's book, is lying to her new teacher about her name.

Ms. B. concluded her remarks about the moves with a puzzling pronouncement. For all that was bad about moving, she said, "I'd rather move than be on a farm."[21]

She told me she hated farming, stating each word with a finality that seemed to dare me to press on. These points usually came when the other woman was approaching a topic that was very hard. I had found that if we could stay in such uneasy moment, her voice might begin to change. The words would start coming like water, first a few drops, then a trickle, then a stream. Gradually, she would find a way to say what it felt to her body to be wronged.

LW: *Why don't you like farm work?*

JEB: *The picking cotton. I don't like picking cotton. I never could pick much no way. And my back hurted me.*

LW: *What didn't you like about it? Tell me.*

JEB: *I didn't like anything about farming. Not one blessed thing did I like about farming. Nothing.*

LW: *Okay. And to pick cotton, you'd what? Bend over?*

JEB: *You had to bend over, and the burrs sticking all in our fingers, kept your fingers all picked up, and when you put your hands in the dishwater to wash the dishes, your hands would be burning and stinging. Around the cuticles, turning back on your fingers. I just didn't like it.*

LW: *Oh.*

JEB: *From the burrs sticking your fingers. Yes. You pull the cotton out, some of it is real hard to pull out. You got to get down in there and dig it out. And carrying the heavy sack on your shoulder. That's hard work. Carrying this cotton around on your shoulder and then picking it. It's rough on your hand, it's rough on your shoulders, and it's rough on your back. It's just three things about you tolerating with the cotton. You've got to carry that heavy strap sack on your shoulders, then bending your back and then when you raise up it feels like your back is just about broke. Stiff as a board. My lord.*

LW: *Would you do that as a child?*

JEB: *Yes. Come in from school, right to the field. Go, get off of the school bus and go in the house, let your books down, change your clothes, go to the field. Go to the cotton field. Till dark. I didn't like to pick it when I came home from school. You are tired from being in school all day. I didn't feel like picking no cotton.*[22]

I looked down at my own swollen fingers, the nails, the pads, the cuticles. In the summer when I was ten, I had spent four weeks at a children's music camp on the UNC at Greensboro campus, learning to finger the notes of children's songs on a rented violin. After that summer, I switched to the piano, which was easier on my fingers.

Michel de Certeau has written about how the knowledge of injustice gets "A*marked on the . . . body . . . inscribing an identity built upon pain.*" The challenge for those who seek a future that redeems those wrongs is complex. They must resist either *confirming or denying* that those marks carry an indelible meaning. Rather, they must seek to interpret those marks in a way that seeks hope without denying the continuing presence, through the body, of the history of wrong.[23] I though about the hurt that still must be there in Ms. B.'s back and fingers, and remembered a passage from Dr. King:

The way of acquiescence leads to suicide. The way of violence leads to bitterness and brutality. But, the way of nonviolence .. . . [24]

In an award winning picture book, thirteen year-old Annika George, an African-American migrant to a large urban city, describes her *Life in the Ghetto*. She dreams of a quiet space for studying in the afternoons while her mother is still at work and a safe stretch of sidewalk for playing hopscotch and riding her bike. She pictures the downward spiral of urban poverty as the blast of noises when she tries to study, and the trickiness of stepping over bodies to get her bike down the steps from her apartment to the street. In the last pages of her story, Aninka seeks to shake herself loose from these feelings. She draws a picture of Dorothy, still inside the safety of her own house, swept up from the cornfield, into the magical Land of Oz.

As a child picking cotton, Jo Elaine B. also spun dreams about going to Oz:

I always have dreamed of traveling. I said, when I get me enough money, and I be a big girl, I'm gonna do some traveling. To see some other part of this world, other than Polkton. Polkton is not the only town there was. I know there were other places. I read about them, seen pictures of them in magazines in school. I just wanted to go further; see some of the world.[25]

By the time Ms. B. had graduated from high school, her girlhood daydreams about the city's adventures had matured into a plan. In March of 1960, she moved North from Polkton to work as a maid for a Jewish family on Long Island. She would get a room and board and free time on Thursdays, with more pay than what her mother made in Polkton, which, in 1960, was about seven dollars a week.[26] Indeed, she was likely to make enough cash on Long Island to send some money back home. She had lined up the job through a girl friend from Polkton who had gone to the same Long Island town.

JEB: *I had a friend who went to New York because she had a sister up there before her. She went to get her a job, and I wanted to get me a job too. After she got there and get settled down, she said she was going to see if the lady she was working for wanted someone. She was going to send for me.*[27]

LW: *And this was the lady you stayed with?*

JEB: *For sixteen years and a half.*

LW: *Before you went up there what were you hoping would be different about the other side of the world, the North?*

JEB: *That the white people there would be more friendly to you. That's one thing I was looking forward to.*[28]

"That the white people there would be more friendly to you." This might seem like too simple a reason for a 20-year-old farm girl to move so far from home. Yet in Ms. B.'s experience, white people's meanness, and the hope that they might be nicer, was hardly a simple concern.

When she was in high school, Ms. B. had spent one summer working in Charlotte, the city that lay forty miles to the west of Polkton on the federal highway. She worked in a laundry owned by a white man and lived with her sister. Charlotte was one of those Piedmont mill-towns that grew fast, along with the railroads and the fences, after the Civil War. It had always been a town of rural people, Baptists, and Methodists, and Presbyterians, who had come to the Piedmont from the hill country of Scotland and Wales. They made Country Music, but were taught by their preachers not to like to dance. The city did not fulfill Ms. B.'s girlhood dreams of adventure; but the white people treated her different than she had been treated back home.

LW: *How did they treat you different?*

JEB: *They were more friendly than they were in Polkton. They were much kinder to you. In the laundry, the man, the owner, was nice. He was a white man. I went to a supermarket, and they were nice there, too. And they were white people. This person held the door back for me to come out the door. And it was a white person.*

LW: *And you remember that all these years?*

JEB: *Yes. Yes, I remember that.*[29]

When Ms. B. said more about how the white folks in Polkton would treat her, the importance of that summer in Charlotte "that summer when that white person held the door back . . . for me to come out the door" became clearer for me to understand.

> LW: *How would white people treat you different in Wadesboro?*
> JEB: *White people were hateful. You could tell that they had something against us. You could feel it. If you didn't see it, you could feel it.*
> LW: *Can you say more about what you could feel?*
> JEB: *You felt funny and strange, like you were in the wrong place at the wrong time. I'm not supposed to be here, because I'm black, and this here is the white people's place. I'm not supposed to be here.*[30]

When black people worked at white people's houses, they had to go to the back door:

> *They had to come to the back door to get the water. They would hand it out to them at the back door. I heard peoples say if you're hired to do a work in the yard of a white person's house, you have to go to the back door to get your water.*[31]

Even the white children had learned the moves of their parents' racial code:

> *Even little kids would call you nigger. Their parents were teaching them to be prejudiced against the black. "Don't touch. Look, kids. Don't touch black kids. The black gonna come off on you, you know." I seen it and heard it amongst the kids. The white kids thought if they touched the black kids, that the black would come off on them.*[32]

When Ms. B. described the children, her eyes got distant. My mind began to recite the jump-rope chants from my girlhood. ". . . *Catch a nigger by the toe* . . . " The voices were still high-pitched and eager. Martin Luther King once observed that *it is pretty difficult to like somebody threatening your children.*[33] He went on to note that one need not *like* those who hurt you. But if you do not learn to *love* them, your bitterness will destroy you.[34] To love your enemies, according to King, you must learn to distinguish between an "*evil system,*" and "*the individual who happens to be misguided, who happens to be misled, who was taught wrong.*"[35] Perhaps it is a little easier to make this distinction when those who threaten one's children are themselves children. But then the very project of making distinctions, between villains and victims, between actors and systems, start to seem like those white women's efforts that Lillian Smith had remembered, futile efforts to shield their children from a world of wrong. Nell Painter describes how a part of the damage that a slave system does to white children is to draw them into enacting, as well as witnessing, its violence:

> *Despite what black and white scholars assume about the rigidity of the color bar, attachment and loss often transcended the barrier of race. The abuse of slaves pained and damaged nonslaves, particularly children.*[36]

* * *

So Jo Elaine B. went North, to Long Island, in March of 1960. She was not quite twenty years old. She lived with a doctor's family, where she had her own room. His wife did not work.

> *She had appointments she would go on. Maybe to the beauty parlor, maybe with her friends and have lunch, or maybe go and play cards.*[37]

Jo Elaine raised the children:

> *Part of my job there was to be a waitress. I was like a short order cook. The boy might want pancakes for breakfast. Well, I'll serve him pancakes. The other one might want bacon and toast. I took care of three kids. I raised them.*[38]

After sixteen and a half years on Long Island, Ms. B. was tired. For one thing, she had developed health problems that were eventually diagnosed as lupus.

> *They had me thinking that I had rheumatoid arthritis for many years. So one morning I woke up, and I put my feet on the floor, and my feet were numb. I didn't have a bit of feeling in my toes. I wanted to come back home and live with my family.*[39]

When Ms. B. moved back to Polkton, her first impression was that things were somehow different:

> *The whites were mingled with the black people more than they was when I left. . . . That's what made the change in the environment. You can feel it when you go in stores and things. It was different.*[40]

She credited this difference to the work of Martin Luther King.

> *Martin Luther King got together with that group and start fighting for white and blacks to go together. I never did dream that I would ever see what I'm seeing now.*[41]

But gradually, after living for a few years back in Polkton, Ms. B. got a better sense of how much, and how little, the world had really changed. It was true that blacks and whites were working together in the few remaining textile factories, but whites were still on top in terms of seniority and supervision. And most of the clean jobs, in the front offices, in accounting and personnel and public relations, were still held by whites. The schools had been merged, but the staffs had never been integrated. By the 1990s, nearly all of the principals, and most of the teachers, in the county's public schools were white, even though almost two thirds of the students were African American.[42] And the Klan was expanding.

For some young people, the changes that had happened gave them new opportunities. These were the ones who had seemed more like adults than children from the moment they were born, and had learned how to act in ways that would not make white folks feel uneasy. You couldn't look too sullen when you turned the other cheek to racial insults. You couldn't carry a "chip" if you wanted to succeed. But there were other young people in Polkton, children who were without such talent. These children, like Jennifer's mother Salina, and Jo Elaine's own father, could not stay in Polkton, even after the color line had supposedly disappeared. When Ms. B. came back to Polkton, she made it her business to take in some of the children that these other young people had to leave behind. The first child that she raised was named Rita. Rita's mother hadn't gone north, but she had nonetheless disengaged herself from her daughter's needs:

> *When Rita came to me, she was six or seven years old, and she stayed with me until she got sixteen years old. She wasn't getting treated nice at home. I growed up with her mother. She didn't comb her hair when she needed it and the guy that was living there was busting at her all the time, and they stayed on Rita's back all the time. I said "I want to take her home and take care of her for a while" and I did. Her mother let her go.*[43]

When I met Ms. B. for the first time, Rita was playing with her own young child on the front porch of the house next door.

The second child that Ms. B. raised was Jennifer, the baby of her own nephew and his girlfriend Salina. One day Salina disappeared.

> *She ran off to New York with another man. She abandoned Jennifer, and she wasn't but four months old. My nephew told me that he needed someone to take care of Jennifer, because Salina had ran off and left the baby in the crib. He was working at the hospital, and he couldn't take care of the kid, so I brought her down to the house, and kept her a while.*[44]

Later on, Salina came back to town to take back her baby. But her mind was still elsewhere.

> *She wouldn't pay her baby a bit of attention. The same Pamper that I had put on that baby when it went over there was still on when she came back. So the brother brought it back. I said, "My God. What's wrong with you? Why you bringing Jennifer back over here? Where is her mother? What is wrong with your sister?" And he said, "I don't know what's wrong with my sister." I said, "Well, my God. You mean to tell that this woman won't take care of her baby. Lord, this poor old child, she going through it. She going through a rough time."*[45]

This poor old child. She going through it. She going through a rough time. The line we like to draw between the mothers and the children "going through it" began to blur.

From then on, Ms. B. stayed close to Jennifer's life, taking her in and then giving her back to Salina when she reappeared. Finally, when the child was fifteen months old, she came to Ms. B.'s house to stay.

She told me to keep Jennifer till she go in the hospital to have her baby. This was her third one. She gave all her girls away, the ones who were older than Jennifer. And the police were looking for her down here in Polkton and then she asked me to keep Jennifer. When it was time for me to take Jennifer home, Jennifer didn't want to stay. She couldn't talk, but she kept asking for someone back here. And Salina said, "I can't do a thing with that child. She's asking for somebody, someone."[46]

When Ms. B. described how she remembered Jennifer coming back to her house to stay, her voice became intense:

Salina called me on the phone. "I'm going to bring your little girl back to you, because I can't do anything with her." I said, "Well, I got an appointment, Saline. I can't miss my appointment." And I left. When I came from the doctor's office, it was about 5:30. I went in the house. I sat down, and I made a fire. I had a wooden heater in the house at that time. It was drizzling rain, and I was sitting down all by myself. All of a sudden I heard a knock at the door. I said, "Who knocking?" . . . "I got something for you." I said, "Got something for me? What in the world you got for me? . . . Lord have mercy Jesus!" When I saw her hands, she had her big coat wrapped, a box of Pampers, and a suitcase.
LW: *And you have kept Jennifer ever since?*
Since then she was with me.[47]

Soon after she had graduated from high school, Ms. B. had determined that she would not bear any children of her own. Instead, just like Winsie B., the midwife who assisted her own mother, Ms B. has tried to be there, when she was needed, to help with other women's children.

Whenever someone got ready to have a baby, they would go for Winsie B., and then she'd come and help deliver the babies. She was good, because a lot of them was born under her. Winsie and me would talk about different things when I was a child, just chat. She told me "I'm the one that delivered you." She had delivered so many children.[48]

If you count the three Jewish children that Ms. B. raised on Long Island, and Rita, and Jennifer, Ms. B. has raised five children.

Head Start's Redemptive Practices

In my research on Project Head Start, I heard stories like Jo Elaine B.'s from most of the sixty women I interviewed. It was the repeated instances of racialized exclusion, humiliation, and abuse that caused me to shift the focus of my research from Head Start's legal framework to the question of race. But the stories that I heard from Head Start women were not just stories of racial injustice. They were also about the women's lifelong work of caring—within and across race boundaries—and they were about how those practices of caring helped them to maintain hope in a world of pervasive racism. The stories were about how women sought to redeem themselves and their children from the blight of racism, and how Head Start sometimes helped them in that effort.

When I began researching the program's legislative record, I came upon hundreds of public testimonials by Head Start women about how the program had changed their lives. This testimony, though undoubtedly scripted, reminded me of the informal talk that I remembered from Head Start women back in North Carolina. For example:

> *Before I entered the Head Start Program, I was afraid. I wouldn't talk; my voice got shaky, and my knees would tremble, and I couldn't talk in front of anybody. I was afraid to open my mouth. But my program director pushed me. She told me I could do it, and I kept trying. I kept getting up. She kept pushing me and I didn't stop trying. Today, I'm a new person. I'm not afraid to talk anymore.*[49]

* * *

> *I felt a sense of despair, with little self-esteem. I thought my life was without meaning. One day I heard there was a Head Start class down the street, at a time when I had lost all hope of ever being anything but an outcast. I learned that I was not the only young mother or dropout. I started putting time in at the class. The teacher would give me work to do with the children. I remember picking up a book to read to the children and the fear I felt. I realized that I needed a Head Start.*[50]

* * *

> *I began writing poetry. I was never interested in writing before, but the frustration of a bad marriage, a houseful of babies needed a mode of expression. The staff at Head Start found out about [my poems] and I gave them permission to print them in the Head Start parent Newsletter. Head Start was there once again, providing outlets for my frustrated, creative urges. Having a voice is one thing, but being able to express that voice is another, and having someone to listen when you express your opinion is the greatest success of Head Start. They listen!* [51]

* * *

> *The moral support I got from Head Start down through the years has helped me to climb up the ladder. Many times it seemed like the next rung was missing or would break under the pressure – but I could always count on Head Start to be there. I think the most important thing is that through the support I have received, I have learned how to support others.*[52]

* * *

If it had not been for Head Start, I might still be a maid. Head Start gave me the first job I ever had that did not include pushing a mop.[53]

This testimony—its cadences, its images, its narrative flow—sounded out of place in Congressional oversight hearings of a federal welfare program. These women were testifying to how Head Start had enabled them to cope with despair, transform hurt and anger into redemptive energy, and feel connected to something larger than themselves. This was the language of witness. These women were testifying to experiences of spiritual change.

During my year of ethnographic research, I had many conversations with Head Start women about the dynamic through they perceived these changes to occur. Those conversations, as well as my participant observation of the program's parent involvement activities, pointed to features of African-American spiritual practice as critical to this process of change. For instance, women often linked their experience of change to their participation in public testimonial events in which they offered public testimony that the change process through a stylized narrative of sin and redemption. As many scholars have shown,[54] this practice of testifying can be traced to the creative interweaving of African, Evangelical Christian, and Hebrew traditions into the distinctive religious practices of Afro-American slaves.

Even in a contemporary secular, indeed bureaucratic, institutional setting like Head Start, these spiritual practices have given thousands of low-income women a common ritual language, a cultural ground, from which they could not just survive race hatred, but turn it around into what Elaine Scarry might call world-making power. Thus, in 1992, the year that more than 50 Los Angeles residents, mostly people of color, were killed in a race-linked urban riot, I witnessed recent immigrants from Mexico, El Salvador, and Guatemala join with second and third generation African-American migrants to testify about how their South Central LA Head Start experience had given them the power to work together across a chasm of ethnic distrust, and thus change their lives.

Head Start's Constitution

My research suggests that African-American spiritual practices are embedded in the local culture of many Head Start programs because of the confluence of several historical circumstances. Head Start was launched by Lyndon Johnson in the summer of 1965, as a key program in his War on Poverty. This was the peak of the Civil Rights Movement. It was also a time when social projects inspired by that movement, such as the Welfare Rights, Legal Aid, and Black Power movements, were mobilizing low-income African Americans to demand greater dignity, equality, and democratic participation in both public and private systems of welfare provision.[55] At the community level, particularly in cities, African Americans were reaffirming distinctively Black cultural, artistic and spiritual traditions, and reweaving those practices into new forms of grassroots institutional innovation and political practice.

Head Start was designed by a presidential committee, called the Cooke Committee, in which Lyndon Johnson brought progressive mental health and child development experts together with African-American educators and grassroots leaders. The academics on the Committee set forth the basic idea around which Head Start was shaped. The crux of this idea, drawn from the work of progressive developmental theorists like Urie Bronfenbrenner, was that the clients of social welfare programs, like all human beings, should be understood not as isolated individuals, but rather as developing social beings, linked in a dense and dynamic human *ecology* that includes the self, the family, the neighborhood, and the public sphere. Therefore, according to this idea, programs of social provision and support should be holistic, development-enhancing, family-focused, and embedded in family, community, and wider political worlds. The goal of human and social welfare, even when it is delivered by the government, is not merely to distribute income or services to individuals through bureaucratic frameworks. Rather, systems of social welfare should have as their overriding goal to protect and enhance social ecologies, thereby helping to ensure optimal human development.

The African-American activists on the committee did not challenge this idea. Rather, they revoiced it from the standpoint of their own life experiences and race identities, thus placing new emphasis on two bedrock normative themes. The first was the theme of democracy, and the second was status equality. They viewed these themes as critically important to human development and flourishing, not just in the political sphere, the market, and civil society, but within the institutional practices of social welfare programs as well.

The African-American members of the Cooke Committee placed such weight on democracy and equality in social welfare programs like Head Start for a straightforward pragmatic reason. They did not believe that a social program like Head Start could gain the trust or tap into the energies of low-income women without paying close attention to the real life experience, in all of its emotional and moral complexity. Their own experiences of race informed them that many low-income African-American women, like Jo Elaine B., were likely to have deeply embedded memories of racial injury, and repeatedly merging their own needs into the care of others. Some of these others were in their extended families: younger siblings, aging parents, neighborhood children like Rita and Jennifer, whose mothers had left them. But because of the world that race made, many of the persons that these women had been called on to care for were inevitably white. The African-American members of the Cooke Committee suspected that low-income women of every race identity, even including whites, were likely to have similarly anguished, similarly powerful, life experience. Poor white women in Head Start would not have been likely subjects of direct *race* injustice. Yet many would have been targets of ethnic or cultural insults, and none would have escaped the persistent erosion of one's dignity that comes with the status of being poor in America. Nor would she have been spared the restriction of voice, ban on empathy, and denial of sexual desire that comes with whiteness for a woman, even if she is poor. She would not have been spared the risk of gender violence. And she would not have been spared the need to care. In the view of the African-American members of Head Start's design committee, low-income women would not be likely to engage with social programs that appeared to ignore or deny the challenge and complexity of their inevitably race-inflected life experience.

Thus, Head Start's African-American architects urged their colleagues to understand race through the lens of social ecology. They argued that race is not a thing, like a biological trait or a set of social categories. It is not the sum of all the bad actions committed by biased individuals, or all the cultural traditions devised by African Americans throughout their history of slavery. Rather, race, in their view, is a constitutive feature of America's social ecology. In every part of the American landscape, the effects of race are woven into the fabrics of memory, action, and aspiration that constitute selves, families, communities, and the nation itself. Race choreographs people's interactions. It channels their relationships. It infused their memories. It silences, amplifies, and inflects their voices. A social program like Head Start cannot promote the development of children, families, and communities, it cannot support social welfare, unless it recognizes the overwhelming salience of race in the American experience.

The tension and dialogue between the academic and African-American voices on the Cooke Committee shaped a policy vision for Head Start that was unique among American social programs. This is not to say that Head Start does not borrow many features from earlier traditions of social provision. Its community-base, its holistic philosophy, its empowerment-orientation harks back to Jane Addams's settlement house model. Its fiscal structure is typical of many federal-state grant-in-aid programs in the child and family welfare domain. Yet in its fusion of the ecological model, a strong vision of programmatic democracy, and a determination to view race both as a constitutive feature of every Head Start Center's social landscape and as a systemic impediment to every Head Start client's social equality, the program's basic policy blueprint was unique.

With the Cooke Committee's blueprint, President Johnson, in the summer of 1965, launched a Head Start summer program in several thousand communities. Because Head Start funding came through the 1964 Economic Opportunity Act, every local grantee was required by law to provide "maximum feasible participation" to its clients. This vague legal mandate was wholly consistent with the Cooke Committee's philosophical vision, so it was not likely to be resisted or dismissed by Head Start's administrators. And indeed, far more than in any other OEO program, Head Start's early bureaucrats embraced the idea of programmatic democracy worked hard to make it real. Because of the effects of the Civil Rights Movement on the federal civil service, those bureaucrats included several African Americans with social movement experience.

For instance, Bessie Draper, the first chief of Head Start's parent involvement component, was an African-American woman. Prior to her appointment, Draper had grown up in Harlem, attended law school, and worked in an Urban League employment counseling center in St. Louis. Because of their own vision and the strong mandate from Head Start's constitutive law, Draper and other early federal bureaucrats made unusual efforts to promote a culture of participation in local Head Start programs. Draper, for instance, toured the country to learn about the grassroots beliefs and traditions for caring for children, nurturing adult women and families, challenging race violence, and promoting racial reconciliation that infused the day to day practices of Head Start's first generation of teachers and parents. She and others then drafted Head Start's first parent involvement regulation so as to encourage all programs to draw on their clients' grassroots traditions and beliefs into the program's official practices.

Thus, Head Start's first parent involvement regulation, issued in 1970, required programs to bring parents into the classroom as volunteers and to hire them as teachers. It charged parents to design and offer enrichment activities for themselves as well as their children, and gave them great leeway to draw on the values, beliefs, and traditions of their own families, communities, racial and ethnic identity groups, and spiritual traditions in doing so. Finally, it gave parents, acting through a parent policy council, the right, and indeed, the obligation, to set basic educational policy for their program.

Thus, Head Start's policy blueprint and foundational law set forth a porous institutional framework. It left ample space for the parents, teachers, and community members in each local program to bring their own race-charged memories, identities, spiritual beliefs, and cultural practices inside of the walls of the program. Indeed, that constitution did something more than permit local programs to draw on their client communities' spiritual rituals and values when designing parent involvement activities. It actually required local programs to do so, in order to create a distinctive democratic culture for the adults as well as children that the program served.

From these beginnings, a national Head Start culture began to take shape in the mid-1970s. Several specific practices, all funded by the federal government, helped with this project of shaping a national Head Start parent culture. These included a national Head Start parents' newsletter, a national organization of Head Start parents, with state, regional, and national tiers of elected officers, and annual national conventions of Head Start parents. Through these institutional channels, specific values, traditions, and practices associated with emancipatory African-American spirituality, such as public witnessing, gospel singing, evangelical-style public speaking, and the like, became deeply connected with "the Head Start experience" for parents, and began to define a unique Head Start identity for the public. As this nationwide Head Start culture began to take hold, new parents became initiated into the program's core cultural practices, even in places that were far removed from the local worlds from which these distinctively African-American traditions had first been introduced into the program.

As the testimonials in the Congressional record suggest, these cultural practices have since become identified by many Head Start women with the "secret" or the "magic" of Head Start's success.

* * *

What lessons about the culture and constitution of programs of social provision—whatever their source—might be drawn from the Head Start experience? I would list two. The first is that in order to be successful with disadvantaged communities, our programs of social provision should be infused with a consciousness of how deeply race cuts through all of America. Race cuts through our memories, lived experiences, relationships, imaginations, spiritual traditions, and institutional practices. It cuts through our psyches, our families, our communities, our national imaginations, whether we see ourselves as privileged or impoverished. Indeed, our understanding of the deepest meanings of concepts like wealth and poverty, or adaptation and pathology, rests on a bedrock of assumptions and values that have racial valence.

Second, spiritual traditions, particularly those that have been shaped in settings of racial oppression and resistance, offer invaluable cultural resources in the domain of social provision. The introduction to this volume emphasizes three important roles that organized religious *communities* can play in "revitalizing the social fabric and re-knitting the safety net": creating community; shaping moral dialogue; and participating with other institutions in social provision. My Head Start research suggests that traditions of religious or spiritual *practice*—musical, performative, rhetorical—can be a critically important resource in shaping the relational and public cultures of social provision programs. There are two obvious dangers in infusing programs of social provision with traditions and practices of particular religions. The first is that such practices can give a program an exclusionary or coercive feeling to people of other faith communities or cultural groups. The second is that these practices will indoctrinate clients, in subtle as well as more overt ways, in the values and beliefs of that religion. This is especially true if those clients are required to enact those practices in return for the program's services, singing a particular denomination's blessing, for instance, to get a meal. But the risk of coercion or indoctrination is also present if clients are simply required to sit in silence while other diners sing.

Spiritual traditions can inform practices social provision in ways that minimize these risks of exclusion, intimidation, and indoctrination. Several best-practice guidelines, drawn from the Head Start experience, suggest some of the ways that this might be possible. The first guideline relates to *who* brings a spiritual or cultural tradition into a program's practice. In the case of Head Start, African-American spiritual traditions were introduced into the program's culture not because either the program's architects or administrators dictated, or even advised, that this should happen. Rather, what the policy architects, legislators, and regulators endorsed, and indeed, required, was that the program's local practices be rigorously egalitarian, strongly democratic, and deeply committed to acknowledging the reality of race injustice in this country and the value of the distinctive beliefs, values, and spiritual practices of racially subordinated groups.

Thus, the program's official values were liberal, secular, and, especially, pluralistic. It was the serious implementation of these values at the local level that enabled African-American women, both clients and staff, to bring their distinctive spiritual practices into the program's local practices. Democratic and pluralistic legal norms and race-conscious, participation-oriented federal bureaucrats encouraged African-American clients to bring their own spiritual practices into the program's culture. It was local Head Start women who found ways to bring these rituals into the program in ways that would feel accessible and inviting to many women and would further the program's goals. This process worked because the overarching norms of secular pluralism and equal participation were vigorously and effectively implemented by Head Start's administrators, at every level. The reasons for this vigorous enforcement of pluralism and participation are largely historical. The legal rules and bureaucratic practices of Head Start were shaped at the height of the integrationist phase of the Civil Rights movement, in which assimilation of African Americans to the dominant white culture was a widely accepted norm. And the particular African-American spiritual practices that were woven into the culture of local Head Start centers stresses *love*, rather than vengeance, as its foundational norm. Although not pluralist, per se, this ethos is in tension with ethnic intolerance.

A second guideline for incorporating spiritual practices into social programs without creating a climate of indoctrination or exclusion relates to *how well* particular spiritual practices fit with a social program's intrinsic priorities. The African-American spiritual practices that Head Start programs incorporated did not have the effect of indoctrinating clients with a particular set of religious beliefs because those practices reflected the program's ecological vision and pluralist norm. Thus, those practices worked well to enable *all* Head Start clients, not just African Americans, to give voice to dignitary injuries, avoid racially fueled anger and retaliation, and, where possible, seek cross-racial reconciliation. It should be no surprise that spiritual practices which evolved in communities that were subject to extreme race oppression would fit particularly well in a social program, like Head Start, in which countering the negative effects of racism on human development is a clear program goal. One can ask whether the rigid secularism of government-linked social programs unnecessarily limits the capacity of those programs to address racial concerns.

The third best-practice guideline for bringing spiritual practices into the culture of social programs without compromising pluralist values relates to the *way* that the spiritual practice is woven into the program's activities. Although there is no real distinction between the form and the substance of a spiritual practice, these concepts offer a helpful vocabulary. Spiritually-informed practices are less likely to feel exclusionary, intimidating, or indoctrinating to clients from other religious traditions when those practices offer rituals through which all participants can express shared values or common concerns, without thereby subscribing to particularly doctrinal tenets. In the case of Head Start, African-American-inspired spiritual rituals give women a ritual language for voicing, and sharing, remarkably widespread personal experiences of despair, hope, and transformation. To many non-African-American women, those rituals do not seem religiously intrusive because they do not offer doctrinal interpretations or responses to those conditions. Nonetheless, it should be noted that women from different religions will find the same rituals to carry different levels of doctrinal meaning. Thus, I have observed Latina and Arab women, of Roman Catholic or Islamic faiths, adapt the African-American practices as their own, and improvise through them. These women have not felt those practices to carry a strong doctrinal message. Yet the same practices may be experienced as strange and coercive to Buddhist women, for example, who come from a tradition that values silence and place, rather than voice and movement.

Questions

These lessons from Head Start suggest several questions that might be posed to every American program and practice of social provision, whether it be funded and managed by government, faith communities, or private sector sources. Can programs of social provision pursue the goals of individual dignity, social equality, and our communal welfare without addressing race explicitly, on the *inside* of the program's culture and practices? It is an easy matter for those at the top of social programs to turn away from the race question. Raising the race issue directly will only get them into trouble. It is likely to reinforce rather than challenge racial thinking and divert their limited resources from their own important goals. To the street-level players in these programs it is no less vexing to confront the race issue, but neither is it so easy to turn away.

Can the street-level actors in programs of social provision develop relationships of trust with their low-income clients—or indeed, with themselves—if they fail to confront the race question directly? The question is most urgent in programs of social provision that seek to do more for their clients than distribute handouts. Such programs include all of the current welfare-to-work programs, for example—employment and training, job readiness, job retention, family support, and the like—that seek to promote the education and development of their clients. They also include programs, like Head Start, for example, or community economic development initiatives, that seek to engage their clients in making changes in their neighborhood, community, civic, and political institutions. They may also include traditional charity or income maintenance programs—ranging from food and clothing pantries to general relief, Food Stamps, and TAFDCC that, at the very least, must enlist their clients' commitment to follow their rules. Can such programs succeed at their own objectives without weaving race awareness deeply into their practice and culture, as Head Start has done?

Yet how can such social programs engage the race question without doing harm? How can social programs enable clients to remember and express racial trauma without aggravating their anger? How can social programs help their clients confront race discrimination, challenge racial segregation, and counter racial violence without diverting scarce resources from their clients' survival needs? Can social programs get any help in negotiating these issues from practices that evolved in African-American faith communities for surviving and redeeming race injustice? And even if religious traditions can offer some guidance on these hard questions, how can spiritual practices be woven into the fabric of social programs in ways that protect pluralist values and further ecumenical social projects?

It complicates the question of "Who will provide?" to put race at the center of our attention. It is much more comfortable to bring race in as an afterthought, as the last on a litany of obvious concerns. It is much easier to relegate the race question to other domains on the social landscape—religion, for example, or the family, or the antidiscrimination agencies of government. The ultimate question for our peculiarly American democracy is whether it is simply wrong to bend to this temptation. Bringing race to the center of our attention means seeking practices, through which the pervasiveness of past racial trauma and ongoing racial injury can be acknowledged, among all participants in a program. It might also mean seeking to weave into the program's cultural fabric those spiritual practices that can enable participants to bear witnesses to that injustice, and to seek redemption.

Notes

1. Martin Luther King, "Nonviolence and Racial Justice," in James M. Washington, ed., *Testament of Hope: The Essential Writings and Speeches of Martin Luther King, Jr.* (San Francisco: HarperSanFrancisco, 1991), p. 8.

2. See Edward Zigler, *Head Start: The Inside Story of America's Most Successful Educational Experiment* (New York: Basic Books, 1992).

3. See William H. Chafe, *Civility and Civil Rights: Greensboro, North Carolina and the Black Struggle for Freedom* (New York: Oxford University Press, 1981).

4. The syllabus for the Colloquium Series, a hand-out from Clemmons on the racial demographics of her county's public school system, and an audiotape of the April 3, 1996 seminar are on file with the author.

5. The field work was funded by the National Science Foundation's Law and Social Sciences Grant Program and the UCLA Law School. The Bunting Institute at Radcliffe College and the Harvard Law School have also supported this research.

6. See Elaine Scarry, *The Body in Pain: the Making and Unmaking of the World* (New York: Oxford University Press, 1985).

7. Jacquelyn Dowd Hall, writing about Katharine Du Pre Lumpkin's *The Making of a Southerner* (unpublished manuscript, 1995), p. 4.

8. Jo Elaine B., Interview A (Polkton, NC, August 24, 1992), pp. 3–36.

9. Lillian Smith, *Killers of the Dream* (New York: Norton, 1949), pp. 142–3.

10. Jo Elaine B., Interview A, pp. 42–8.

11. Smith, *Killers of the Dream*, pp. 142–3.

12. Jo Elaine B., Interview A, p. 8.

13. Ibid., pp. 31, 35.

14. Ibid., pp. 4–5.

15. Ibid., pp. 39–40.

16. Ibid., p. 7.

17. Ibid., p. 37.

18. Ibid., pp. 60–1.

19. Nell Irvin Painter, "Soul Murder and Slavery: Toward a Fully Loaded Cost Accounting," in Linda Kerber, Alice Kessler-Harris, Kathryn Kish Sklar, eds., *U.S. History As Women's History: New Feminist Essays* (Chapel Hill: University of North Carolina Press, 1995), pp. 138, 146.

20. Dorothy Allison, *Bastard Out of Carolina* (New York: Dutton), pp. 64–7.

21. Jo Elaine B., Interview A, pp. 60–1.

22. Ibid., pp. 61–4.

23. Michel de Certeau, "The Politics of Silence: The Long March of the Indians," in Michel de Certeau (translated by Brian Massumi), *Heterologies: Discourse on the Other* (Minneapolis: University of Minnesota Press), pp. 226–7ff (quoting from a speech by 21-year-old Bolivian Indian activist Quispe Balboa in the presence of Paraguayan authorities).

24. .Martin Luther King, Jr., "My Trip to the Land of Gandhi," in Washington, *Testament of Hope*, p. 25.

25. Jo Elaine B., Interview A, pp. 61–4.

26. Ibid., pp. 57–8.

27. Ibid., pp. 55–6.

28. Ibid., p. 56.

29. Ibid., p. 45.

30. Ibid., pp. 46–7.

31. Ibid., p. 51.

32. Ibid., p. 47.

33. Martin Luther King, Jr., "Love, Law, and Civil Disobedience," in Washington, *Testament of Hope*, p. 47.

34. In King's words: "The way of acquiescence leads to moral and spiritual suicide. The way of violence leads to bitterness in the survivors and brutality in the destroyers. But, the way of nonviolence leads to redemption and the creation of the beloved community." See King, "My Trip to the Land of Gandhi," in Washington, *Testament of Hope*, p. 25.

35. Ibid.

36. Painter, "Soul Murder and Slavery," p. 141.

37. Jo Elaine B., Interview A, p. 66.

38. Ibid., p. 34.

39. Ibid., p. 71.

40. Ibid., p. 71.

41. Ibid., p. 50.

42. See compilation of personnel statistics from the Union County Public Schools prepared by Head Start parent Sallie Clemmons for a lecture at Duke University, April 1993.

43. Jo Elaine B., Interview A, pp. 76–7.

44. Ibid., pp. 78–9.
45. Ibid., pp. 78–80.
46. Ibid., pp. 79–80.
47. Ibid., p. 82.
48. Ibid., p. 54.
49. Ann O'Keefe, *What Head Start Means to Families* (Washington: Department of Health, Education and Welfare, 1979), p. 25, quoting a parent from Alabama.
50. Lula Malone, Head Start Reauthorization Hearing Before Subcommittee On Children, Family, Drugs, and Alcoholism of the Senate Committee On Labor and Human Resources, 101st Congress (1990), 2nd Session, p. 97.
51. Myrtha Andrews, Head Start Reauthorization Hearing Before Subcommittee On Children, Family, Drugs, and Alcoholism of the Senate Committee On Labor and Human Resources, 101st Congress (1990), 2nd Session Children, Family, Drugs, and Alcoholism Hearing, pp.105–6.
52. Ibid., p. 106.
53. Frankie King, Reauthorization of the Head Start Act, Hearing Before the Subcommittee On Family and Human Services of the Senate Committee On Labor and Human Resources, 98th Congress (1984), 2nd Session, pp. 35–6.
54. See Albert Raboteau, *A Fire in the Bones: Reflections on African-American Religious History* (Boston: Beacon Press, 1995); Zora Neal Hurston, *The Sanctified Church* (Berkley: Turtle Island); Paul E. Johnson, ed., *African-American Christianity: Essays in History* (Berkeley, CA: University of California Press, 1994).
55. See Martha Davis, *Brutal Need: Lawyers and the Welfare Rights Movement* (New Haven: Yale University Press, 1993).

CHAPTER 11

Religion and the Boston Miracle: The Effect of Black Ministry on Youth Violence

Jenny Berrien, Omar McRoberts and Christopher Winship[1]

Despite concerns over the practicality and political expediency of "faith-based" anti-poverty programs, the success of organizations such as the Ten Point Coalition suggests that social welfare programs that lack the depth dimensions of faith may be inadequate.

DURING THE 1990S, MANY LARGE CITIES IN THE U.S. saw dramatic declines in their homicide rates.[2] Boston's rate of homicide has dropped further than has that of any other large city, a full 80 percent between 1990 and 1999, creating what is now termed the "Boston Miracle." Perhaps more impressive is that Boston has achieved this precipitous decline in homicides through a process involving a unique partnership of the city's police and probation departments with community leaders. This strong partnership has helped establish broad support for police actions. This is in sharp contrast to New York City, where the declines in homicide rates have also been impressive, a 72 percent drop over the same eight year period, but where there have been open and hostile conflicts between the police and community leaders over the methods that police have used to reduce crime.[3]

In Boston, the key community group working with the police has been a set of black churches known as the Ten Point Coalition. The coalition consists of more than 40 churches, though only three ministers, Reverends Jeffrey Brown, Ray Hammond, and Eugene Rivers, pursue its agenda on a daily basis. The coalition's major contribution, we have argued, has been to change the relationship between the police and Boston's inner city communities from one of open antagonism to one of partnership. This has allowed Boston to succeed in substantially reducing homicide rates without imposing a "police state," as some people fear has happened in New York City. Specifically, we suggest that the coalition has created an "umbrella of legitimacy" for the police to work under. To the degree that the police pursue policies and activities that are beneficial to the community, the coalition provides public support and thus legitimacy for police efforts. If those efforts, however, are not constructive, the police are open to explicit public criticism in the press by the ministers; in short they may be put "out in the rain." Furthermore, we describe the ways in which church efforts to minister to at-risk youth complement work done by police. In particular, the ministers appear to increase police effectiveness by providing a "remote surveillance capacity" for neighborhoods. Finally, we detail the ways in which police and the ministers work together to determine which youths should be given a second chance and which ones pose such a threat to the community that it is best to get them off the street. This process both increases police effectiveness and the perceived legitimacy of the judicial system.

Boston is in many respects a most positive picture of police-community partnership. The critical question is whether the Boston experience can be replicated in other large cities. If so, a key secondary question is whether it is important, perhaps even critical, that the key community leaders in this partnership are ministers with inner city congregations. Specifically, if other cities were to attempt to replicate Boston's salutary experience, would it be essential to involve ministers, or might other community based strategies be as, or even more, effective? This question is key for two reasons. First, from a policy perspective, it is desirable to know what are the essential ingredients of the Boston story. Other cities, New York perhaps most notably, have also reduced their crime rates substantially but at the cost of curtailing the civil liberties of its citizens. Boston is being looked at by some as a model of how to reduce crime precisely because it has achieved success without such negative side-effects.[4] Second, as we have already briefly discussed, the Ten Point Coalition has possibly contributed to the Boston Miracle in a variety of ways. Examining whether their religious identities are important to these contributions provides a method for assessing the varied ways in which they have contributed.

After presenting the story of the Boston Miracle, we then examine why the Ten Point Coalition may have been an important contributor to reducing Boston's homicide rates. The importance of having ministers as community partners is examined from two perspectives. First, there is the question of whether and how the legitimacy and authority of the Ten Point Coalition ministers have been based on they're being ministers. Second is the question of whether their message, which often has been explicitly religious, has been effective precisely because of that religious content. Specifically, are there ways that Ten Point's religious based messages have allowed them to simultaneously influence both the police and at risk youth? We conclude by suggesting that although there are strong theoretical reasons why it has been important that the partnership between Boston's police and the community has involved ministers, the true empirical assessment of this importance awaits the development and analysis of other programs that do and do not include ministers.

The "Boston Miracle"

Guns, Drugs, and the Police Response. Although Boston has never been considered a violence-plagued city to the extent that Los Angeles or New York has been, in 1990 a record-breaking 152 homicides stunned Boston with the realization that it had a serious violence problem.[5] The roots of this violence took hold with the introduction of crack-cocaine into Boston's inner city in 1988, relatively late in comparison to other major U.S. cities. As the crack market developed, so did turf-based gangs. When they realized how much money they could acquire through crack sales, gangs became increasingly protective of turf divisions. Gang colors and geographically based gang names such as "Corbett Street Posse" all showed evidence of family-type loyalty and respect.

Rival gangs turned to firearms to protect and defend their turf and gang identity. One gang's disrespect of, or show of aggression towards another, would inevitably be followed by retaliatory attacks. The extent of gang ties and turf delineation often led individuals who formerly avoided the temptation of gangs and the drug trade to pursue membership for protection and camaraderie. With firearms serving as the primary means of aggression, the level of violence grew to a rate and severity never before seen in the Boston area.

Since Boston law enforcement agencies had little experience with turf-based violence and criminal gang activity, their initial response to the situation in the late 1980s and early 1990s was disorganized. Until 1990, a department-based policy directed police officers and administration to publicly deny the existence of a "gang problem." In interviews, many current Boston police officers vouched for the fact that the department truly had no policy for dealing with the problem of violence in certain Boston neighborhoods in the late 1980s. Rather than creating a plan of attack to address the specific characteristics of gang-related violence, the police engaged in a fallback to the aggressive riot-oriented tactics of the 1960s. In addition, because homicide traditionally has been handled on an individual case basis, the police department became primarily focused on making the "big hit" and arresting the "big player," rather than addressing the significance of the group-based quality of gang violence.

In 1988, the City Wide Anti-Crime Unit, which was traditionally responsible for providing intense, targeted support across district boundaries of the city, was permanently assigned to the most violent neighborhoods of Boston's inner city. In 1989, the police department issued a policy statement that any individual involved in a gang would be prosecuted to the full extent of the law. Thus the department finally acknowledged the existence of a "gang problem." According to one current police captain, the unit, known as the CWACU, was expected to "go in, kick butts, and crack heads," and it adopted a mentality that "they could do anything to these kids" in order to put an end to their violent activity. This mentality resulted in highly aggressive and reportedly indiscriminate policing tactics.

Community Backlash. Two events in 1989, the Carol Stuart murder investigation and the Stop-and-Frisk scandal, focused community attention on the police department's initial approach to the violence crisis. Carol Stuart, a pregnant white woman, was murdered in the primarily African-American neighborhood of Boston's Mission Hill. Her husband, Charles Stuart, who was with her at the time of her death, reported that a black male committed the crime. Relying on Charles Stuart's account, the Boston Police Department "blanketed" the Mission Hill neighborhood looking for suspects. There were widespread reports of police abuse as well as coerced statements that implicated a black male suspect, William Bennet. Charles Stuart himself was later identified as the alleged perpetrator of the crime, but committed suicide before an investigation could be completed. The Boston Police Department's unquestioning acceptance of Charles Stuart's story about a black assailant, and subsequent mishandling of the murder investigation, created an atmosphere of extreme distrust of the department within Boston's African-American community.

This community suspicion was further intensified by the Stop-and-Frisk scandal, which also occurred in 1989. A public statement by a precinct commander that labeled the then-current police approach to gang-related violence as a "stop-and-frisk" campaign shocked the community and solidified the public's suspicion of the Boston Police Department.[6] There is some dissension within the police department about the extent to which their policy was to indiscriminately stop-and-frisk all black males within high crime areas, a policy known as "tipping kids upside down." According to several officers, they targeted individuals who either were previously spotted performing some illegal activity or were known gang members. However, officers also acknowledged that this approach was critically flawed because it was often very difficult to "distinguish the good guys from the bad guys." In addition, current members of the police force agree that there were "bad seed" cops who acted far too aggressively and indiscriminately. Accusations of unfairness about the stop-and-frisk tactics led to a court case in the fall of 1989 in which a judge threw out evidence acquired in what he viewed as an instance of unconstitutional search and seizure.[7]

As a result of the Stuart case and the Stop-and-Frisk scandal, the CWACU was disbanded in 1990. The department, however, began to see significant rewards from their aggressive street policies as Boston's homicide rates fell from 103 in 1991 to 73 in 1992.[8] This drop reinforced belief in the efficacy of their heavy-handed tactics. The police continued to view their actions as simple compliance with departmental orders. Despite this success, however, most officers acknowledged that the department's aggressive actions during this time brought community mistrust to an extreme level.

These two scandals, combined with smaller-scale, less visible incidents, eventually led the Boston press to question the police department's capacity to effectively handle even basic policing activities. In 1991, the *Boston Globe* published a harshly critical four-part series called "Bungling the Basics,"[9] that detailed a succession of foul-ups by the Boston Police Department during the previous few years. The series reported serious failings in the department's Internal Affairs Division. Misguided investigations, problematic policing and bad press eventually led to the appointment of the St. Clair Commission to conduct a thorough review of the Boston Police Department and its policies.[10]

At this point, the Boston Police Department was in desperate need of an overhaul in order to deal with all the negative publicity. Steps were taken to publicly exhibit a changeover in law enforcement policy in Boston. "Bad-seed" cops were weeded out. The disbanded CWACU was reorganized into a new unit, the Anti-Gang Violence Unit, or AGVU, which took a "softer" approach. The aggressive and indiscriminate, but effective street tactics of the past were sharply curtailed. Apparently as a result, the decrease in homicides during 1991 and 1992 were followed by a sharp increase in 1993.

The St. Clair Commission Report, released in January 1992 after a yearlong investigation, cited major corruption within the department and recommended major changes[11]. In 1993, Mayor Flynn resigned, and Bill Bratton, then head of the New York transit police, replaced Police Commissioner Mickey Roache.

Innovation in Law Enforcement. Bratton brought a new philosophy and a commitment to innovation to the Boston Police Department. Fundamental shifts occurred in its overall operations. According to current police officers, the neighborhood policing tactics, that formerly "just existed on paper" and had never been implemented under Roache, were actively pursued under Bratton. Many officers also agreed that the new administration was simply more open-minded and willing to break away from the institutionally embedded policing practices.

Street-level officers had learned from their constant exposure to the complexities of gang-related violence. They realized the need for innovative law enforcement strategies to address the current problem specifically and intelligently. The reorganized Anti-Gang Violence Unit looked for new ways of managing gang activities. First, it realized the need for community support and thus was determined to exhibit "squeaky-clean" policing strategies. Previous strategies had also failed to include collaboration with other agencies, so the AGVU began to pursue an increasingly multi-agency approach to combat youth violence. In 1993, the AGVU was renamed the Youth Violence Strike Force, retaining the same key members.[12]

Other agencies within Boston's law enforcement network were concurrently revamping their activities. Certain individuals within the probation department in particular became quite disillusioned with the "paper-shuffling" nature of their job. Fearful of the extreme levels of violence in certain Boston districts, probation officers had abandoned street presence and home visits. Consequently, there was no enforcement of probation terms such as curfew, area, and activity restrictions. Without enforcement of probation restrictions, a term on probation became viewed as a "slap on the wrist" within the law enforcement community and was essentially ineffectual in combating youth violence.

A few probation officers began to respond to this crisis of ineffectiveness and took strong, proactive measures to readjust their approach. Informal conversations between probation officers and police officers who regularly attended hearings at Dorchester District Court led to an experimental effort in agency collaboration. A strategy labeled "Operation Night Light" was developed that enabled probation officers to resume the enforcement component of their job.

On the first outing of the Night Light team, three probation officers and two police officers went out in a patrol car on the night of November 12, 1992. With protection provided by their police companions, probation officers were able to venture out after dark and enforce the conditions placed on their probationers. Youths began to realize that they could no longer blatantly disregard the terms of their probation because their "PO" might be out on the streets, at their house, or at their hangouts after curfew to check on them. Probation violations would have repercussions, such as lengthened probation sentence, stricter probation terms, or ultimately time in jail. Operation Night Light eventually became an institutionalized practice of Boston law enforcement agencies that has been heavily praised by policy experts and the media across the country.

Inter-agency collaboration to address the issue of youth violence has become standard practice in Boston. Participation of policy researchers (primarily David Kennedy and his associates at the John F. Kennedy School of Government) also served a vital role in bringing about the fundamental overhaul of Boston's policing strategies. The Boston Gun Project, begun in 1995, was a three-year effort that brought together a wide range of agencies including the police department, the city probation department, the Boston School Police, the Suffolk County District Attorney, a federal agency, Bureau of Alcohol, Tobacco, and Firearms, and many others to address youth violence.

The Boston Gun Project was innovative, not only for its collaborative nature, but also because it utilized research-based information to address the youth violence problem from a new angle. The gun project coalition was able to attack the problem at the supply side by cracking down on dealers of illicit firearms. On the demand side, gun project research led to the specific targeting of 1,300 individuals who represented less than 1 percent of their age group citywide but were responsible for at least 60 percent of the city's homicides.[13]

This type of inter-agency collaboration helped implement a variety of additional innovative strategies. In 1994, "Operation Scrap Iron" was initiated to target people who were illegally transporting firearms into Boston. Gun trafficking within certain areas of the city was shut down. Additionally, "area warrant sweeps" were used to target dangerous areas. For example, police would arrest all outstanding warrants within a particular housing project. Multiagency teams of youth and street workers then came in to provide follow-up after police presence subsided. As one police officer noted, these strategies made sure that "everyone was involved and brought something to the table. Everyone had a piece of the pie and, therefore, would get the benefits."[14] Even more impressive is that, according to this same police officer, not one civilian complaint was filed in response to the warrant sweep tactic.

In May 1996, this collaboration culminated in Operation Cease-Fire. Operation Cease-Fire fully institutionalized inter-agency collaboration among

Boston's crime-fighting agencies—the city's police and probation departments, the Massachusetts Department of Youth Services, special agents from the federal Drug Enforcement Agency and the Bureau of Alcohol, Tobacco, and Firearms, among others. Key community members, primarily from faith-based organizations were also involved in the operation's development and implementation. These groups worked together to identify gangs responsible for violence in specific hot spots around the city. Subsequently the group executed a forceful intervention by developing "zero tolerance" enforcement within the specific targeted area and sending an explicit message to gang members themselves that violence will no longer be tolerated.

Ten Point Clergy and Community-Level Intervention. Individuals within Boston's religious community were some of the most vocal critics of the police department's aggressive tactics during the late 1980s and early 1990s. Rev. Eugene Rivers, in particular, became a controversial figure in the media during these years because of his harsh criticism of both local law enforcement agencies and the city's black leaders. Remarkably, these same religious leaders later became active participants in law enforcement agency strategies such as Operation Cease-Fire. This turnaround suggests that the Boston Police Department has been effective in improving community relations. It is also likely that Boston's faith-based leaders experienced a shift in their own attitudes toward the police.

Boston's faith-based organizations did not begin working together as a group until 1992. Until then, most African-American clergy leaders in Boston had been following separate agendas. Their activities did not generally involve much street-oriented action to address youth violence within their communities. Although Rivers was on the street establishing strong outreach to gang members and other community youth, his constant criticism of other clergy leaders made his effort a partnerless endeavor.

A tragic event in May 1992 finally spurred collaborative action among Boston's African-American clergy.[15] Violence broke out among gang members attending a funeral for a youth murdered in a drive-by shooting. The shootout and multiple stabbing in the Morning Star Baptist Church threw the service and the congregation into chaos.

The brazenness of this attack, taking place within a church sanctuary, inspired many of Boston's black clergy to take action. They realized that they could no longer effectively serve their community by remaining within the four walls of their churches and ignoring the situation on the street. Instead, youth and others in the surrounding troubled neighborhoods needed to become extensions of the church congregations.

This incident led to the founding of the Ten Point Coalition, a group of some forty churches, with Reverends Ray Hammond, Eugene Rivers, and Jeffrey Brown as key leaders. A "Ten Point Proposal for Citywide Mobilization to Combat the Material and Spiritual Sources of Black-on-Black Violence" was drawn up and published as a call to churches to participate in the effort to address the violence crisis in their communities. The creation of the Ten Point Coalition represented a major step towards active collaboration within Boston's African-American religious community.

As of 1992, however, the relations between the African-American community leaders and Boston's law enforcement agencies were still very strained and often antagonistic. Rivers was constantly "in the face" of Boston law enforcement and was viewed as a "cop basher" in police circles. He established a constant presence in the troubled streets of Dorchester and made repeated contact with the same kids as the Anti-Gang Violence Unit. As an aggressive advocate for local youth, both in and out of the courts, Rivers had many confrontations with members of the AGVU and other patrol officers.

Eventually this antagonism subsided and was replaced with effective collaboration. The turnaround resulted from a combination of influential events and the strong effort made by key law enforcement officials to show that the Boston Police Department had a new attitude. In 1991 shots were fired into Rivers's home in Four Corners, one of the most violent areas of Dorchester, making him painfully aware of the dangers of carrying out a solitary campaign against youth violence. He has acknowledged that seeing the lives of his wife and children placed in jeopardy caused a shift in his attitude. He became more open to the possibility of allying with both other ministers and individuals in the law enforcement community.

When Rivers and other key clergy members such as Rev. Ray Hammond and Rev. Jeffrey Brown formed the Ten Point Coalition in 1992, their public stature and media influence increased. They wielded their power effectively for the purpose of maintaining a check on police practices in Boston. In 1992, the Ten Point Coalition partnered with another community based organization, the Police Practices Coalition to establish an organized, community-based police-monitoring group.

The Ten Point Coalition, and especially Rivers, had habitually criticized the Boston Police Department. Increasingly positive interactions with individual officers, however, began to convince the clergy group that the department could change their behavior. The ministers acknowledged the department's progress in an awards ceremony called the "People's Tribunal" initiated in 1992 to publicly honor "good cops." These positive steps eventually led to collaborative efforts like the previously mentioned Operation Cease-Fire. Cooperation among law enforcement agencies and clergy leaders, as well as various community-based groups, has continued to evolve and expand during recent years.

Current Relations. Currently, there is extensive inter-agency and community-based collaboration in Boston. A primary venue for this work is the Bloods and Crips Initiative. It was established in spring 1998 as an aggressive street-level mobilization of lay and pastoral workers to intervene in and prevent youth involvement in Bloods, Crips, or any other gang activity. By combining the effort of a wide range of agency representatives, the initiative aims to approach the problem comprehensively.

Members of the clergy, the Boston Police Department, the Boston Probation Department, street and youth workers for the city, the state Department of Youth Services, the Massachusetts Bay Transportation Authority Police, the Boston School Department, and the school police met weekly to share information on important developments on the street. For example, several disturbing incidents of sexual assault and harassment occurred on the city's public transportation system. MBTA Police and city youth workers as well as clergy brought up the importance of addressing these incidents at the weekly Bloods and Crips Initiative meetings. A task force on sexual harassment and assault was established in order to address these issues effectively. School presentations on the subject are planned in the future.

Another objective of this collaboration is to exhibit strong, supportive and unified authority to the targeted youth. This is achieved through the participation of multiple agencies and clergy representatives in all of the initiative's activities: school visits and presentations, home visits to youth suspected of gang involvement, regular street patrols, and strong presence in popular "hang-out" areas during peak hours. The collaborative approach serves to notify youth of alternative options and brings them into contact with a network of resources designed to serve their specific needs.

More informal cooperation among the wide array of agencies and community groups participating in operations such as the Bloods and Crips Initiative plays an important role in achieving quick responses to tense situations, and effective distribution of resources to problematic "hot-spots" in the city. Recently, for example, a particular youth repeatedly instigated dangerous confrontations in Dorchester—holding a gun to another youth's head; firing shots in the air in the midst of young "trick-or-treaters"on Halloween night, shooting holes in parked cars—all within a period of a couple of weeks. Each incident had the potential to aggravate tensions among various neighborhood "crews" and destroy any sense of community security. Because of this risk, Rivers utilized his connections with law enforcement to ensure a quick and effective handling of the situation.

In this case, "handling" the situation meant getting the individual off the street, for a long time.[16] At the weekly Bloods and Crips Initiative meeting, Rivers identified this particular youth and made law enforcement officials aware of his threat to peace in the neighborhood. Rivers and a youth worker also spoke with the youth personally to explain to him why he was being targeted. The youth was arrested and the "noise" he was causing in the community was quieted. Clergy leaders and law enforcement officials have thus achieved an uncommon level of collaborative action in Boston.

Ten Point's Possible Contributions

How has the Ten Point Coalition been important to the Boston story? Is it critical that Boston's community leaders have been ministers? If so, has it been crucial that they have been ministers of a particular type? Certainly, there are other cities that have substantially reduced their crime rates without the involvement of local ministers or other community leaders.

We suggest that there are four different ways that the Ten Point Coalition has contributed to the Boston Miracle: (1) ministering to youth; (2) adjudicating the outcomes of criminally involved youth; (3) increasing police efficiency; (4) creating an umbrella of legitimacy. In the following discussion we present each of these possible contributions. We then examine in each case how significant it is that the community leaders partnering with the police have been ministers.

Ministering. A recent article by Joe Klein analyzes Ten Point's contribution to Boston's efforts to reduce youth violence in terms of the ministering they do for at-risk youth.[17] Klein's article tells a series of stories about the Ten Point ministers confronting and dealing with youth involved in so-called gang-banging. He suggests that the ability of Ten Point ministers to work with these hard-core youths has been critical to Boston's success in reducing youth violence.

Brown, Hammond, and Rivers have been the principle ministers involved in working with at-risk youth. There are also several other ministers, less closely associated with Ten Point, who have their own youth programs. The three clergy work both individually with youths, as well as speak to groups of youths either identified or gathered together by the police or in schools. In these respects, the ministers' activities are not substantially different than those of a community or social worker.

The ministers' message to the youths, nevertheless, is quite different. In essence, when the ministers do home and school visits, they partner with police officers to play "good cop – bad cop." Ministers offer resources and support to youth, encouraging youth to make the right choice and avoid turning to violence. In this capacity, therefore, the ministers are the voice of compassion, hope, honesty, not of inevitable doom. On the other hand, the ministers advocate "tough love" after the model of Jesus and of the prophets who presented stark choices and painted vivid pictures of what would happen with each choice, but doing so out of compassion and hope, not sarcasm or nihilism. The ministers are quite explicit in telling youth that they have a choice about how to live their lives. To paraphrase their message: "You have a choice. Stop your gang-banging and we will help you—help you get back in school or get a job, help you deal with your family, your girlfriend; help you straighten out your life. Continue to gang-bang and we will work as hard as we can with the police to see that you are put in jail, both for your own good, and the good of the community. As long as you are gang-banging you are a danger to yourself and to others. What I ultimately want to avoid more than anything is presiding over your funeral."

The message here is multi-faceted. First, there is the strong implicit message that the youths can live their lives in different ways. Second, it is a demand that youth take personal responsibility for their lives. Third, it is a message of the possibility of redemption. If you choose to give up gangbanging and "go with

God," your life will be redeemed. Fourth, if you choose incorrectly, you will be punished. In essence, you must choose between life and death.

There are clear parallels between this message and specific Bible passages. For example, consider Deuteronomy 30: 17–19 where Moses says to the Israelites:

> But if your heart turns away and you will not obey, but are drawn away and worship other gods and serve them, I declare to you today that you shall surely perish. You shall not prolong your days in the land where you are crossing the Jordan to enter and possess it. I call heaven and earth to witness against you today, that I have set before you life and death, the blessing and the curse. So choose life in order that you may live, you and your descendants.[18]

Some black Pentecostal clergy use ideas rooted in Christian scripture and teaching to justify "worldly" activism on behalf of the poor and oppressed. Ten Point clergy use religious ideas in similar ways. Rather than confining them to narrowly religious activities, these clerics' understanding of "salvation" involves the satisfaction of the entire spectrum of human needs, including physical and social, as well as spiritual ones. This "whole person" interpretation of faith demands that the ministers recognize the ways that societal structures limit the life opportunities of poor people. Such faith underlies the clergy's early criticisms of the law enforcement and criminal justice communities.

At the same time, though, the clergy subscribe to traditional Christian tenets that emphasize the sanctity of human life, the divine offer of personal salvation and the necessity of making a fundamental choice. Therefore, individuals are required to take clear responsibility for their own lives before God. The ministers demand moral accountability from individuals and specifically from youth in the community as they would from members of their own congregations. Indeed, these clergy have extended the ordinary intra-congregational community ethic to support neighborhood and metropolitan-wide community building.

The notion of a highly committed faith-based community serves as a kind of middle point between congregation-based religious practice and community-based activism. Within the community, moral consistency, trust, and mutual respect provide a basis for collective survival, as well as unity against perceived adversaries, such as unresponsive criminal justice agents or repressive police. Thus, while the Ten Point clergy began by critiquing power structures, it was natural for them also to acknowledge and try to check *individual* behaviors that threaten community well being, particularly the violent behaviors of a minority of young people.

The moral authority of the Ten Point Coalition *qua* ministers is obviously critical to their ability to hold individuals in the community personally accountable. Their authority is further enhanced by the fact that much of their work with at-risk youths consists of street ministry. These are a particular kind of inner-city ministers. They often work by walking neighborhoods both during the day and at night. This is important in for two reasons. First, it provides them with an understanding of the streets, which lends greater legitimacy to their actions and positions *vis-a-vis* those streets. When the ministers act in concert with the police, youths know that the ministers are doing so in an informed way. Second, the ministers' street work with youths sends a strong, visible message to the community that they truly care about these children and are committed to helping them live a good life. When the ministers advocate that a particular youth should be arrested and/or sent to jail, all know that the ministers are doing this out of concern for the youth as much as for the sake of the community. Thus, the ministers' one-on-one work with youths contributes legitimacy to their work with the police department. Of course, any community worker can increase their legitimacy by being knowledgeable and by visibly working in the open in the community. The ministers, however, intrinsically hold significant authority and legitimacy, because of their clerical status. Their knowledge of and work in the streets acts to further reinforce their moral status.

Adjudication. When a young male is potentially violent, an inner city community faces a vexing problem: Should the youth be given a "second chance," supported and helped with the hope that he will be able to turn his life around? Or, for his own safety and that of the neighborhood, should he be put in jail? The conflict here is between the desire for safe streets and the desire to keep one's children out of jail. These are difficult questions, ones that will provoke disagreement in many cases. Often there is no "right" answer. Rather the issue of concern is whether or not the decision is made in a way that is considered fair and just.

But how can this be accomplished? The police are seen as being, and are likely to be, too concerned with having safe streets. The judicial system as a whole may also be suspect. Social workers, street workers, parents, and relatives are likely to identify too closely with the youth's interests.

In Boston, the Ten Point ministers have come to play an informal role in determining how particular individuals will be treated by the judicial system. In some circumstances this means that the ministers contact the police and ask for certain youths to be arrested. The ministers will encourage judges to sentence these troubled youths to alternative programs or regular check-ins at their churches, rather than serve time in jail. In other cases, it means that the ministers appear in court to argue either for leniency or for a stiff sentence. An example was related above in which Rivers contributed to the arrest of the young man responsible for repeated incidents of violence during Halloween 1998.

The fact that Ten Point consists of ministers here is critical. As noted previously, clergy are seen as being able to discern the "right" answer for particular youths because they are directly involved in the lives of young people. More unique is the ministers' status as *independent* youth advocates. That is, the clergy are not parole officers, social workers, or other agents with formal connections to the state. This leads young people and their families to trust the motives of the clergy more than they might trust some other agent. In other words, their status as independent leaders as well as ministers grants the Ten Point clergy legitimacy among a population that has grown cynical of the politics of crime prevention.[19] Such legitimacy not only enables the clergy to serve as effective adjudicators, but also creates broad community acceptance of the particular specific cases.

Effectiveness. Both the police and the ministers believe that only a small number of youths are responsible for most of the violence. There is empirical evidence to support this assertion. David Kennedy estimates that 1 percent of the city's youth age group—1,300 youths—constitute the core group of youth at risk for serious violence.[20]

One of the critical aspects to the partnership between the police and the ministers has been the willingness of the ministers to help the police concentrate their efforts on this small group of youth. This happens in two ways. First, ministers help screen which youth are out of control and present a danger to themselves and the community. The ministers may then identify a particularly dangerous youth to the police and indicate the need for the youth to be arrested. Since most of these youths will have outstanding arrest warrants, they will be arrested even if the minister's call has not been precipitated by an actual crime. In this regard, the ministers and those working with them have come to provide a type of remote surveillance capacity for the police.

Second, the ministers make the judicial system more efficient by helping the police identify which youths in fact are likely to get involved in violence. This allows the police to increase surveillance of these youth. Both the police and ministers let these youths know that if they are gangbanging they will be prosecuted for even small infractions of the law. One youth who was suspected of being involved in several homicides was given a twenty year jail term for having a bullet in his pocket. This story is now legend among Boston's inner city youth.

The danger to the ministers in working so closely with the police is that the community may believe that they have been co-opted by the police department. Here, the perceived moral authority of the ministers is critical. The fact that they are responsible to a "higher" power creates trust in the community that the ministers are not simply doing the police's bidding. Furthermore, as already discussed, depending on the case, they may advocate for leniency or severity of punishment. As a result, at least some of the time they are perceived as arguing against the position of local law enforcement.

The ministers have also engaged in activities that indicate their independence from and willingness to criticize police. Recently, in partnership is a law professor at Northeastern University, Debra Rameris, Ten Point has been working on the problem of racial profiling by the police department. Activities such as this send a strong message to the community that the coalition has not simply become surrogates for the police.

While the clergy's adjudicating role indicates a degree of *public* trust in the clergy, the relationship between the clergy and the police points to the *state's* trust in the clergy. The law enforcement community perceives Ten Point clergy as indigenous leaders possessing a unique combination of street savvy and trustworthiness. This perception has led the former to have faith in the latter's ability to take on certain functions previously reserved for the police; namely, separating the proverbial wheat from the chaff among youth who are in trouble.

An Umbrella of Legitimacy. An enormous problem for the police force in any major city is the need to establish the legitimacy of their activities. As the Amadou Diallo killing in New York City in February 1999 has illustrated, the legitimacy of a highly successful and conscientious police force can be totally undermined by one tragic and highly visible incident of questionable police behavior.

In most major cities the police department has exceptionally poor relations with its inner city community. As Randall Kennedy has thoroughly documented in his book, *Race, Crime, and the Law,* this is due at least in part to a long history of racism in our country's judicial system.[21] As a result, in many cities, police activities are seen by many minority residents as illegitimate. This in itself can be an important instigator of criminal behavior. In *Why People Obey the Law,* psychologist Tom Tyler argues that an important factor in people's decisions to engage in criminal behavior is whether or not they see the judicial system as legitimate.[22]

If one were looking for legitimacy through a relationship, there could perhaps be no better partner than a group of ministers. Throughout society ministers have unique moral standing. It is assumed that they are fair and that they will protect the interests of the less fortunate. In the inner city, ministers and their churches are among the last formal institutions committed to the welfare of their neighborhoods. Within the black community, they often have been looked to for leadership. All three of the core Ten Point clergy are well known for their extensive work with inner city youth. These factors give Ten Point considerable credibility to speak for Boston's inner city community.[23]

In Boston, the ministers have created a context in which police can deal with the problem of youth violence without recrimination from the press or the community. We describe it as an "umbrella of legitimacy." It is an umbrella, however, that only provides coverage under specific conditions: (1) when police focus on the truly problematic youth; (2) when they deal with these youth in what is perceived as a fair and just way; and (3) when this is done in cooperation with the community through the ministers.

Activities that fall outside these boundaries will be publicly criticized in the media. The ministers' past criticism of the police in *The Boston Globe* is well remembered. Furthermore, Rivers, as the most outspoken of the ministers, is known for his willingness to criticize anyone, whether it is the police, the Urban League, or Harvard's Department of Afro-American Studies. The ministers thus provide informal oversight of police actions. They are able to do this in part because they are ministers, in part because they are community leaders and members, and in part because they exhibited a willingness in the past to be highly critical of the police.

By providing an umbrella of legitimacy for police work, the ministers help legitimize the whole system. But this also makes their own legitimacy more precarious. If the ministers are too supportive of the police then they are vulnerable to being accused of selling out. If they also concur with the police or the district attorney in their recommendation with respect to the treatment of a particular youth, then they will be perceived as partial. It is critical that their relationship with the police be seen as being at "arm's length." The fact that they have advocated that some kids be given jail sentences and that others be put into alternative sentencing programs also contributes to their credibility in the community. However, their legitimacy in Boston in fragile. There are other groups of actors within the black community that would be thrilled to see them discredited. If a case of serious police abuse were to occur where the coalition could have done something to prevent it from occurring and did not, its standing with Boston's inner city communities could be short lived.

Discussion

In terms of whether it is important that the Ten Point Coalition consists of ministers, we have suggested that this may be significant in two ways. First, as a coalition of ministers, Ten Point enjoys important moral authority and legitimacy both within their particular communities as well as in greater Boston. We have argued that this is important to their adjudication efforts, their efforts to increase police efficiency, and most importantly, in their ability to bestow legitimacy to police efforts and the judicial system more generally.

Second, we have suggested that the religious theme in the coalition's message to youth in its ministering efforts has been important. The ministers have argued that youths need to take responsibility for their actions, and that they deserve support and the opportunity for redemption. In important ways this position cuts across political lines since it rejects the liberal position that these youths need to be solely thought of as victims, but also rejects the conservative position that these youths alone should be responsible for straightening out their lives. Their status as clergy, then, has allowed the core Ten Point actors to uniquely transcend antagonistic politics and reconcile contrasting interests. Meanwhile, religious ideas have provided an ideological toolbox with which to assemble the umbrella of legitimacy.

These analyses point to the unique position of the black church within inner city communities. Here the role of faith is critical, albeit in ways that have little to do with explicit proselytization. On the one hand, the concerned public and agents of the state alike have faith in the good intentions and political purity of the most visible Ten Point clergy. Such faith has been well documented in previous scholarship. In *A Bridging of Faiths,* Demerath and Williams argue that organized religion wields far less influence over urban politics than it used to. The power of religion, nevertheless, persists in part through the public activities of the clergy.[24] The clergy are able to influence local politics largely because of the moral authority they bring to the public arena. In her review of *A Bridging of Faiths,* Nancy Ammerman eloquently sums up this residual, yet consequential, impact: "[T]he clergy (and other religious professionals) retain a kind of symbolic moral power that can be invoked in the public arena. Their presence reminds citizens and officials alike of the moral realities that transcend their individual interests, of a 'sacred' realm that stand over against mere profane considerations."[25]

Public awareness of such "moral realities" translates into a special variety of political capital that allows clergy to transcend stale partisan political debates, even while injecting their political views into those debates. This special legitimacy has little to do with public belief in specific religious tenets, although not all religious clergy can be assumed to enjoy it equally. Sikh and Rastafarian leaders, for example, do not carry as much moral weight in the American public arena as do Jewish and mainline Christian clergy. Nevertheless, the clergy have special political power because they are clergy. When Rev. Jesse Jackson recently announced his decision to forgo a third bid for the Democratic presidential nomination, he indirectly admitted that his power as a moral authority might be better used outside of the formal political process. The formal political arena, he noted, would continue to be a critical one. Yet,

> . . . we also need people who are willing to wage the moral fight that lies beyond politics. We need people who are willing to go wherever that moral cause takes them: to corporate boardrooms, to sweatshops overseas, to Appalachia, to the Delta, to Wall Street and LaSalle Street, to shop floors and picket lines, to the ghettos and the barrios. We need people willing to speak the truth. We need people willing to push the envelope. We need people willing to give voice to the voiceless. . . . I'm not going to run for President. But I am going to act. I am going to march. I am going to roll up my sleeves and work as hard as I know how to work. I am going to speak out. I am going to raise uncomfortable issues. I am going to be an unabashed advocate for the least of these in our society. I am going to demand accountability from those with power and wealth and clout.[26]

Similarly, the Ten Point Coalition has used the moral capital of the clergy to create the umbrella of legitimacy so crucial to the Boston story. The Ten Point clergy's moral authority rests in two forms of public trust: the black community's trust in the independence and integrity of clergy, and a public administrative recognition of the centrality of religious institutions to the concerned public. Such dual trust has enabled the Ten Point clergy to proclaim a sort of divine pragmatism, which ignores partisan debates and unites traditionally opposing social views.

Among black churches, in particular, there is ample precedent for this model of public religion. The tradition is rooted in the central, yet independent, status of the historical black church in African-American life. As Aldon Morris notes, "Scholars of the black church have consistently argued that it is the dominant institution within black society. It has provided the organizational framework for most activities of the community—economic, political, and educational endeavors as well as religious ones."[27] In addition, the black church provided an independent, black-controlled alternative to the institutions of white society, which overtly and systematically excluded blacks well into the twentieth century. The combined independence and centrality of the black church produced a cadre of charismatic, often educated, religious leaders, particularly in the urban North and South. These leaders proved critical to the black Civil Rights Movement, not only because they were charismatic voices, but also because they were independent voices. That is, they were beholding not to the white political structure, but to an indigenous, autonomous black institution. Their simultaneous independence and centrality allowed them to mediate between the black masses and the agents' oppressive institutions.

The Ten Point Coalition perpetuates the tradition of the black cleric as independent, indigenous critic of powerful institutions. To be certain, these clergy have explicitly pointed the public toward "moral realities" beyond profane political debate. It is clear, nevertheless, that the public's dual faith in Ten Point clergy has little to do with a public subscription to specific religious beliefs. Rather, this faith has mostly to do with the historic structural role that the clergy has played in the black community. In other words, Ten Point clergy have been successful in their public activity not so much because they are perceived as holy by all parties involved, but because their unique structural position as black church leaders has granted them the opportunity to serve as intermediaries.

The clergy themselves interpret their religious faith in such a way as to demand social activism on behalf of the disadvantaged, while demanding moral accountability from the same. Their interpretation of religious ideas demands that they, as clergy: a) get involved with the struggles of disadvantaged people, while critiquing structures of power; and b) demand moral accountability from the communities they represent.

The first factor implies that the Ten Point clergy believe in their own mission and are willing to "walk the walk" as well as "talk the talk." More importantly, though, they construct the idea of "the walk" in ways that demand activism as well as ministering from within church walls. This aspect of faith is crucial, for it distinguishes the core Ten Point clergy from those who limit their ministry to more traditional forms of evangelism. Meanwhile, the second factor obliges clergy to hold young people responsible for their own behavior, and to present clear and viable opportunities for personal transformation.

In traditional political discourse, emphases on structural determinacy and individual responsibility are at odds. Yet, the clergy, through an application of their personal religious faith, are able to represent both of these perspectives simultaneously. So, just as public faith in the clergy gave the latter the political capital to reconcile conflicting social groups, the clergy's own religious faith allows them to hold contrasting political opinions in tension. Both are central to the umbrella of legitimacy. In fact, the umbrella in question can be thought of as consisting of two "halves": a political half that reconciles potentially opposing constituencies (police and the inner city community), and an ideological half that accommodates contrasting social views (the need for individual responsibility and outside assistance).

Conclusion

The New Testament demands action on behalf of others.[28] Hundreds of organizations around the country, including the Ten Point Coalition, have taken this mandate seriously, developing a plethora of "faith-based" responses to human suffering in urban cores. Much of the current debate over the practicality and political expediency of "faith-based" anti-poverty programs, nevertheless, revolves around the possibility of that social welfare programs that lack the depth dimensions of faith may be inadequate.

The Ten Point Coalition's work with the Boston police represents one type of faith-based intiative. In this paper we have argued that police ultimately cannot be efficacious in a community that does not view their activities as legitimate. Furthermore, over the long run it is difficult if not impossible for police activity in the inner city to be successful unless it is seen as legitimate and supported by local residents. In this respect, police efforts to curtail youth violence are inherently problematic. Communities want safe streets but they also want their kids to stay out of jail. Difficult choices need to be made that are likely to be seen as unjust by some. In this environment, it is difficult to establish legitimacy for police actions, no matter what those actions are.

The Ten Point Coalition has evolved into an institution that has at least partially ameliorated this dilemma. By supporting police activity that the coalition believes is beneficial to the community and being critical of activities that are not, they have created what we have called an umbrella of legitimacy for police to work under. This in turn has allowed the police to effectively deal with youth violence by pursuing a focused strategy targeting truly dangerous youth. This situation, which is far different from most major cities, has significantly contributed to the spectacular drop in homicide rates observed in Boston.

Our analysis provides a particular interpretation of what has happened in Boston. If it is correct, it suggests that police need to create strong community partnerships. These partnerships should involve both a cooperative effort to deal with youth violence and a delineation of what constitutes legitimate police behavior. Police strategies can only acquire true legitimacy within inner city communities if the community partner is willing to both support police tactics when they are appropriate and provide harsh, public criticism of activities that are not.

Ministers may possibly be ideal partners. Because of their moral authority and the nonpartisan nature of their message and actions, they enjoy both considerable legitimacy themselves and are able to confer, when and where appropriate, much legitimacy on the police and the judicial system more generally. Other community leaders may be able to play this role. This is something that will need to be analyzed in the context of other cities. However, given the ubiquitous presence of churches within most inner city neighborhoods and the considerable moral authority enjoyed by black clergy, coalitions such as the Ten Point Coalition arguably should be the partners of first choice.

Notes

1. Brent Coffin provided us with useful criticisms as did participants in the Kennedy School's Summer Institute and Social Inequality seminars. We want to thank Reverends Jeffery Brown, Ray Hammond, and Eugene Rivers of the Ten Point Coalition for providing information and insight as well as a variety of members of the Boston Police Department. This research has been support in part by National Science Foundation grant and a grant from the Smith Richardson Foundation.

2. Between 1990 and 1996, the homicide rate dropped 58.7% in New York, 27.9% in Los Angeles, 54.0% in Houston, 15.9% in Washington, D.C., and 17.7% in Philadelphia. Other cities, however, have not experienced similar drops in their homicide rates; for example, Baltimore, Phoenix, and Las Vegas have seen rises of 7.5%, 45.3%, and 103.8% respectively.

3. Tensions in New York between the police and community leaders have been long standing. In February of 1999 they mushroomed after the killing of an unarmed black immigrant and street vendor, Amadou Diallo by four policemen. The four policeman have been indicted for second degree murder, a first in the history of the NYC police force. Subsequently they were found innocent of all charges by a mixed race jury.

4. Orlando Patterson and Christopher Winship, "Boston's Police Solution," *New York Times*, March 3, 1999.

5. The Federal Bureau of Investigation Uniform Crime Reports state that 143 homicides were committed in Boston in 1990. However, current Boston Police statistics and current police officers report 152 homicides for the record breaking year.

6. Globe Staff, "Events Leading to St. Clair Report," *Boston Globe*, January 15, 1992.

7. The question of causality and timing here are complex. The most aggressive period of stop-and-frisk tactics stopped in 1990. Yet the homicide rate continued to fall in 1991 and 1992. If one believes that the causal connection is contemporaneous, then this is evidence of a lack of a causal effect. However, if the causal effect of police enforcement is lagged, then this is evidence for a causal effect.

8. Federal Bureau of Investigation, Uniform Crime Reports, 1991–1992.

9. Globe Staff, "Boston Police: Bungling the Basics," *Boston Globe*, April 7, 8, 9, 10, 1991.

10. Globe Staff, "Events Leading to St. Clair Report."

11. Ibid.

12. Conversation with David Kennedy, October 1997.

13. Conversation with David Kennedy, October 1997.

14. Jenny Berrien, "The Boston Miracle: The Emergence of New Institutional Structures in the Absence of Rational Planning," Harvard University Department of Sociology Senior Thesis, March 20, 1998.

15. Robert A. Jordan and Globe Staff, "Clergy's Anger Can Bring Hope," *Boston Globe*, May 16, 1992.

16. Information concerning this Halloween incident is based on a conversation that took place during the Bloods and Crips Initiative Wednesday meeting in November of 1998.

17. Joe Klein, "Can Faith-Based Groups Save Us?" *The Responsive Community* (Winter 1999/98).

18. *New American Standard Bible: Reference Edition.* (Philadelphia: A. J. Holman Company, 1973).

19. It should be noted that the Ten Point Coalition's legitimacy as a representative of the black community has been challenged. Both prominent black politicians and political leaders have questioned Ten Point's authority.

20. Conversation with David Kennedy, October, 1997.

21. Randall Kennedy, *Race, Crime and the Law* (New York: Vintage Books, 1998).

22. Tom Tyler, *Why People Obey the Law* (New Haven: Yale University Press, 1990).

23. This is not to say that the Ten Point Coalition is universally seen as the legitimate representative of the black community within Boston. There have been numerous conflicts between Ten-Point, particularly Reverend Rivers, and other representatives of Boston's black community.

24. N.J. Demerath, and Rhys H. Williams, A Bridging of Faiths: Religion and Politics in a New England City (Princeton: Princeton University Press, 1993).

25. Nancy Ammerman, "Books in Review: *A Bridging of Faiths*," *Society* 31 (November 1993): 91.

26. "Jackson Decision" 03/24/99 Press Release.

27. Aldon Morris, The Origins of the Civil Rights Movement: Black Communities Organizing for Change (New York: Free Press, 1984).

28. *King James Version*, James 2:20: "But wilt thou know, O vain man, that faith without works is dead?"

CHAPTER 12

Faith Communities and the Post-Reform Safety Net

Mary Jo Bane[1]

Religious politics has often enough been intolerant and threatening to democracy. But the real threat to democracy now is more likely to come from the rampant self-interest that thwarts all efforts at social and political reform. At their best, churches bring into the public arena a politics of community and of compassion.

IN THIS CHAPTER, I RETURN TO THE ISSUE OF WELFARE, with which the seminar that generated this book began. The pivotal event, for welfare reform in the 1990s as well as for the thinking of contributors to this volume, was the passage of the 1996 welfare reform legislation, the Personal Responsibility and Work Opportunities Reconciliation Act. Now, almost five years after its passage, it seems clear that there has been a dramatic change in both the size and the character of the welfare system in the United States without a similarly dramatic decrease in poverty or hardship. This, in turn, has changed the context of the debate about poverty and injustice, has expanded the range of relevant policy alternatives and has the potential for changing politics and the rhetorical framework in which the debate is conducted.

This chapter examines the challenges and opportunities for involvement by religious organizations in this new context. It examines the role that churches, and in particular the Catholic Church, played in welfare reform during the 1990s. The examination is offered as a useful background for considering a possible new role for churches in the new policy context. It then argues that the times provide both a new need and a new opportunity for more effective involvement.

The Role of the Church in the 1990s

I focus on the activities of the Catholic Church in advocating for welfare policy and in providing social safety net services as an example of a large (indeed the largest), well-organized, mainstream and largely progressive religious organization, with a well developed and authoritative theological and moral tradition. I believe the lessons that can be inferred from examining Catholic participation in welfare reform are relevant for understanding both the promise and the perils of religious involvement more generally. Because I am myself Catholic, I am deeply involved in these debates, and may be simultaneously more sympathetic and more critical than I might be of other traditions or than others might be of mine.

In looking at the role of the Catholic Church in both policy advocacy and service provision, I distinguish between the actions of official national bodies and the actions of congregations and their members. Despite the hierarchical structure of the Catholic Church, and despite its often authoritarian history, these are not identical. Both are worth looking at, and both should, I believe, be considered actions of the Church.[2] The actions of official church bodies are, of course, easier to describe and analyze since they are well documented and public. In this paper, I can bring only limited evidence and some speculation to bear on the question of congregational and individual participation.

The Catholic Church and welfare policy. Official Catholic organizations were active participants in welfare reform debates throughout the 1990s. At the national level, the National Conference of Catholic Bishops, or NCCB, and Catholic Charities USA spoke and lobbied on behalf of the church. At the state level, state Catholic Conferences, affiliated with the US Catholic Conference, which is the policy arm of the NCCB, and state Catholic Charities agencies reflected national positions adapted to the specifics of individual states.

The documents produced by NCCB and Catholic Charities USA represent the official position of the Church. They are of several types.[3] The foundational document is the 1986 pastoral letter of the bishops, *Economic Justice for All*.[4] This letter lays out a biblical and theological rationale for a set of principles about human dignity, human rights and the special obligations to the poor and vulnerable that are then applied to a set of social and economic issues including poverty and welfare. Although the specific recommendations about welfare in the 1986 letter have in many ways been overtaken by events (it recommends, for example, national eligibility standards and a minimum national benefit level for welfare), the basic principles that were debated and agreed to by the bishops continue to provide the justification for Catholic positions on welfare and poverty policy.

In 1994, Catholic Charities USA issued a position paper on "Transforming the Welfare System,"[5] and in 1995 the US Catholic Conference issued its "Moral Principles and Policy Priorities for Welfare Reform."[6] These documents argued that welfare reform legislation ought to both encourage work and protect family life. They asked for recognition that some individuals are unable to work but entitled to support from the community, that mothers of young children have important roles in the home and that children deserved support independent of the behavior of their parents. They argued for retaining entitlements to welfare, food stamps and Medicaid, for realistic and compassionate work requirements, and for supports to assist those making the transition to work. The bishops opposed "family caps" (not increasing welfare benefits when a child is born to a welfare recipients), opposed denying welfare benefits to minor mothers and opposed benefit cutoffs for immigrants. These positions were very much on the liberal side of the welfare debates that were taking place at the time, generally consistent with Clinton administration positions but opposed to some aspects of the administration's work requirements, family cap, teen mother and immigrant proposals.

Catholic Charities and the NCCB elaborated and specified these positions in a number of documents, letters, position papers and educational materials over the course of the welfare reform debates. Washington staff members and individual bishops also made their arguments in congressional hearings and through interactions with individual staffs and members of Congress. Both their policy analysis and their lobbying activities were quite sophisticated. The Clinton administration and Democrats in Congress considered them useful and effective, though unofficial, allies. Because their positions were well thought out, well argued and compellingly presented, they were conscientiously attended to by most serious participants in the welfare policy debate.

There is little evidence, however, that members of Congress saw these positions either as morally binding or as representative of a large and active constituency. Despite the fact that the Catholic Church has 60 million members in the United States, and despite a hierarchical structure within which bishops allegedly speak authoritatively for the Church, my impression was that the Catholic positions were accorded approximately the same level of respect and weight as those of The Children's Defense Fund, The Center for Budget and Policy Priorities or the Child Welfare League of America.[7] Politicians who are or represent Catholics appear to worry about both sin and electoral retribution if they oppose the Church's position on abortion. This did not appear to be the case with regard to welfare. The overwhelming House and Senate bipartisan votes in favor of the 1996 legislation suggests the limits of the Church's effectiveness in influencing welfare reform policy.

I do not propose to argue that the official Church ought to have threatened its members with mortal sin if they voted for the 1996 welfare legislation, or that it ought to have instructed pastors to make sure that their parishioners wrote their representatives. Since Vatican II, the Church has rightly recognized and largely respected the autonomy of all people to develop and follow their own consciences in matters of personal and public morality. The social teachings are considered binding on Catholics at the level of general principle, but not at the level of specific policy. Indeed, men and women of good will can come to different judgments on particular provisions of specific welfare legislation. At the same time, the Catholic Church could and, I will argue later should, be more than just another Washington policy analytic and lobbying group, given the clarity and power of its teachings on justice and charity and the sheer size of its membership.

Figuring out a political role consistent with both democratic politics and the mission of the Church is no easy task. A start would be to note the ways in which the Church did and did not participate in the welfare discussions of the 1990s. It engaged in ethically and theologically grounded policy analysis and in professional lobbying at the national level. It also distributed informational materials on the issues and the Church's positions to local congregations and organizations. It did not, however, engage in large-scale deliberation with or mobilization of its potentially huge base. The vast membership of the Catholic Church did not participate in developing, discussing or reflecting on its policy positions, and saw no particular reason to either adopt or promote these positions.

The Catholic Church and social safety net provision. The involvement of the Church with welfare and poverty is not only about policy and politics but is also about the "doing" of welfare and anti-poverty work, that is, the provision, singly or in partnership, of assistance and support to the poor and to actual or potential welfare recipients. Indeed for many the important question about the churches and welfare reform is whether churches could or should replace the public welfare system, as it shrinks, with a network of programs rooted in faith, motivated by religious compassion and charity, and focussed on personal transformation and involvement. This is the hope of the most fervent advocates of Charitable Choice, the fear of the most progressive, and one of the issues that instigated the seminar that led to this book. Here too the Catholic Church provides an interesting case study. Here too the distinction between the large, official, national agencies and local congregations and members is important.

There is a tradition within the Church of radical evangelical ministry to the poor, from St. Francis of Assisi to Dorothy Day's Catholic Workers. And there is also a history of parish-based personal ministries, such as the St. Vincent de Paul Societies that still exist in nearly every parish. By and large, though, these are relatively small-scale operations. The history of Catholic charities over the century[8] suggests that charity work, for a variety of good and bad reasons, by and large became centralized and professionalized over time, moving from parishes to professionally staffed diocesan agencies. Dioceses developed centralized, hierarchically controlled, professional Catholic Charities agencies that displaced parish work and relied on trained paid staff rather than volunteers. Catholic philanthropy, too, became professionalized, adopting the money raising techniques of professional fund-raising and de-emphasizing both small giving and personal volunteering.[9]

By the 1990s, the network of agencies collectively known as Catholic Charities USA was very large, very professional and very dependent on government funding. Catholic Charities agencies were involved with most aspects of the social safety net. They ran food pantries and homeless shelters, day care centers, job training and ESL programs, foster care and adoption programs and many others. Their collective budget amounted to over $2 million in 1996. About 62 percent of this budget came from state and local governments, through contracts to provide publicly defined, funded and regulated services.[10] These agencies met all the contracting requirements for professional delivery of services, and also lived comfortably with the requirement that no public funds be used for sectarian activities or ends.

The Charitable Choice provisions of the 1996 welfare reform legislation seemed not to affect these arrangements very much. These provisions were designed by their proponents to make it easier for religious groups, especially local congregations, to contract with welfare agencies to provide services. They required states to open contracting to religious groups, and loosened somewhat the strictures on groups in terms of religious symbols, activities, and hiring. Catholic Charities did not support the Charitable Choice provisions, arguing that their agencies were able to participate fully in service provision under the old rules and that their operations would not change as a result of Charitable Choice.[11]

At the congregational level, participation in welfare work, both before and after Charitable Choice, is harder to document. In 1996, the Independent Sector's survey found that Catholics volunteered at about the same rate as the population as a whole, that they did less volunteer work for their churches and about the same amount of volunteer work for human services organizations—slightly less that ten percent of survey respondents reported such volunteer work. About the same percentage of Catholics contributed to the nonprofit sector as the general population, but those who did contribute gave a much lower percentage of their income (about one percent) to the Church than did members of other religious groups.[12]

Charitable Choice could potentially increase the involvement of parishes. The National Survey of Congregations, while finding that very few congregations in fact contracted with government to provide services, also found large numbers of congregations, including a majority of the surveyed Catholic parishes, expressed an interest in doing so. The barriers to congregational participation in the welfare system are, however, not likely to be limited to those addressed by the Charitable Choice provisions. Few congregations have the expertise or resources to bid for, enter into or manage government contracts. And because of the professionalization of Catholic social service provision, congregations seem to see their mission mainly as contributing money to diocesan or national charities, rather than directly providing services themselves.

It is possible that local welfare agencies might make more efforts to enlist congregations in the tasks of welfare reform, making use of the Charitable Choice provisions. If they begin to focus, for example, on the multiple problems of the most disadvantaged who remain on the welfare rolls, welfare agencies might look to churches to provide mentors or counselors, faith based recovery programs or families to "adopt" welfare families. Such programs have been developed, with some success, in some places. Congregations may also respond, with increased St. Vincent de Paul or other individually based assistance, to families that are left without resources by welfare cutoffs. But at least thus far it does not appear that a vast new network of congregational partnerships with government is developing.

Community-based organizing. Another avenue through which parishes have been indirectly involved with welfare reform and poverty policy is through congregation-based community organizing. There is certainly a history in this country of the Church as an institution and of individual parishes organizing and exerting political power on behalf of their members and specific Catholic causes.[13] The prosperity and suburbanization of American Catholics to some extent breaks down the correspondence of self-interest and concern for workers and the poor that characterized the immigrant church earlier in the century. But this tendency may be partially countered by another demographic fact. Immigration of traditionally Catholic Latinos and Asians is dramatically changing the character of Catholic congregations in some parts of the country, especially in big cities. And an important congregation-based organizing effort, spearheaded by the Industrial Areas Foundation (IAF), is growing in many areas.

A relatively mature example of IAF work comes from Texas, particularly from Austin and San Antonio. The San Antonio organization, Communities Organized for Public Service (COPS) had 26 member congregations in 1990. It has become a major political force in city politics, and generated housing and infrastructure development in several very poor Latino neighborhoods. Austin Interfaith has been successful in organizing parents, teachers and community leaders around school reform. The Texas IAF is also the sponsor of QUEST, a successful but small training program for welfare recipients and other disadvantaged workers.[14]

Another example of involvement with the welfare issue comes from Baltimore. There, the Industrial Areas Foundation[15] affiliate organized its member congregations to not provide workfare slots themselves and to pressure Johns Hopkins University and other employers to do the same. The organization's action against workfare was part of a larger campaign for economic justice for low wage workers, involving pressure on employers to pay a living wage and to not displace existing low wage workers, many of whom were supporting families, with "free" welfare workers. The IAF thus appealed to basic values of social justice as well as to the interests of both welfare recipients and low-wage workers, building a board based coalition built of member congregations. It generated in its member congregations not only deliberations about welfare issues but also organized political action in the service of broader social goals.

The IAF is currently attempting to large, broad-based large, metropolitan-wide organizing efforts in both Chicago and Boston. In Boston, the founding assembly of the Greater Boston Interfaith Organization (GBIO) was held in November 1998, with about 100 congregations and 4,000 participants in attendance. About half of the member organizations in GBIO are Catholic parishes. The Boston organizing effort has engaged in process of convening a delegates assembly and holding house meetings in order to identify the issues that members will work on, currently education, housing and crime. The primary organizing tool of the IAF is the one-on-one meeting, a half-hour semi-structured meeting between two individuals, in which they explore each other's backgrounds, values and interests. Thousands of such meetings have already been held in the Boston area, and have generated new relationships and new appreciations, based on personal encounters, for the diversity of situations, problems, and potentials across the metropolitan area. GBIO has also provided the impetus for serious congregational renewal in at least two Boston parishes.[16]

Community-based organizing efforts provide quite a different model for church involvement in welfare reform and anti-poverty efforts than either the policy advocacy or service delivery models described above. As we examine a new role for the Church in the future, they present intriguing possibilities.

A New Role for the Church

Looking back at welfare reform in the 1990s, it seems to me that official Catholic participation in both politics and service provision was responsible, moral, and professional. As a participant in the welfare debates, I saw their policy analysis and advocacy as thoughtful and helpful, bolstering the more liberal voices in the debate—though I would have liked them to be more effective. As a (lower case d) democrat, I believe that their modes of political participation and service provision were respectful of diversity and supportive of the constitutional boundaries between church and state. One can imagine an equally responsible and professional role in the next decades, of policy analysis and advocacy looking at the problems of the working poor and the unemployed, and of professional agencies expanding their menu of programs and services to include new partnerships with government to meet new needs.

As a Catholic, however, I was and remain disappointed by the limited scope of the Church's participation, which seems to me inconsistent with the radical message of the gospels and with the call for all Christians to act in the world on behalf of the less fortunate. Nor does the Church's current activity seem to me consistent with the magnitude of the problems of poverty and injustice that face this country in the aftermath of welfare reform. Catholics can and should do better in terms of their own call to discipleship.

An integrated role. My basic argument is that the role of the Church should encompass policy, service and politics; that these three elements ought to be integrated; and that they ought to be practiced at the parish as well as the national level. National Catholic bodies ought to supplement their current roles of policy analysis, advocacy and program development with the role of leading this broader effort. The pieces of this new role, as I see it, are: authoritative articulation in the parishes of the basic Church teachings on social justice, human dignity, concern for and service to the poor; parish-based community building; parish-based service; parish-based deliberation of policies and positions; and the provision of opportunities and encouragement for participation.

The more open, local and participatory approach that I am suggesting would be a departure from earlier Church practice. The centralization and professionalization of policy advocacy and service provision reflect (though they are not required by) the hierarchical structure and tradition of the Church. In this tradition it is for the hierarchy of the Church to decide what should be done, for the clergy to convey those decisions to the faithful, and for the laity to obey. In the past, that was considered an appropriate model not only for basic doctrinal teachings but also for specific decision making about both personal and public morality. In the past, the model worked. But both the development of Church teachings as reflected in Vatican II and the growth of a more educated and independent laity make it inappropriate in the current situation. The bishops recognized this, at least implicitly, in not presenting their conclusions on welfare policy as binding teachings of the Church that Catholics voters and office holders would be required to adopt and act on, or as representative of the membership of the Church. Their current modus operandi of policy analysis, advocacy and program development may, however, sacrifice opportunities to teach more powerfully, act more effectively and engage the whole Church in a commitment to justice.

The new model I propose is, I believe, consistent with the conclusions of Vatican II about religious freedom, freedom of conscience and the role of the laity, as well as with the Council's conclusions about the importance of the Church to the world, especially in its special concern for the poor and the vulnerable.[17] The Church is clearly struggling with issues of authority and the appropriate balance of hierarchy and democracy. Nonetheless, the distinction between authoritative teachings and issues open to debate and personal decision has always been made, and underlies my proposals here.

The teachings of the Church. The first element of my proposal for a new role for the Church is that it articulate forcefully at both the national and the parish level its basic teachings on human dignity and social justice. The official teachings of the Church are articulated, rightly, at a quite general level. Only parts of the 1986 bishops letter on the economy are presented as essential teachings; they are the principles of equal human dignity and basic human rights, the special position of the poor and vulnerable, the mandate to work for justice in the world and so on. These principles are solidly grounded in scripture and long church tradition. But they do not lead inevitably to specific policy positions, as the bishops themselves note in describing the policy sections of their letter as illustrative and as "related to circumstances which can change or which can be interpreted differently by people of good will."[18] Despite the hierarchical structure of the Church, it recognizes (most of the time) that it has no standing or mandate to promulgate binding teachings on, for example, how old children should be before their mothers are required to work or the proper benefit reduction rate for the Earned Income Tax Credit. This is all to the good, both theologically and practically.

The basic gospel teachings about justice, the worth of human persons and obligations of the rich toward the poor are, however, unambiguous. Nor is there any ambiguity about the mandate on those who would be disciples to structure their communities and live their lives in accordance with these principles. So it cannot be the case that all public positions and attitudes about welfare are equally consistent with Catholic faith. Attitudes and policies that degrade and stereotype, for example, are out of bounds, as is public and private indifference to the plight of the poor. A major challenge for the Church, then, is to teach and act forcefully about basic principles as foundation and background for more open deliberations about specific policies and about how members can effectively and responsibly fulfill their obligations as Catholics and as citizens.

Building community. Much of the politics and the rhetoric of the 1996 welfare reform debates were quite ugly. Even in the public debates on the floor of the House of Representatives, divisive, racially based stereotyping was apparent. One member of Congress used a "Don't Feed the Alligators" sign as a prop for a speech against welfare dependency. Others made sharp contrasts between "people riding in the wagon" and those "helping to pull." Opponents of the legislation, in turn, compared supporters to Nazis.[19] A sense of the brotherhood and sisterhood of humanity was not much in evidence.

Given the political context within which the welfare reform debates took place, just months before the 1996 election, it seems clear that politicians had calculated that such rhetoric would appeal to their voting constituents. This could only be true if voters lacked empathy and compassion for welfare recipients; if they neither knew nor cared about them personally; and if they felt no strong moral obligation to see and treat them as brothers and sisters.

The stereotyping and ugliness of some of the welfare debate clearly violated principles of the basic dignity and equality of every human person. These are strong teachings that ought to be forcefully communicated to Catholics, bounding the arena of acceptable discourse. Congregations could also make an important contribution to at least the civility and perhaps the compassion of future debates about poverty and welfare by making explicit efforts to create and nourish genuinely inclusive worshipping communities. Individual congregations do often tend to racial and economic homogeneity. But the Church is not homogeneous and neither are dioceses. Opportunities abound to bring people together for worship, service and socializing. Such efforts could noticeably change the terms of the debate about poverty and welfare in the future, and could be a genuine contribution.

Providing safety nets. Some conservatives have argued that churches and other private charities ought to replace the government in providing assistance and support for the poor. Others advocate partnerships between churches and government in providing services, specifically by expanding the scope and applicability of the Charitable Choice provisions of welfare reform. Some on the left, in contrast, argue that churches should not, in fact, expand their charitable activities, so as not to let government off the hook.[20]

As in many areas of the welfare and poverty debate, there are legitimate differences of opinion on this topic. Clearly inconsistent with Catholic faith, however, is indifference to the plight of the poor and refusal to take action to alleviate it. The injunctions to feed the hungry, and so on, are directed at individuals; public action would also seem to be required when it is necessary. Here, too, foundational Church teachings bound the range of acceptable opinion and action.

Most parishes are not in a position to become major contractors for the provision of welfare services.[21] But they could expand their local activities. In some places, they will literally find the needy on their doorsteps and should respond. In others, they will be urged by local civic authorities to partner in mentoring and other programs. Such activities are clearly consistent with the injunction of the prophets and the gospels to care for the poor. If only for the ultimate good of their better-off members, churches ought to feed the hungry, clothe the naked, shelter the homeless and welcome the stranger. Such activities, coupled when possible with reflection, are also likely to both expand the resources available to the poor and increase the understanding and compassion of the larger society. This too could provide an important contribution to the welfare debate.

Shaping the moral dialogue. The Catholic welfare policy debates of the 1990s took place mostly in elite national organizations and in private interactions with policymakers. The debates of the next decades ought to take place in the parish pulpits, in bible study groups and in local social justice committees. Only if parishioners understand and work through the issues will they be involved participants and committed witnesses.

Shaping these dialogues is tricky business. Although gospel mandates and Church teachings are clear, their application to different circumstances and specific policy questions requires empirical analysis, interpretation and judgment. People can come to different conclusions based on their reading of the evidence or predictions about the future. Presentations from the pulpit ought to be clear about Church teachings but also generate dialogue. Pastors often do not know how to lead such deliberations, or do not have the necessary empirical background for an informed debate. Some of their parishioners undoubtedly have the required knowledge and skills, however, and can be utilized in the effort. A broader based discussion of poverty and welfare, based on theological and moral reflection, could genuinely transform the coming debates.

The kind of deliberation I am urging brings together reflection on basic values grounded in faith, personal experience based on community and service, and empirical analysis. I do not believe that there is one right answer about policy that will emerge from these deliberations correctly conducted; and I do not propose to develop my own version of what that answer is here. I do, however, believe that faith, personal experience and empirical evidence all, and together, narrow the range of plausible policy alternatives. Church teachings rule out indifference to and inaction toward the plight of the poor. Both experience and statistics rule out a conclusion that poverty and hardship are no longer problems in this country. They also rule out simple conclusions about the characteristics of the poor and the reasons for their poverty; an analysis of the post-welfare reform world clearly cannot support a conclusion that the only problem is that people do not want to or have no incentives to work. Historical data and programs evaluations narrow the range of policy alternatives that can be expected to be effective.[22] Judgments will differ, based on analyses of the current situation and predictions about the future, about what policy approaches ought to be tested or enacted. The process of deliberation proposed here, however, should increase both consensus and civility among participants, and should lead to a more humane set of choices than policy makers considered in 1996.

Urging and facilitating participation. Political action is one venue through which obligations to the poor can be fulfilled. Parishes can provide opportunities to their members for developing and exercising the skills of deliberation and political action. According to Verba et al, many citizens, especially minorities and low-income individuals, develop civic and political skills in their faith communities, where they often have opportunities and incentives to speak in public, run meetings, write letters and work together to solve problems.[23] Some churches devote considerable attention and resources to developing leadership skills among their members. As noted above, congregation based organizing efforts, like the one in Boston, have had considerable success in eliciting leadership from a wide range of people who had never before spoken in public, run meetings or debated an issue. Catholic parishes, according to the Verba data, are less likely to provide leadership opportunities for their members than Protestant congregations, no doubt because of the large size of most parishes and the hierarchical structure of the Church. But again, parishes could do more and in so doing could enrich both the spiritual and the civic lives of their members and communities.

Finally, churches can offer their members opportunities and incentives to take political action. The largely white, evangelical churches of the Christian Coalition have proven very effective in mobilizing their members, and have become a formidable political force in many campaigns and on many issues. Catholic churches can turn out formidable numbers of letters and petition signatures opposing abortion despite the fact that Catholics in general have attitudes on abortion that are very similar to those of the population as a whole. In a very different way, congregations organized by the Industrial Areas Foundation have proven effective in organizing and taking action at the local level, developing specific proposals and demands and mobilizing large numbers of people to hold accountable the public officials with the power to solve problems. Most parishes, around most issues, however, do not provide opportunities of this sort. There are obviously pluses and minuses to doing so, for both churches and the broader society, but without them, the fulfillment of the Church's mission to do justice on behalf of the poor is unlikely to be realized.

Religious Involvement—A Good Thing?

Although my analysis of the 1990s welfare reform focused on Catholic involvement, my suggestions for a new role can be at least partly generalized to other traditions. Both the interests of their members and the theological traditions of the major faiths point toward engagement with poverty and welfare issues.

Within the Judeo-Christian tradition, engagement with the poor, very simply, fulfills a biblical mandate. The Hebrew scriptures are rich with the notions of covenant and community, and of the mandate to do justice, and of the obligation to provide for widows, orphans and strangers. Christians cannot read their gospels seriously and ignore either the plight of the poor or the duties of the rich. Early Church history reinforces the importance not only of individual acts of kindness but also of community responsibilities. Serious individual Christians and Jews must provide for the poor. And good sense suggests that they should do so using the various institutions of social provision that societies have created—individual, communal, and political. Churches should approach the political realm carefully, of course, avoiding partisanship and dogmatism. But they should not content themselves with rhetoric about general principles, and to translate their principles into genuine provision they will need to engage both policy and politics quite concretely.[24]

The broader, civic polity, I believe, should encourage service provision, community organizing and nonpartisan politics by faith communities. I am arguing here for policy and political participation grounded in and bounded by religious faith and articulated in religious language. History does, of course, provide some grounds for caution about this kind of involvement. Churches and religious leaders have at times abused their power and authority over their followers. Religious politics has often enough been intolerant and threatening to democracy. But at this point in history we have some experience with protecting against the abuses. The real threat to democracy now is more likely to come from the rampant self-interest that thwarts all efforts at both social and political reform. The churches at their best bring into the public arena a politics of community and of compassion that can bring out our better natures. They bring into service provision an ethic of respect, equality and personal involvement. These qualities, I believe, are desperately needed in our public life. They might help us respond to the question of "Who will provide?" with what has to be the right answer: "All of us."

Notes

1. Thorton Bradshaw Professor of Public Policy and Management, John F. Kennedy School of Government, Harvard University. Full disclosure also suggests that the reader should know that I was an appointed official in the Clinton administration with responsibility for welfare reform; that I resigned after the President signed the welfare bill; that I am a practicing Catholic; and that I am currently working with the Industrial Area Foundation's organizing effort in Greater Boston.

2. From the perspective of a social scientist, this distinction is surely interesting and important. But even from the perspective of the church it is worth making. Without getting into ecclesiological debates, it is worth noting that Vatican II took great pains to define and elaborate the notion of the church as the people of God.

3. The analysis in this section relies heavily on Thomas Massaro, *Catholic Social Teaching and United States Welfare Reform*, (Collegeville MN: The Liturgical Press, 1998).

4. National Conference of Catholic Bishops, Washington DC, 1986.

5. Catholic Charities USA, Alexandria VA, January 1994.

6. United States Catholic Conference, Washington DC, March 1995.

7. At the time of the debates over the 1996 welfare bill I was Assistant Secretary for Families and Children in the federal Department of Health and Human Services. My responsibilities included both administering the welfare system and participating on behalf of the department in welfare policy making and interaction with the Congress. I testified on welfare many times, and had at least weekly meeting with administration and congressional staff involved in welfare reform. My impressions of the debate came from these interactions, as well as from closely following the public debates and the press coverage. In general, political scientists find that religion is not a major influence on voting by members of Congress, with exceptions for a few issues, most notably abortion. See Robert Booth Fowler and Allen D. Hertzke, *Religion and Politics in America,* (Boulder CO: Westview Press, 1995).

8. The history of both Catholic charities and Catholic Charities is thoroughly and interestingly explored in Dorothy M. Brown and Elizabeth McKeown, *The Poor Belong to Us* (Cambridge, MA: Harvard University Press, 1997).

9. This history is documented by Mary J. Oates, *The Catholic Philanthropic Tradition in America* (Bloomington: Indiana University Press, 1995).

10. Data available at the Catholic Charities website, *www.catholiccharitiesusa.org.*

11. See Anna Greenberg's chapter in this volume for discussion of these issues.

12. Independent Sector *Giving and Volunteering in the United States 1996 Edition; and Giving and Volunteering in the United States 1994, Volume II: Trends in Giving and Volunteering by Type of Charity* (Washington DC: Independent Sector, 1995 and 1996).

13. This history is documented in David J. O'Brien, *Public Catholicism* (New York: McMillan, 1989), chapter 3.

14. *IAF 50 Years: Organizing for Change* (Franklin Square, NY: Industrial Areas Foundation, 1990).

15. A good summary description of the Industrial Areas Foundation approach is found in Robert Fisher, *Let the People Decide: Neighborhood Organizing in America* (New York: Macmillan, 1994), pp. 192–196.

16. In early 2000, *The Boston Globe* ran stories about the revitalization of St. Peter's and St. Mark's parishes, both of them in the Dorchester section of Boston: Nathan Cobb, "Divine Interventionist at 73," *Boston Globe,* January 19, 2000; Marcella Bombardieri, "Diverse Parish Looks in Mirror and Learns," *Boston Globe,* February 9, 2000.

17. Several of the Vatican II documents are relevant, including the Dogmatic Constitution on the Church, the Pastoral Constitution on the Church in the Modern World, the Decree on the Apostolate of Lay People, and the Declaration on Religious Liberty. A new translation of the documents is available in Austin Flannery, OP, *Vatican Council II: The Basic Sixteen Documents* (Northport NY: Costello Publishing Co., 1996).

18. *Economic Justice For All: Catholic Social Teaching and the U.S. Economy* (Washington: Catholic Conference, 1986), p. 68.

19. These debates took place on the floor of Congress in early August 1996.

20. See especially the Theimann, Minow and Greenberg chapters in this book for further discussion of these issues.

21. See the discussion of congregational capacity in Greenberg's chapter in the volume.

22. An excellent, though now slightly out of date review of statistical, historical and evaluation data is provided by Rebecca Blank, *It Takes a Nation: A New Agenda for*

Fighting Poverty (Princeton: Princeton University Press, 1997). Unfortunately, both data collection about and evaluation of welfare reform are less extensive than is needed for thoughtful policy making. Better research might well end up being a recommendation of many deliberative bodies.

23. Sidney Verba, Kay Lehman Schlozman, and Henry E. Brady, *Voice and Equality: Civic Volunteerism in American Politics* (Cambridge, MA: Harvard University Press), pp. 317–330.

24. The papers by Thiemann and Hehir in this volume speak directly to the theological issues.

List of Contributors

Mary Jo Bane is Thornton Bradshaw Professor of Public Policy and Management at Harvard's Kennedy School of Government. From 1993–1996, she was Assistant Secretary for Children and Families at the U.S. Department of Health and Human Services, and co-chair of President Clinton's working group on welfare reform. In 1992–1993, she was commissioner of the New York Department of Social Services. She is the author of a number of books and articles on poverty, welfare, and families.

Jenny Berrien is an analyst at Abt Associates, Inc., working in the Housing and Community Revitalization Area. She graduated from Harvard University in 1998 with a degree in Sociology. After graduating, Ms. Berrien spent a year at Public/Private Ventures conducting research on national models of faith-based initiatives working to reduce youth violence.

Brent Coffin co-directs a new program on religious organizations and practices in public life, sponsored jointly by the Harvard Divinity School and Kennedy School of Government. From 1997–2000, he served as Executive Director of the Center for the Study of Values in Public Life at Harvard Divinity School. An ordained Presbyterian minister, Coffin served congregations in the South Bronx, Trenton, and Minneapolis/St. Paul. His dissertation, *A View from Below: Justice in the Welfare Reform Debate* (Harvard, 1997), examined how conflicting views of justice influence a public policy debate. His current research examines the public character of congregations and their civic engagement, particularly with respect to issues of inequality.

Francis Schüssler Fiorenza is the Charles Chauncey Stillman Professor of Roman Catholic Theological Studies at Harvard Divinity School. In addition to publishing more than one hundred essays in areas of fundamental theology, political theology and hermeneutics, his publications include: *Foundational Theology: Jesus and the Church*; *Systematic Theology: Roman Catholic Perspectives*, co-authored with John Galvin; *Habermas, Modernity, and Public Theology*, co-edited with Don Browning; and *Modern Christian Thought*, Vol. 2. *The Twentieth Century*, co-authored with James Livingston.

Samuel D. Herring is Vice President of Content Development for LGUIDE.COM. He holds a masters degree from Harvard Divinity School, where he focused on religious ethics and social policy. While at Harvard, Herring wrote and conducted research for the Center for the Study of Values in Public Life on topics related to welfare reform and faith-base organizations.

Peter Frumkin is Assistant Professor of Public Policy at Harvard University's Kennedy School of Government where he is affiliated with the Hauser Center for Nonprofit Organizations. His current research focuses on public policies shaping the nonprofit sector, the management of nonprofit organizations, and the performance of private philanthropic foundations. His most recent publications have examined compensation policies in nonprofit organizations, the impact of fundraising strategies on private foundations, and the impact of public funding on nonprofit mission definition.

J. Bryan Hehir is Professor of the Practice in Religion and Society, and Chair of the Executive Committee at Harvard Divinity School. He also serves as Counselor to Catholic Relief Services in Baltimore. From 1973–1992, Father Hehir served in Washington at the U.S. Conference of Bishops and taught at Georgetown University. He was Director of the Office of International Affairs (1973–1983), Secretary of the Department of Social Development and World Peace (1984–88), and Counselor for Social Policy (1998–1992). His publications include: *Military Intervention and National Sovereignty; Expanding Military Intervention: Promise or Peril?; Catholicism and Democracy: Conflict, Change and Collaboration*; and *The Just-War Ethic Revisited.*

Omar M. McRoberts is Assistant Professor of Sociology at the University of Chicago. His interests straddle the sociology of religion, community and urban sociology, collective action and urban poverty. McRobert's previous work includes a dissertation (Harvard University, 2000) on the multicongregational environment in Four Corners—a depressed, mostly black neighborhood in Boston. His ongoing research examines the tension between human community and place in contemporary urban settings.

Martha Minow has taught at Harvard Law School since 1981. Her books include *Between Vengeance and Forgiveness: Facing History After Genocide and Mass Violence; Not Only for Myself: Identity Politics and Law; Making All the Difference: Inclusion, Exclusion, and American Law*; and *Civil Procedure: Doctrine, Practice, and Context*, coedited with Stephen N. Subrin, Mark S. Brodin, and Thomas O. Main. She is a member of the Harvard University Press Board, the Harvard Society of Fellows, the American Academy of Arts and Sciences, and several child welfare organizations.

Betsy Perabo is a doctoral candidate studying ethics in the Department of Religious Studies at Yale University. She is a graduate of Harvard Divinity School, where she worked as a research assistant at the Center for the Study of Values in Public Life from 1997–1999.

Theda Skocpol is Victor S. Thomas Professor of Government and Sociology at Harvard University and Director of the Center for American Political Studies. She is author of *Protecting Soldiers and Mothers: The Political Origins of Social Policy in the United* States, which won five scholarly awards. Her most recent books are *Civic Engagement in American Democracy*, co-edited with Morris P. Fiorina, and *The Missing Middle: Working Families and the Future of American Social Policy.*

Ronald F. Thiemann is Professor of Theology and Religion & Society at Harvard University. An ordained Lutheran minister, Thiemann served as Dean of the Faculty at Harvard Divinity School from 1986–1998, and was founding Director of the Center for the Study of Values in Public Life from 1992–1998. He is author of *Revelation and Theology: The Gospel as Narrated Promise, Constructing a Public Theology: The Church in a*

Pluralistic Culture, and *Religion in Public Life: A Dilemma for Democracy.* He is currently working on a book-length project entitled "Prisoners of Conscience: Public Intellectuals in a Time of Crisis."

Richard Weissbourd currently conducts research and teaches at the Graduate School of Education and the Kennedy School of Government at Harvard University. He is the author of *The Vulnerable Child: What Really Hurts America's Children and What We Can Do About It* (Addison-Wesley, 1996). He is the principal founder of ReadBoston, a city-wide initiative, led by Mayor Menino, intended to unite schools and communities around the common goal of all children reading by third grade. His work focuses on vulnerability and resilience in childhood and on effective schools and services for children.

Lucie E. White is the Louis A. Horvitz Professor of Law at Harvard Law School. She teaches and writes in the fields of poverty, social welfare, and democratic participation. He current research examines race-based obstacles to democratic governance among low-income women in Project Head Start.

Christopher Winship is Professor of Sociology and Department Chair at Harvard University. He is currently doing research on the estimation of causal effects with non-experimental data; the Ten Point Coalition, a group of black inner-city ministers who have been working with the Boston Police Department to reduce youth violence; and racial differences in educational performance in elite institutions of higher learning. He is also investigating the changing racial composition of prisons, the effects of education on mental ability, and the effects of different components of mental ability on different dimensions of social and economic success.

Selected Bibliography

Abbott, Walter, ed. 1966. *The Documents of Vatican II*. New York: Guild Press.

Addams, Jane. 1910. *Twenty Years at Hull-House*. New York: Macmillan.

Allison, Dorothy. 1992. *Bastard Out of Carolina*. New York: Dutton.

Altshuler, Alan A., and Robert D. Behn. 1997. *Innovation in American Government*. Washington: Brookings.

Ammerman, Nancy. 1997. *Congregation and Community*. New Jersey: Rutgers University Press.

Axinn, June, and Herman Levin. 1982. *Social Welfare: A History of the American Response to Need*. New York: Harper and Row.

Bane, Mary Jo. 1976. *Here to Stay: American Families in the Twentieth Century*. New York: Basic Books.

Bane, Mary Jo and David T. Ellwood. 1994. *Welfare Realities: From Rhetoric to Reform*. Cambridge, MA: Harvard University Press.

Barry, Norman. 1990. *Welfare*. Minnesota: University of Minnesota Press.

Beer, Samuel. 1978. *The New American Political System*. Washington, D.C.: American Enterprise Institute.

Bellah, Robert, et al. 1985. *Habits of the Heart: Individualism and Commitment in American Life*. Berkeley: University of California Press.

Bell, Daniel. 1991. The Winding Passage: Sociological Essays and Journeys. New Bruswick, NJ: Transaction Publishers.

Belle, Deborah, ed. 1982. *Lives in Stress: Women and Depression*. Beverly Hills: Sage Publishers.

Benhabib, Seyla. 1992. *Situating the Self: Gender, Community and Postmodernism in Contemporary Ethics*. New York: Routledge.

Berger, Peter L. and Richard John Neuhaus. 1996. *To Empower People: From State to Civil Society*, 2nd ed. Washington: American Enterprise Press.

Bernstein, Richard. 1986. *Religion and American Public Life*. New York: Paulist Press.

Bernstein, Susan. 1991. *Managing Contracted Services in the Nonprofit Agency*. Philadelphia: Temple University Press.

Blank, Rebecca. 1997. *It Takes a Nation: A New Agenda for Fighting Poverty*. Princeton: Princeton University Press.

Boff, Leonardo, Virgilio P. Elizondo, and Marcus Lefebure, eds. 1986. *Option for the Poor: Challenge to the Rich Countries*. Edinburgh: T. & T. Clark.

Borowitz, Eugene B. 1991. *Renewing the Covenant: A Theology for the Postmodern Jew*. New York: The Jewish Publication Society.

Bowen, William G., Thomas I. Hygren, Sarah E. Turner, and Elizabeth A. Duffy.

1994. *The Charitable Nonprofits*. San Francisco: Jossey-Bass Publishers.

Brown, Dorothy M., and Elizabeth McKeown. 1997. *The Poor Belong to Us: Catholic Charities and American Welfare*. Cambridge, MA: Harvard University Press.

Brunner, Emil. 1945. *Justice and the Social Order*. New York: Harper.

Bryk, Anthony S., Valerie E. Lee and Peter B. Holland. 1993. *Catholic Schools and the Common Good*. Cambridge, MA: Harvard University Press.

Buchanan, Constance, H. 1996. *Choosing to Lead: Women and the Crisis of American Values*. Boston: Beacon Press.

Carter, Stephen L. 1993. *The Culture of Disbelief: How American Law and Politics Trivialize Religious Devotion*. New York: Basic Books.

Chafe, William H. 1981. *Civility and Civil Rights: Greensboro, North Carolina and the Black Struggle for Freedom*. New York: Oxford University Press.

Christian, William A. 1964. *Meaning and Truth in Religion*. Princeton: Princeton University Press.

Chubb, John E., and Terry M. Moe. 1990. *Politics, Markets and America's Schools*. Washington: Brookings.

Cohen, Jean L. and Andrew Arato. 1992. *Civil Society and Political Theory*. Cambridge, MA: MIT Press.

Cohen, Lizabeth. 1990. *Making a New Deal: Industrial Workers in Chicago, 1919–1939*. New York: Cambridge University Press.

Coleman, James S., Thomas Hoffer, and Sally Kilmore. 1982. *High School Achievement*. New York: Basic Books.

Constantelos, Demetrios J. 1991. *Byzantine Philanthropy and Social Welfare*. New Rochelle, NY: Caratzas.

Danziger, Sheldon H., and Daniel H. Weinberg, eds. 1986. *Fighting Poverty: What Works and What Doesn't*. Cambridge, MA: Harvard University Press.

Davis, Martha. 1993. *Brutal Need: Lawyers and the Welfare Rights Movement*. New Haven: Yale University Press.

Derthrick, Martha. 1979. *Policymaking for Social Security*. Washington: The Brookings Institution.

DiMaggio, Paul J., and Walter W. Powell, eds. 1991. *The New Institutionalism in Organizational Analysis*. Chicago: University of Chicago Press.

Douglass, R. Bruce, and David Hollenbach, eds. 1994. Catholicism and Liberalism: Contributions to American Public Philosophy. Cambridge, U.K.: Cambridge University Press.

Dworkin, Ronald. 1977. *Taking Rights Seriously*. Cambridge, MA: Harvard University Press.

______. 1985. *A Matter of Principle*. Cambridge, MA: Harvard University Press.

Edin, Kathryn, and Laura Lein. 1997. *Making Ends Meet: How Single Mothers Survive Welfare and Low-Wage Work*. New York: Russell Sage Foundation.

Eigo, Francis, ed. 1991. *The Works of Mercy*. Villanova: Villanova University Press.

Ellwood, David T. 1988. *Poor Support: Poverty in the American Family*. New York: Basic Books.

Erikson, Erik H. 1968. *Identity, Youth and Crisis*. New York: Norton.

Fahey, C.J., and Mary Ann Lewis. 1992. *The Future of Catholic Institutional Ministries: A Continuing Conversation*. New York: Fordham University.

Fahey, David M. 1996. *Temperance and Racism*. Lexington: University Press of Kentucky.

Finke, Roger and Rodney Stark. 1992. *The Churching of America, 1776–1990*. New Brunswick: Rutgers University Press.

Fiorenza, Francis Schussler. 1983. *Foundational Theology: Jesus and the Church*. New York: Crossroad.

Fiorenza, Francis Schussler and John Galvin, eds. 1991. *Systematic Theology: Roman Catholic Perspectives*. Minneapolis: Fortress.

Fisher, Robert. 1994. *Let the People Decide: Neighborhood Organizing in America*. New York: Macmillan.

Flannery, Austin. 1996. *Vatican Council II: The Basic Sixteen Documents*. Northport, NY: Costello Publishing Co.

Flora, Peter and Arnold J. Heidenheimer, eds. 1981. *Protecting Soldiers and Mothers: The Political Origins of Social Policy in the United States*. Cambridge, MA: The Belknap Press of Harvard University Press.

Fowler, Robert Booth, and Allen D. Hertzke. 1995. *Religion and Politics in America*. Boulder: Westview Press.

Frank, Robert H. 1999. *Luxury Fever: Why Money Fails to Satisfy in an Era of Excess*. New York: The Free Press.

Frazer, Nancy. 1983. *Unruly Practices*. Minneapolis: University of Minnesota Press.

Freedman, Marc. 1993. *The Kindness of Strangers*. San Francisco: Jossey-Bass.

Fuller, Millard. 1994. *The Theology of the Hammer*. Macon, GA: Smyth and Helwys Publishing, Inc.

Gannon, Thomas, S.J., ed. 1987. *The Catholic Challenge to the American Economy*. New York: Macmillan Publishing Co.

Garland, Diana S. Richmond. 1994. *Church Agencies: Caring for the Children and Families in Crisis*. Washington: Child Welfare League of America.

Giddens, Anthony. 1987. *Social Theory and Modern Sociology*. Oxford: Polity Press.

Gidron, Benjamin, Ralph Kramer, and Lester M. Salamon, eds. 1992. *Government and the Third Sector: Emerging Relationships in Welfare States*. San Francisco: Jossey-Bass Publishers.

Greeley, Andrew. 1990. *The Catholic Myth: The Behaviour and Beliefs of American Catholics*. New York: Charles Scriber's Sons.

Gremillion, Joseph. 1976. *The Gospel of Peace and Justice: Catholic Social Teaching Since Pope John*. Maryknoll: Orbis.

Gronbjerg, Kirsten A. 1993. *Understanding Nonprofit Funding: Managing Revenues in Social Service and Community Development Agencies*. San Francisco: Jossey-Bass Publishers.

Gustafson, James M. 1984. *Ethics from a Theocentric Perspective: Ethics and Theology, Volume 2*. Chicago: University of Chicago Press.

Habermas, Jurgen. 1996. *Between Facts and Norms: Contributions to a Discourse Theory of Law and Democracy*. Cambridge, MA: MIT.

Hall, Peter Dobkin. 1992. *Inventing the Nonprofit Sector and Other Essays on Philanthropy, Voluntarism and Nonprofit Organizations*. Baltimore: Johns Hopkins University.

Hansen, John Mark. 1991. *Gaining Access: Congress and the Farm Lobby, 1919–1981*. Chicago: University of Chicago Press.

Harris, Fred. 1999. *Something Within*. New York: Oxford University Press.

Heubert, Jay P., ed. 1999. *Law and School Reform: Six Strategies for Promoting Educations Equity*. New Haven: Yale University Press.

Higginbotham, Evelyn Brooks. 1993. *Righteous Discontent: The Women's Movement in the Black Baptist Church, 1880–1920*. Cambridge, MA: Harvard University Press.

Hilfiker, David. 1994. *Not All of Us Are Saints: A Doctor's Journey with the Poor*. New York: Hill and Wang.

Himmelfarb, Gertrude. 1984. *The Idea of Poverty: England in the Early Industrial Age*. New York: Random House.

Hochschild, Jennifer. 1995. *Facing Up to the American Dream: Race, Class and the Soul of the Nation*. Princeton: Princeton University Press.

Hodgkinson, Virginia, Murray Weitzman, Arthur Kirsch, Stephen Norga, and Heather Gorski. 1993. *From Belief to Commitment: The Community Service Activities and Finances of Religious Congregations in the United States*. Washington: Independent Sector.

Hoffman, Alexander von. 1994. *Local Attachments: The Making of an Urban Neighborhood, 1890–1925*. Baltimore: Johns Hopkins University Press.

Hollenbach, David. 1979. *Claims in Conflict: Retrieving and Renewing the Catholic Human Rights Tradition*. New York: Paulist Press.

Holtaman, Abraham. 1963. *The Townsend Movement: A Political Study*. New York: Bookman.

Hooper, J. Leon. 1993. Religious Liberty: Catholic Struggles With Pluralism. Louisville: Westminster/John Knox Press.

Hurston, Zora Neal. 1981. *The Sanctified Church*. Berkeley: Turtle Island.

Ignatieff, Michael. 1985. *The Needs of Strangers*. New York: Viking.

Ingram, Helen, and Steven Rathgeb Smith, eds. 1993. *Public Policy for Democracy*. Washington: Brookings.

Jernegan, Marcus Wilson. 1980. *Laboring and Dependent Classes in Colonial America*. Westport, CT: Greenwood Press.

John, Richard. 1995. *Spreading the News: The America Postal System from Franklin to Morse*. Cambridge, MA: Harvard University Press.

Johnson, Paul E., ed. 1994. *African-American Christianity: Essays in History*. Berkeley: University of California Press.

Joseph, Stephen M. 1969. *The Me Nobody Knows: Children's Voices from the Ghetto*. New York: Avon Books.

Katz, Michael. 1986. *In the Shadow of the Poorhouse: A Social History of Welfare in America*. New York: Basic Books.

Katznelson, Ira, and Margaret Weir. 1985. *Schooling for All*. New York: Basic Books.

Kauffman, Christopher J. 1992. *Faith and Fraternalism: The History of the Knight of Columbus*, revised edition. New York: Simon and Schuster.

Kegley, Charles W. and Robert W. Bretall, eds. 1956. *Reinhold Niebuhr: His Religious, Social and Political Thought*. New York: Macmillan.

Keohane, Robert O., and Joseph S. Nye. 1989. *Power and Interdependence*. Boston: Little Brown.

Kerber, Linda, Alice Kessler-Harris, and Kathryn Kish Sklar, eds. 1995. *U.S. History as Women's History: New Feminist Essays*. Chapel Hill: University of North Carolina Press.

Kingson, Eric R., Barbara A. Hirshorn and John M. Cornman. 1986. *Ties That Bind: The Interdependence of Generations*. Washington: Seven Locks Press.

Komisar, Lucy. 1982. *Down and Out in the USA: A History of the American Response to Need*, 2d ed. New York: Harper and Row.

Kotlowitz, Alex. 1991. *There Are No Children Here*. New York: Doubleday.
Kramer, Ralph M. 1981. *Voluntary Agencies in the Welfare State*. Berkeley: University of California Press.
Ladd-Taylor, Molly. 1986. *Raising a Baby the Government Way: Mothers' Letters to the Children's Bureau, 1915–1932*. New Brunswick: Rutgers University Press.
Lagemann, Ellen Confliffe, ed. 1999. *Studying Philanthropic Foundations*. Bloomington: Indiana University Press.
Lincoln, C. Eric, and Lawrence H. Mamiya. 1990. *The Black Church in the African American Experience*. Durham: Duke University Press.
Lindberg, Carter. 1993. *Beyond Charity: Reformation Initiatives for the Poor*. Minneapolis: Fortress.
Lovin, Robin W. 1995. *Reinhold Niebuhr and Christian Realism*. New York: Cambridge University Press.
Luhmann, Niklas. 1982. *The Differentiation of Society*. New York: Columbia University Press.
______. 1990. *Political Theory in the Welfare State*. Berlin: Walter de Gruyter.
Marmor, Theodore R. 1973. *The Politics of Medicare*. Chicago: Aldine.
Marshall, Thomas H. 1977. *Class Citizenship and Social Development*. Chicago: University of Chicago Press.
Mason, David E. 1996. *Leading and Managing the Expressive Dimension*. San Francisco: Jossey-Bass Publishers.
Massaro, Thomas. 1998. *Catholic Social Teaching and United States Welfare Reform*. Collegeville, MN: The Liturgical Press.
McConnell, Stuart. 1992. *Glorious Contentment: The Grand Army of the Republic, 1865–1900*. Baltimore: Johns Hopkins University Press.
Mead, Lawrence. 1986. *Beyond Entitlement: The Social Obligations of Citizenship*. New York: The Free Press.
Miller, Richard M. 1991. *Interpretations of Conflict*. Chicago: University of Chicago Press.
Minow, Martha. 1990. *Making All the Difference: Inclusion, Exclusion and America Law*. Ithaca: Cornell Press.
Mollat, Michel. 1986. *The Poor in the Middle Ages: An Essay in Social Theory*. New Haven: Yale University Press.
Monsma, Stephen V. 1996. *When Sacred and Secular Mix*. Lanham: Rowman & Littlefield Publishers, Inc.
Morgan, Edmund S., ed. 1965. *Puritan Political Ideas: 1558–1784*. Indianapolis: Bobbs-Merrill Company.
Morris, Aldon D. 1984. *The Origins of the Civil Rights Movement: Black Communities Organizing for Change*. New York: Free Press.
Morris, Charles R. 1996. *The AARP*. New York: Times Books.
Mosch, Theodore R. 1975. *The G.I. Bill: A Breakthrough in Educational and Social Policy in the United States*. Hicksville, NY: Exposition Press.
Murnane, Richard, and Frank Levy. 1996. *Teaching the New Basic Skills*. New York: The Free Press.
Murray, Charles. 1984. *Losing Ground: American Social Policy*. New York: Basic Books.
Murray, John Courtney, S.J. 1960. *We Hold These Truths: Catholic Reflections on the American Proposition*. New York: Sheed and Ward.
Nathan, Richard P., and Thomas L. Gais. 1999. *Implementing the Personal Responsibility Act of 1996: A First Look*. Albany: Nelson Rockefeller Institute of Government.

Niebuhr, Reinhold. 1968. *Faith and History*. New York: George Braziller.
______. 1972. *The Children of Light and the Children of Darkness*. New York: Charles Scribner's Sons.
Nordin, D. Sven. 1974. *Rich Harvest: A History of the Grange, 1867–1900*. Jackson, MS: University of Mississippi Press.
Nozick, Robert. 1974. *Anarchy, State and Utopia*. New York: Basic Books.
Nussbaum, Martha. 1995. *Poetic Justice: The Literary Imagination and Public Life*. Boston: Beacon Press.
______. 2000. *Women and Human Development: The Capabilities Approach*. Cambridge: Cambridge University Press.
Nussbaum, Martha, and Amartya Sen, eds. 1993. *The Quality of Life*. Oxford: Clarendon.
Nygren, Anders. 1969. *Eros and Agape*. New York: Harper and Row.
O'Brien, David J., and Thomas A. Shannon. 1992. *Catholic Social Thought: The Documentary Heritage*. Maryknoll, NY: Orbis Books.
Offe, Claufe. 1984. *Contradictions of the Welfare State*. Cambridge, MA: MIT Press.
Olasky, Marvin. 1996. *Renewing American Compassion: How Compassion for the Needy Can Turn Ordinary Citizens into Heroes*. New York: The Free Press.
______. 1992. *The Tragedy of American Compassion*. Wheaton, IL: Crossway Books.
Olson, Keith W. 1974. *The G.I. Bill, the Veterans, and the Colleges*. Lexington: University of Kentucky Press.
Osborne, David. 1990. *Laboratories of Democracy*. Cambridge, MA: Harvard Business School Press.
Osborne, David, and Ted Gaebler. 1993. *Reinventing Government*. New York: Penguin.
Outka, Gene. 1972. *Agape*. New Haven: Yale University Press.
Parsons, Talcott. 1971. *The Systems of Modern Societies*. Englewood Cliffs, NJ: Prentice-Hall.
Pencak, William. 1989. *For God and Country: The America Legion, 1919–1941*. Boston: Northeastern University Press.
Peterson, Paul E. 1981. *City Limits*. Chicago: University of Chicago Press.
Piven, Frances Fox, and Richard A. Cloward. 1993. *Regulating the Poor: The Functions of Public Welfare* (updated edition). New York: Vintage Books.
Powell, Walter W., and Elisabeth S. Clemens, eds. 1998. *Private Action and the Public Good*. New Haven: Yale University Press.
Powell, Walter W., ed. 1987. *The Nonprofit Sector: A Research Handbook*. New Haven: Yale University Press.
Raboteau, Albert. 1995. *A Fire in the Bones: Reflections on African-American Religious History*. Boston: Beacon Press.
Rawls, John. 1993. *Political Liberalism*. New York: Columbia University Press.
______. 1971. *A Theory of Justice*. Cambridge: Harvard University Press.
Reynolds, Charles, and Ralph Norman, eds. 1988. *Community in America: The Challenge of Habits of the Heart*. Berkeley: University of California Press.
Ricoeur, Paul. 1995. *Figuring the Sacred: Religion, Narrative and Imagination*. Minneapolis: Fortress.
Riesebrodt, Martin. 1993. *Pious Passions*. Berkeley: University of California Press.
Roof, Wade Clark. 1999. *Spiritual Marketplace: Baby Boomers and the Remaking of American Religion*. Princeton: Princeton University Press.
Ross, Davis R. B. 1969. *Preparing for Ulysses: Politics and Veterans during World War II*. New York: Columbia University Press.

Rutter, Michael. 1979. *Fifteen Thousand Hours*. Cambridge, MA: Harvard University Press.

Ryan, Mary P. 1981. *Cradle of the Middle Class: The Family in Oneida County, New York, 1790–1865*. New York: Cambridge University Press.

Salamon, Lester. 1995. *Partners in Public Service: Government Relations in the Modern Welfare State*. Baltimore: Johns Hopkins University Press.

Salamon, Lester, and Alan J. Abramson. 1982. *The Federal Budget and the Nonprofit Sector*. Washington: Urban Institute Press.

Salamon, Lester M., and Alan J. Abramson. 1997. *Holding the Center: America's Nonprofit Sector at a Crossroads*. New York: The Nathan Cummings Foundation.

Sandel, Michael. 1996. *Democracy's Discontent: America in Search of a Public Policy*. Cambridge, MA: Belknap Press.

Scarry, Elaine. 1985. *The Body in Pain: the Making and Unmaking of the World*. New York: Oxford University Press.

Schorr, Lisbeth B. 1997. *Common Purpose: Strengthening Families and Neighborhoods to Rebuild America*. New York: Anchor Books, Doubleday.

Schudson, Michael. 1998. *The Good Citizen: A History of American Life*. New York: Free Press.

Scott, W. Richard, and Soren Christensen, eds. 1995. *The Institutional Construction of Organizations*. Thousand Oaks, CA: Sage.

Sen, Amartya. 1999. *Development as Freedom*. New York: Alfred A. Knopf.

Sherman, Amy. 1997. *Restorers of Hope*. Wheaton, IL: Crossway Books.

Shklar, Judith N. 1991. *American Citizenship: The Quest for Inclusion*. Cambridge, MA: Harvard University Press.

Shneewind, Jerome, B., ed. 1996. *Giving: Western Ideas of Philanthropy*. Bloomington: Indiana.

Smith, Lillian. 1978. *Killers of the Dream*. New York: Norton.

Smith, Rathgeb Steven, and Michael Lipsky. 1993. *Nonprofits for Hire: The Welfare State in the Age of Contracting*. Cambridge, MA: Harvard University Press.

Solow, Robert M. 1998. *Work and Welfare*. Princeton: Princeton University Press.

Stack, Carol. 1974. *All Our Kin: Strategies for Survival in a Black Community*. New York: Harper and Row.

Taylor, Charles. 1993. *Sources of the Self: The Making of the Modern Identity*. Cambridge, MA: Harvard University Press.

Thiemann, Ronald. 1996. *Religion and Public Life: A Dilemma for Democracy*. Georgetown: Georgetown University Press.

Thompson, Ross A. 1995. *Preventing Maltreatment Through Social Support: A Critical Analysis*. Thousand Oaks, CA: Sage Publications.

Tillich, Paul. 1954. *Love, Power and Justice*. New York: Oxford University Press.

Trattner, Walter I. 1984. *From Poor Law to Welfare State: A History of Social Welfare in America*, 3rd ed. New York: Free Press.

Tyack, David, and Elisabeth Hansot. 1982. *Managers of Virtue: Public School Leadership in America, 1820–1980*. New York: Basic Books.

Verba, Sidney et al. 1995. *Voice and Equality: Civic Voluntarism in American Politics*. Cambridge: Harvard University Press.

Walzer, Michael. 1983. *Spheres of Justice: A Defense of Pluralism and Equality*. New York: Basic Books.

Washington, James M., ed. 1991. *Testament of Hope: The Essential Writings and Speeches of Martin Luther King*. San Francisco: HarperSanFrancisco.

Weisbord, Burton A. 1977. *The Voluntary Nonprofit Sector*. Lexington: Heath.

Weissbourd, Richard. 1996. *The Vulnerable Child: What Really Hurts America's Children and What We Can Do About It*. Reading, MA: Addison-Wesley.

Wilensky, Harold. 1975. *The Welfare State and Equality: Structural and Ideological Roots of Public Expenditures*. Berkeley: University of California Press.

Will, George F. 1983. *Statecraft as Soulcraft: What Government Does?* New York: Simon and Schuster.

Williams, Harold S., Arthur Y. Webb, and William J. Phillips. 1995. *Outcome Funding: A New Approach to Targeted Grantmaking*. Rensselaerville, NY: Rensselaerville Institute.

Wilson, William Julius, ed. 1993. *Sociology and the Public Agenda*. Newbury Park, CA: Sage Publications.

Wilson, William Julius. 1996. *When Work Disappears: The World of the New Urban Poor*. New York: Alfred A. Knopf.

Wind, James P., and James W. Lewis, eds. 1994. *American Congregations, Volume 2: New Perspectives in the Study of Congregations*. Chicago: University of Chicago Press.

Withnow, Robert. 1994. *Producing the Sacred: An Essay on Public Religion*. Chicago: University of Illinois Press.

Wolch, Jennifer. 1990. *The Shadow State: Government and the Voluntary Sector in Transition*. New York: The Foundation Center.

Wuthnow, Robert. 1997. *The Crisis in the Churches: Spiritual Malaise, Fiscal Woe*. New York: Oxford University Press.

______. 1998. *Loose Connections: Joining Together in American's Fragmented Communities*. Cambridge, MA: Harvard University Press.

______. 1988. *The Restructuring of American Religion: Society and Faith Since World War II*. Princeton: Princeton University Press.

______. *Sharing the Journey: Support Groups and America's New Quest for Community*. New York: The Free Press.

Zigler, Edward. 1992. *Head Start: the Inside Story of America's Most Successful Educational Experiment*. New York: Basic Books.

Index